IROQUOIS
Supernatural

IROQUOIS
Supernatural

Talking Animals
and
Medicine People

**MICHAEL BASTINE AND
MASON WINFIELD**

Bear & Company
Rochester, Vermont • Toronto, Canada

Bear & Company
One Park Street
Rochester, Vermont 05767
www.BearandCompanyBooks.com

Text stock is SFI certified

Bear & Company is a division of Inner Traditions International

Library of Congress Cataloging-in-Publication Data
Bastine, Michael.
  Iroquois supernatural : talking animals and medicine people / Michael Bastine
and Mason Winfield.
      p. cm.
  Includes bibliographical references and index.
  Summary: "Brings the paranormal beings and places of the Iroquois folklore
tradition to life through historic and contemporary accounts of otherworldly
encounters"—Provided by publisher.
  ISBN 978-1-59143-127-5 (pbk.) — ISBN 978-1-59143-944-8 (ebook)
  1. Iroquois Indians—Folklore. 2. Iroquois mythology. 3. Iroquois Indians—
Religion. I. Winfield, Mason. II. Title.
  E99.I7.B235 2011
  398.2089'9755—dc23
                                                                    2011024900

Printed and bound in the United States by Lake Book Manufacturing
The text stock is SFI certified. The Sustainable Forestry Initiative® program
promotes sustainable forest management.

10 9 8 7 6 5 4 3 2 1

Text design by Virginia Scott Bowman and layout by Priscilla Baker
This book was typeset in Garamond Premier Pro with Arepo and Twylite Zone
used as display typefaces

To send correspondence to the authors of this book, mail a first-class letter to the
authors c/o Inner Traditions • Bear & Company, One Park Street, Rochester, VT
05767, and we will forward the communication.

Contents

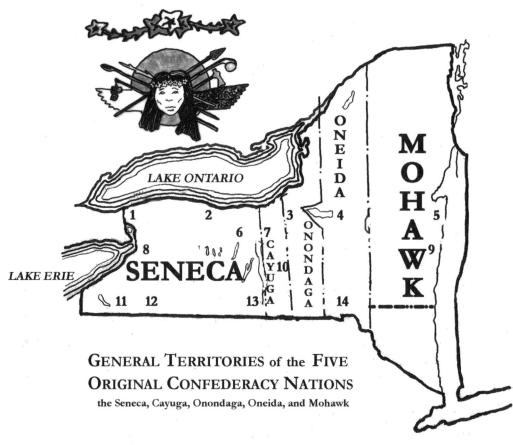

GENERAL TERRITORIES of the FIVE ORIGINAL CONFEDERACY NATIONS

the Seneca, Cayuga, Onondaga, Oneida, and Mohawk

Approximate Positions of Today's Cities

1. Niagara Falls
2. Rochester
3. Syracuse
4. Oneida
5. Saratoga Springs
6. Canadaigua
7. Auburn
8. Buffalo
9. Albany
10. Ithaca
11. Jamestown
12. Salamanca
13. Elmira
14. Binghamton

The Iroquois Supernatural

Reaching Beyond the Sacred

The Native Americans known collectively as the Iroquois have had an impact on world destiny out of all proportion to their numbers and territory. They have been deeply admired for their leaders as well as for their national character, their League of Six Nations, and their simple moxie, but they have had a hold on so many far-flung imaginations that isn't easy to explain. People all over the world who have no particular interest in anything Native American have found themselves strangely haunted by these industrious, adventurous, mystical Iroquois. What could be the source of it?

The Iroquois are unmistakably and for all time native North Americans, but they might be unique even among their native New York neighbors. Something drew these five, then six nations—the Cayuga, the Mohawk, the Oneida, the Onondaga, the Seneca, and latecomers the Tuscarora—into a single distinctive unit, this outfit we call the Confederacy, the League of Six Nations.

Enough books have been written about the character and history of the Iroquois. This book is devoted to the supernatural traditions of these first historic New Yorkers, from as far back as we can trace them, to the present day.

Figuring out what to include in this book has been tricky. Where do you draw the line between miracle and magic? Between religion and spirituality? Between the sacred and the merely spooky? This book doesn't try to choose. How could anyone?

All religions are at heart supernatural. Throughout history most societies have had both a mainstream supernaturalism and others that are looked upon with more suspicion. The "out" supernaturalism is often that of a less advantaged group within the major society. What the mainstream culture calls "sacred" is *its* supernaturalism; terms like "witchcraft" are applied to the others. Someone's ceiling is another's floor, and one culture's God is another's Devil. To someone from Mars, what could be the objective difference?

Although all Iroquois supernatural belief may seem "superstitious" or "magical" to some observers, Iroquois society itself makes its own

Dhyani Ywahoo, Mad Bear, the Dalai Lama, and Michael Bastine
in Dharamsala, India, in 1980

distinctions between the sacred and the spooky. Still, one often overlaps the other.

This book is not about the sacred traditions of the Iroquois. It is a profile of the supernaturalism external to the religious material recognized as truly sacred. This is a book largely about the "out" stuff: witches, curses, supernatural beings, powerful places, and ghosts. It includes things on the spiritual side: healings, power people, visions, and prophetic dreams. Some of the material is historic, archaeological, and anthropological. Much of it is as alive and current as a paranormal report.

Algonquin coauthor Michael Bastine and I have written this book from the belief that one of the world's great spiritual traditions is that of the Iroquois, and that it's been under the radar for too long. A broader familiarity with Iroquois traditions would help world spirituality—and hence the world.

We also believe that the world might develop more sympathy for Iroquois causes if it knew the Iroquois better.

The partnership between us is an equitable one. I did most of the book research and keyboarded the words. The voice of the narrative is mine. Michael, a highly respected elder, trained with many people mentioned in this book. Vast stretches of its words—and most of the wisdom—are his.

MASON WINFIELD

AND

MICHAEL BASTINE

1

The Longhouse Folk

You must forgive me, therefore, for not always distinctively calling the creeds of the past "superstition" and the creeds of the present day "religion."

JOHN RUSKIN,
THE QUEEN OF THE AIR

THE IROQUOIS

In 1609 on the west bank of the lake named for him, French explorer Samuel de Champlain had the white world's first encounter with the Iroquois—symbolically, a violent one. Two hundred Native American strangers had cheerfully attacked a much larger party of Algonquin, among whom Champlain stood. They were bold, confident, and well-formed men, Champlain reported, and he made an impression himself. At the first blast of his gun, three attackers fell dead, including two chiefs. The rest scattered at their first experience of firearms.

When Champlain asked the name of these scrappers—almost certainly Mohawks—the Algonquin called them a word that sounded like "Iroquois," which meant something like "real snakes." It was an indignant term, but it held respect. Another possible derivation for the word *Iroquois,* pointed out by archaeologist Dean Snow, is "Hilokoa," a pidgin Basque/Algonquin name meaning, "the killer people." Then, as now, they were admired as warriors.

The Iroquois called themselves *Haudenosaunee,* "People of the Long House." They were a union of five, later six, nations who held most of New York state at the time the Europeans arrived.

The Iroquois were hunters, farmers, and warriors. They lived in small, semipermanent villages across most of what is now upstate New York. Their influence ranged far beyond. Their greatest arts were things they could carry with them: their songmaking, their storytelling, their language and their use of it. It was in the last capacity that the Six Nations folk so impressed the white world. The best of them were the greatest orators any European had ever seen.

The Iroquois were never numerous. Sir William Johnson estimated in 1763 that there might have been ten thousand of them. Two centuries later, Edmund Wilson figured that there were about double that number of mostly Iroquois people. In the 1995 New York census, 62,651 folks chose to call themselves Iroquois, which is still only about 0.3 percent of the state's population.

Because of their political unity and prospects of empire building, the Iroquois were nicknamed "the Red Romans." They may have been on their way to controlling a continent at the time the Europeans landed. Power brokers in all the colonial wars, the Iroquois helped shape the North America we see today. Their League of Six Nations has often been considered the model for today's United States, and thus of democratic unions all over the world. It's no stretch to suggest that the Iroquois were the most influential Native American political body that has ever been.

ORIGINS

The origins of the Iroquois are still debated. Until recently most historians envisioned the ancient Northeast along the model of Dark Ages Europe: a borderless, nationless land mass in which culturally distinct bodies of people—tribes—pushed each other around or ate territory whole. The Seneca scholar Arthur C. Parker (1881–1955) thought this way at the start of the twentieth century, envisioning the boundaries of Iroquois Nations—Oneida, Cayuga—moving across the map of prehistoric New York like cloud shadows along a ridge on a gusty day.

A century later, we have dramatic new tools for understanding the past, among them linguistics and genetics. We also have different ideas about the Iroquois. To understand them we need to separate for a moment the idea of *culture* from that of *people.*

Culture—language, lifestyles, artifacts, religion, customs, ways of thinking—can develop within a population. Contact with new people can change it. It can be brought in with new people who take over territory. These models—it grew here, it came here, they brought it here—are not mutually exclusive when it comes to the roots of "Iroquois-ness."

The first Iroquoians were named after a lake—Owasco Lake near Auburn, New York—where their oldest identifiable sites were found. Currently, there are two predominant models for the origins of the Owasco culture. The more popular of them is a mix of "it grew here" and "it came here." In this scheme, the people who became the historic Iroquois were already in place. They were the indigenous folk of the Northeast Woodlands who may have been here since the last glaciers. They may have had an Iroquoian language—that we'll never know—but the artifacts, customs, and lifestyles that go into what we consider Iroquois-ness developed among them later, maybe as recently as a thousand years ago.

In this picture, hunting-gathering bands of eighty or so people grew into more static villages of several hundred, probably due to the practice of agriculture spreading from Mesoamerica through the Mississippian

Culture of the Midwest. Owasco artifacts and lifestyles developed as innovations and through contact with other groups, and spread around upstate New York. The Iroquois nations developed as cultural identities when these villages banded together for mutual support.

There is still another picture of Owasco origins: "they came here." Some scholars believe the relatively sudden appearance of agriculture, longhouse-style buildings, and compact villages in upstate New York means that an influx of newcomers brought them. It may have been a complete takeover. If so, it was probably Iroquoians supplanting Algonquin-speaking aboriginals. Where did these Iroquoians come from?

Archaeologists have discovered what they take to be signs of an immigration from the St. Lawrence River Valley. Linguistic historians think the push could have come from the south through the Appalachians. Iroquoian languages were spoken in the Southeast by nations like the Cherokee, from whom today's Iroquois may have broken off before the pyramids of Egypt were built.

The Iroquois have their own traditions, of course. National and religious creation tales feature them sprouting right out of the ground or from a single hill. Those are widely regarded as mythical. As for Iroquois storytellers, their only conflict with the archaeologists may be one of timing. The Iroquois carry tales of distinct nations wandering into ancient New York from other parts of the continent, usually the Northeast, the Southeast, or the Great Lakes. There are faint traditions of an old home in the American Southwest. This seems the least likely legend to be directly true; however, we think most of the ancestors of today's Native Americans came from Asia. Thus North America was populated by groups migrating from the general direction of the west.

Even the pros admit that the choice between evolution and immigration is too simple. The real answer might be a mix of all factors: in-place development, new cultural influences, immigration, and at least one X-factor. (The Iroquois always seem to toss you one of those.) All everyone agrees on is that by the sixteenth century, the Iroquois were a political union of New York nations, sharing language and many other aspects of culture.

THE LEAGUE OF SIX NATIONS

According to legend, for many centuries the Iroquois nations had no sense of kinship. They warred with each other continually. Then an Iroquois, possibly Mohawk, chief had a vision of a mighty tree that never lost its leaves, with Iroquois people sheltering under its boughs. His message of unity was not readily taken, and this visionary chief, usually called the Peacemaker, had many adventures as he spread his word. Eventually the five original nations accepted his guidance and banded together. Strong and supple like the fingers of a hand, their Confederacy had flexibility and reach. It could also draw together into a fist for attack or defense.

Some Iroquois historians set the Confederacy's founding date between 900 and 1450 CE. A few white historians place it as recently as 1600. What's clear is that by the time the Europeans were settling New England, this was the strongest native power on the continent.

Though the Confederacy was never a big body by the standards of the Old World or of Central and South America, it had an impressive form of representative government based not on cultural or ethnic factors, but political ones.

The semiofficial fracturing of the League came during the American Revolution. When the British and the colonials split, the Six Nations were understandably confused. To which set of English-speakers had they sworn their oaths? They covered the holy council fire at Onondaga, meaning that each Iroquois nation was free to decide for itself. Most Oneida and Tuscarora sided with the Yanks. The other nations went with the British. The first blows one Iroquois nation had struck at another in centuries came at the Battle of Oriskany in 1777.

In the 1970s, a renaissance of Native American self-awareness and political power brought the League back into closer communication, and many other nations came with them. The League may never again be like it was, but the world around it has changed—and for the better—due to its influence.

THE LONGHOUSE

The Iroquois called themselves Haudenosaunee, "People of the Long House," and many today insist on the term. To those who think we should have used it instead of "Iroquois" throughout this book, we should explain. The term *Haudenosaunee* has not been used much in print until recently, and its spelling is still variable. There are four centuries of references to the Iroquois. Our point in commemorating these Longhouse Folk is lost if our readers don't know who we are talking about. We should talk about the structure that is the source of their name.

Big stone buildings were nonexistent in the Northeast before the whites came. Most Native North Americans lived in single-family structures like teepees or wigwams.

A characteristic feature of Iroquois life was the use of rectangular, multifamily dwellings called longhouses. Wood framed and walled with skins and bark, these longhouses surely developed in response to the cold winters of the Northeast. Some longhouses were 100 feet long, 25 feet high, and 20 feet wide.

Families lived in close quarters in the longhouse. A central aisle usually ran through them, and people slept on hammock-like bunks on each side. At the center of the longhouse was a fire pit. A hole in the roof above it let out the smoke and fumes. This fire was the center of cooking, warming, socializing, and teaching. An entrance was usually at each end.

Longhouses weren't intended to be permanent. Most Iroquois communities picked up and moved to another site within their national territory about every seven years. They had to. Their subsistence crops of corn, beans, and squash—the Three Sisters—exhausted the soil after a few seasons, and the fields took years to recover. Structures like long-houses have been found among other societies of the Northeast, but they are separate from the concept of "the Longhouse" found among the Iroquois.

The Longhouse is more than a signature building; it is the symbol of Iroquois identity. The inclusive, sheltering, protective image is a figu-rative way of looking at Iroquois society. Its physical form is even the outline of Iroquois territory in New York state.

We doubt that UFOs were taking Iroquois elders on periodic sky rides, but somehow the Longhouse folk came up with a correct impres-sion of the shape of their traditional lands. It's a breadloaf across the New York map, a rough rectangle whose longest sides stretched from the Hudson to the Alleghenies. Lake Ontario and the Pennsylvania border formed the lines of its northern and southern walls. This geographical figure is remarkably close to the shape of the longhouse, and since the spots in the material longhouse had their traditional associations, the Confederacy's five original nations were nicknamed by the position of their territories.

The Genesee Valley Seneca and the Mohawk Valley Mohawk were Keepers of the Western and Eastern doors, respectively. Since the usual position of the firekeeper, storyteller, and teacher was by the fire at the middle, "Firekeepers" was one of the nicknames of the Onondaga, who held the center of Iroquois territory. Between the end and the middle in the material longhouse were stationed the children whose duties were to tend the fire. On the landscape-longhouse, these were the positions of the west-central Cayuga and the east-central Oneida, called "the Younger Brothers."

THE NATIONS

The Iroquois nations spoke closely related languages. They shared cus-toms, lifestyles, religion, and a body of cultural tales, as well as attitudes about the supernatural, the focus of our book.

The Iroquois were adopting societies, bringing many non-Iroquois people—thus genetic and cultural diversity—into their villages. Before the Europeans came, these would have been Native Americans of all Northeastern nations. In historic times, many white and black Americans were taken in by the Iroquois, too. Newcomers became instant Iroquois. They were discriminated against in no perceptible ways and were judged solely by the contributions they made to the society. Some of the great leaders in Iroquois history have been of mixed blood. It could well be that this unusual inclusiveness plays some part in accounting for the Iroquois mystique.

The formation of the League brought the separate nations into closer contact. It all melded into something we might call, without stereotyping, the Iroquois character. Some sign of that character may be found in the League's tribal names.

Celtic tribes often named themselves for animals and trees. The Brannovices may have been Folk of the Raven. The Chatti were the Cat People. The Eburones were People of the Yew. Some Germanic tribes named themselves for weapons. The Franks were known for the *francisca*, a short-handled throwing-ax and close-quarters weapon that was probably the model for the tomahawk. The Saxons' namesake was the *seax*, a long-handled bowie knife.

The Iroquois nations named themselves after things of the earth: hills, swamps, stone. We're not sure what this may say about them, but it could symbolize their spiritual rootedness in the New York landscape. No wonder it ached so much to lose their lands.

We tend to think of the Iroquois League as a single entity. Never forget that these are six nations with histories and identities as distinct as those of England and Italy and they bear examining this way. Let's start with what may have been the first nation, the Onondaga.

The Onondaga

The Onondaga's upstate homeland lies between Cazenovia Lake and Onondaga Creek. Today's city of Syracuse is their heart center. Like their western neighbors the Seneca and Cayuga, they hunted as far north as Lake Ontario and as far south as the Pennsylvania state line. Their name for themselves—sometimes written as Onotakekha—means, roughly, "People on the Hill."

The Onondaga have a tradition that their nation is the mother of the rest of the Iroquois. In that sense, the Onondaga are the proverbial turtle of the nations, the base of the Iroquois world. They hold the center of its territory.

In one of the nation's origin traditions, the Onondaga once lived near the St. Lawrence River. Weary of wars with a much bigger society, they came to their historic home centuries before Columbus. Archaeological evidence may back the Onondaga; some of it suggests the midstate influx of an Iroquoian population from northern New York. Others believe the Onondaga, like every other Iroquois nation, developed a cultural identity only after they had lived many centuries in New York.

All Iroquois nations have legends of ancient wars, and the archaeological evidence suggests that there was pressure on early Onondaga territory. Many of the earliest Onondaga sites were fortified hilltops, indicating that the need for defense may have drawn them to unify.

Located in the heart of the Iroquois world, the Onondaga may be the heart of Iroquois tradition. They were the Firekeepers of the nations in the symbolic longhouse that must always be kept in mind when thinking of the Iroquois. The Onondaga were culture preservers. They were holders of the Peace Tree, the white pine of the Peacemaker's vision, under whose evergreen branches the Iroquois buried the weapons they had once used on each other.

Many figures legendary to all Iroquois were Onondaga. The wizard king Atotarhoh (or Tadodarho, "the Tangled") became the first presiding high chief of the Confederacy. Like Julius Caesar, his name, Tadodarhoh, has become a title. Hiawatha, the Peacemaker's helper, may have been the most memorable Onondaga (though he's sometimes claimed by other Iroquois nations). The unity of the Iroquois is symbolized by a wampum strip made in a pattern called Hiawatha's Belt (shown on page 4 superimposed on the state of New York). Even the tomb of Prophet Handsome Lake (1735–1815) is in Onondaga territory.

Because of early white settlement of the Syracuse area and the work of white historians like William Martin Beauchamp (1830–1925), the Onondaga are particularly well represented in the literature—as they are today by the young Buffalo, New York-based writer Eric Gansworth. SUNY Buffalo professor and "Faithkeeper" Oren Lyons and Buffalo State College professor Lloyd Elm are other Onondaga teachers of note.

The Seneca scholar Arthur C. Parker wrote in 1901 that the Onondaga (with the Seneca) were the least "Whiteman-ized"—his word, our hyphen—of the Iroquois nations. By that we think Parker meant "assimilated." Only the Iroquois can decide how right he was, but the Onondaga Nation has consistently refused state or federal grants that might compromise its independence. (Gifts from the U.S. government have been known to come with a sting, at least for Native Americans.) The Onondaga Nation seems to have served the Onondaga well. They've reclaimed much of their ancient territory near Syracuse.

The Seneca

The Seneca were the largest of the Iroquois nations and usually stereotyped as the most warlike. Though the Seneca core area was the lower Genesee Valley region around today's Rochester, their sphere of influence was wider, including all of New York state west of Seneca Lake. Since the 1794 Treaty of Canandaigua, most Seneca have lived on three reservations in western New York, at Alleghany, Cattaraugus, and Tonawanda.

These Keepers of the Western Door were the defenders of the western entrance to the Six Nations territory. They were major players during the colonial wars, including the American Revolution.

The historic name of the Seneca—that of the Roman playwright—is not their own. The Seneca called themselves Nundawaono, usually taken to mean "People of the Great Hill." The name that comes to us through the Dutch and French, who first heard of them from their Northeastern rivals, is A'sinnaker, usually said to mean "standing stones." A'sinnaker is likely a corruption of a willful misunderstanding of the Seneca's original name—thus an enemy sneer gives history its name for a most influential Native American nation.

Onondaga tradition suggests that the Seneca may have been spin-offs of the Cayuga. In the Seneca's own origin myth, they hail from a hill at the top of Canandaigua Lake. They may have given us more famous people than any other Native American nation.

The fabled Peace Queen was a Seneca, as was the hero-trickster Skunni Wundi. The warrior Cornplanter (1736?–1836), Prophet Handsome Lake, and the orator Red Jacket (1750–1830) were illustrious Revolutionary-era Seneca. Mary Jemison (1743–1833), "White Woman of the Genesee," was an adopted Seneca who declined several chances to return to the white culture. Attorney Ely Parker (1828–1895) was an aide to Union General Ulysses Grant and drew up surrender terms at Appomattox. His polymath grandson, Arthur C. Parker, was a scholar, folklorist, historian, translator, author, and the first New York state archaeologist.

Among recent Seneca spiritual leaders are the author and teacher Twylah Hurd Nitsch (1920–2007) and author and storyteller DuWayne "Duce" Bowen (1946–2006)—one of the few writers of any origin who has published still-living Iroquois folklore. But the image the Seneca may always leave to the world is that of the scrapper. In April 2007, Seneca Nation President Maurice A. "Moe" John was asked if things might turn rough if the state tried to collect taxes on reservation tobacco sales. "I hope and I pray every day that there will be no violence," John said. "I can't guarantee it. We are a nation of warriors."

The Cayuga

The Cayuga have a penchant for picking up nicknames. Sometimes called People of the Pipe or Keepers of the Great Pipe, the Cayuga call themselves something similar to the name by which history knows them: Kayoknonk, or Gayogohono. The term might have meant "Where the Boats Are Taken Out" or "People of the Landing." Others take it to mean "People of the Great Swamp," since, according to the late chief Jacob Thomas, most Iroquois who visited the Cayuga came in canoes and looked for their settlements by following the marshy ground along the lake. The Cayuga (with the Oneida and Tuscarora) are sometimes called the Younger Brothers, probably to distinguish their position in the grand Longhouse that symbolizes Iroquois territory. The Cayuga's turf lay between the central hearth (Onondaga lands) and the western (Seneca) door.

The Cayuga lived on both sides of Cayuga Lake, and today's city of Auburn is the nucleus of their territory. They hunted north all the way to Lake Ontario and south to the Susquehanna River. Conflict was common, too, during the Cayuga's cultural birth. Many early Cayuga sites are high fortifications.

In the Cayuga's own origin legend, they followed their prophet Hiawatha from Oswego to Cayuga Lake, wandering the upstate woodlands like Aeneas after Troy. They had many adventures, including clashes with other nations and fearsome giant beasts. They surely impressed the Jesuit fathers, who described the Cayuga as the boldest, fiercest, most political, and most ambitious "savages" the American forest had ever produced. Memorable Cayuga include John Logan, the Revolutionary-era warrior whose monument stands today in Auburn, New York, and Peter Mitten, the twentieth-century medicine man mentioned a number of times in these pages.

We wish the Cayuga had more to show for the grandeur of this legacy now. Approximately 450 Cayuga live on reservations, mostly in western and central New York. There may be 2,000 or so more across the United States. The Cayuga Nation still holds the traditional Council of Chiefs and Clan Mothers. Their chiefs sit on the Haudenosaunee Grand Council that meets regularly at Onondaga. The Cayuga own only two tiny pieces of their former land. They're still pursuing their claims with New York state, in which we wish them luck. On second thought, though, they've had a lot of luck, and little of it's been good. Let's wish them justice.

The Mohawk

The folk we call the Mohawk call themselves Kanyukehaka, "People of the Flint," maybe because of the abundance of tool-making flint in their core area of the Mohawk and upper Hudson river valleys. Whatever its source, the name is a suitable description of the Mohawk character: ancient, unbending, sharp, with glittering highlights and hidden depths.

The name *Mohawk,* as with the origins of the name *Seneca,* is a slur, bestowed by their northeastern rivals, who probably figured they could tell white people anything. The name might mean "people eaters," in short, cannibals. We take this more as a sign of their foes' dread than any direct proclivity.

In the hairstyle named for the Mohawk, you have a hint of their reputation. Peeling a fully haired scalp off a corpse could be awkward. The ideal leverage, it was said, was given when a head was shaved but for a single narrow strip from forehead to nape—like a horse's mane or the plume of a Corinthian helmet. The coif of choice for Mohawk warriors was a standing challenge: *Come and get it.* The tough part of getting the scalp, of course, was getting its owner dead.

The Mohawk are also called the Elder Brothers, possibly because they were the first nation to accept the Great Law of Peace. Indeed, the Mohawk language was the first one learned by important Iroquois of other nations, since it may have been the language used at the Great Council and at important pan-Iroquois religious events. Another Mohawk nickname is Keepers of the Eastern Door, since they protected the Confederacy from trouble at the eastern entrance to the heartland. The Mohawk River was the spine of their territory. Their conquest of the Hudson Valley inspired James Fenimore Cooper's Leatherstocking tales.

In the seventeenth and eighteenth centuries, the British and French fought over control of North America. Mohawk land lay between French outposts at Quebec and British ones at Albany. The Mohawk were generally skilled at working political situations, though they picked the wrong side in the Revolution, and the cards fell from there. Most Mohawk moved to Canada after the war.

Mohawk war parties distinguished themselves in the War of 1812. In 1813, Mohawk, British, and French-Canadian forces defeated Americans near Montreal during a small campaign some Canadians like to call "the American invasion." At the 1813 skirmish at Beaver Dams on the Niagara Frontier, the Mohawk contingent was credited with beating the Americans single-handedly.

The great Peacemaker who unified the Iroquois tribes is generally considered a Mohawk. The Freemason and war chief Joseph Brant (1743–1807) and the religious leader Kateri Tekakwitha (1656–1680) are two of the most famous historic Mohawks, the latter blessed by the Vatican and possibly on her way to becoming a saint. Brant's son John Brant and half-Scottish Mohawk John Norton were major players in the War of 1812 on the Niagara Frontier. One of the most curious figures of the nineteenth century was "Lost Dauphin" Eleazar Williams (1787–1858), rumored to be the son of Louis XVI and Marie Antoinette, spirited out of France during the Reign of Terror and raised in an American Mohawk community. The most famous Native American in the history of television was the Lone Ranger's sidekick Tonto, played by actor Jay Silverheels (1912–1980), born on the Six Nations Reserve in Ontario. Contemporary Mohawk of note include the storyteller, healer, and community founder Tom Porter and Robbie Robertson, founding member of Bob Dylan's former backup band, the Band.

Today, the Mohawk live in a handful of major communities, several of them in Canada. Many twentieth-century Mohawk worked in steel and construction, particularly on skyscrapers. It was noticed in the early twentieth century that few Iroquois—and no Mohawk—have any fear of heights. Many Mohawk walk a six-inch beam twenty stories up as comfortably as most readers would walk one resting on the ground. One of them explained the national nonchalance: "If you slip, the result is the same if it's fifty or five thousand feet." The Mohawk seem to like the challenge of the work—and the danger.

The Oneida

Oneyoteaka is what the People of the Standing Stone (sometimes "People of the Boulder") used to call themselves, and you can see it Anglicized in the word *Oneida*. Like the Scots and their Stone of Scone, the Oneida treasured a special boulder that was kept near the main national settlement. Each Oneida village had its own lesser rock by which local ceremonies were held.

The Oneida heartland was the high ground southeast of Oneida Lake, between today's cities of Utica and Syracuse. Their hunting lands stretched from Pennsylvania to the St. Lawrence River. Possibly the smallest of the Iroquois nations, the Oneida were considered the most arrogant by some missionaries.

Some Oneida historians saw their folk as spin-offs of the Onondaga, their neighbors to the west. Archaeological and linguistic evidence suggests closer ties to their eastern neighbors the Mohawk. In one of their own traditions, the Oneida sprouted right out of the ground. Their website proclaims that the People of the Standing Stone have stood on their land for 10,000 years. Who are we to argue? The coming of the Europeans, though, would be disruptive.

While other Iroquois nations sided with the British, the Oneida—with a plucky band of Tuscarora—stuck by the American colonies. The 1777 Battle of Oriskany, New York, was a traumatic moment for the Confederacy, the first time in centuries that Iroquois nations had fought one another.

The Oneida may have saved the Revolution through a delivery of 600 bushels of corn to George Washington that wicked winter at Valley Forge. The Continental Congress praised the Oneida, their love "strong as the oak," and their fidelity, "unchangeable as truth." The Congress promised to love, honor, and protect the Oneida "while the sun and moon continue to give light to the world." Nice words.

The Oneida paid for backing the Americans in the Revolution. Other Iroquois, particularly the Mohawk, attacked Oneida forts and villages. The Oneida lashed back in spades. Many Christian Oneidas took off with a Mohawk preacher to eastern Wisconsin in 1820. Another so-called pagan faction settled on the Thames River near London, Ontario. A third group stayed on the Onondaga Reservation near Syracuse, while a fourth hung on to a few acres outside Sherrill, New York. The state of New York gnawed into Oneida lands throughout the nineteenth century until even their stone was lost. It wasn't until 1985 that the U.S. Supreme Court would listen to them.

By 1987, the Oneida were down to thirty-two acres of the Onondaga Reservation. The Turning Stone Casino, which opened in 1993, may be turning things around for them. The Oneidas have bought back 3,500 of their former New York acres and have a thriving community today.

Two of the most memorable Oneida may be women. The fearless Polly Cooper stayed with Washington's troops at Valley Forge to show them how to use and ration the Oneida corn. She may have taken water to soldiers in battle. Our contemporary Joanne Shenandoah is a Grammy-nominated composer, singer, and performer. The Revolutionary-era Oneida chief Hanyerri had many adventures in the service of the United States and seems to have engaged in a lifelong feud with the formidable Mohawk Joseph Brant. The valiant old Oneida chief Hanyost Thaosagwat bears honorable mention. A guide to the 1779 Boyd-Parker mission in the Genesee Valley, Thaosagwat lost his life in the Revolutionary War incident remembered as "the Torture Tree."

Many world cultures have a central stone that represents the world navel, the center of things. It's surprising that the other Iroquois nations don't have an object or place as concentrated as the Oneida stone. Maybe non–Native Americans just haven't heard about it yet; maybe the other nations don't need it, with the Oneida holding the crystalline heart for all the rest.

The Tuscarora

The Tuscarora call themselves Skaruren, meaning something like "Gatherers of the Hemp," or "The Shirt-Wearing People," possibly because they wore woven hemp shirts. They are the only Iroquois nation whose name for themselves doesn't come from an earthly feature. Whatever this might say about them, these shirt-wearers were the latest addition to the Confederacy.

The Tuscarora were an Iroquoian-speaking nation whose home was around today's city of Raleigh, North Carolina. How Iroquoians wound up in North Carolina is lost in prehistory, but Iroquoian language and culture ranged far afield. The Cherokee, an Iroquoian-speaking people we think of as western, hailed from the Carolinas.

By 1700, their homeland was getting hot for the Tuscarora. They were pressured and affronted by the incoming whites. (Tuscarora children may have been taken from their parents and sold into slavery.) Other Native nations of the region used white contact as an opportunity to chip away at them. The same thing happened to the Aztecs, and with better reason. The Tuscarora took about all they could and lashed back, but the odds were against them. The wars they fought with the English and other Native nations ate into their lands and population. By 1713, most Tuscarora had left the Southeast.

The story of their adventures en route to their new home would be a real saga, could it ever be written. Eventually they took refuge in Oneida territory and were admitted to the League in 1722 at Oneida sponsorship. At first the Tuscarora settled in several areas about New York—the Hudson Valley, the Genesee Valley, and midstate.

Maybe because they knew something about a fight for independence, most Tuscarora sided with the young United States in its first struggle with the British Empire. A few joined the Iroquois allies of the British and lived after the Revolution in Ontario. Those who stayed in the States established a national home by buying their lands near Lewiston, New York.

Memorable nineteenth-century Tuscarora include the historians

David Cusick (1780–1831) and J. N. B. Hewitt (1857–1937). A major figure in this book is the late twentieth-century activist, celebrity, and medicine man Wallace "Mad Bear" Anderson (1927–1985). His friend, and another of coauthor Michael Bastine's tutors, was the late author and medicine man Ted Williams (1930–2005). Our contemporary, the tobacco tycoon "Smokin' Joe" Anderson, is a powerful, influential figure.

By the early nineteenth century, many Tuscarora were Christians, and most of the nation is Christian today. Among some of them is a feeling that those Tuscarora who took up the Longhouse religion of Handsome Lake from the beginning may be "the *real* Indians." No Tuscarora should have a need to envy anyone.

"The Shirt-Wearing People" fought like tigers in 1813 for their new neighbors, the whites of Lewiston, after the fall of Fort Niagara. That December massacre of unarmed civilians would have been a lot worse had not a small force of Tuscarora roused the village, sheltered refugees, and held the line just long enough against the British and Native American storm coming up from the Niagara River.

IROQUOIS LANGUAGES

Iroquois refers to a language family. It's a lot like the word *Celtic* in that regard. There are Iroquoian language speakers who are not members of the Confederacy. There are Celtic speakers who aren't Irish—or Welsh or Scottish.

Each of the six Longhouse nations has its own distinct language. To a linguist, the languages are very similar, sharing many word roots and grammatical principles. That doesn't mean the speakers can understand each other. In fact, pronunciation, accent, and other variables make many Iroquoian languages as mutually unintelligible as German and English. ("Mohawk is *really* weird," said one of our Seneca confidants.)

The sounds of Iroquois languages are so non-European that any attempt to transcribe Iroquois words into everyday English is doomed.

Two whites could hear an Oneida word and spell it so differently that you wouldn't recognize it. This situation accounts for a lot of confusion in the general reader looking over historic sources.

In this book, we try to keep things simple. We try to render Iroquois words into pronounceable syllables and leave the technicalities to specialists.

IROQUOIS RELIGIOUS INFLUENCES

This is not a book about Iroquois religion or anything else we knew was sacred enough to be sensitive. Not only is that not our purpose, but, as a Mohawk friend said recently to me, "If it's sacred, you don't know it." And coauthor Michael Bastine would not reveal it. But lines between spirituality and supernaturalism are not always easy to draw, and many developments in this book will be incomprehensible without a little primer.

The old Six Nations religion featured a head god often called the Good-Minded One. He had legions of helpers, including demigodly figures like the Thunder Beings. Not everyone agrees that he was a separate figure from the Creator, the Great Spirit. The two names are often used interchangeably.

The Good-Minded Spirit also had a powerful, ambiguous sibling with his own legion of helpers. You may see him referred to as "the Evil-Minded One," and no one mistakes him for the Creator. Actually, his name in the various Iroquois languages could mean a number of things, including "circuitous" or "indirect."

While the impulse of any westerner is to presume that this character was the Iroquois Devil, things might not be so clear-cut. We should remember that the writings of the Christian missionaries give us our first glimpse of the Iroquois, and they have shaded centuries of interpretation after. It would have been a reflex for the Jesuits to look for a Devil. But few world religious systems are as dramatically "dualist"—good guy vs. loathsome bad guy—as Christianity, and it would be remarkable if things with the Iroquois plugged right into any other model.

The Iroquois Evil-Minded One might be more Loki than Satan, more of a trickster than a lord of demons. He just doesn't do things transparently and straight up. It's his nature to be subtle, indirect, and devious. The natural world has room for a lot of things and beings like this. The Evil-Minded One might be the Bacchus/Dionysus figure of the classical world. He's the opponent of order and clarity. In the Asian way of looking at things, he could represent the yin side of existence—diffuse and less definite but not evil. For the Iroquois he might even symbolize an alternative principle to the light and the domestic. He could represent the shadowy, forbidding, and craggy places in the landscape.

There were echelons of other supernatural beings, too, ranging from figures legendary to all Iroquois (like Little People and Great Flying Heads) to localized individual bogies that might have been unknown outside the folklore of a certain swamp or creek valley in the territory of a single nation. There were mortal culture heroes, too. Figures like Hiawatha and the Peacemaker were virtually deified, much like the Greek Hercules or Roman Aeneas. This ancient, indigenous tradition survives today partly in supernatural folklore and in the dances and chants that are as sacred to many Iroquois as anything in life.

Many Iroquois today are Christians. It's a miracle. The early missionaries often hit brick walls. (The Iroquois thought "the Black Robes" might be witches, and not without reason. One of the prime witch job descriptions is to be the bringer of plagues, which the first Europeans certainly were.) Only when they respected the Iroquois as they were did the missionaries start to reach them. Today the Christian Iroquois are often guarded about old supernatural traditions.

A third major influence upon the Iroquois was their own prophet, Handsome Lake. A half brother of the Seneca war chief Cornplanter, Handsome Lake was troubled by the deterioration of Iroquois society due to alcohol, relocation, and the loss of traditions. A series of famous visions led Handsome Lake to create a code of conduct or Gaiwiio, which means, "the good word." In 1913, Arthur C. Parker published and annotated the Gaiwiio in *The Code of Handsome Lake*. The prophet's code adapts the old traditions to a new way of life, seemingly including Christian influences. This Longhouse religion is still quite influential. Handsome Lake the man became known as a witch finder, and you will find many of your most serious witch-dreaders today among his followers.

INTO THE WOODS

Traditions

The old Iroquois historians kept a significant body of myth and legend, but none of it was written. The first European visitors were more interested in proselytizing and grabbing resources than in preserving native traditions, and it took centuries for the Iroquois material to be written down. Most sources consider the nucleus of it to be at least four centuries old.

Some of the whites who saw the Iroquois before the Revolution considered them the most avid storytellers on Earth and suspected that the body of their tales would dwarf that of any other society. Even in the early twentieth century it was said that whenever parties of Iroquois met, sessions of storytelling followed the initial greetings. Few, though, would tell their tales within earshot of outsiders, which may be why this tradition is not better understood.

We should be aware from the start that we have only parts of the body of legend that was once that of the Iroquois. No source anywhere is considered a bible of preserved Iroquois tales and stories, either.

We should also remember that folklore everywhere is a plastic art, always growing and absorbing. Iroquois storytellers used elements and even motifs—story outlines—from other societies, including ones brought to them by whites. The church had a big hand in this, and it's no wonder that biblical elements occasionally appear, including the Western Devil.

The "golden age" of Iroquois folklore has been said to be from 1880 to 1925. Hope Emily Allen, William Beauchamp, Harriett Maxwell

Converse, Jesse Cornplanter, Elias Johnson, Arthur C. Parker, Lewis Henry Morgan, Henry Schoolcraft, and others had the advantage of talking to Iroquois folk when the traditional wisdom stories were still strong. A lot may have been lost quickly thereafter, and the Iroquois have been notably quiet since. There is also a living supernaturalism on the reservation and among Iroquois folk everywhere. Most non–Native Americans would be stunned to know the prevalence and survival power of this ancient tradition.

Never forget that there are people who talk about the subjects of these stories as if they are true. They will look you in the eye and tell you about an experience of the Little People, a curse, a witch light, a magic charm, or a visionary dream. And not all of them are Native Americans; New Yorkers of any origin describe things they still see on the Iroquois homeland that could have stepped right out of ancient Iroquois legend. Take tales like these with no less respect than you would give to a UFO report, a Bigfoot sighting, a ghost story, or any psychic or religious experience. We want to show where it all came from and how it so gloriously survives today.

The Storyteller's Bag

The old Iroquois tales fall into three main subject areas. When delivered live, the storyteller introduced each tale with a formulaic phrase that alerted listeners to the story type they were about to hear.

The first category is creation tales about the origins of the world and of the nations: "These are things that really happened," the storyteller often began. These are mythic or religious. Another category is animal tales: "It's as if an animal walked. . . ." Many of these tales are ingenious and familiar: "How the Skunk Got His Stripe" or "How the Bear Lost His Tail." Most of them are whimsical and remind us of jokes or riddles. Both these categories have been well preserved from their ancient forms, and neither belong in our book.

The forest tales make a third category: "They went into the woods." These stories can change by the decade. To the Iroquois, field and village were the domain of humans. Like the Celts of Europe, the Iroquois considered the forest and remote regions to be the realms of the supernatural. Though the supernatural could reach into the community—usually with a bit of inviting—even witches left their village homes for their dark rites and spells in the woods. The forest was also home to the most famous Iroquois supernatural beings: Flying Heads, Stone Giants, vampire skeletons, Little People, and the rest. This book is about the subjects of the forest.

In addition to the formulaic introductions, traditional Iroquois storytellers abided by a number of conventions. Particularly when entertaining children, the storyteller might bring a bag to the event and spill it at the start. It was always filled with small objects, often curious, sometimes junk: a bone, a stone, a feather, a broken pipe. Before starting, the storyteller picked one of these items and improvised a way that it reminded him of the upcoming tale. The children's eyes widened.

This book is a bag, and we empty it before you. A few things in it remind us of this and that. *And now we're going into the woods. . . .*

The Witches' Craft

If one can forget the twentieth-century preoccupation with black magic (which is a comparatively recent innovation), it becomes clear that the real witchcraft is more than likely to be yet another variation on the ways in which the old practices were perpetuated.

JANET AND COLIN BORD,
THE SECRET COUNTRY

IROQUOIS WITCHES

Like preindustrial people everywhere, the old Iroquois had an outlook on the world that might be called animistic. Spirits were thought to animate everything, including animals, plants, and earthly features. They could be the invisible causers of storms, floods, natural disasters, and plagues. But what powered the spirits?

Many world societies have words for the life force: mana, prana, pneuma, ch'i, kaa, manitou. The power of life, landscape, spirituality, and divinity for Iroquois society was often called something that sounded like *orenda*. There is debate about the prevalence of this exact word, but not the concept. To simplify things, let's think of it like the Force in the *Star Wars* motif.

Orenda was a titanic, universal, inexhaustible power that could be channeled to do almost anything. It was also carried around as part of a being's life package. By their nature, gods and supernatural critters had big batteries of orenda. One supernatural could spot it in another by sight, through any disguise. Humans could enhance their own orenda through virtue, training, and life experience. Chiefs, heroes, and shamans packed plenty of it. Someone who could master the use of orenda or gain the aid of spirits who wielded it could do almost anything.

But orenda—the Force—could be turned. It could be refocused into a weapon.

Otkon is a broad term for negative things, beings, energy, or forces. It was thought that otkon, the other side of orenda, could be launched like a fateful laser beam at human targets. It could be projected into objects like dolls or trinkets, turning them into psychically radioactive land mines that work to the grief of all who come near them. Who would do such a thing with orenda?

The old Iroquois had a powerful belief in witchcraft. They feared it, they hated it, and they quickly killed anyone convicted of practicing it. The witch—and any other wielder of otkon—was thought to hold the power to cause death, drought, sickness, blight, storms, and almost any other calamity that could befall people and the natural environment. Anyone—man, woman, child—could become a witch. Some could even turn themselves into animals. But is this all witches are? Supernatural evildoers? People who reroute orenda and use it selfishly? It could well be that some witches were more.

The difficulty of making sharp and current distinctions in matters of ancient supernaturalism is one of the themes of this book. We see that in many world cultures, some form of proscribed supernaturalism operated in the shadow of the mainstream, and that it was often vigorously persecuted. The handiest example may come to us from medieval and Renaissance Europe, where a Christianity struggling to solidify itself made witches out of herbal healers and the practitioners of older, pagan religions, as well as whatever "devil worshippers" might truly have been out there. Things aren't even that clear-cut with the Iroquois.

The Iroquois had their own alternative god, sometimes called the Evil-Minded One. His name would have been different in each Iroquois language and virtually unpronounceable in this one. As we have said, he could be more of a Trickster than a demon. But in some of the tales we have, some Iroquois witches are portrayed as the Evil One's devotees. Maybe so. We should not presume that a few people might not have given up asking the Good-Minded One for what they wanted and figured to give his rival a try. The first deed of every initiated witch of this type was to magically kill a treasured friend or family member.

In 1989 the anthropologist Annemarie Anrod Shimony (1928–1995) estimated that about a third of the residents of the Six Nations Reserve in Canada were "traditionalist Indians," and that it was about this percentage who still believed in the power whites call witchcraft. While few contemporary Longhouse folk would ever think of working a curse in the traditional way, few would deny that others have the power to do it. In fact, witchcraft is alive and well, or at least the faith in something that answers to it. Only those who categorically deny the existence of psychic phenomena could say that the Iroquois are completely wrong. The Iroquois were not alone in their belief.

A faith in something we would classify as witchcraft has developed in so many unconnected parts of the world that we have to conclude there could be something interesting and original going on. Witchcraft of the European style—along with occultism of many types—came across the Atlantic with the first wave of immigrants to North America. Even in the nineteenth century, the territory once owned by the Iroquois was so proverbial for its alternative white cults and religious movements that the region drew nicknames like "the Spirit Way" and "the Burned-over District"—meaning that all spiritually flammable souls had been set alight. Some of the eclectic tenets of this period included Christian spin-offs like Evangelism and Adventism. Some other indigenous isms like Spiritualism and Mormonism looked a lot like witchcraft to some mainstream Christians.

Ethnic supernatural customs and traditions could be found among many New York families well into the twentieth century, and some whites may have known plenty about the Iroquois dark arts. In 1923, Seneca scholar Arthur C. Parker claimed to know a white doctor with a reputation for diagnosing and curing victims of witchery on the Tonawanda Reservation. Never forget that our own day has its trends that to many materialist thinkers look no less magical: feng shui, homeopathic healing, past-life regression, reiki, and psychic communication.

Though direct terms like *magic* and *witch* aren't used on the reservations very much any more, some Iroquois today will give you a sly glance and acknowledge that they know someone who. . . . They tell a lot of stories about people who do "extra" things. They may also be guarded. It's never been good form on the rez to talk much about witchcraft. Seeming to know too much about it, even showing signs of a talent like ESP or prophecy, could get people wondering.

Michael and I don't know much about witchcraft, either, by the way. He's just telling you what he's heard. And I'm just telling you what I've read. This chapter details stories and incidents about the dark art in Iroquois country.

TWO KINDS OF WITCHES

There is a hierarchy among Iroquois witches. Anyone working a spell out of a handbook and hoping for a new job or a new lover might be called a witch. But there's a big difference between this and a seasoned witch working a spell out of malice or for hire.

There may also be categories among Iroquois witches. Arthur C. Parker tells us that they come in two styles, distinguished by their methods.

With some witches, the power is innate. They can blight with a thought—they need not even voice it—or by casting a cold eye. The only tool of the trade they need is the occasional bit of tobacco, a generic offering. Natural witches like these are the original black magicians, using the power of "malefic mental suggestion," which seems to be mostly psychic. They may be helped by training, but they need only practice. They can take the forms of animals, even ancient monsters like the *niagwahe,* the demon bear.

The second and more modern style of witch works his or her will through objects and spells, a general style of magic found all over the world and often classified as sorcery. Though we have never heard this word used on the reservation—they call it all "witched" or "medicine"— this is what sorcery is: magic done with spells and implements. It's like baking: get the ingredients and follow a recipe. This is what most of us would do if we tried black magic.

An Iroquois version of this type of cursing was to introduce something small into the body of a victim by supernatural means. The object was often a worm or a splinter from a deer bone, but sometimes it was more intricate, like a wooden needle, pointed on either end and with a hair from the witch threaded through the eye and wrapped around it. A wasting death was certain unless these cursed things were found and withdrawn. Another technique was planting a charm—the dreaded otkon—by the target's house.

SPOTTING A WITCH

Traditional witches can do their deviltry safely and effectively as long as they stay hidden. Sometimes just finding and confronting a witch is enough to back him or her off. Does that surprise you? Let it not.

You see, some witches aren't really evil. Some have been driven to their practice by poverty, despair, or even jealousy. Some of them haven't even thought through what they are doing. Practicing magic is a guilty little power game. Discovering them, calling them out, and getting them to realize what they've done to others can make them break into tears and give it all up. One might presume that these are entry-level witches.

And many witches are shy individuals, neither personally nor socially powerful. Most of them are afraid of their victims, which is probably the reason they choose witchcraft; it's a way to strike from hiding and at long range. Simply showing up on the witch's front door—armed and raving—is often enough to make the witch back off.

Witches are thought to travel as witch lights (*ga'hai*), which probably ought to be considered their astral bodies. Sometimes their faces are even visible inside these fuzzy light spheres. You can't hurt witches in this form, often called the witch's torch, but they come back to their natural bodies sooner or later. Of course, if you see one of these witch lights leaving or entering your neighbor's chimney, the case is made that someone who lives in that house is a witch. That's an ad for otkon the way a neon Bud Lite sign proclaims a bar. Such a witch has to be a rookie, or an old one, absent-minded enough to be careless or too powerful to care.

Another light is inside the witch. They say when Iroquois witches are outdoors at night, a red light shines through their mouths and nostrils as they breathe, as if forge fires burn inside them and their lungs work like bellows. This "internal luminosity" is reported of shamans and power people worldwide. The only way to recognize an Iroquois witch by sight is to see this fire glowing through them. ("When you see one coming down a road," said the Seneca Cephas Hill, "you get the effect of a flashlight being turned on and off.") The sight is particularly atmospheric on frosty nights on those wooded trails between villages in the Alleghenies, the Finger Lakes, and the Mohawk Valley.

One of the distinctive powers of the Iroquois witch (like the Celtic druid) was shape-shifting: the ability to become another being, usually a bird or mammal, and still think like a human. (This, of course, is connected to shamanism, a type of religious expression once found all over the world.) Not all metamorphosis is witchcraft, nor are all witches shape-shifters. Still, the Iroquois have many stories of witches becoming animals. Though some can do this with the aid of the right charm, most witches who shape-shift are the old kind of witch with innate powers.

Not only are these witches well disguised, but they travel quickly in their animal forms. Sometimes they do things directly to hurt their human enemies, but so much of the time they just spy and do their real business later. If you know what to look for, you can often spot them. They don't act like normal animals. Their movements are atypical and strange. They may even look weird.

If you recognize one of these witch critters and track it to somebody's house, you've narrowed the field. Someone who lives or visits there is the witch. Animal tracks between the homes of the victim of a curse and a suspected witch are a giveaway—especially if the tracks start or end as human footprints.

Sometimes one of these shape-shifting witches is spotted in the act. One might be disguised as a strange pig or cow in the barn or an extra cat or dog in the yard. Somebody might lash out with a stick or whip. A passing hunter might take a shot. The wounded critter splits. A few hours later and not too far off someone is found with a matching injury—someone perhaps long suspected of being a witch. A bloody trail of the prints of hoof or paw may even lead to the house. This, too, is an Old World motif.

In the late and desperate stages of a curse, some bewitched people can even see their tormentors, particularly when they are coming to visit. Often, they say, in this sort of vision trance, the sufferer can narrate the witch's movements as if watching a surveillance video.

Recognizing your hexer is critical to any defense. It's rare that it's easy. The witch could be anyone. The best thing, of course, is to spot someone engaged in some act or practice—say, making a charm—which would take away all doubt. But most witches train and work in secret.

We hear stories about witches who learned the dark art at the private tutelage of a friend or family member. The tutor may even be someone no longer alive. But often a semipublic ceremony seems part of the process of becoming a witch, and a sip of a magic brew completes the initiation. Witches often go into the deep woods and work their rites and spells by small, slow fires. If you spot one of these in progress—and make it back—you may know several witches.

If you chance to be out in the New York countryside and come across one of these midnight rites, you can start by being quiet. *Rrreeeaaallll* quiet. You might see a slow blaze, a steaming kettle, and a ring of human countenances in the glow. Note the faces. Hear what the voices are saying. You may be able to figure out what they're up to. If someone in the community has been suffering, you may know why.

The old Iroquois believed that the spirits of exceptional witches could inspire living ones long after their physical deaths. Like the European vampire, this spirit witch lingers in the grave in a queer state of death-in-life. A living witch with such a disembodied friend is especially powerful. The spirit witch will lead the living one to prosperity and luck. In some tales, the live witch occasionally visits the graveyard, showering the dead one with grisly gifts and tokens. If you go by a cemetery and see someone paying homage to an open grave, you may have spotted one of these eerie transactions. When it's discovered by the medicine people, the witch body has to be specially dealt with. This is another parallel to the European vampire.

If you're bold enough to poke around in the house of a suspected witch, you might find ritual objects, particularly totems and animal parts used in cursing or shape-shifting. But be careful what you play around with. If you hold one of these otkon objects, you may, against your will, learn how it works. You may curse or kill the next living thing you see. If you put on the wrong hat or glove, your next move may be in something other than your natural form. If one of the veteran practitioners spots you flitting around in your animal body and asks you a few questions, you may not make it back in any form.

GETTING TO THE ROOT OF THE HEX

Once you realize that you or someone you know is the target of a curse, the source of it has to be identified before any effective cure can be found. This won't always be easy. Witches usually attack in secret.

The stroke could have come anywhere or any time in the past few months. It could have been launched quickly, with a powerful witch blinking the victim with an evil eye. It could come slowly, a traditional hurting curse wrought with spells and implements in a private ritual and from far away. Like an avenging spirit, its energy keeps escalating.

There might also be a charm targeting the victim, an inanimate, metaphysical time bomb as traditional as a charm-bundle or as seemingly non-Iroquoian as a simple effigy representing the victim. Like a voodoo doll, it might have burns or scratches in selected places. It could be a tiny object magically placed within the victim's body. It could be witch powder fed to the victim by "sprinkling"—tossing charmed dust on a dinner or drink.

If you or someone you know happens to be suffering from a curse, knowing who your attacker is can be very helpful. That way you may be able to handle things on your own. As we've seen, you might be able to buffalo that witch into dropping the business.

It might sound easy at first. Most of us have a real small list of people who might be both mad at us and magically inclined. But it can take a long time to spot a pattern in a wave of disasters and come to the conclusion that something magical might be involved. And just because you're suffering from a curse doesn't mean you're the real target.

You see, Iroquois witches don't always hurt their intended victims, at least not at first. Some of them work toward their targets by knocking off the people they love, thus making them suffer the more. Fiendish and clever. Think of it as a national refinement.

ARTHUR C. PARKER ON WITCHCRAFT

Arthur C. Parker stated in 1901 that no understanding of his own Seneca people was possible without taking into account their belief in witchcraft. No matter how reluctant they were to admit it to anyone they didn't trust, many Seneca of Parker's day still dreaded the evil art.

It didn't matter whether one was a traditionalist, a Christian, or a follower of Handsome Lake. There was no general agreement on the origin of the craft and its entrance into Iroquois society.

Some Mohawk claim that witchcraft was introduced to them by members of an Algonquin-speaking nation whom they had taken in. Some Seneca trace theirs to the Nanticoke Nation, which the Seneca adopted—if not the Eries or Kah-Quas (Neutrals), nations they absorbed or displaced. The Onondaga fought wars with the fierce Andaste Nation, suspected of being a race of enchanters. The Tuscarora came to upstate New York with occultism, which was possibly influenced by the traditions of African slaves in their North Carolina home.

In Europe, there is a similar pattern of a dominant society associating traditions of magic with a culture it has supplanted, repressed, or absorbed. Every tribe or nation that migrated to or invaded the British Isles—Celts, Romans, Saxons, Normans—attributed occultism to those it displaced. Occult traditions are also found among marginalized groups within a society or among immigrants who bring occult traditions with them.

The gypsies have always been the wizards of Europe. Occult and mystical traditions came to imperial Rome in waves from its provinces. Voodoo came to the American colonies with displaced Africans. Still, the tradition of witchcraft seems so entrenched in Iroquois culture that it's hard to believe all their customs could be imports.

In Parker's version of *The Code of Handsome Lake,* the Longhouse prophet was so ruffled by witchcraft that it became his personal quest to warn all the Iroquois against it. Handsome Lake begins one of the sections of his Code by noting that the Creator was unhappy at the piles of dead, all people killed by the actions of magic, and in particular, charms. The prophet forbids all types of magic. In doing so, he describes a few spells:

1. If someone dies keeping a secret from you, you might discover it by sleeping on the ground with a handful of dirt from the per-

son's grave under your head. If everything goes right, the dead person will reveal the mystery in three successive visions.

2. The Iroquois were great runners who could send messages one hundred miles a day along their upstate trails. A man hoping to be a runner might keep a bone from the grave of a famous runner in his belt. Most celebrated Iroquois runners were said to carry such charms.

3. A warrior could protect himself from ambush by making three cuts in the back of his neck and rubbing them with an oil made from the scalps of enemies. The cuts would heal into three white, protruding scars. If an enemy came up from behind, these queer tattoos would tingle.

4. At least two Iroquois nations, the Seneca and Onondaga, held the belief that an exact number of children is predestined to every woman. These children, they believed, were fastened within each woman on a vinelike runner they called the string of children. The Creator, who made life so that it should live, was distressed when people interrupted the natural process, hence the prophet condemned abortion charms and potions.

5. The most effective charm for getting rich is the tooth of a *niagwahe,* the demon bear.

One thing the prophet failed to add is that attempting to get a tooth off one of these critters is the most effective charm known for committing suicide.

Parker's observation of the two styles of Iroquois magical practice may illustrate the traditional distinction between the magician/witch and the sorcerer. As Peter Partner observes in his book about the Templars (*The Murdered Magicians*), the sorcerer—like Shakespeare's Prospero—needs book and staff. Keeping a sorcerer away from the magical tools and techniques takes away all his or her power. You can let one of these off with a lesson.

But the old kind of Iroquois natural witch or magician is a far more dangerous figure. The magician/witch is inseparable from his or her power. You are only safe from one of these characters when he or she is dead. Thus, for the old Iroquois, there was only one solution to a danger like this. It was extreme.

ONONDAGA WITCHES
(Syracuse-Oneida, Nineteenth Century)

Artist and folklorist De Cost Smith (1864–1939) was born in Skaneateles, New York, and spent time at Onondaga in 1887 and 1888. He heard enough about witchcraft to inspire an article, "Witchcraft and Demonism of the Modern Iroquois." Smith was familiar with rumors about a double execution for witchcraft at Oneida in 1825. He was shocked to hear that an old man suspected of witchcraft was ambushed and shot to death on one of the Canadian reservations as recently as the 1880s.

"What did the man's friends do about it?" Smith asked those who told him.

"Nothing," was the reply. "They thought he had been at that business long enough."

"And the white people?"

His Onondaga friends shrugged. "They didn't know about it."

A middle-aged Onondaga man told Smith about an old reservation woman he had thought for years to be a witch. Once, as he was going home around eleven at night, he came around a wooded hill and saw the woman ahead of him on the same trail. Her long hair kept her from seeing him, and he decided to slow down and play it cool.

He caught an eyeful. With each breath she took, many-colored flames blew from her mouth, licking the locks of her hair. The display even lighted her way. He followed till she neared a certain longhouse used for national councils. As if sensing she was being followed, the old gal ran around the building, came to a long log home said to have housed a couple of witches, gave a last huff and puff, and disappeared within.

The Onondaga Reservation quarries used to have an odd geological feature called the Cat Hole, a slot in the rock said to be the dumping place for the bodies of executed witches. The bodies needed special treatment. You didn't want to bury nonwitchy folk on top of them. The witch bodies might bear toxic charms. You didn't want to live near the dead bodies, either. As with radioactive waste, you wanted generations ahead to know where the bodies were buried. Onondaga Reverend Albert Cusick (1846–?) knew a man whose sister was killed for witchcraft and dropped into this space.

In his book *Onondaga* (1849), white historian Joshua Clark (1803–1869) tells us of four women accused of witchcraft in 1803. One confessed, repented, and was spared. Two clammed up and were killed. The fourth admitted her guilt, was taken to the top of the hill east of the Castle, killed with an axe, and buried among the rocks.

Ephraim Webster (1762–1824), first white settler on Lake Onondaga, believed there could have been something to witchcraft. He testified to having seen the marks of the fingers of a phantom strangler on the neck of a victim who died overnight. He also heard about a serious witch-incident from before the whites had settled. It started in a big Onondaga community that may already have been cursed.

During the 1696 invasion of Quebec, governor Frontenac burned and dispersed the villages on the east side of Onondaga Creek. The Onondaga returned and rebuilt many of these, including one on the flats east of Jamesville. An old man of this community claimed to have gone for an evening walk and been sucked into an immense cavern lit by countless torches. It was a gathering of witches and wizards. They ejected him quickly. They should have done the same with his memory.

The next morning he told the story to the chiefs and led them about the village pointing here and there at people he said he had seen in the witches' cave. Hundreds of the accused may have been executed; others were driven off and became refugees. The incident sent shock waves throughout the Confederacy. The Onondaga Nation nearly came apart. The village was abandoned for good around 1720. Heaven help whoever lives over the site of it now.

Onondaga Reverend Albert Cusick was a confidant of white historian William Martin Beauchamp, to whom he reported hearing about fifty witches who had been burned to death near Onondaga Castle. This may be part of the case reported by Webster, above. According to Cusick, the witches were sort of an occult mafia whose secrets no one could reveal and then expect to live. These witches could turn into foxes and wolves and run quickly through the night, all the while accompanied by flashes of light. They could fly in the forms of turkeys or owls. They could blow hair and worms into people they wanted to curse. If they were stalked, chased, or surprised they could turn themselves into stones or rotting logs and be completely hidden.

The Midnight Service
(Onondaga, Traditional)

Three Onondaga siblings were especially close. Their parents had died when they were children, and they'd been brought up with their late mother's cousins in a village somewhere near today's Syracuse. They were all teenagers when the oldest took to his bed with an illness so strange and unexpected that his brother and sister sensed witchcraft. The younger brother set out to investigate.

As a boy he'd heard rumors about one old woman in the village. Someone said they'd seen her breathing fire one night as she walked. One afternoon, he sidled up to her and commenced an indirect conversation that went nowhere. Finally, he told her he wanted to be a witch. She looked him over without much enthusiasm.

"I hear there are such things," she said, "but you better be real serious about what you say."

He assured her that he was and looked at her steadily. She looked back as if reading him. Then she gave him a special look. She opened one of her eyes wide, rolled it back in her head, looked away quickly, and wiped her nose.

"All right then," she said. "Go home and point your finger at your sister the instant you see her. In a while she'll get sick, and in days she'll be dead, but that's

how I'll know you mean business. If you don't do it just like I tell you, you better point the finger at yourself, because what's coming to you will be worse." She told him where and when to meet her next.

The lad didn't believe his finger could be loaded, but he had no intention of trying it out on anyone he loved. On the way home, he pointed high into the trees, heard a squeak, and jumped when a squirrel flopped at his feet. Then he told his sister the whole story. She went along with the plan and pretended to be sick. Soon the whole village was talking about her illness. The witch must have smiled.

A night or two later, the young man walked through the woods to the witch's meeting spot. Well before he'd reached it, someone startled him by coming up behind him. It was the old girl herself. They walked together a while, and she startled him again: She took a run at a tree as if she were going to ram it, then leaped up and held to it as if her hands and feet were claws. What turned to look at him was a full-grown panther, spitting and snarling. Even in the dim light, he could see the fiery eyes, the gleaming teeth, and the muscles rippling beneath the furry coat. He stood his ground and looked at her evenly.

She let go of the tree and stood again on two legs. "Scared you good, didn't I?"

"Not really," the young man said. "Actually, I want to be like you. I want that power."

The witch chuckled. "We'll see," she said.

They came to a clearing in the woods at which a number of people were gathered around a small fire. A kettle not much bigger than a cup hung over it, and a bundle of snakes dangled above, dripping blood, venom, and fluids. Faces glowing like goblins, people waited around it for the drops to mount and took turns passing cupfuls of the fearful brew. It was easy for the youth to pretend to drink and step back with others who had already sipped.

Most of the folks were older men and women. Some were from his own village, and the lad was surprised by some of the ones he recognized. He decided that he wasn't very good at guessing witches. He didn't see any other males his age and figured that this might have been why it was so easy to infiltrate the group. They wanted young men.

He noticed movement at the edges of the clearing. People's forms leaped and cavorted out of the circle of light, jumping high like human grasshoppers. Others frittered in the trees like squirrels, and some even made leaps that became brief flights in and out of the clearing. Others changed more slowly.

He'd been thinking about a girl he was sorry to see here, and when he saw her again she had cat's ears. In another minute she bounded into the shadows like a mountain lion. Someone who had turned into a squirrel started chasing someone who'd become a bobcat. The antics ended in a wrestling match that had everyone hooting and snarling with laughter.

Too fascinated to be afraid, the youth stood and stared. At first no one seemed to wonder why he, too, didn't transform, but soon a couple came over to him. Their horns and feathers, he thought, concealed veteran witches, and he was terrified that they would know he hadn't tried their potion. Then he noticed a handful of others still in human form, all of them young women and girls. He thought quickly.

"I can't turn into anything," he said to someone next to him.

"It's hard the first time," said an old man with drooping hound ears.

A woman's voice beside him said, "What would you like to be?" He turned and saw a squat pile of tusks, nostrils, eyes, and fur that he thought might have been a wild pig.

"A screech owl," he said. They greeted this with snorting and huffing that he took to be approval.

"We've got just the thing," said a man with stag antlers coming out of his long gray hair. Other mostly human folk went into the dimness and came back with a hat made out of a horned owl's head. They handed it to him but told him to wait before wearing it.

"When you put that on," one said, "you'll take the owl's form instantly. You'll fly like a bird. But if you don't practice a bit before you put it on, you might kill yourself and take our hat with you."

"How do you practice being an owl?" the youth said.

"Practice acting like an owl," said a stag with the voice of an elder he knew.

"Practice thinking like an owl," said a girl still in her own form. "That's what they always tell me." The young man recognized her, an orphan being raised by a great aunt he'd seen around the fire earlier. He noticed how pretty she was.

He started making the movements of the owls he'd seen: preening beneath his arms with his nose as if it were a beak, moving his elbows as if they were folded wings, turning his head sharply, even trying out a few screeches. There was howling around him that he took to be laughter. "He'll be a boss witch once he gets going," said a big dog.

"Boss owl, anyway," said a big old man with a panther nose and teeth.

The meeting started to break up. The handful who had kept their human forms took separate trails into the woods, including the orphan girl who cast him a glance as she left hand in paw with a bear. Others went off as foxes, wolves, panthers, hawks, and owls. A handful of animals, people, and animal people still surrounded him, watching him curiously. He put on the hat. Its beak covered his nose. He looked through its eye sockets. The world changed.

Before he knew it, he was flapping wings. In a few strokes, he was aloft, straight up through the trees, and then soaring and darting on the currents. At first he was ecstatic. The speed, the wind! The moonlight silvering the treetops below! He could see in the darkness as if the moon were a sun. He saw the sudden movement of a small animal by a creek and could hardly stop himself from diving after it.

But even after practicing, he was a beginner owl. It was hard to flap and steer, and he was not used to looking with those eyes. How different the world was through them, and from above! All he saw were treetops, hills, and creeks.

In sudden terror of losing his way, he thought only to get back to his village. He flew in ever-widening circles from where he thought he'd started, hoping to spot the fires, rooftops, or fields of a settlement. He knew his village was the closest to the clearing from which he'd started, but how far had he flown?

He saw smoke in the distance and headed toward it. Soon he saw a stream and cleared fields. He heard a dog barking and knew he was near a village. He got closer and tried to hover. Surely it was his own village. He tried to perch on the peak of the roof of his family's longhouse, but he landed too hard, and the magic headpiece toppled into the smoke hole. Immediately, he took back his own form, and plunged feet first through the opening after the hat.

He clung with his elbows to the edges of the hole in the roof, his legs dangling. The dogs went crazy, leaping for his ankles, and his cousins jumped up reaching for war clubs. Before he let go, he tried to yell out who he was, but he landed in the cold ashes and came up covered in them. Only his sister's shouting kept him from being clobbered. The mood was only lightened by his sick brother, laughing from his bed for the first time in weeks. The owl cap, though, had been stomped into uselessness, and the dogs were having a tug-of-war with what was left. It was a while before anyone got to sleep.

The next day the young man called his brother's friends together and told them the whole story. It was not as hard as you might think to convince them. Many of them had their own suspicions about the illness. They went to the chief with a plan.

An elite group of warriors stayed ready in their homes for several nights. On the first twilight that people were spotted leaving the village, the warriors assembled. The sick man's brother led them on a stealthy trek through the trails to the clearing in which his adventure had started. There the witches were gathered.

Still in their human forms, the witches were easy to identify. They were also distracted, listening to their officers and sages engaged in many a fine speech. Six Nations witches, it seems, love rhetoric, like all other Iroquois. Each warrior was able to creep up close to a witch undetected. The sick man's brother took a place close to the orphan girl who'd helped him before.

The leader of the witches stood by the fire. "Enough of these reports," he called. "To business. Where's our new young friend, Owl Boy? We'll have to settle for him soon. He may be able to recognize some of us." There was a murmur of assent among the group, already mixed with a few half-animal sounds.

"But first I have to tell you something serious. If we were all to die today, not one of us would go to the Evil One who is our patron. Not one of us has done enough evil deeds. The Good-Minded Spirit would take us to him. Let's vow, each of us, to leave here tonight and curse and murder at least one person apiece. Let's start with that boy who has our fine owl hat."

At that second, the lad they spoke of jumped up. "You don't mean me, do you?" He took the hand of the orphan girl who'd helped him and hauled her out of the glow of the fire. Every witch took a breath to snarl or roar. Furry faces wrinkled, and fangs bared.

But before any of them could move, each warrior leaped from the darkness beside his appointed target and struck. Every witch fell dead. The men went back to

*their homes, heroes, having saved the local villages more suffering than they would
ever know.*

The Witch of Otisco Lake
(Onondaga, Traditional)

*A vain, pretty woman was the belle of the village. All the young men courted her, all
but one fine hunter who didn't pay her much attention. After a while, this was the
only one she wanted, but he either minded his own business in life or went about
with young women who were more grounded.*

*The pretty woman used a charm to bewitch him. It worked so well that he
wanted to be with her all the time. Once the shoe was on the other foot, she put him
off just as she had all the other young men. In a few weeks he was so thin, weak, and
sick that his friends started to worry about him.*

*A couple of them took him to Otisco Lake, hoping to get him away from his
worries. Still he roamed, wandering in the moonlight, moaning for the woman who
had witched him.*

*One day, his friends took him on a lake cruise in a patched canoe. In the
middle of the lake, it started leaking. The sufferer was too weak to paddle with the
others, but he bailed water as fast as he could with a gourd dipper. In the middle
of the lake the boat went under. The strong fellows took turns helping their witch-
struck friend get back to shore, but he was unconscious when they reached land and
lived only hours longer.*

*His best friend gave the death whoop when the small party neared the village.
The people gathered, and among them was the witch, who gave a loud cry, ran to
the body, knelt in tears, and confessed what she had done. The procession moved
silently past her.*

MARY JEMISON ON WITCHCRAFT
(Genesee Valley, Late Eighteenth Century)

The autobiography of Mary Jemison is a window into the Iroquois
character. In its pages we meet people of deep virtue, true to the death
to their own codes. We see harsh lives, nationalistic conflict, desperate

brutality, and superhuman courage. We see people in times of change. We learn plenty about their supernatural belief.

The Seneca people Jemison knew may have shed their faith in some of the more exotic folkloric beings like the Giant Mosquito and the Legs. They had a little less doubt about the Great Flying Heads, sensing that they might just be getting rare. They hadn't lost a shred of their faith in witchcraft.

Jemison's Seneca believed that, next to their own Evil-Minded One, the world's many witches were its greatest scourge. To them it seemed their duty to do whatever they could to destroy this dangerous source of evil.

A number of people presumed to be walking on the dark side got along fine within the community—as long as they didn't go too far. Those accused of witchcraft were tried like those accused of anything else, and the Iroquois had an admirable legal system. There was no parole or forgiveness, though, for those convicted of practicing an art as dangerous as the dark one. The only chance was to make tracks, as many did on first hearing they were suspected. Others were hauled to trial before they could get away.

In her time with the Seneca in the Genesee Valley, Jemison could hardly recall a year in which she did not hear of at least one execution for witchcraft. She cites an incident in which a Native American man with lust in his heart pursued a woman near Little Beard's Town along the Genesee River. A strong lass, she fought him off and made her escape. The man—boy, perhaps, we should say—went back to his village and reported that he'd seen fire in the woman's mouth and that she must have been a witch. The woman was arrested, and Jemison witnessed her execution. Another time, Jemison saw a supposed witch killed and tossed into the Genesee River.

Some reservation folk tell us that Jemison herself was suspected of being a witch and that several times she ran from her home and hid out in the woods till things subsided. This she never mentioned in her book. We asked a pair of our Seneca friends what they thought about the odds that the White Woman of the Genesee was into the otkon.

"Maybe she just had some of the wrong friends," Jean Taradena suggested.

Pam Bowen shrugged. "She might have been trying a little too hard to be Indian."

THE HEART OF A BLACK BIRD

There's another way to deal with being witched: fight back with the same medicine. But even in small communities, it can be hard to identify an occult tormentor. Arthur C. Parker in his book *The Code of Handsome Lake* describes a deliciously sinister ceremony for finding a witch.

Get a living bird, black in color. A crow might be best, but a black hen will do. Take it into the woods at midnight and make a small, slow fire. Split the bird's body, take out its heart, and hang it by its arteries over the fire. Roast it slowly and wait. Whoever did the witching to you will know about your ceremony soon enough and get to the spot immediately. The witch will have no power over you and will tell you why he or she is witching you, or anything else you want to know.

But suppose whoever's witching you is too far away to get there in person? This is when things get really interesting. Your witch will put in an appearance in an astral form and roost in the leaves of a tree above you. At other times you may not even see this apparition of your witch; all you'll hear will be a voice from somewhere overhead. You'll find out who it is, though, and why he or she is witching you. The answers may surprise you. The questioning is especially critical here because so much of the time you may not be the true target. You may not even know the witch. He or she may really be targeting someone who loves you and will be hurt by any pain you suffer.

Once you have your witch, there's nothing but dawn between you and the answers you want. There shouldn't be any need to kill the witch, either. Come to think of it, you have a pretty powerful enforcer in your back pocket, and a time may come when you will need one. Just hang on to that scorched heart, keep it safe somewhere, and this character will do your bidding. If you really mean business, though, let the heart burn all the way through. The witch will be found dead in the morning of a malady the Iroquois call burnt heart.

There has to be more to this than Parker described. No doubt there's a conference with an elder, probably a medicine person, who will prescribe the exact steps, even the ideal night for the ceremony. There might be other moves and ingredients. But based on the way the Church of Rome rations its exorcisms, you don't want to overuse this powerful ritual. Keep it for that rainy day.

WITCH BONES

Many of the old Iroquois witches worked their spells through a little object called a witch bone that they placed in the body of the victim. It was often a tiny, double-pointed, needlelike splinter with a hole in the middle. Sometimes a single hair from the head of the witch would be threaded through and around. This magic trinket could be bone or wood, and other objects, even living ones like tiny worms, have been reported. Stories about objects like these being drawn from witched people are common.

There's not much agreement on how a witch bone gets into the body of a sufferer. Most of these witch totems sound small enough to be planted in food or drink. But customarily, witches "blow" these things wherever they want at the end of a ceremony. From the sounds of it, once the job is done right, the object just ends up where it's supposed to. From there—usually in the guts of the victim—it does its damage, ruining happiness, health, even life.

If you get hit by this kind of traditional curse, burning the hidden, charmed object will heal you. The difficulty is finding it and hauling it out. For that, you need the help of a traditional healer. The ceremonies are often uncomfortable and take a lot of time. Once you find one of these witch bones, though, you're in a position of power. Burning it can hurt the witch, killing him or her within hours. You can also throw it in almost any direction, even from inside a building, with a word of guidance, such as "Now go, and fly into her heart!" The fiendish object will become a guided missile, finding the witch the same way it found you.

But as with the bird heart ceremony, the medicine people don't always burn these things. Why bother? You don't need revenge, do you, if the curse failed? You have a weapon against whoever sent it. You can get whatever you want out of the witch from then on. Twentieth-century Tuscarora medicine man Mad Bear, we hear, had quite a collection of these charms.

A WITCH'S BAG

As we mentioned earlier, witchcraft may be no more than a diversion of orenda for selfish and hurtful purposes. It changes its name when so used. The otkon can be concentrated—incarnated, if you will—into objects. Put the right bunch of them together, each with its own power, and the concatenation can work up a mojo that's greater than the sum of its parts. Iroquois witches often mixed up these recipes, which were partly traditional and partly intuitive.

These witch bundles come in small, medium, and large, from a charm that might be a single energized object to a necklace bag, a satchel, or even a whole cauldron. A number of these witch-kettles have been found buried about upstate New York, including a fearful one in Buffalo surrounded by a ring of skeletons and filled with human skulls. Undoubtedly a bunch of the grim things are still out there, all over Iroquois territory. They only turn up by accident, when people dig. For those who happen to live above one unknowingly—enjoy.

The Erie lakeshore folk always thought the old woman was a witch, and no one entered her house for a long time after her death. The first who dared was a white man, and no slouch when it came to the spooky.

Irving, New York, historian and antiquarian Everett Burmaster (1890–1965) found a bag in the house and listed its contents in his memoirs.

The bag, like the three witches' cauldron in *Macbeth* ("fillet of a fenny snake," "eye of newt and toe of frog"), had ingredients that were macabre but mundane and easily acquired: tiny weapons, dolls, animal hearts, thread, dried snake blood, a bottle of "eye oil," various powders, hair in many shades, nail clippings, wet blood, a small sharp bone, various greasy substances, a dried human finger, and the skins of snakes, a black calf, and a big dog.

The miniature weapons were probably totems made to the supernaturally powerful Little People, "the Iroquois fairies," in hopes of enlisting their energy into rituals. The pelts and skins could have been used with the aim of shape-shifting. Most of the other stuff has analogies to magical practices all over the world.

From his earliest days of experience with the Iroquois, our late East Aurora friend Bill Bowen (1940–2009) found them superstitious. If you were threatened or harassed by an angry Iroquois male and the situation got extreme, all you needed to do was clasp a hand over a spot on your chest about the level of an imaginary locket and look him in the eye. "That's OK," you might say. "I'll just go get my bag, and we'll take care of everything." Presuming that you might have a witch working for you—or that you might be one yourself—your harasser would almost instantly recoil. It was a radical move, though. Bowen saw the trick in action in his youth in the 1950s on the Tonawanda Reservation.

Two Seneca men were arguing at a meeting, and one tugged the imaginary bag. The other marched out as if he'd seen a ghost. An undercurrent of grumbling broke the peace, and before long a near-riot started. A couple of friends dragged the air bag man out the door. "Are you crazy?" one of them said. In a culture that still dreaded magic, this gesture was the nuclear bomb of arguing, just a step short of pulling a gun. It could be dangerous in many directions, including to the man who made the threat.

THE WITCH JOHN JEMISON

In 1897, a Cayuga woman told white ethnologist William Beauchamp a strange story. During Mary Jemison's days in the Genesee Valley, a curious pounding was heard coming from inside a nearby hill. Folk drew near just as a giant, one-horned serpent dug its way out like a hatchling. It retreated when it saw them, but came back later and was soon tame. Jemison tapped the horn with an awl. Out flowed blood, and she filled a cup with it and served it like Guinness to her children. Maybe this explains how one of her brood, John Jemison, became a witch.

Just after the War of 1812, a Seneca hero called Young King fell into a heated argument with the government blacksmith at Buffalo. A blow from a scythe cost Young King an arm and outraged the Seneca. While the Great Hill folk took the matter to court, John Jemison appointed himself the national executioner and stalked off for Buffalo.

Somewhere on his way along old Route 5, John was spotted by the white writer Orsamus Turner. To the author of the *Pioneer History of the Holland Purchase,* John looked like " the Angel of Death": face painted red and black, horse-hair fetishes on each arm, war club in one hand and tomahawk in another. People kept the smith out of sight until John quit looking for him. It was clear to all that Mary's son by her second husband, the lethal Chief Hiokatoo, was no one to mess with. He may also have been a witch. There were signs of it early on.

One of Rochester's first white settlers, Ebenezer "Indian" Allan (1752–1813), spotted something unsettling in John when he met him as a boy, and Allan—former member of the Crown's Revolutionary terrorist outfit Butler's Rangers and a frontier scumbucket of the first order—should have known. Some strange incident happened in John's boyhood, something witnessed only by his younger half brother Thomas. Their mother either never knew what it was or didn't include it in the autobiography she dictated to Doctor James Seaver. But brother Thomas always called John a witch, and the rumor stuck.

John Jemison was a renowned healer who made long nocturnal

forays into the Genesee woods gathering his ingredients. The site of his medicine garden may be a grove in the northwest area of today's village of Mount Morris, just yards from the top of Letchworth State Park. While no one but brother Thomas ever called him out as a witch, accusations of witchcraft were mighty serious in that society. Even a wisecrack could have led to a trial and a potential death penalty. Their mother believed this was the cause of the hatred between these two.

Witch or not, John was a seer. He dreamed that he killed his brother Thomas and forfeited his own life. He told this to an old sage called the Black Chief, who advised him to watch his temper. The dream turned out to be prophetic.

On the first of July 1811, Thomas came to his mother's house and encountered brother John. A quarrel commenced. John grabbed Thomas by the hair, dragged him out, killed him with a tomahawk, and fled to Caneadea, New York. His mother found Thomas on her doorstep. It was a bitter loss to the community. Though he enjoyed a drink, the fifty-two-year-old Thomas was a model Seneca. The council weighed the matter but decided that this was just a fight, a simple brawl that got out of hand.

Mary's youngest boy, Jesse, was thought the finest of her sons by a long shot. At twenty-eight, he was the main support of his widowed mother and a very "white" Indian in manners, dress, and work. Mary ordered him to steer clear of brother John, in whom, according to Doctor Seaver, something had incited "so great a degree of envy that nothing short of death would satisfy it."

In the spring of 1812, Robert Whaley of Castile sold a raft before it was built. The planks to be used for it were at the top of a hill on the banks of the Genesee, and he needed extra hands to get them to river level. Unaware of the family tension, Whaley recruited a crew that included Mary's son-in-law George Chongo and both of her feuding sons.

Whiskey joined the work and stayed when it was over. A fight broke out between Jesse and George Chongo. Hiokatoo's youngest son pounded his brother-in-law and started heading home. At that point, brother John pulled a knife and stood before the white raft builder, face lit with a demonic intensity. "Jogo!" he snarled. "Get lost!" Whaley made tracks.

"So, you want more whiskey and more fighting," said Jesse, trying to take away the knife. The pair clinched and tussled, and Jesse was struck repeatedly. "Brother, you have killed me!" he cried out. Any one of his eighteen wounds could have been mortal.

The bravest thing John did in his whole life was to tell his mother what he had done. There was no legal consequence to this deed, either, probably looking to the council like no more than a drunken knife fight. But John was a pariah—till people needed medicine.

In the spring of 1817, John Jemison went to Buffalo to work as a healer. He came back to Mount Morris in midsummer just after the Great Slide of the Genesee. He took a look at the hillside that had collapsed in that event and considered it a sign of his own death. In a couple of days, he fell to drinking on nearby Squakie Hill with three Seneca, two remembered only as Doctor and Jack, and a third from Allegany.

In the afternoon, a quarrel started, and the two local Seneca decided to kill John Jemison. He may have threatened to witch them, and the pair dared not let him get a head start. As the party broke up, the two conspirators hauled John Jemison off his horse, hit him with a rock, and finished him with an axe. He was fifty-four when he died at the end of June 1817 and was given a white funeral.

Blood feuds and revenge figured in preindustrial life everywhere, but among the Iroquois, a death didn't always merit a death. If someone killed a member of a rival clan and sent an offering, usually white wampum (a symbolic beaded sash), to the victim's family, the quarrel was over—if it was accepted. This the two murderers tried. Mary Jemison refused. She told the council that she didn't want the pair harmed; she just never wanted to see them again. This meant banishment from their families, their villages, and their ancestral lands.

Doctor and Jack ended up wandering Squakie Hill, despised, despising even themselves. Troubled by dreams and visions, they soon took their own lives.

The Seneca always considered the hill haunted because of Jemison's death there, and his revenge could be said to have come from the spirit world. Does his influence linger? White campers today report all kinds of apparitions about Squakie Hill. Is he behind the psychic play, still stalking the shades of his murderers?

TWO SENECA WITCH TRIALS

Son of a white trader and a Seneca maid, Garyanwaga, or Cornplanter, became a chief among the Seneca. His name turned blood cold in colonial hearts during the frontier wars, like those of Mohawk Joseph Brant and the white Loyalist ranger John Butler (1728–1796). Cornplanter was surely with those two at the infamous Cherry Valley, New York, massacre. He fought against the 1779 counterstroke at Sullivan's Hill until the day was lost.

Cornplanter was more than just a fighter. In 1790, he spoke nobly to George Washington on behalf of all Native Americans. One of the tracts given to the Seneca after the Revolution is still largely in their possession: the Allegany Reservation, to which Cornplanter and many Seneca retired after the Revolution.

But things didn't stay peaceful. The young U.S. government relocated a party of Munsees/Delawares to the Allegany, not seeming to understand that they and the Seneca were traditional enemies. Tension bloomed into trouble.

Cornplanter's daughter Ji-wi fell ill in 1800 after giving birth. Led by Cornplanter's half brother, the soon-to-be-prophet Handsome Lake, the Senecas accused the child's Delaware father of trying to kill Ji-wi through witchcraft to spare himself "the responsibility of matrimony." Things got out of hand quickly. War nearly broke out between the rival nations. Negotiators were called in from Ohio and Canada. State militias in Ohio, Pennsylvania, and New York went on alert, and reports were made to the U.S Secretary of War.

Ji-wi recovered and the matter cooled, but not before serving as a testament to the power of witchcraft in the Iroquois world.

Rhetoric was one of the transcendent arts of the Six Nations. Their speechmakers were world renowned in their day, and the man we call Red Jacket (Sagoyewata) was the greatest known to history. Red Jacket's familiar English name was likely due to his fondness for a British soldier's coat. By the end of the eighteenth century, he had made a most powerful enemy.

Partly under Cornplanter's guidance, the Seneca had backed the losing side in a couple of conflicts, most importantly the Revolution. Cornplanter also had a hand in land sales to the whites, and Red Jacket's dagger-wit was letting no one forget. Cornplanter had the great Sagoyewata charged with witchcraft, possibly accused of making a curse or spouting witch fire at night.

It was far from the first time a powerful Iroquois was suspected of cutting corners to gain "extra" abilities. And word wizards—riddle masters, poets, and songmakers—in many world cultures were sensed to be magicians. It may also have been a political hatchet job orchestrated by Cornplanter's half brother, the witch finder and soon-to-be-prophet Handsome Lake. It was a dangerous moment, and it came to trial in 1801 in a council meeting at Buffalo Creek, remembered in John Mix Stanley's famous painting.

Red Jacket got up and gave it back—for three hours—along the Buffalo Creek. He was acquitted and never challenged again. It was presumed thereafter that his sorcery involved nothing but words.

KAUQUATAU

It was momentous when an Iroquois chief fell ill. His orenda was that of the nation, and when his illness seemed magical, it was presumed that only a powerful figure could have launched the curse. This would either be the chief of another community—which could lead to a war—or a mighty witch, possibly within the chief's own community.

In the spring of 1821, an important Seneca man fell ill at his home on the Buffalo Creek Reservation. He seemed to need no more than simple nursing. Kauquatau, a Seneca woman who was considered a healer of great power, was appointed to tend him. Everyone was shocked when her patient died. The community sensed witchcraft and blamed his magical nurse.

A delegation of chiefs approached Kauquatau and got ready to knock her off, but at the critical moment, the appointed executioner choked. According to rumor, the witch froze him and his fellows with an instant spell, possibly the evil eye. Chief Soonongise, commonly called Tom Jemmy, broke free of the spell, drew his knife, and slit the witch's throat. They left her body where it lay, on the banks of Buffalo Creek, possibly near the foot of Michigan Street in Buffalo.

The whites of the region threw Tom Jemmy into jail. Red Jacket came to his trial, took a bit of scolding from the white prosecutor, then thundered back. The Seneca were a sovereign nation, he argued, and the execution was legal in their society. He reminded the white court of the American witch trials in Salem, even their culture's treatment of their own Savior, one no Christian is allowed to forget. Convinced or maybe just cowed, the State Supreme Court let the prisoner go.

Witches' bodies were considered so toxic that they were always specially handled. Kauquatau seems to have been buried under her house, one no Seneca would touch thereafter. The land was sold in the winter of 1842 to the Ebenezer religious society, and shelter was so scarce that a family of German fundamentalists took over the witch's collapsing cabin. Soon, they reported terrifying psychic eruptions. Only the intervention of group leader Christian Metz and the burning of the cabin put the matter to rest. Today, the witch's presumed grave is still a conspicuous bare space in a white burial ground. The Old Main Cemetery in West Seneca is a regional legend, with many reports of the apparition of a "woman in white."

The Stealer of Children's Hearts
(Seneca, Late Nineteenth Century)

An old reservation woman was especially solicitous at the deaths of children. She consoled families and helped with funerals, and for a while it was appreciated. But late one night, a neighbor walking by her house saw a head-sized ball of light shoot out the chimney toward the graveyard. This was a witch light, in which some witches were thought to travel. "So," she said to herself, "The old girl must be up to it."

The next time a child died, the old woman came to help, taking a turn sitting with the corpse. But the woman who'd seen the witch light told her husband to keep an eye open around the body that night.

Sure enough, at midnight when the old woman thought she was alone, she took a knife, cut the heart out of the child, and left the house while everybody slept. The neighbor's husband followed her. In a while, a ball of fire flew out the chimney of her cabin and streaked to the cemetery.

Frightened but game, the husband followed it to the old section in which many of the graves were sunken. He watched the woman dig and scrape for a while, put something into a hole, and cry out, "There! I've got you another. Now we're friends again, and you'll lead me to money."

The neighbor's husband took off as quickly and quietly as he could. He dove for cover and lay still when the light soared over him again, doubtless heading back to the witch's chimney.

The next day he went to the dead child's father and said what he'd seen. They found no marks on the body; the witch had magically healed the cut. But at the cemetery, they found the grave the witch had visited, with signs of fresh digging. They dug up the grave and found a corpse with a tender heart in its teeth and its shockingly fresh and contented face covered with blood. They ran for the witch doctor.

At twilight they watched him pour kerosene down the hole of the open grave, stuff it with rags, and set the mess afire. Soon red and black smoke poured out, and the leaves of the trees above it fluttered in the glow. Toward the end they thought they heard a horrid gibbering through the crackle of the flames, as if a vent to hell had opened in that grave.

They broke into the old woman's house and found bloody rags on a table. They approached her at the funeral. "You're nothing but a witch!" the bereaved father shouted. "Now I know why you go to funerals. Admit it!"

She burst out crying. "I never hurt the children. I gave their hearts to my friend after they were dead. My friend in the ground was my friend in life, and she makes luck for me now. I'd starve without her."

"You should have told people you needed help," said the father. "You can do without luck like that. Go home, and give up this business."

A witch doctor made a charm above the heartless child so that she might rest in her grave. The witch woman died not long after, so maybe her time was due. And maybe only the power of the spirit witch had kept her alive that long.

The Swig of Flying
(Seneca, Early Twentieth Century)

One young Seneca man was visiting another at his cabin. The two were enjoying a summer evening and discussing a couple of ladies they hoped to know better. One of them mentioned the fine opportunity the evening's dance at the Tonawanda Reservation Long House could provide, ten miles away. Neither of them had a car, and it would all be over by the time they could walk there. The host went to his cabin and brought back a reused wine bottle. "Take a sip of this," he said.

Both took swigs of something that tasted like sweet wine. After putting the bottle away, the host trotted down the dirt road in the direction of the Long House. His guest followed. Soon both were running in great, effortless bounds. Thirty, forty, fifty feet. Tracts of road and trail flew under them with every stride. They tossed their heads and laughed. The sky above them hurtled by.

In only minutes, their airy courses glided to a walk. Lights and music came to them from the Long House and reminded them where they were heading. Just as they entered, the guest cleared his throat and coughed. He got a shock. Red light glowed in his cupped fingers as if a fire inside him shot light through his mouth and nostrils—one of the traditional giveaways of the Iroquois witch. Folks sure to know what it meant would be inside the Long House.

"I wouldn't do that in there," said the owner of the magic wine, and his guest nodded. They had a good time, but as the night came to an end, the guest was starting to wonder if he had been made into a witch for good. He was happy to find *when he left the dance that the effects of the flying liquor were barely noticeable. His strongest cough made no more than a spark, and in another hour, he was all the way back to himself. Still, he stayed a long way away from that witch-Seneca ever after.*

WITCH CHILDREN

Belgian ethnologist Frans Olbrechts (1899–1958) spent time among the Cherokee of North Carolina and reported on a strange custom in 1932. Some Cherokee families chose certain children, often twins, to be witches. They were brought up specially, undergoing a sort of life initiation supposed to endow them with supernatural abilities. The most critical period of this training was the first fortnight of life.

Infants so chosen were given no mother's milk for their first twenty-four days. They were fed only the white liquid of corn hominy and only at night. No strangers were allowed to visit them.

Once this three-week cycle was over, the parents of these witch children never worried about them, even when they didn't know where they were. It was presumed that the children could take care of themselves. Even in infancy, Olbrechts reported, "whatever they think happens." Throughout their childhood, their constant playmates were the Little People, usually invisible to everyone else. By adulthood, they could fly through the air, project themselves underground, walk on sunbeams, and take the forms of certain animals.

Olbrechts wondered openly why anyone would want to add to the number of witches in the world. He sounded, though, as if he had become a believer. When these witch children grew up, he reported, "They are most annoying individuals. They always know what you think, and you could not possibly mislead them. What is worse, they can make you ill, dejected, love-sick, or dying merely by thinking of you in that condition."

The Cherokee are linguistic cousins of the Iroquois and once lived near the Tuscarora in the Carolinas. When the Tuscarora came to New

York, some Carolina customs surely came with them. Our confidants have been ominously quiet about practices among the Iroquois that might be related to this.

The Hair-Bone Token
(Seneca, Early Twentieth Century)

A strong young man got sick, and no one knew what was wrong. He saw doctors, took medicine, got rest, and got worse. By the time he quit work and went to stay with a friend, he was in bed most of the day.

A witch doctor from the Tonawanda Reservation made a potion of unspecified stuff and put a poultice of it on the sick man's belly. Calling for quiet, he covered it carefully with rags and moss and sat back to wait. Those who touched the mass said it felt hot.

In a while, the sick man groaned, as if something was being drawn out. At a moment he seemed to be waiting for, the witch doctor grabbed the poultice, ran to the kitchen, and dumped it into the ash pan of the stove. He rummaged around in it and pulled out a small sharp bone wrapped in a white hair—a traditional witch token. Jaws dropped. The healer communed with the quirky object for a while and ventured that a certain neighborhood widow was behind the witching. Friends and family had a hard time with this. "She calls every day to see how he is," said the woman of the house.

"Just see what happens next time she visits," said the witch doctor, tucking the hair-bone token into the patient's hand. His recovery wasn't instant. He tossed and mumbled, covering himself with the sheet.

By the end of the next day, he was coherent and, as he held the bone-and-hair trinket, sounded as if he was narrating a film. "Here she comes. She's leaving her house. Now she's down by the well. Now she's on the road . . . crossing the bridge, the gate, the path. She's by the apple tree. Now she's at the door." There was a knock.

"I couldn't sleep last night," said the widow when the introductions were done. "I worried so much about poor Bill."

"You're the one!" the sick man yelled from under the blankets. "You leave me alone after this or I'll kill you!" With apparent pity, the old woman took her leave.

That night the sufferer talked to the bony item as if spectators didn't exist, chanting phrases and verses from a language none knew he'd ever learned. At the end, he wrapped one of his own hairs around the object and shouted, "Go back to her, and stick in her heart!" He threw it in the direction of the witch's house. Everyone heard it tap against the wall. It vanished as if it had flown right through.

The next day the sick man's friends went to see the old widow. Her neighbors were already gathered outside her house. They had found her dead with the bone in her chest. Those who knew the situation felt sorry about it, but not for its victim. "She had no business witching people," said one of the sick man's friends.

The Witch's Daughter
(Seneca, Late Nineteenth Century)

When the Salamanca woman died, her husband and daughter went through her belongings and saw that she'd been a witch. The Christian father wanted to burn the bundles and potions, but his girl told him it might be dangerous even to touch them. But maybe she had something on her mind. Her heart was set on a handsome young Seneca who visited her father on business. One night, she dosed the lad's drink with a love potion, snuck out as he left, and waited for him by the path. Things turned amorous. When the frolic was over, she asked, "Why don't we get married?"

"No need in it now," the lad said, heading home. "We've had our fun."

Weeks later he was near again on business. He meant to avoid the house that had gotten him in trouble, but something pulled him to it. This time the witch's daughter double dosed his cider and headed to the same wood. Things went as before, but this time he left singing love songs. The girl came home announcing marriage. "That's interesting," said her father. He knew that the lad had just married a girl from Cold Spring.

The new wife gave the lad a good long talking. He promised he'd learned his lesson, and in a few days things had cooled. He also got sick. He lost weight. He had sharp pains every night and couldn't sleep. Soon he couldn't work. It seemed clear that he'd been witched.

A witch doctor had a feeling about the swamp nearby and sent the sufferer to a certain spot to see for himself what was happening. Something swinging in the moonlight across a creek caught the lad's attention; it was a bark doll dangling from a tree, and soon someone he knew came to it.

Calling the doll by his name, the witch's daughter caressed it like a newborn, then scraped it with a knife. "When the string rots, you'll fall and die. Till then I'll scrape away." The lad felt every stroke, once even crying out from his hiding place. He huddled in terror, but there was no need. The girl laughed aloud, thinking it more of her own long-range magic. "Ha! I can even hear you from here."

The next day from his bed at home, he heard her voice. She had come to his house, bringing soup and asking about his health. "Go away," he yelled from his bedroom. "And leave me alone. I'm sending for a crow."

"What good's that going to do you?" she said, leaving in a huff. She should have read the whole witchcraft manual.

"So she's been here," said the witch doctor on his afternoon visit. "Just as I thought. Now we can do it." He had with him the body of a crow. The young Seneca cut the heart from the bird, held it up, and called it the name of the witch's daughter. They hung the heart from the kettle frame and ran a splinter through it. They lighted another splinter and passed it under the heart a couple times, singeing it and giving it a gentle toasting. Then they set it aside and waited.

The next day the witch's daughter came over crying, showing a burn mark on her breast that had blistered. "Now quit witching me," said her victim, "or I'll burn the heart out of you."

No one knows what happened to the doll, but the young husband recovered, so she must have taken care of it the right way. She never witched anybody again, either, and in time became a good friend to the young family she'd offended. She even looked after their children when the couple traveled.

Sassafras Charley

Autumns are moody in Iroquois country. The one of 1929 brooded trouble on the Cattaraugus Reservation.

Recently widowed Nancy Bowen was a spry sixty-six-year-old tribal healer. Svelte, thirty-six-year-old Lila Jimerson worked at the reservation school and was known as a seer. The Cattaraugus power pair started using a Ouija board to reach

Bowen's late husband, a part-Cayuga medicine man whom many white Buffalonians knew as Chief Sassafras or Sassafras Charley.

Sassafras Charley Bowen sold trinkets, herbs, wood carvings, and sassafras, the dried bark and leaves of a tree used in many a cure. He was also into the otkon, and had had many adventures related to it. Once some Christian Senecas found red witch powder in the snow outside their cabin and figured Sassafras Charley was to blame. The discovery got him kicked off the reservation for a couple of weeks.

Charley Bowen's recent death had been outwardly natural. To his widow and her friend, though, the voice of the Ouija said otherwise. The moving planchette spelled out the news that Sassafras Charley had been murdered and would wander in a spiritual netherworld until his killer was punished. Soon the messages named her: Clothilde Marchand, the slight, pretty white wife of an illustrator at the Buffalo Museum of Science. Her husband Henri Marchand had done some painting at the Cattaraugus Reservation, even using Lila Jimerson as a model. Her long-range maleficence, the board's messages said, was behind other Cattaraugus deaths as well.

The Ouija—"the devil board," as some call it—is not native to the reservation. Still, it is not strange that it would be found there and in use. The Iroquois are no supernatural snobs. They adopt any tools and techniques they fancy. What was strange was the coherence of the messages that came through on this one, naming and describing Mrs. Marchand and even giving her Buffalo address: 576 Riley Street, near the museum.

By the winter of 1930, an odd series of untraceable letters had been delivered to Sassafras Charley's widow, all supporting the same conclusion. For weeks Jimerson and Bowen had been aiming traditional magic at Clothilde Marchand. Its failure must have convinced them of her power. On March 6, they took the next step.

The two women walked five miles to the trolley line and took the ride to Buffalo. The younger met Henri Marchand at the museum and got him to drive her around the city in his car. The widow went to his Buffalo home and met Mrs. Marchand at the door.

"Are you a white witch?" she asked

"Maybe I am," said the artist's wife, making a joke and turning to let her guest in. With a hammer bought that morning, the widow gave Mrs. Marchand a tap or two on the temple. Chloroformed cotton tamped down her throat made sure her life was done. Her twelve-year-old son found her body after school.

By the same time the next day, the two Cattaraugus women had been caught and charged. They readily admitted to the killing. Why not? She was a witch.

At first the motive seemed ludicrous. Most Buffalonians thought well of the suave French-born artist. They presumed Jimerson had a mad crush on him and had his wife killed to clear the way. The case was not simple to the government, which sent a high-powered team to defend the women.

Experts like Seneca scholar Parker have attested to the power of witchcraft in the Iroquois soul. One Iroquois would kill another, he said, if convinced that this would end a hex.

A Seneca crone led investigators to the graves of three mighty Seneca warriors. Jimerson and Bowen had planted whiskey and vittles among their bones. Found with those tributes were little white wood-and-cloth dolls, doubtless portraying the wife of the artist. One was even dressed with paper from one of those mysterious letters sent to the widow.

When a Buffalo newspaper printed some of the letters Henri Marchand had sent to Lila Jimerson, it was clear that artist and model had been more than friends. In fact, Marchand had had more affairs than he could reliably estimate. The scandal made headlines.

Sex and sorcery made for lurid newspaper reports, but Native American sovereignty and religion were the subjects of the trial—which became a lightning rod. Shouts of racism and conspiracy from the women's defenders would be familiar today. The Jimerson-Bowen trial woke people up to supernaturalism on the Cattaraugus Reservation. Otherwise, it's hard to understand why the two women were virtually acquitted, let off with little more punishment than the ordeal of the trial. The all-white, all-male jury clearly despised Marchand's escapades and may have decided it was no mystery that something finally blew up. They may even have suspected that Marchand had a hand in the murder. (There were those anonymous letters in handwriting a bit like that of Henri Marchand.) The artist-widower did nothing to help his image, taking an eighteen-year-old girlfriend by the time of the trial.

Then again, the jury may have come to believe that a dead Cayuga witch had driven two women to murder.

The Last Act
(Tuscarora, Early Twentieth Century)

Nobody ever said much about Davey Roy's background. He'd been adopted as a boy by Lulu Gansworth, a Christian, and raised with her brood in the farmhouse on Indian Hill on the Tuscarora Reservation. He grew into a shy, dark, good-natured young man whom Tuscarora author Ted Williams remembers as not the world's alpha male. He had a girly throw with a baseball, for instance. He also had an Asian cast to his eyes that reminded Ted of the First Nations people he had seen from Georgian Bay. Davey Roy was a helpful, hard-working lad—maybe a bit too *helpful.*

One of Davey Roy's adopted brothers was nicknamed Heavy-Dough, and these two used to trade off the chore of bringing the cows in and milking them every night. One early evening Heavy-Dough took his turn, setting off on the dirt road that curves around Indian Hill and leads to the back pasture. It was well out of sight of the Gansworth farmhouse, and a gigantic dead tree once stood beside it.

The stark form of that tree had fascinated Ted as a boy. He had spent many a moment staring at it, scrying it against the sky from various angles and weighing the impressions it gave him. That day, though, Heavy-Dough was in no mood for admiring. In fact, he came running back without a single cow. When he got to Davey Roy, he was almost too rattled to get his story out.

He was within sight of the herd when he noticed something bright and eye-catching in the sublime tree. Perched on a branch fifty feet over the road was a gleaming being that the son of Lulu could only process as "an angel." It was a man-bird, and it was making motions to him to come closer.

Who is ever sure what any apparition really is? Many a routine ghost may have been mistaken as the Virgin Mary by a Christian witness. Something about this "angel" scared Heavy-Dough out of going anywhere near it. Davey Roy set off down the path to finish bringing the cows home. In the morning, Davey Roy was found, pounded to death, on the side of the road that goes up Indian Hill.

Nobody knew of any enemies that Davey Roy had, and none had a clue who might have killed him, evidently helped by the conjuring of supernatural apparitions. Late in his life, though, Ted Williams found a possible connection.

For some time, Ted had been keeping records of the lives of reservation folk so that they might be remembered when they passed away. In the 1960s, he was looking over his decades-old notes and spotted a reference to Davey Roy's grandmother Emily Gossey. His recollection of her contained the cryptic comment that she had been engaged in a bitter, lifelong feud with a dreaded witch with the Tuscarora name of Kreegi(t)uh. Grandma Gossey must have been a power person herself, one who kept her brood safe while she was in the world. Was Davey Roy's death the last act of the feud?

Big I'sic's Desire
(Tuscarora, Early Twentieth Century)

Big I'sic was a large man, and he did justice to his meals. By his thirties, he was the biggest Tuscarora anyone had ever seen. He also had a secret crush on a woman on the reservation.

One day, Big I'sic spotted Asa Williams talking kindly to the object of his desire. There was nothing unusual about this gesture: Asa Williams was a shy homebody who talked kindly to everyone. But the sight of this filled Big I'sic with an impulsive rage. He quickly contrived a situation in which he and Asa worked with axes in the same wood. Asa and his head were separated before the third tree was felled. Big I'sic covered the body with trunks and branches, then went home as if nothing had happened—minus one imagined rival. But his victim had a brother, and Dan Williams was no gentle soul.

Like the Seneca John Jemison, Dan Williams was well-known as a healer. His expertise was prized in Native American circles, and he traveled widely dispensing it. But both he and the girlfriend who shared the family farmhouse had, like Jemison, another reputation. As was said of them both in direct translation of the Tuscarora phrase, "They know poison" (they were witches). This was a factor that Big I'sic had left out of his calculations, if any were made at all. They say love—if you can call it that—does that to many of us.

When it was clear that Asa Williams had disappeared, brother Dan got out the medicine and made a single potion. He poured the steaming mixture into a bowl, loomed over it, draped a shawl over his head, and rocked and chanted for a long time. At last he gained one vision he was sure of: his brother's head and body covered by branches. He found the body, arranged the funeral, and got the honoring and grieving done. The next step was finding the killer.

Big I'sic had seen enough of the medicine that could find a body that fast. Before the funeral was over, he took off for the Six Nations Reserve in Canada where at least one long arm—white American law—couldn't get him. But Uncle Sam isn't the only one with a reach.

Before long, Dan Williams had the killer's name. Everyone knew payback was coming, one that was going to be greater than the crime. Dan Williams confessed years later to his cousin Ted that he had his victim on a leash, and he gave it plenty of snaps.

Big I'sic developed a psychotic addiction to food. The more he ate, the more he craved. Maybe his supernatural attacker had sent him the spirit of Sagodadahkwus, "He Who Eats Inwards," the Seneca personification of gluttony. He died a ghastly death of self-indulgence and one with a distinction: He was the only Tuscarora Ted ever knew so big that he was buried in a piano crate. He never revealed the name of his secret love, even when he had nothing else to lose.

A Wayward Youth
(Tuscarora, Early Twentieth Century)

From his boyhood, Ted Williams remembers an older woman everyone called Cassandra. Who could forget her? She had her own style: high-top shoes, broad-brimmed sunhats, and flowery dresses that flapped in the wind. She lived with her daughter's family on an old farm.

Her grandson was a lad nicknamed Less, and he was the man of the house after the early death of his father. Cassandra hoped that he would become something in life—a lawyer or doctor, perhaps. He had been taught well at the reservation school, but it could all change for the worse in his teens. There were obstacles and so many distractions for reservation youth.

The pivotal moment came when Less neared the legal age for dropping out. One day he announced that he was tired of school and didn't see why he should keep going. His grandmother sent him with a note asking his teacher, Miss Felsy, not to let him flunk any more courses.

A few afterschool conferences took place, and something changed. Young Less started to like school and often stayed late to work on his grades. This was encouraging on the home front, but he was slacking on his chores, and one day the cows got loose because he'd forgotten to mend a fence. Gramma Cassandra hitched up a horse and buggy for the first time in years and took off for the school for a word with her grandson.

Ted Williams was on the scene as the grandmother drew up to the building and looked down into a window. Whatever she saw almost made her fall out of her seat. She turned the carriage around and tore off on a track that led into the woods. The only thing at the end of the track was the log cabin of a woman with the nickname of Old Shrinkable—a known witch.

Ted wondered what could have given Less's grandmother such a start. He looked in the same window in time to see Miss Felsy stand up, straighten her clothing, and button her dress. Equally disheveled, young Less tore out of the school and after his grandmother. He had an expression, a flushed face, that Ted would not understand until he was older.

Less wasn't back in school the next day. Miss Felsy left the school shortly thereafter. One day she just didn't show up. Once Ted got to know the male teacher who replaced her, he asked about Miss Felsy. "She grew three funny warts on her face," the man said. "She didn't want anyone to see her. When they got out to about half an inch long, she had them taken off. Three more got growing in different parts of her face. The doctors couldn't figure anything out about these. Now, how about that?"

Ted told the story to his father, Eleazar Williams (1880–1968), a celebrated medicine man. Eleazar sat him down. "Ted, Gramma Cassandra was worried that her grandson was going to run off with his teacher, and the farm and all her dreams for him were going to fall apart. She went to Old Shrinkable the witch and got her to fix the teacher. That's one thing Shrink can do—put warts on you. But Old Shrink doesn't work for free, and Cassandra and her daughter will be paying her off the rest of the way. I may have to put a stop to the cycle. It's too bad we didn't know about those potato eyes before this," he concluded. "We might have done something to keep them from growing."

The great healer reached into his medicine cabinet and came out with some dried squirrel corn, a northeastern herb with white heart-shaped leaves, which he pounded and made into a tea. "We'll have a little ceremony just between us," he said to his son. "This tea is really good for secret keeping. If either of us talks about this, those potato eyes will start growing on us." When the mixture cooled, Eleazar and his son touched cups, met glances, and drank. Young Ted was terrified by the thought of those warts. This was one secret he was going to keep!

A couple of days later, Ted looked out the window and saw his medicine man father hop onto a horse. He had the expression of somebody off to do business. "Where you going?" Ted called out.

"Shrink's place," said the father. "Don't forget about those potato eyes."

Because nothing more was ever said about this, we presume that Old Shrink stopped demanding payment from certain people and warts stopped growing on others. We will never know whether Ted's father was serious about the wart-growing potion. The tale appears in Ted's book Big Medicine from Six Nations, which wasn't published until 2005, just after Ted left this world.

3

The Witches' Torch

The lights have been with us since the beginning of time,
and they will be with us until the end of time.

DuWayne Leslie Bowen, *One More Story*

WITCH LIGHTS

The strange, nocturnal lights known in Seneca as *ga'hai*—witch lights—are fixtures of Iroquois storytelling. Sometimes the lights appear as pale, slow-moving, head-sized spheres that, but for their variable hues, could be the lanterns of distant hikers. Sometimes these luminous balls swarm, drifting across the landscape like pastel balloons. Sometimes they seem atmospheric and even site-bound, rising like tallow marsh gas from invisible vents. Other witchy lights are dynamic, fiery, and even self-directed, hurtling through the treetops like low-level comets and coming to rest in dire places like graveyards, battlefields, or swamps.

In some tales, these flying lights are flares leading a witch or wizard to victims or targets. They might be static markers indicating the hiding places of charms or other treasures. If one springs to light by the course of your evening stroll, watch your step: Its controller is near.

The lights themselves are virtual characters in other tales, going through their impish, seemingly intelligent maneuvers to the amazement of human onlookers. Ones like these are more likely to vary in size, to flock in numbers, to fill a grove or graveyard, and dart or hover like hummingbirds. The presumption is that some supernatural being that inhabits or causes them might be out for a little fun with us. We're surprised that these lights are not routinely associated with the Little People in Iroquois country. They were in Europe.

In the most developed stories, witch lights are regarded as alternate forms that witches take in order to travel. If you are near a witch light as it passes, you might see the faint image of a human face inside the sphere. It's probably the countenance of a power person, living or dead, presumably the witch or wizard directing it. It's best if it does not notice you noticing it.

Though unassailable in this form, called the witch's torch, witches come back to their natural bodies sooner or later. If you follow one of these lights to its destination, you may see it snap out of existence. In its place will be the human you now know to be a witch.

Whites in the Northeast have been reporting these lights for centuries, offering no explanations for them in local folklore. The ga'hai are still seen with frequency about upstate New York, and by all types of people, especially in traditionally haunted sites and areas. In contemporary accounts, they seem to be simple paranormal phenomena, almost like spontaneous and unintelligent offshoots of the territory around them. Maybe this is what they really are. Though some fit the profile of the folkloric witch lights, others are surely will-o'-the-wisps or swamp gas. Their high-density sites are often on reservations, prehistoric ruins, battlefields, or other "places of ancient sanctity" (as John Michell called them) to Native American societies.

ANOMALOUS LIGHT PHENOMENA

What is often called ALP (anomalous light phenomena) is commonly reported around the world. Regarded most often as signs of fairies or ghosts in European and Asian traditions, these earthbound mystery lights are among the most commonly reported sights at haunted locations. Like ghosts, they seem site specific, associated with particular areas that often have historic, religious, or geological peculiarity.

Two of the most prominent contemporary paranormal scholars started their careers in search of the answer to the UFO phenomenon, whose early peak was in the 1960s. British authors John Michell (1933–2009) and Paul Devereux found levels of complexity to the matter. Michell noticed general paranormal connections to UFOs, including the witness experience. People either witnessed the lights when they were suspiciously close to ancient sacred spaces or when the lights themselves were above these features.

Devereux backtracked on earlier reporting and reinterviewed witnesses cited in media reports. He noticed that a lot of things first reported as UFOs may not have been the classic sky lights presumed to be extraterrestrial vehicles, and that the eyewitnesses may have been reporting something different altogether. He concluded that a different type of phenomena was getting lumped in with UFOs, the confusion likely caused by news stories written by hasty and disbelieving newspaper and TV reporters. Many so-called UFO witnesses were describing more terrestrial types of lights—a European version of the Iroquois witch lights. Devereux decided that most of these "Earth Lights," as he calls them, come from the natural energies of the earth. He separated them into categories:

1. *Ball lighting.* This is a many-colored nexus of light that manifests, cavorts, and then escapes. Once thought to be paranormal, ball lightning has been recently accepted as a real physical phenomenon. It often shows itself inside enclosed spaces like buildings or airplanes.

2. *Will-o'-the-wisp.* These mysterious lights seen at night or twilight over bogs, swamps, and marshes were personified in the British Isles as Will of the (lighted) Wisp, or sometimes Jack of the Lantern. Will (or Jack) was fated to wander the world's lonely places with his woeful searchlight till the Judgment Day. The decay of organic matter and the subsequent oxidation of phosphine and methane in the air is one explanation for these lights.

3. *Earthquake lights.* Nicknamed EQLs, these strange lights manifest near the surface of the earth just before seismic disturbances. When tectonic plates grind beneath the surface, they create natural electrical charges, called piezoelectricity, which have been photographed and videotaped. It's like the spark set off when steel hits flint. Though EQLs weren't recognized by seismologists until the mid-1960s, Charles Fort (father of American phenomenalism, 1874–1932) listed appearances of them in his books as early as 1919.

The witch lights reported in Iroquois country include all three of these forms. Some act like natural ball lightning, starting in one place and moving irregularly to another. Others haunt marshy ground, and still others just might be the EQLs of Devereux's third classification, trooping about the Onondaga Formation and many of the geological faults that underlie upstate New York. There are also witch lights in folklore that don't fit into any of these categories. These the Iroquois might know better.

Like Walt Disney turning a house mouse into Mickey, folklore personifies natural phenomena, giving them character and personality, and spinning them into stories. Even if you believe that this is what has happened with the witch lights, regional traditions of sightings could also indicate some kind of metaphysical energy about sites or regions. When witch light appearances permeate a place, this is regarded as a sign of many spirits, as if there were once a battle or an old tradition of occultism.

THE HILLS OF ROCHESTER

Western New York has been Seneca country for at least a thousand years. Before the Seneca's arrival, other Native Americans lived here, including communities of Algonquin on a couple of Rochester's damp hills. The Algonquin's heyday was probably during the European Middle Ages, around the 1200s and 1300s. It's fairly certain that they were driven out or absorbed by the Seneca. We may never know exactly where any of the clash points were. But sites linked to battles and bygone populations attract supernatural folklore everywhere. It was no different along the Genesee River. For the Seneca, the five Rochester hills made a zone of spirits.

One of them, Oak Hill, has been leveled off and made into a country club. Highland Hill and Cobb's Hill are recreation spaces today. The other two, Pinnacle Hill and Mount Hope, are the most interesting from paranormal perspectives. What do we do with pieces of land no one wants to live on? Sometimes we give them to the dead. This was the case with both hills.

First named Mount Monroe, Pinnacle Hill is the highest point in Rochester and just might be the object visible from Buffalo on the northeastern horizon at the end of Genesee Street in Joseph Ellicott's (1760–1826) 1804 city plan, which is very likely Masonic. A lawyer, surveyor, and city planner, Ellicott's name has surfaced in connection with mysticism many a time. (A prominent artist, lecturer, and self-described "urban shaman" in Buffalo, Franklin LaVoie has this and many other innovative theories about local landscape.) Pinnacle Hill hosts a church, park, St. Patrick's Roman Catholic Cemetery, and legacies of witch lights.

Mount Hope by the Genesee River may have been even more powerful. The Seneca didn't cross the hill or the marshy area below it after dark. Even the white settlers drove carts and wagons far out of their way to avoid it. The much-storied Mount Hope cemetery has a huge late population, hosts of ghosts, and several proverbially haunted regions.

Strange lights have been reported at night about Mount Hope, floating, drifting, and hovering. Several buildings at the nearby University of Rochester are thought haunted, though the ghosts may be related to more recent events. Even the campus newspaper has reported various supernatural sightings over the years, not the least of which are the lights.

THE LIGHTS OF OSWEGO BITTER

In the early 1800s, Revolutionary War veteran John Marshall (1755–1835) gave land for a cemetery near his house in Oswego Bitter, a hamlet ten miles east of Syracuse. From the start, the settlers reported strange lights at night in the gravestones on Bennett's Corners Road.

The lights moved with apparent purpose—along walking lanes, around obstacles, and over streams. Some witnesses thought they might be people with lanterns. They always came from or vanished into the graveyard, though, and those who saw them up close had different stories.

A farmer's horse knew its route between barn and tavern so well that its owner could have as many as he wanted "for the road" and trust it to lead them both home. Their course went past the burial ground at Oswego Bitter. On one such night the over-served rustic woke up at the graveyard gate, the cart parked, and the horse mesmerized by a dancing ball of light. Only when the light drew into the cemetery and blinked out could the horse be persuaded to move.

Another time two farmers spotted one of these lights and stopped their wagon to watch. The glowing sphere came right at them, drifted over the harness, passed between them over the center of the seat, then disappeared in the graveyard.

By 1952, newspapers were still referring to will-o'-the-wisps in the hilly country near Bennett's Corners Road. The term may have comforted reporters, who likely surmised they were nothing but swamp gas, but the sightings created a buzz among the locals.

No wonder. The lights in Oswego Bitter seem nothing other than the ga'hai.

By 1987, Robert Fletcher, a resident of Oswego Bitter, had been seeing these luminous balls for thirty years. Fletcher lived near Bennett's Corners Road and had used parts of John Marshall's original house to build his own. Most often, Fletcher said, the lights came down the hill, entered the graveyard, and disappeared. He presumed the phenomenon was natural, though he ventured no opinions on the cause. Others on the road thought the business was rooted in the ancient spirits. The area is at the margin of Cayuga and Onondaga territories, and it would have been fun to talk to the old-timers two centuries ago and find out what they made of the lights.

Since the late 1980s many who have spotted the lights heard an animal call that no local hunter could identify. The sound reminded some of the recorded cries of an alleged Bigfoot in a western state. The Big Hairy has been reported in most parts of the Empire State, and in many zones associated with mystery-light phenomena. Maybe this graveyard near Oswego Bitter is one of those places.

INDIAN HILL

New York state has several sites called Indian Hill. One at the edge of the village of Gowanda not far from the Cattaraugus Creek is getting pretty famous. The road cutting over it to the Cattaraugus Reservation has accidents with a suspicious frequency. Maybe that explains its deep legacy of supernatural folklore. Anyone bold—or silly—enough to be here on certain nights might hear eerie sounds coming from the hollows holding old graves and homesteads. Phantom forms are reported in the woods at twilight and around distant fires, seldom distinct enough to be studied. One presumes they may be simple human ghosts, possibly those of earlier inhabitants.

But mystery lights are the specialty at Indian Hill, widely reported by drivers using the road. Depending on when and where they appear, they could have many natural causes. Those who have encountered them at close range are not so sure.

One of the most elaborate reports from Indian Hill is of a distant sphere of dim light drifting through the trees that, as it nears, becomes the complete image of a wolf in a sort of glow. Thought to be some type of wizard in animal guise, witch lights like this one are regarded as very dangerous.

Maybe a great medicine person lived nearby and did a bit of nighttime wandering in a form like it. It's possible that this apparition was seen at times of turmoil for the neighborhood, hence it could be interpreted as a protest from the collective psyche. We think it was just one more aspect of the witch lights.

Native Americans on all of western New York's reservations think of Indian Hill as a whole zone that's active and enchanted. A word to the wise, though: this would be a bad place for thrill seekers of any type. It is part of the Cattaraugus Reservation and hence sovereign Seneca territory. Ask permission before you start poking around.

TRAIN TRACKS AND WITCH LIGHTS

By the winter of 1887–1888 people living near the Peanut Railroad between Corfu and Indian Falls were starting to worry about strange nocturnal lights. In February 1888, the *Batavia Daily News* even ran a curious report titled "Supernatural Lights." Newspaper reporter G. Ranger claimed to have seen one himself while driving north from Attica. It first appeared north of Alexander on the Central Railroad and kept up with his horse and cart almost to Batavia. From a distance, it looked "like the headlight to a locomotive," though not as bright. Ranger got home without further incident. As he neared his house, the light drifted off and disappeared into the woods.

Years before, a local named Philander Shippy was out for an evening drive in the same general region and was ambushed by a flurry of these lights. The air was full of them as he left Batavia. They danced around his cart "like flies in the summer," lighting on the horse, the harness, and even his hat. He snapped at them with his whip, but they easily dodged every stroke. He set his horse running to get away from them. They followed him the length of the turnpike, but they disappeared when he hit the high ground.

Ranger noted that these lights were nothing new to the area but that they were getting rarer in recent decades. He felt confident in saying that they "belong to the Jack-o-lantern or the will-o'-the-wisp family, are without heat, and perfectly natural and harmless." He was untroubled by the seemingly intelligent behavior of the one he claimed to have seen, or its difference from the ones that beleaguered Shippy. The idea that these could be fireflies or swamp gas seems ludicrous. It seems as if the whites were encountering witch lights, which are known to play pranks.

The fact that these witch lights are associated with railroad tracks or beds makes us wonder if there might not be some geological or geo-magnetic component to their appearances. But why would anything psy-chic favor these broad straight channels through the landscape? It almost makes us wonder if it's hard for a post-colonial shaman to see when dis-guised as a light. Maybe these artificial paths make for easy navigating.

THE HILL OF DEAD WITCHES

One of New York's folkloric hotspots is a piece of territory on the side of a hill in Allegany State Park. To the Seneca this is Ga'hai Hill, a region of magic and mystery where anything otherworldly is likely. It's an "X-zone," in other words, an area whose magic affects many who come here. From a distance, witch lights can be seen at night on this hill. The northern Alleghenies are part of a region that has long been a major zone for UFO reports. Ga'hai Hill is one upstate site like the English ones noted by Paul Devereux, in which earthly lights and celestial ones—the classic UFO—may be linked. There may be more to it than that.

In 2007, we interviewed a woman of Onondaga ancestry who reported that she was the descendant of a woman who had been considered a witch. Possibly during the hard-to-date Onondaga witch scare, this woman fled to Seneca territory near Salamanca, where either her practice or the accusations caught up to her. Eventually she was executed and buried on a hill in Cold Spring—Ga'hai Hill where other witches may have been laid to rest.

Few of the Salamanca Seneca admit knowing of this association to the hill, but there was witch trouble in this area before, as we've seen during the time of Cornplanter. And reports of the lights are still around. Residents of Cold Spring, Steamburg, and Salamanca persistently see them on Ga'hai Hill. Many Salamanca motorists are terrified of breaking down anywhere near that hill, even in the section of I-86 that arcs the base.

The Gold of Ga'hai Hill

Allegany Seneca storyteller George Heron (1919–2011) heard most of his tales from an uncle who was born before the Civil War. The interchange included many legends about the ga'hai on Bay State Hill across the river from Cold Spring, about four miles southeast of Red House Lake. The ones Heron's uncle described floated about as high as a human knee, "like a car headlight but with no explanation."

Heron's uncle told a tale about three Union deserters en route to Canada carrying bags of money through the Allegany Reservation. They recruited three young Seneca to round up food and civilian clothing and get them directions to Lake Erie. In payment, the soldiers offered each Seneca a full grab into a bag of gold coins, a fistful that would have been the sum of a lifetime. "But don't go spending it right away," they warned as they left. "It's hot money."

The joy of the three Seneca was mixed. Their first worry was losing their treasure. Their second was being caught with it. The oldest had a plan: He'd bury it on Ga'hai Hill. He'd fill his pipe at the bottom of the trail, start smoking, and walk with the gold to the top. When the tobacco ran out he'd bury it, and that would be the way to find it again. The three would wait a few years to start spending it. This *made sense. "Nobody will poke around for it up there," they reasoned, because of the dread of the witch lights.*

The oldest Seneca did as he had planned, found a tree special enough to remember, and dug. Over the winter he caught an illness and died before he could show his friends to the spot. All anyone knew was that the gold was somewhere on the trail up Ga'hai Hill, about as far as a single pipeful would last.

For years, the two surviving friends prowled Ga'hai Hill, their thirst for gold evidently greater than their fear of witches or lights. After their deaths, one of the men's sons took up the search. Storyteller Duce Bowen told me this is thought to be a true tale in Salamanca. Even today, when the witch lights are out on the hill, people wonder if the souls of the treasure hunters might be among them, still looking for their gold.

The Boys Who Hooked a Witch Light

One summer evening in the 1930s, two young men from Cold Spring trolled lines from their little boat on the Allegheny River. By dusk, they had some fish to show for their efforts, including a couple of the suckers that were such a delicacy to the family cats. One of them spotted a mysterious light along the nearby railroad tracks. At first, it was a bright sphere moving slowly at ground level. He called to the other to look, and it sped up.

The light hopped to the treetops, came back to the earth, and bounced up again. It made long, majestic arcs, bounding like a luminous ball tossed by a giant along the railroad tracks. It disappeared when it landed on the riverbank. A small fire soon started on the spot. The boys were alarmed to see a shadowy human form in the glow. It could only be a witch. "Let's get out of here," one whispered. They paddled as quietly as they could, with occasional backward glances.

The fire on the shore faded into a white light. It came down the bank, entered the water, and came at them under the dark water like a glowing torpedo, making one small wave. It overtook them with such speed that they rested their paddles and watched. It passed under them, scraping the hull and rocking the boat, then drove out into the river and curved back. Again it hit and rocked the boat, this time so wildly that they clung to the sides.

A fishing pole shot up, slapped one boy's leg, and leaped into the water. "We hooked it!" he cried. It seemed true. As if the witchy light were a swimming wizard who had snatched their line, it and their pole had started following its wake. The light took another bend under the water and came back, this time a bit slower. It shook the boat even harder, splashing in water and pitching one boy on top of the other. Then the unknown force let them go, and they paddled madly for the shore. The light headed in another direction and crept out of the water like an animal. The little fire on the bank started up again, and a shadow form beside it shook like a dog shedding water.

They hauled up the boat, left their catch, and ran to the nearest boy's home, where they gasped out their story. The father listened impassively and at the end said, "Did you remember to bring the suckers for the cats?" His eyes twinkled above his pipe. He knew they had been teased by a witch light. Mojave-dry wit is an Iroquois characteristic.

ONONDAGA WITCH LIGHTS

Onondaga faith keeper Tony Gonyea is a prominent teacher, elder, and activist whose home base is the reservation near Syracuse. In 2004, I ran into him in a Syracuse bookstore, the legendary *Seven Rays,* and asked him about witch lights.

Tony started by recalling that he grew up in a home under a hill that was locally famous for these lights, a little like Ga'hai Hill near Salamanca. He disclosed few details, but conceded that some lights had been spotted there in living memory. "My brothers and sisters used to see them all the time when we were kids," he said. Once they even saw one bouncing down the hill and crossing the yard.

Tony remembered the night that he and a friend had spotted a brilliant light sphere coming down the same wooded hill. It should have been zigzagging because of the dense trees, but its course was as fast and smooth as if it had been immaterial. It couldn't have been a motorcycle with a single headlight, not moving like that through those woods.

Years later, Tony saw one of these lights, this one bright blue, on the same hill. An adult by then, he was walking home from work in

Lafayette at the end of day when he saw it. He studied it as long as he could see it. Then it disappeared like a match burning out, and he took off running to the exact spot. He found what he was sure was the place, a clearing as naturally circular as if the trees had parted in their growth to leave a nurturing space. This would have been a spot the old-timers might have called "a Little People place."

I pressured him for more details. I asked him why we only hear about the lights in certain hot locations. "I'd say the witch lights are all over the state," he reflected. "People kind of pay attention to things at a different rate."

A METAPHYSICAL CONTRACT

Generally good-natured supernatural characters like the European and Native American Little People love it when someone makes a kindly gesture toward them, and they will often dispense good fortune to the giver. Many sinister supernaturals, though, in world folklore can act against someone only after a similar overture. When the unsuspecting human being either offers hospitality to the supernatural one or accepts it in return, that exchange becomes the signature on a metaphysical contract. The gesture that seals the deal can be simple and surprising, but this stricture—the fact that an invitation must be made and accepted—is one of the few fixed protections we mortals have.

Also like the European fairies, the Iroquois Little People are sometimes associated with strange lights, usually different in size, shape, and behavior from the mistrusted witch lights. One must not be treated as the other.

The Girl Who Fed the Witch Lights

One family on the Tonawanda Reservation lived near a railroad bed by which they saw these ga'hai often on winter nights. They thought of them as no more sinister or conscious than supernatural wildlife. As a joke in the 1980s, another child told one of the family's daughters that these witch lights were the Little People. The girl "fed" the witch lights, probably by leaving leftovers at spots outside the home where they had been seen.

The lights appeared more often and steadily nearer the house. The neighborhood was soon on edge. One night a neighbor called and told the girl's mother to look out the kitchen window. She pulled back the curtain and was shocked to see a handful of the lights hovering five feet from the house, as if waiting for someone to open a door and ask them in for a meal. The closest light held a faint, hollow human face. This was an emergency.

One of their neighbors was a Navaho man people remembered only as Marvin. He had married a woman of the Tonawanda Reservation, and he must have seen something of the lights in his own native Southwest. For four nights he camped around the house of the girl who fed the witch lights—burning tobacco, offering prayers, and conducting ceremonies. He couldn't keep the lights from their habits of favoring train tracks, hills, and winter nights, but they stayed away from this house after that. A worthy medicine man, this Marvin.

GHOSTLY WALKS AND PHANTOM HOSTS

The grandfather of one of my Mohawk confidants was a farmer on the Tonawanda Reservation. In the summers, he and his hands worked till darkness every day in his field near Judge Road. One July dusk, three of them were shutting off the machines in the field when a couple of head-sized light spheres streaked by them, crossing a hundred yards in seconds and disappearing behind the tree line. None doubted what these were: ga'hai.

As they followed the lights with their eyes, they heard an odd sound effect in the wake of their course: dozens of running human feet and people talking to each other in Seneca. It was as if an invisible host of spirits had crossed the open field in the guise of the lights and let the sounds they'd made follow them after.

This strange story sounds particularly antique and European. In Iroquois folklore, the typical witch lights are not often associated with anything but witches, or mystery in general. In the Old World, phantom lights can be presumed to be anything, though most commonly they are thought to be fairies and spirits of the human dead. The fairy host often moves, too, with the sweep and sound of a phantom caravan. Maybe the continents weren't that far apart, or else the supernatural is the same everywhere, and our accounts vary because we see only pieces of the picture.

The Ghosts of Niagara on the Lake

In July 2005, fifteen people on a Haunted History Ghost Walks tour stopped by a bend in the road in Niagara-on-the-Lake, Ontario, Canada. The broad green of a lakeside golf course curved around them. Down the slope to their right was the Niagara River; across it in clear sight was the famous Fort Niagara. Ahead of them to the north was the inland ocean, Lake Ontario, and above it, a sky of contrasts. The parting day was stretching peachy fingers into the graying clouds to the left. The air ahead of them was deep indigo. To the east it was already night.

This was Mississauga Point, a site with a dramatic, even mysterious past. Scott Jones, the young tour guide, waved his arm toward the lake across the curving green and told his group about old tunnels between the town and reconstructed Fort Mississauga. He motioned toward the heavy river once lined on both sides with prehistoric castles and helped them imagine historic and possibly ancient battles the site had witnessed. He waved again toward the lake as he mentioned the mystery lights in the sky and the UFO flaps of the 1970s, all above this very point charged by geology, legend, and history. He noticed them looking hard at something closer and along the ground. He turned and stared with them.

A hundred yards away, on and around the site of the old fort, was a flock of possibly a dozen hazy head-sized lights. Everyone saw them clearly. They were strange and eerie. What were they?

The tour group included thirteen young women and a big young fellow who'd been scornful the whole night. He'd laughed at stories about Niagara-on-the-Lake's ghosts and tried to find natural explanations for all the reports and encounters. Even while studying the head-high, earthbound lights on the course, he kept at it. For sure it was just "a ship on the lake in the distance" with a high mast and a handful of blue lights on it, all moving independently. At first he'd been ready to charge them. At last even he gave up and admitted wonder. They were clearly just above the surface of the land.

The humans could have stared until their eyes glazed over: the witch lights glowed and moved as long as anyone watched, though they were fainter as the group turned to leave. On the back of his sign-up sheet, Jones wrote a statement about the marvel. All his clients signed their names underneath.

Lady of the Blue Light

Two men went fishing in a little boat on the Niagara River well above and south of Niagara Falls. It was summer, and the river was calm. After hours of little luck, they moved on and passed under the Peace Bridge and into the broad mouth of northeastern Lake Erie. Their luck changed quickly. They caught one fish after another.

One fisherman was ready to pack it in. It was getting dark, and there was a different tone in the air. But the owner of the boat insisted on following their fortune. They headed out into the lake and caught more in that one hour than they had the rest of the day.

Then the fog came. Thick clouds pressed down on them, and they lost their bearings. They had no idea how close they were to the nearest shore or which direction it could have been. They couldn't see any anything but the glowering, ever-darkening gray. Anxiety chilling every vein, they started the motor and headed the boat in a direction they thought was toward land. They couldn't even be sure they were heading in a straight line. For hours, they wandered lost in the fog.

A stray wave splashed over the side, knocking the host's spectacles from his eyes. He yelled for his friend to take the wheel while he fumbled for them. As if nothing could go right, even their voices were lost in the wake and fog. They had to shout to each other unless they were side by side. Then they saw the light.

It was a blue sphere that appeared to be static. It had to represent either a big still boat or a solid shore. It was faint, though, and a long way off. The boat owner found his glasses, took over the wheel, and floored the boat, heading to the sphere. It was two in the morning.

Around that time, a little girl woke up crying in a Buffalo home. She had had a dream she couldn't remember and tried to convince her mother that her father *needed help. It was just a nightmare, she was told, and she fell back to sleep.*

The boat hit something hard. Both men were pitched into the water. Other than being near a stony shoal, they had no idea where they were.

The blue light was above them, and bright enough to show in its glow someone standing on the rocks. It was a woman, her arm out to the side, the blue light in her hand like a lantern. She was in settler-era native clothing of moccasins, a long dress, and a rope belt from which hung some feathers and a round, dark object like a turtle's shell. She seemed out of time. One of the men realized, to his astonishment, that the woman had the face of his daughter. Either the fog shifted briefly or the light grew brighter, and the two men were able to see clearly enough to scramble out of the river onto the rocks.

They clambered to the top, ready to thank the oddly dressed woman with the light and ask her if they were on a river or lake, in New York or Canada. But she was gone as if she had never existed. The men had their own problems.

Their craft was damaged, and they stayed where they were. The horrid fog lifted just before dawn, and they found they were on the long break wall that comes out of Buffalo Harbor. When full daylight came, they were shocked to realize that the light had led them to a place not far from where they had set out. They also saw that their boat was partly swamped. Helped by another passing boat, they made it to their truck near the launch, and after that to their homes with a story to tell.

So sure was one of the men that their deliverer had worn his daughter's face that he sat quietly with the girl some time after the event. He asked her, a seven-year-old, how she had known where to find them on the Niagara River. It was this little girl who, thirty years later, told us this story, in which many mysteries remain.

What are these mystery lights, anyway, seen so commonly in upstate New York? Our Iroquois friends might call them all witch lights and add a new facet to their legacy or zoology. Others would call them UFOs, spirits, incompletely formed ghosts, or nonsense. Our ghost-hunting friends might even call them orbs if they turn up on film and nowhere else.

Have the Iroquois hit the nail on the head? Is all this stuff a projection of the power people? Is there some realm that sometimes shows itself into this, a realm in which no boundaries exist and all psychic actors—spirits, ghosts, witches, Little People, and the projections of the minds of living humans—are one?

JOE BRUCHAC ON WITCH LIGHTS

As we've seen, the Iroquois tend to be suspicious of all moving outdoor lights. For Algonquin groups, only the ones with a greenish cast are likely to be witches or nether beings, thus objects of dread. Lights of pure white are often thought to be clear human souls on their journey after the body's death.

The Algonquin-speaking Abenakis have a custom that young and confused souls can become lost and need help finding their way to the realm of the ever-blessed. When these innocents come back as tender light forms, they are saved by the big buck deer, who find and catch them with their broad-spreading antlers, race them to the highest hill nearby, and toss them into the hereafter. What a spectacle that would be! Those broad tines linked by streaks of light like an astral cat's cradle! It's said that sometimes these beautiful creatures are too good for their own good, mistaking car headlights for human souls that need saving, and rushing into them.

The Dance of the Two Orbs

The flu swept the Northeast in the Great Depression, and the family of Abenaki author Joe Bruchac (b. 1942) lost several members. One of the stricken was Joe's grandfather, Grandpa Bowman, a revered elder taking his last breaths in the family home near Cole Hill in the Saratoga County town of Greenfield.

Early on the evening that would be Grandpa Bowman's last, someone looked out the window and called everyone's attention. There on the open ground outside the home was a small, white, luminous orb, clearly one of the spirit lights. It moved timidly, as if confused. No one could account for its movements. It neared the house as if it wanted to enter, then backed off as if afraid.

Grandpa Bowman came to for the last time and asked about Eddie, his youngest grandson. No one had the heart to tell him that, only hours before, Eddie had been taken by the same plague.

Soon after Grandpa Bowman passed, someone looked out and spotted a much larger, more brilliant orb, as abnormally large as the other had been atypically small. The little one drew up and circled the bigger and danced like a water bug on the surface of a pond. Then the little light's movements slowed and became more like those of the big. The pair moved smoothly together into the trees and up Cole Hill.

It was interpreted that the confused, earlier passing soul of the grandson met the more solid form of its elder. Grandpa Bowman's soul would know its way to the Great Spirit. One like his could have led a herd of others with him.

Whatever they are, these witch lights, bless yourself and all creation when you see them, that the world still has wonder.

Medicine People

The shaman . . . not only dies in and of himself, but serves as a sacrament to the spiritual forces of the universe. In this way he mystically unites himself with a sacred order of being, beyond the dimension of this or that person in this particular body.

STEPHEN LARSEN, *THE SHAMAN'S DOORWAY*

AN AURA OF THE SPIRIT

You've had a serious run of bad luck. You know the drill: bounced checks, fender benders, lost jobs, runaway pets. If it can go wrong, it has. The string of disasters is so unlikely that you can almost laugh about it. What next? You might turn to a shrink or a life coach, but he or she can't do much about what appears to be fate.

Or maybe you're sick with a malady so lingering and draining that it's starting to affect your outlook on life. The doctors keep trying new remedies with the same old result. The feeling grows on you that something more than coincidence is behind the picture, and you start looking for new ideas. You need the medicine people.

Today, most of us think of sickness and healing in purely material terms. To us, our doctors are plumbers, carpenters, and chemists of the human body. Preindustrial societies had doctors, too, but they were regarded as much more than physical healers.

In fact, an aura of the spirit has always clung to indigenous medicine workers, and it's no wonder that it would be that way. To people who believe that Spirit animates everything in the world—rocks, trees, grass, weather—the suffering of a body could quite well be an imbalance in the soul, if not an outright metaphysical attack. The customs and duties of preindustrial doctors, therefore—like, probably, all humanity's arts and all other practices considered expressive or spiritual—evolved from the idols, drawings, rites, dances, and customs of the original spirit talker of humanity's ice age societies: the shaman.

The shaman was *the* culture preserver for his or her community, combining the functions of priest, poet, historian, musician, wizard, teacher, doctor, and many others. You can see images of this figure, often half animal, on the walls of the caves in France, in the paintings of the ice age critters, many now extinct, which he hunted, consulted in spirit, or mystically became. The shaman might even have been the first artist.

Popular interest in shamanism and neoshamanism soared in the late twentieth century. A lot has been written about that journey, some of it personal, imaginative, and elaborate. Little is known about the most ancient shamanism, and only a few fundamentals can be taken to be true.

Arctic explorer Knud Rasmussen (1879–1933) encountered societies whose lifestyles and outlooks must have changed little in ten thousand years. They were still led by shamans, one of whom summarized his duties for Rasmussen: He had to lead the tribe to the best hunting grounds and appease the spirits of the animals whose lives they had taken. He was qualified to do this because, in trance, he could leave his body and commune with the world of spirits. He could learn almost anything this way. Some of the spirits he pacified on behalf of the tribe, "explaining" to the souls of the animal victims why humanity had killed them and thus protecting his community from the potential vengeance of a spirit legion. While he was at it, he might take the opportunity to get in a few words about other things. He might even intervene with the spirits of disease and get them to back off of suffering individuals or his entire community.

By the time the first Europeans encountered the Iroquois, all these shaman duties were no longer embodied in one individual. The healer became one of the spin-offs. The medicine societies lasting to this day probably show some vestiges of their ancient shamanic roots, as do the private contractors, still called medicine people.

Iroquois healing societies like the False Faces (or Medicine Masks) are keepers of the ritual songs and chants. These are precious items of national personality, and they should be respected and preserved. During performances of these rites, the celebrants are believed to reach and even speak for otherworldly presences and beings. Even if you don't believe in the powers of these healers, a look into their nature is valuable.

BEAR AND TED

Steady lives of selfless good aren't "sexy." The headlines of history favor drama: curses, murders, trials, and bad ends. We have less historical information about medicine people than we do about witches, but through Michael Bastine's friendship with two important twentieth-century medicine men—Wallace "Mad Bear" Anderson and Ted Williams—we have unparalleled access to contemporary Native medicine. Furthermore, a book has been written about Mad Bear, and Ted Williams wrote two books himself.

Wallace "Mad Bear" Anderson (1927–1985) was Michael's long-time tutor and the subject of Doug Boyd's 1994 book *Mad Bear*. Mad

Bear, always known by his family nickname, served in the U.S. Navy on Okinawa and worked for years in the Merchant Marine, where he was a spokesman for his fellows of all colors.

Author Edmund Wilson (1895–1972) met Mad Bear in his twenties. "A young man in a lumberjack shirt," he wrote in 1957, "broad of build, with a round face and lively black eyes." Envision Mad Bear as a less melanin-challenged version of baseball player Babe Ruth. Wilson was convinced that Mad Bear could be the leader the Iroquois needed. Several times he was asked to be Tuscarora tribal chief, but that would have kept him close to home and hopping to a council's beat. Mad Bear's goals were neither Tuscarora, Iroquoian, Native American, nor even simply human. They were global.

Mad Bear believed that the best way to help Native Americans and aboriginal people everywhere was to raise the spiritual consciousness of the world. He believed, as do we, that this was also a great way to help the world. His transcendence, his care for all life, brought in people from all quarters.

The breadth of Mad Bear's friendships was indeed imposing. He conferred with Martin Luther King Jr. on some issues, and his wide-faced image appears like an orb in many photos of luminaries like Ted Kennedy, Fidel Castro, Bob Dylan, and the Dalai Lama, a friend he took Michael Bastine to visit. His late-1960s North American Indian Unity Caravan brought many far-flung Native nations together. At first this movement started as a rolling coalition of activists who toured reservations, gave speeches, led rallies, and inspired many indigenous American nations to work together on behalf of common causes. Before the end of its six-year run it drew the attention, sympathy, and involvement of well-wishers of all ancestries. It is hard to overestimate Mad Bear's impact in bringing Native American issues to the awareness of the mainstream. It was certainly the seed of much of our admiration today for Native American character and wisdom.

As with most visionaries, the burly Tuscarora was mighty fixed on his purpose, and that simple sense of human closeness was not always with him. Though Michael trained, tutored, and traveled with Mad Bear for years, he wonders sometimes even today how well he knew the man who taught him so much.

This was not the case with Ted Williams. If Mad Bear stands out as a medicine man willing to be profiled, Ted Williams may have been the first to profile himself, albeit indirectly. Ted's two books, *The Reservation* (1985) and *Big Medicine from Six Nations* (2005), are as valuable for their characterizations of reservation life as their inside look at the magic that we describe as *medicine.*

Ted was raised around the traditional ways and witnessed many a miracle. Most of his life he lived off the reservation and worked at a number of "white" jobs. He was a paratrooper, a partier, a jazz player, and, word has it, a ladies' man. One could see that. Even in his late sixties, when I first met him, he was a sturdy, active, handsome man, with a long aquiline nose and a profile that could have gone Hollywood. He was charismatically direct of expression.

Ted came to the medicine late in his life, but things moved fast for the son of Eleazar Williams, one of the most admired healers in living memory. Ted became a member of the False Faces Society, and through him I learned a lot about it.

Ted and Mike Bastine never made a big deal out of their friendship. They just hung out. But the only time I've ever heard a catch in Michael's voice was when we talked at the end of Ted's memorial service in 2005. Till then I'd had no idea how close the two were.

By now the image of the Native American medicine man or woman is a media icon. August, patient, transcendent, nearly omniscient—people this uncomplicated are only found in books and movies.

"These medicine people are still people," says Michael. "They can have all the flaws of any of the rest of us." There is also, we both think, a little something extra about them. We profile Ted, Mad Bear, and all other people and events in this chapter as representatives of the Iroquois medicine tradition, one meriting the deepest respect.

WITCH DOCTORS

We've all heard stories about apparently supernatural displays of power and awareness. In parapsychology they're called "psychokinesis" (PK) and "extra sensory perception" (ESP). In the old days it might all have been called magic.

Some of us these days have too much faith in these subjects and others may have too little. Maybe we all should have some. Successful experiments with faith healing and the mind-bending feats of martial artists, Zen masters, and Indian yogis ought to confirm that "mind over matter" exists in people to some extent. Even animals seem to know things sometimes that they simply shouldn't be expected to know. Who hasn't seen a family dog frisking by the door minutes before its owner arrives home?

Preindustrial shamans could have had even greater special abilities, which might have spelled the difference in personal or cultural survival. The living preservers of their tradition may have them, too.

We hesitate to encourage wild assumptions about Iroquois power people, but we have to say that psychic healing and communication does seem to occur far more often on the reservation than in the society around it. Today, in the twenty-first century, the Western medical establishment shows more than a grudging realization that the world holds a lot we can't explain. To its credit, the American Medical Association is beginning to consider the effectiveness of alternative treatments, ones that have been used in other parts of the world for thousands of years. Not everyone gets better with Western treatment. Sometimes traditional healing works—sometimes so miraculously that psychic or supernatural factors could be involved.

Western medical doctors themselves often use hunches in curing their patients. They get that funny feeling, prescribe an extra test, and end up lengthening a life. And let's not forget that many famous discoveries have come to scientists suddenly as a psychic flash or an insightful dream, in which at least the unconscious mind was at work.

Until the advent of modern medicine, Iroquois traditional healers could set broken bones, treat wounds, and cure ailments at least as well as Europe's physicians. They were also skilled herbalists who knew every plant in the Northeast Woodlands. Their potions and poultices would be valuable to us today. These were the body healers.

Other healers were teachers and culture-preservers whose religious and spiritual function was incalculable. They were the keepers of a body of age-old wisdom, memorialized in rituals, memorialized in song. Since the Iroquoian word root for *power* was the same as that for *song,* you can see the respect in which these incantations were held. They were thought at least as valuable for the healing of the patient as any physical remedy. Those who kept the tradition were also the first line of defense against the attacks of witches.

Early in the twentieth century, Arthur C. Parker acknowledged several forms of occult practice among the Iroquois, among which he included healing. Parker understood the spiritual discipline driving the gatherers of medicinal roots and plants. Still, he profiled most of his occultists in terms of witchcraft. The question could be one of terminology.

Even in the middle twentieth century *witched* was still used as a catchall word by reservation folk for a state that could be described with a variety of terms: cursed, enchanted, charmed, spellbound. Parker found among the Iroquois two styles of witch doctors, the metaphysical wing of the medicine people.

The first category is the anti-witch, someone who has made a special study of curses and countermeasures. An expert in diagnosis, he or she knows the signs of the varied curses and the exact means of combating them. A doctor of body and soul, this type of witch, says Parker, usually works free of charge.

The other type of witch doctor—or at least someone who will occasionally work as one—is simple: This is *your* witch, an occult practitioner you recruit against other witches who may have attacked you. In a metaphysical sense, you "find a dog who'll eat a dog." He or she cures you by outcursing the curse, usually turning it on its senders.

A bit has changed since Parker's time. Our late contemporary Ted Williams acknowledged three categories of healing medicine:

1. *Simple medicines that are purely physical cures.* Good examples are herbs such as wild cherry bark for calming a sore throat or slippery elm for drawing out boils, slivers, or infections.
2. *Medicines that take preparation.* These medicines are often concoctions of herbs and other ingredients, which have to be carefully gathered and measured, sometimes according to cycles of the year or moon. They are aimed at curing chronic conditions and diseases, such as gallstones, pleurisy, and arthritis, not just sicknesses and wounds.
3. *Medicines "that hide."* These are spiritual and anti-witch. This, Ted tells us, is the type of medicine that brought people to the east door of his family's house, the sheltered side, to see his father, Eleazar the healer.

Mount Holyoke and Wellesley professor Annemarie Anrod Shimony made a penetrating study of twentieth-century Iroquois witchcraft. She found two categories of spiritual healers: those who diagnose ailments and those who diagnose *and* cure. Because many of today's spirit healers take on some of the techniques of Western psychics, a lot of them give the appearance of fortune-tellers or tea-leaf readers. In fact, the term *readers,* a word Mad Bear used himself, is sometimes applied to all of them.

The English words used to describe the effects of magic have changed, too. Not many people talk anymore about witches, though they may surely think in terms of witchery. By the late twentieth century *medicine* had become so common a term for most redirections of the omnipresent psychic force orenda that reservation folk use it almost the way Spiritualists use the word *spirit.* In 2005, some healers/medicine people might say they "did some work" on behalf of this or that result. There seems to be the understanding that the force they use is one. "Good" or "bad" depends on its uses or its interpretation.

The healers we have today are usually solo operators, made, we figure, by some blend of natural talent—most likely psychic—and a period of training with at least one great healer. People with the potential to be healers often give some sign of it at an early age. Some have a natural gift, and some are made. The greatest, like athletes, are doubtless both.

Your first encounter with a healer can be a surprise. The rites may not seem elaborate. "Work" almost always begins with generic ceremonies and gifts of tobacco—a common offering to the spirits and the four quarters as a commencement to any worthy undertaking. Smudges of sage and cedar are customary for healing and purifying, following which might be moments of meditation and praying or chanting in one of the Iroquois languages. Other things these healers use may seem unlikely. Humble items, even ones made of plastic and mass-produced, could have their uses. The point seems to be to focus the intent of the practitioner and invoke the energy of generations of tradition behind it.

DIVINERS OF MYSTERIES

"Diviners of mysteries have always been prominent characters" among the Iroquois, according to Parker. The work of these spirit doctors could be as specific as finding lost children or possessions and solving crimes, or it could be as diffuse as telling fortunes and interpreting dreams. It could be as simple as deciding on the proper ceremony and medicine society for the patient's complaint. It could be as dire as naming the supernatural assailant behind a spell causing a sickness.

Handsome Lake Uncovers the Truth

In the early 1800s, during the hunting season, a father and son from Cattaraugus came to Cornplanter village in Allegany while Prophet Handsome Lake was on hand. After a short stay, they took off into the woods.

The young man came back alone with their horse and cart. "My dad is lost,"
he said. "I spent a week looking for him. I walked and searched and signaled with
gunshots hoping to find him."

Members of the community sensed that things were more than they seemed.
They went to the local diviner, who said, "I think this guy killed his dad." Handsome
Lake was called in to the proceedings. The visionary told them to get a knife, a bullet,
and a tomahawk and put them on a blanket before the suspect. "If there's anything
to this," the prophet said, "one of them will move without being touched."

They set things up as Handsome Lake directed and brought the son in. Others
talked, and the objects were still. The minute the suspect spoke, the bullet moved.
This not only told the prophet that the father had been shot by the son but somehow
revealed to him the hiding place of the body. He could even describe the spot.

A Taint of the Supernatural

One night in the early twentieth century, three men came to the home of a healer
on the Cattaraugus Reservation. One carried a spade and another a lantern. The
third was a Tonawanda Reservation witch doctor.

A Cattaraugus family had been plagued with bad luck. Strange ailments
had taken several children, and the affair had the taint of the supernatural. The
Cattaraugus healer had been asked to do something about it, and he'd called on a
specialist from Tonawanda.

The four walked into the swampy woods. Now and then, the Tonawanda man
stopped, took a forked stick out of his bag, and held it like a dowsing rod, one arm
of the Y in each hand. He pointed it in various directions, studied it briefly, and
then tucked it away. Once the rod took on a subtle gleam. They went the way it
indicated, trying to keep it trained on its target as they negotiated the paths and
obstacles. The forked stick glowed like it was red hot as they converged on an old
stump. Its holder tapped the ground between two roots. "Here we dig."

The spade bearer set to. At the sound of metal hitting stone, the witch doctor
took over. The lantern revealed a cubical box made of thick slabs from the creek
bottom. "It's there," the witch doctor whispered. He put some white powder on top
of the rough container and covered it with earth again.

The party went back to the house of the suffering family and dug a hole at the corner of the woodshed. Into it the witch doctor put a five-gallon crock with a large piece of silk weighted at the corners, covering it like a drumhead. He made a small fire, threw medicine powder into it, and chanted, commanding the witch bundle to come from its box through the air into this container. In just a while, a ball of fire hurled itself across the night sky and arced down toward them. They dove for cover, all but the witch doctor, who saw it pass through the silk without burning it.

Inside, they found a bundle of rags soaked with blood, and in them a sharp bone, bloody red: the otnäyont, *the blood bone, the cursed totem that had been drinking the blood of children. The witch doctor made off with it, and there were no more mystery ailments. The last sick child got well.*

These witch bones can be laid in an area to curse it, and they'll siphon the heart-blood of children until seen to in the traditional way. No wonder the Iroquois hated witches. At least it wasn't a bomblet in the shape of a toy. Hell waits, too, for the deviser of that one.

HERBS AND HEALINGS

Prophet Handsome Lake had a lot to say about the occult practices of his people, including the healers. Herbal healers weren't just magical gardeners who plucked what they wanted in the woods. They gathered herbs with the attitude of Iroquois hunters taking game: reverence. And the power of the plant was more than physical.

"It's wrong to take a plant without first talking to it," said Handsome Lake in his code. "Offer tobacco, and tell the plant in gentle words what you want of it. Then pluck it from the roots." This was probably a way of both empowering the herb and involving it in its intended function from the moment it left the earth.

When the old Seneca healers came to a site to gather medicinal herbs, they often built small fires. Into the embers they cast tobacco at intervals, chanting prayers. They called on the spirits of the medicines, reminded them of the suffering people, and told them which of their powers were needed. The gatherer had a routine chant:

They say that you are ready to heal. Now I claim you for medicine. Let me use your healing powers to purge and cleanse and cure. I won't destroy you when I take you, but instead I'll plant your seed so you can grow and thrive. Herb-spirits, I take you with purpose, to make you agents of healing. It was said that all the world might come to you. Here I am. I thank you for your powers. I thank the Creator for the gift of you.

After the last puff of tobacco smoke, the herb gatherer dug the plant from the roots. He broke off the seed stalks, though, dropped the pods into the hole, and gently covered them over with fertile leaf mold. He never left this ceremony without announcing: "The plant will come again, and I have not destroyed life but helped increase it. So the plant is willing to lend me of its virtue."

For Handsome Lake, it wasn't right to take payment for healing with an herb. The patient should offer only tobacco in the name of spirits greater than the healer.

More to It Than That?

Once a year around the anniversary of Appomattox, some Civil War veterans used to get together for a few days and rough it near the Evans farm off Blakeley Road in the Erie County town of Aurora. As long as they lived, they did this, camping and recalling old friends and historic battles. Doubtless another companion—Sir John Barleycorn—was with them in abundance. A small natural spring was nearby.

The late historian Herb Evans (1905–2005) who hailed from the town of Wales, New York, spent time at these gatherings as a boy, and he got an earful. He also saw a few things that impressed him.

One of these vets had a skin condition due to his stay in a prison camp, and it got worse as he aged. He grumbled about it within earshot of the others, one of whom was an old Seneca who knew something about that spring on Evans's property. "Chief Carpenter," as he was nicknamed, told the sufferer to get into it and bathe in the water. He also told him to drink a bit every few hours. It soon cured him. The spring had a lot of sulfur in it, but there must have been more to it than that.

Turning a Spell Around

Artist-author Jesse Cornplanter (1889–1957) was the last lineal descendant of the Revolutionary-era war chief Cornplanter. Soon after he came back from World War I, a family on another reservation developed some hard feelings for him. He got sick, lost weight, and couldn't eat. White doctors hadn't been much help. In recollection, he chuckled, "I could almost taste strawberries," an Iroquois way to say, "pushing up daisies." Strawberries line the road to the Iroquois heaven.

One of the elders of the Tonawanda Reservation informed him that he had been witched. On four straight mornings, the old fellow gave him an emetic of touchwood fungus and twelve quarts of water to drink. Jesse Cornplanter threw up countless times into a hole the old man dug in the ground. The healer told him to stay out of sight of anyone before coming to see him on the fourth day. Sure enough, on that morning, up came a little sliver of wood. They built a fire, burned tobacco over it, and threw the thing in to turn the spell around. Jesse Cornplanter learned just a short time later that the woman he suspected of hexing him had died. He was sorry, but it was her life or his.

THE SEVENTH SON

In November 1926, the *Batavia Daily News* made an announcement: An eleven-year-old Mohawk mystic—the seventh son of a seventh son—had come to town. Abram George (c. 1916–1948?) of the St. Regis Reservation had moved with his family from Hogansburg and taken up residence at 104 Liberty Street.

Father Mitchell George did the family talking. He declared that young Abram had been traveling the states as a part-time exorcist and full-time healer. He had chased spooks from a Memphis mansion, healed rheumatics and cripples, and found a drowning victim sixty-two feet under the surface of the St. Lawrence River. Young Abram had settled in upstate New York "ready to drive the voodoo man from the ill or solve any occult mystery."

This, though, was only the hype. Abram's powers were those of touch—he was a psychic masseur. He rubbed the ailing parts of his patients' bodies with his strong hands and didn't speak during the process.

Abram was a husky lad with a thatch of jet-black hair and big, commanding eyes. ("A bright-eyed boy of sturdy physique and shy manner," the papers said of "the little red doctor.") His demeanor was strangely unchildlike. More than one observer was reminded of the boy-sage Krishnamurti (1895–1986), likewise making a sensation, who had recently come to the United States from India. Both must have been old souls.

Abram never set himself up as a guru. He gave no lectures, made no prophecies, and claimed no power but healing. There was no trance act or hocus-pocus about his practice, and no black art was the source of his gifts. Being the seventh son of a seventh son, said his father, he had inherited his powers because of his birth. Whatever their source, Abram's gifts made believers.

A Rochester boy paralyzed from infancy developed muscle and even started to walk under regular treatments from "Dr. George." A blind Rochester man claimed to see light and shade for the first time in thirty-two years. A near-blind woman from London, England, was so improved when she left Batavia that she sent presents—toys—back across the Atlantic.

Abram's patients didn't snap to suddenly as if a switch had been turned on. It took regular treatments from those healing hands. (Upstate reporters seemed most impressed by the color contrast, those hands of "the true bronze skin of his race" at work on his white patients.) And Abram couldn't help everybody. A Rochester dame crippled in a fall reported little improvement. (She had seen Abram only twice, though, and said she still had hope.)

Another thing was strange: Neither Abram nor his dad charged for the healing work. People would have been free to accept his treatment and pay nothing. In fact, Abram ministered to many who had no chance of paying. All this is consistent with a good healer.

Abram also treated the affluent, but with an agreement: If he healed a patient, the family would give him what it could afford. He must have been good. Abram's father was able to plunk down $2,500 cash for a new truck in 1927. His family seemed on the verge of wealth and fame. But there were chinks in the armor, and folks were starting to probe.

The dad was clearly a showman, fully bent on capitalizing. The first stop of his Seneca country swing had been at the offices of the Batavia paper. Possibly hoping to keep an air of mystery about Abram, Mr. George let on that his son knew no English. (He spoke only "Indian," according to an, alas, undereducated reporter, who spoke only "European.") Abram endangered no detail of his dad's ad campaign and could have been mute for all he said to whites. But his Batavia teachers were sure he knew what they were saying and that he could have spoken English had he cared to.

That bit about the "seventh son of a seventh son . . ." is worth a look, too. At least the first half of it was true for young Abram, one of eleven born to the George family. As of 1926 his six brothers and a sister were alive. The business of associating the birth-order condition with Iroquois mojo is problematic.

It was news to the Tonawanda Seneca, for instance. There is a Seneca tale predating young Abram's life that does indeed concern a magical seventh son, but it doesn't imply that his birth-order is the source of his powers. One Batavia reporter—possibly the one who implied that all Native Americans speak one language—conjectured that it was either a superstition specific to St. Regis or "the Iroquois tribe." He obviously did not know that the Iroquois were a confederacy that included the local Seneca and that seven, though a sacred number to some world societies, is not known to be one to the old Iroquois. This "seventh son" stuff might even be some feature of American Southern tradition, making its way to St. Regis through contact with African Americans or even an exposure to blues music. This is quite logical. The Iroquois have always been ready adopters, of both people and supernatural customs.

These may be minor points in judging a sacred gift, but any dissembling is a trouble sign. Still, Abram was a hit and seemed on the verge of stardom. The street outside the family's Batavia home was busy enough in 1926. Such mobs came to Abram's Rochester office that the police were called to South Avenue to keep order.

But something was getting to young Dr. George. He had fainted at a healing in Geneva and cancelled his first big Rochester gig because of strain. This should have been foreseen. No healer finds the work easy. No mature medicine person would sign on for the assembly-line healing Abram had been doing.

Trouble started in Rochester. The men who'd arranged one meeting for the Georges had charged admission fees at the door. The Georges may not even have known about it nor gotten a cent from it, but these no longer free healings fell under a different kind of scrutiny.

Others were looking for trouble. Batavia neighbors complained about the traffic at the Georges' home. The Batavia children's court accused Mitchell George of being a poor guardian by keeping his son out of school. Medical organizations protested Abram's "quackery." His own lawyers broke it to the father that the state could indeed keep the son from working. The family went back to Hogansburg, where they had lived prior to Batavia.

The move dodged some short-range trouble, but it was unfortunate for the prosperity of the George family. Batavia was halfway between population centers in Buffalo and Rochester. It was also in the core of the Burned-over District, where people had been used to prophets, healers, and would-be Christs for over a century.

In 1929, the Georges came back to Batavia, proclaiming that Abram was now sixteen and could do as he chose. (How he had aged four years in the two they'd spent away was hard to explain.) His second stay was short and frustrating, and his career was derailed.

In 2002, Batavia reporter Scot Desmit did some digging about Abram the healer. He tracked leads on the St. Regis/Akwesasne Reservation and found a woman of eighty-two who remembered Abram as a boy. He had asked her sister on a date.

They still talked about him on the reservation, curing lameness and eye trouble. For waking someone out of a coma, a New York City family gave him the Cadillac he drove around Hogansburg. He was a shy fellow, they recalled, and he still worked with touch. They remembered him traveling often for healings. If someone on the St. Regis got hurt or sick, he came over and did his thing. He got into drinking, said the St. Regis woman, and died young, possibly in the 1940s. He was a great healer, though, whatever quirks he had, and he had respect on the reservation. It was natural for him to have gifts, the old gal said, even if they brought complications. He was, after all, a seventh son.

MEDICINE BAGS

We've seen witches use their rites, materials, and objects. Sometimes they put collections of things together to make power bundles called witches' bags. For every medicine, there's a countermedicine, and those who would battle malicious witchcraft make caches of their own. Around 1900, Seneca Edward Cornplanter (father of the aforementioned Jesse) itemized the contents of a typical charm holder's bundle:

- The scales of the great horned serpent or a vial of its blood
- A round white stone given by the Little People
- Claws from the death panther or the fire beast
- Feathers of the *dewatyowais,* the exploding bird
- Castor (a natural scent) of the white beaver
- An otnäyont, a sharp bone or blood bone
- A corn bug
- A small mummified hand
- Hair from a ferocious Great Flying Head
- Bones from the *niagwahe,* or the demon bear
- A small flute or whistle made from an eagle wing bone
- Anti-witch powder
- A bag of sacred tobacco
- Claws or teeth from various wild animals

- A small mortar and pestle
- A small war club
- A small bow and arrow
- Miniature wooden bowls and spoons
- A small wooden doll
- Clairvoyant eye oil (a potion giving the second sight)

This is just a generic list; master wizards would have had their own tricks and ingredients. No bundle was broken in, anyway, unless it was "sung for" in the charm holder's ceremony. Great power, though, could be the reward. The holder of a charm bag could overcome a sorcerer's blight or determine which offended spirits were behind a problem. The magic bundle could heal, work a blessing, or turn a curse.

Even in magic, the downhill path is easier. The main test in assembling the witch's bag is one of the stomach. Just acquiring the ingredients of the charm holder's bundle would be a quest, sometimes outright life-threatening. No Great Horned Snake would seem eager to part with blood or hide. Others, such as Great Flying Head hair, sound chimerical, like the kennings (girl beards, cat footfalls, fish breath) that leashed the Scandinavian demon-wolf Fenrir. There may be some truth, though, to the exploding bird. One of these was caught on film in a baseball stadium in March 2001, colliding with a heater from former pitcher Randy "The Big Unit" Johnson.

Twentieth-century shaman Mad Bear Anderson had his own medicine bundles, used for healing, divination, medicine, and, yes, personal defense. We never get a look at what might have been in any of these bags, but he seems to have had three kinds of them.

One was a middle-sized medicine case that he took on important trips. This was a leather satchel he used for quick-developing problems. It probably held herbs, powders, and implements that he used to work cures and blunt curses. A thing of fascination to many supporters, it would have been coveted by some fans and all opponents.

It and most people had to be kept away from each other. Once it was stolen.

The Fifth Spiritual Summit in New York City was a 1975 conference of world religious traditions sponsored by the United Nations. During one of Mad Bear's appearances, the fabled case disappeared from his hotel room. The young Native American appointed to watch it got suddenly sick. He had no idea what had become of the case and displayed all the signs of being magically bamboozled—"overshadowed," as Mad Bear put it. Mad Bear gave him a bit of doctoring and went to find the culprit somewhere in the vast city.

The next time anyone saw Mad Bear, he had his bag back. "I had to use some medicine to find it," was all he would say.

The bag thief was a white man who had been around the conference all week and had drawn attention by his appearance. He had the Johnny Cash "cowboy in black" look. He'd had his hands on the bag, and he needed some "doctoring," too. It was clear that somebody was using him.

Mad Bear also wore a tiny sack on a cord about his neck. This was the immediate line of personal defense. He never took it off in public, and the one time he did so for a dip in a swimming hole, he was struck almost immediately by the bite of a strange-looking insect, one that sent him to a hospital and seriously weakened him thereafter.

From the fact that there was a daypack and a tweener, we deduce that Mad Bear had a master collection, possibly even a cauldron-sized power cache that would have been kept somewhere quite safe, possibly even buried. The concatenation of it all in one place probably made it an orenda-emanator that could work medicine long-range.

We've heard of these medicine kettles being unearthed around New York state. We've mentioned the one in Buffalo at the center of a ring of bodies, and it may not have been a holy one. One wonders if someday someone will find the major storehouse of Mad Bear's medicine under equally cryptic circumstances.

SABAEL AND THE MEDICINE BEADS

The variously named Sabael (Sabile, Sebele) Benedict was probably an Abenaki born in western Maine. At twelve, he ended up fighting at the Battle of Quebec and ever after figured his age based on that 1759 clash. He needed to have some benchmark because he lived a good long life in Mohawk country in the undeveloped Adirondacks.

In his late teens, he'd had enough of white men's wars and ducked out of it all to be the first settler of Indian Lake, seventy miles northwest of Saratoga Springs. He was a legend around Hamilton County, liked and trusted by the whites who came in later. Not all was due to the good in white hearts. Sabael sold the rights to a valuable iron mine at Keesville for a bushel of corn and a dollar. Other decisions went his way. So well regarded was Sabael Benedict that a settler offered his own red-haired daughter as a bride. From what we hear, this was a fine long marriage.

Sabael was a medicine man. Where he got his training is anyone's guess. Maybe he was one of those naturals. Maybe it was all in the medicine necklace he wore. This string of beads was good against many a complaint.

If he was in a canoe when a storm rolled in, all he had to do was drop a bead in the water and the lake would stay at peace. On land, just hanging this necklace on a tree would guarantee that no lightning would strike anyone under it. When the heebie-jeebies came on him in the woods, he took the necklace out of his pouch and held it before him like a torch. The *chepi*—"hostile spirits" in an Algonquin tongue—cleared before him like schools of fish before a skin diver. Something kept him alive over a century.

One night at the end of his very long life, Sabael went on his last ramble, trudging into the trees and elements he had lived among. Maybe the Great Spirit was calling. His body was never found. His worried wife went looking for him, and she was found, frozen and buried in snow, on a small island in Indian Lake. Her apparition has been reported on this island, as well as the sound of his voice calling her.

FOR THE UNBORN CHILDREN

Early in July 1998, I called Mike Bastine to go over a certain story I had heard him tell a couple times. "Heck, there's a guy in town that tells the story a lot better," he said. "Ted Williams. He's who I heard it from. I'm going up to Lewiston to see him tomorrow. Why don't you come on up and meet him?"

Nobody was around when I got to the meeting spot. I set up with my laptop under a tree. In half an hour, a car pulled up and parked beside mine. Pam Bastine, Mike's wife, got out with a long-haired gentleman built like many Tuscaroras—big chested and middle sized. The pair had just returned from lunch, and Michael had gone back to work.

Ted was then in his late sixties. He was a handsome, photogenic man with a still mostly black mane. Pam told him about my work, which didn't knock him over. He was the most naturally short-spoken author I'd ever met. Even his syllables were clipped. He kept his teeth close together when he talked, as if he were determined to hold on to a piece of hide in his molars and someone were tugging on it as he spoke. I wasn't sure he liked me. I was planning the next move of my day when the old healer came up with a small, dense plastic disc. "How about a little game?" he said with a gleam in his eyes.

"Ultimate Frisbee?" I had played that active sport in my teacher days. It also took a team.

"Disc golf," said the healer with a huff.

"Ted's the national champion," said Pam.

"That's really something," I said. "National champion."

"The sixty-fives," said Ted. "Couple years ago. Course I won't win again till I'm seventy and this one guy gets out of the age group. He's one year younger. Then I won't win till I'm seventy-five."

"National champion at anything," I said. "That's something."

"The guys in the fifties are a throw a hole better," he said.

"Just think if they were sixty-five," I said. "You'd get 'em."

"It'd be the same," he said. "I'd be eighty then."

We played nine holes on the state park course, firing the long-soaring discs to the distant, metal-chained baskets on poles. The green was so thick that I could hardly see what we were aiming at. Ted was way ahead at the end.

We sat again back at the start. Ted was curious how the research that became this book was going to go. I started in on the subjects: medicine people, wars, curses, witchcraft.

Ted looked into the tree line as if his vision could soar through it and take his spirit on a romp down the Niagara, into the sparse clouds, and out over the Ontario. Then he turned back and looked at me. "You know, it's an interesting thing about witches. Some of them get pulled in by money, and they get started on the wrong road. Then they can't give up. They get too far in and can't do it any other way. It's just like other people can't get out of the Mafia."

"Fifty years ago most whites thought medicine people were all bad," I said. "Now they think they're all good. I would have thought the medicine people would have been all about the preservation of traditional society and values. Keeping the culture and the teaching. But they come in on both sides of some disputes. Gas. Gambling. Tobacco."

He smirked. "Some of the chiefs thought a casino would be good because the Oneida were doing well with it and everybody had money. Some of the chiefs said, 'No, that won't make a better world for the unborn children.'"

He shifted to face me. "You know, I do some medicine," he said, like it was quite an understatement. "Part of where the trouble comes in . . . people on both sides of a matter come to me and ask me if I can do some work for them. It disappoints them when I tell them I can't. I make my mind up based on what will be the best for the unborn children. It's just a different opinion of what that will be. What will be best for the unborn children."

He gave a little cough of a laugh. "Course it's not something hidden for me to tell you that. That's pretty much the job description of a chief."

He looked at me intently. "You know, it's not like there's evil people on either side of these disputes. You might think of it like the enneagram. You heard of that?"

"Little rusty."

"It's that nine-sided problem you can look at so many ways. There ought to be many insights into the truth. It's not always easy to tell what will be best for the unborn children."

Bluedog

When he was a boy, Ted Williams's family took in a pup to which he was much attached. Sunlight brought azure flecks out of its vinyl-black coat, and while people were figuring out a name they called it Bluedog, which stuck. Every day for weeks, Ted ran home from school to play with it. He was fascinated by its animal manners, its open nature toward all life, and the simple love it felt for him. One day, though, he came home to find its body still and cold on the front step. He ran in crying. His father, the healer Eleazar Williams, was waiting.

"Ted, my son," he said. "You know that all beings have free will. We can choose what might be right for us and others, or we can choose what might be wrong. Just the way we tell you what's good for you, we told that little dog again and again not to go down the driveway and play in the road. But he didn't listen to us, and he ran out with the cars. Now he's learned a lesson that's sad for all of us. But it's the Creator's way. We have free will."

"Daddy, can't you do something for Bluedog?" Ted cried.

"Now, Ted," the father said. "There might be something I can do for him. But this isn't an easy decision. We shouldn't turn back the pattern of the Creator just because we want to. We can only do what's allowed. And some of what's allowed isn't the best thing."

"Daddy, bring Bluedog back to us," said Ted. "Daddy, I know you can."

"I want to be sure you have thought about this," his father said. "It's a lesson for you, too. In the balance of things, there's a cost for everything we do. Someday you may want to change something else the Creator has allowed, and He may already have spoken for you. I just ask you to think about it."

"I won't ask for anything again," said Ted. "Just do it now."

"If you've decided, I'll give it a try," said the father. "You have free will, too. The Creator won't let us do anything that would tip the balance of things. Come watch with me and let's see if that little dog has a job to do that we don't understand right now."

By then the whole family had gathered. Eleazar Williams went to the body of the pup, opened its jaws, tucked something small between them, and closed them gently again. He chanted over the dog's body in Tuscarora. Now and then he looked up through the trees as if asking the sky for guidance. He stroked the soft fur under the dog's chin and called to it as if to wake it gently. He may have done all this for half an hour.

"Now, Ted, let's put him down real easy into that warm grass over there right where the sunlight falls. You just sit here on this step and make sure nothing bothers him while the Creator's deciding."

The tears had dried on Ted's cheeks by the time the grass started to shake, and he heard a tiny cough. The green parted, and Bluedog stood, shivering. A couple of times he stopped and hacked up bits of organ and bone. Once he'd stopped coughing for good, he trembled and looked around as if he didn't know where he was, as if he were about to run into the woods. Then he saw Ted and wagged his tail.

Though he always walked with a shimmy, Bluedog went on to a long and happy life. He had a bit of that quality the Europeans call fey, that was all. Maybe because of his short stay in the other world, Bluedog was always seeing spirits in this one. It was hard getting him to keep a pace sometimes on those late night walks, and some nights he wouldn't leave the yard. But he was the best animal friend any boy ever had. In his seventy-fifth year, Ted's eyes welled whenever he told the story.

Ted became a healer himself. But tragedy came to him later in life, as a father—one he would have given his life to undo. It was an accident that caused the death of a child, an event he thought he had a hand in. He always wondered if he might not have used the Creator's special dispensation when he was a boy.

Mad Bear's Medicine Hat

An old treaty with the British Empire granted the Iroquois hassle-free passage between the United States and Canada forever. Political firebrands are occasionally blocked at the border with the idea of keeping them out of trouble, but sometimes it separates them from councils and family gatherings. Leave it to Mad Bear to make a point: When the authorities tried to block him at one of the Niagara River bridges, he crashed his Jeep through a wooden gate and was on his way. He offered to make up for any damage caused by his exercise of his political rights, but the authorities were not amused. Mad Bear was told that he would be arrested if he tried to attend an early 1970s rally in Toronto.

Mad Bear announced that he would attend, not to disturb the peace, but to carry out his duties to his nation. The problem was following through—the guards at the border were on the lookout, and Mad Bear's photo was in every booth. Native American caravans were sure to get the once-over.

Mad Bear's standoff had made news, and reporters were stalking him. Under his black, wide-brimmed magic hat, he crossed the border in a backseat between two friends. The customs agent peered into the car holding Mad Bear and waved them on. "Hey! That's Mad Bear in that car up there!" yelled a Buffalo reporter hanging out the window of the car behind them.

The agent looked again, studying faces more closely, then waved them all on a second time. As they pulled away from the Peace Bridge, Mad Bear grinned faintly. He was later to say, "Every time that guard looked at me, it felt like sand was sprinkling all down over my face. What he saw was someone else."

White writer Doug Boyd (1935–2006) had heard a lot about the "doctored" hat. Once Mad Bear even let him try it on. It was a bit too big for him, and he felt something different under it, if not cascading sand. Mad Bear looked at him curiously as if he himself was surprised by its effect. Boyd turned for the mirror, but Mad Bear snatched the hat back before he could see himself under it. Next time he visited, it was not on its usual hook.

MAD BEAR'S METHOD OF READING

Mad Bear's curative powers were famous even off the reservation. People came to him with all sorts of problems, including ones they suspected were magical. Mad Bear did his healing only on weekends. Most Saturday and Sunday mornings, a line of cars was parked outside his Tuscarora Reservation home, filled with people waiting for him to start.

He had two strictures: He wouldn't start before sunrise, and he never worked past sunset.

The healing itself was as likely to be physical or emotional as occult. Though Mad Bear's remedies were traditional and Native American, he reached his diagnoses through a mix of occult customs. There were three or four distinct stages to his reading.

Mad Bear always started by letting his guest talk a while, maybe asking a few questions. He tossed a bit of loose tobacco into a glass of water and peered into it. (His favorite cups were mass-produced clear ones that the local Tops supermarket used to package frozen shrimp, sauce included. Mad Bear scarfed down the shrimp and kept the cups, just the right shape, size, and depth for observing the movements of the tobacco.)

There was something different about the tobacco Mad Bear used. People who knew him believed that no tobacco he touched was ordinary, that every time he held any he was talking to it, reminding it of its sacred function, investing it with a sense of mission.

Often he had things figured out in the middle of a client's statement and broke off for a cure. Sometimes he didn't, and it was another toss of the leaves.

If the ailment was psychic, a ceremony burning a certain type of wood or herb often did the trick. If the complaint was physical, Mad Bear often prescribed a treatment involving local plants and substances. The Tuscarora hailed from the Carolinas, so there was a southeastern element to some of Mad Bear's recipes. He often wrapped things up in the same visit. Many cures came in a remarkably short period of time.

Though he proved his fabled powers occasionally, seemingly on a whim, Mad Bear resisted enacting them when asked or challenged, and he never did performances. ("If you want to see a show, get a ticket for the circus," he used to say to those who pressed him. "What we're about is the message.") He never let a third party sit in on one of his readings, either. Still, people were constantly passing through his home and his life, and there are witnesses to some remarkable things.

Mad Bear sent some people to other healers, usually because he could see that they wouldn't follow his directions. "I could prescribe some treatment," he might say. "But I see that you really like wine. I don't think you'd stop what you do long enough to get better." Or, "You eat a lot of greasy food. That won't mix with my medicine, and it could even be worse for you. Maybe another healer can give you something."

It was important to Mad Bear to succeed. If people were running around saying that he was a bust, it would compromise his ability to heal anyone. Some of his prescriptions were irrational, and they had to be followed to the letter. That was his public reasoning. Mike Bastine conjectured that just a touch of pride may have been involved. Mad Bear didn't want any public flops.

Mad Bear often forgot the details of even his most electrifying readings. It frustrated Mike, who had been raised off the reservation. When he first started meeting with Mad Bear, he searched for a Western-style understanding. Time and again he tried to ask Mad Bear about old cases, reminding him of particulars. "Do you remember *that* reading? You can't forget *that* one?" It was hard bringing Mad Bear to admit that he remembered.

This amnesia may well have been sincere. The healing work had to be an exhausting art demanding total immersion, and Mad Bear did so much of it. Once he said that he deliberately put old cases out of thought because he didn't want them clouding up his mind and getting in the way of new ones. But one of the things about Mad Bear that Mike never really got was how he could let such marvelous experiences completely slip from his consciousness. Maybe they weren't marvels to Mad Bear, to the medicine people.

Mad Bear's home region of western New York is known as a cultural melting pot, and he had become a great favorite of its ethnic and immigrant communities. He had come into contact this way with many world traditions and had learned to be respectful of them all. He had also picked up a number of keepsakes, and his cabin had become a den of crazy objects and artifacts. One day when Mike Bastine was helping Mad Bear move, a ragged doll caught his attention. His mentor told him its strange history.

The Devil Doll

Sometime in the late 1970s, a family from a Caribbean island was having some difficulties that they sensed might have a supernatural root. The mother and father came to Mad Bear for a reading, which he commenced in his usual way. He looked in his glass of water and tobacco and studied it hard. "Somebody's jealous of you," he told the couple. "And I bet it's got something to do with where you came from. Have you had any visitors recently?"

They had: people they knew back in the islands.

"Well, they brought a little surprise for you," said Mad Bear. "Knowing what I do about those islands and the way people from there operate, I might guess they left a doll for you. It's most likely somewhere where it'll be close, probably somewhere in your house. These are the early stages, where nothing much is happening, but pretty soon it's going to start interfering in your daily life. You have to go home and see if you can find it. Let me see if I can help you."

Mad Bear looked harder into his glass and tried to visualize the doll's location. As if looking off through his own walls, he spoke out loud about the images that were coming to him. He talked about walls, paintings, and furniture and seemed to be describing a room in a house.

"The object those people left behind will resonate," Mad Bear explained to the couple. "It contains basically the same energy as a good thing. But it's powerful, and people will put their own twist on it in order to interfere with people's lives."

Within days, they found the doll behind a dresser in a bedroom and brought it to Mad Bear. "Those people had it in their luggage," he told the couple. "I'm not sure they were determined to hurt you, and they may have been in the process of deciding whether or not to leave it when something else happened. Or maybe it came out of the luggage by itself. These things have a tendency to work on their own."

Mad Bear conducted a ceremony to reroute the force of the devil doll, and he held on to it after the ceremony was over.

The doll was a rough thing, a human effigy made mostly of the leaves of a plant or tree that was not native to the Great Lakes region. It was likely that its leaves were from a palm tree. The doll had been dyed in some places to make it look more like a person. Ribbons had been tied onto it to simulate clothes, and it had a bit of a headdress. Eyes and features had been drawn onto it, and symbols burned in. Mad Bear recognized the marks designed to make people suffer.

The doll didn't, however, have needles stuck in it. This was no surprise to Mad Bear. "They don't need the needles," he told Mike. "That's for tourists. This doll was designed to hold an energy, and that energy would drain people and create a discomfort that would just get worse. When they make the charms, they put the person's name right into it. It knows who it's supposed to act on.

"We all have days when we're just not feeling up to things. If that lasts too long, you always have to get suspicious. It could be something other than just having a down day. If something lingers a while, you need to go talk to somebody. Geez, there's not too many people left you can go to anymore."

Medicated Goo

One afternoon in the 1950s, our late confidant Bill Bowen was helping two young friends work on a car in a garage along Buffalo Creek in Elma. One boy had an accident with the blowtorch that dealt a sickly wound to the back of his hand. The nearest adult was an old Seneca who lived within walking distance. The three of them rushed over, hoping he would call the hospital.

The old man came out, looked at the hand, then rummaged around his cabin and emerged with a small tin holding a homemade potion—a strange pale green goo. He spread a bit of this fibrous ointment all over the wound. It took the pain away instantly.

"Put some of that on there tomorrow," said the old Seneca. "And the next day, and the next. Then bring back whatever's left. You won't need it after that."

All of them were puzzled. A wound like that should have taken weeks to heal. But the old Seneca had the reputation of a healer. Overnight, the burn scabbed over and stopped oozing. By the second morning, the wound was closing at the edges. By the third, only a fine line remained.

When they brought the rest of the potion back, they tried to find out what was

in it. The healer chuckled and said it was "just something I put together." They tried
a few more times to get it out of him, but he never said any more than that it was
bits of things he'd found along the creek.

This green goo is a common form for herbal medicines to take. An Iroquois
healer brought a tub of something like it to the hospital where the father of a
confidant lay, suffering with cancer and given his last rites. The patient was told to
drink it in hourly doses until all of it was gone. His health took a quick turn for the
better, and soon he was cancer-free. His doctors were astonished.

Mitten's Mysterious Mixture

The remarkable Mohawk Richard Oakes was born in 1942 on the Akwesasne St.
Regis Reservation way upstate in New York. Work on the St. Lawrence Seaway
disrupted reservation life, and he hit the road at sixteen. He did stints as a skyscraper
ironworker and ended up in college in San Francisco. One sunny afternoon in 1969,
he dove into Frisco Bay, swam out to Alcatraz Island, and led a student-Native
occupation that brought a lot of attention to Native American causes.

Charismatic and telegenic, Oakes was the spokesman at many high-profile
events. He was also a scrapper. In 1970, he and some Native Americans had a bar
brawl with a group of Samoans, one wielding a pool cue. A shot to the head sent
Oakes into a month-long coma in which every muscle went into spasm. As his mind
slept, his body labored against itself, endlessly. He was dying.

A Native American power trio came to the hospital demanding to treat
Oakes: Mad Bear, Peter Mitten, and the influential Hopi Thomas Banyacya
(1910–1999). The idea seemed crazy to the hospital doctors, but they gave in,
probably because they thought Oakes was dead already. They watched, though,
as Mitten prepared his potion in the hospital room, all the time chanting in
Cayuga. They asked about everything he did. Mad Bear answered for him. "He
won't speak English during the medicine ceremony. You wouldn't understand
it, anyway."

At the end, Mitten's mixture looked like pond water or green Gatorade. The
doctors gasped to see it wind up in Oakes's IV tube and enter his ashen body. Soon,
though, they noticed color return around his heart and spread slowly over his whole
frame. Oakes relaxed so much that he sank into his mattress. Mitten spoke to the

doctors, and Mad Bear translated. "He's very tired. He will rest for two days and then come back to us."

This was so. It's only too bad Mitten's mix couldn't temper that Mohawk backbone and keep Oakes out of confrontations with armed men. He was shot dead in 1972.

Mitten's Breath of Life

One day in the 1970s, a reservation boy was knocked from his bike by a car and apparently killed. He lay on the road until the white paramedics arrived. Mad Bear came out just as they were loading him into the ambulance. The mother pulled on him and cried, telling them to leave him, but the blanket was over his head. A voice rang out.

"Put him down!" It was Peter Mitten, coming unsteadily down the steps of his house. He was ill, weak, and in bed most of the time by then, but there was something in that voice of his. They set the cyclist back down.

The Cayuga healer bent over the boy, nose to nose, and put something in his mouth, something he must have had in his hand. Then he blew breath onto the boy's face. "Open your eyes. Come back to us!" Nothing happened. "Come back, I told you! You come back here and open up those eyes." The tender lids fluttered. "Open your eyes. Open them all the way, but don't move until I tell you."

The boy jerked awake and looked around him. His mother ran to him, but he didn't know her, and Mad Bear kept her back. Wild and terrified, the boy tried to get up, but the two healers kept him down, talking to him calmly, making sure all the parts of his spiritual self were back in place for good. Only when he could talk and show sense in his eyes did they give him to the medics. The stunned whites had stood and watched. They told it all to the emergency room doctors.

Years later, Mad Bear talked about it to Doug Boyd. "Everybody knew those medics had found that kid dead. But nobody ever put that in writing. See, those things, they're never reported, they're just denied. And even when they're observed and admitted, they just can't be officially acknowledged. But I'll tell you one thing we never discussed with anybody. One of those doctors needed help with his own personal situation and came to Peter Mitten and me confidentially. I'm still in touch with that doctor, although his problem is over."

I give a lot of talks and tours in western New York. I've met several nurses who remember a Native American healer called to various Niagara Frontier hospitals for strange or hopeless cases. None remembered his name or nation, but it had to be Mad Bear.

The Cattail Cure

In his early twenties, Michael Bastine worked in a restaurant whose young waiters delivered their tickets to the cooks by sticking them onto an old-fashioned spike-and-wood device by the kitchen door. Often called a ticket spindle, this was basically a knitting needle sticking up like a flagpole out of a blocky base. It got to be a dramatic little game with them to see how many tickets they could slam at one time onto the giant thumbtack. The record may have been thirteen. As the stack of orders thickened, though, more and more torque was needed. In an attempt to break his own record, Michael reared up for a fearful slam. He made it, but the papers slid just a bit, and the big needle dug into the bone between the top joints of his thumb. It was a nasty, agonizing wound. Though this was early on in Michael's acquaintance with Mad Bear, he decided to give the prominent healer a try.

The second he walked in the door, Mad Bear proposed a bout of chess, a game he was always mad to play. He wouldn't listen to a word Michael said. They got through a diffident game or two, with Mike, in agony, barely moving the pieces. "Boy, you're not yourself today," said Mad Bear. "You're lucky we don't have money on this."

Mike stormed for the door, bent on heading to the emergency room. "Oh, about that hand of yours. . . ." Mad Bear said. He gave careful directions about finding the right cattail, tracking its root under the muck, pulling it up just right, and peeling and cutting a few small pieces. Only an inch or so was needed. He told Michael how to prepare the root as a poultice and apply it to the injured digit.

Not more than a day or so later, the thumb was supple, painless, and infection-free. Mike was sure that conventional medicine would have had him splinted and stitched for weeks, with no certainty the wound would heal better.

The Okra Potion

Simple readings taught Mad Bear quite a bit about other people. Sitting by someone and looking into his cup with its tobacco gave him a window into private moments. Western New York has many long-settled ethnic communities, and through his readings Mad Bear came to know and appreciate their rich and varied folk cultures.

A German-American woman in her nineties came to see Mad Bear for a consultation that turned into a quick friendship. Mike Bastine was working around the house at the time and could hear the two of them laughing. At one point, Mad Bear looked up from his cup and confided to the woman a little secret about herself.

"When you make meatloaf, you always grab a bit of raw meat and eat a little before you bake it, don't you?" Their eyes met. She nodded.

"You do that with everything else you bake, too, don't you? Whether it's batter, cookie dough. . . . It's a little custom with you. No one sees you, you've done it all your life, but it's your little private ritual between you and the things you make for the people you love. You really like that, too, don't you—getting in a little bite before everyone else?" The two of them shared another laugh.

The woman had come for a simple reading with Mad Bear, but he spotted something else. She admitted that she had a bowel obstruction and was scheduled for surgery in two weeks.

Mad Bear gave her a recipe for something that might make her feel better. It was a spicy vegetarian stew whose main ingredients were okra and tomatoes. He told her to have a bit of it three times a day and to be sure to finish the pot. "Mike, you know the recipe," he called to his student in the doorway. "Write it down for her on the way out."

In a week or so, she felt completely better. At the insistence of her family, she went in for the operation, but the doctors scanned her beforehand and couldn't find the obstruction. They sent her home without opening her up.

A Gift with a Return

Things have a way of "happening" for medicine people. In the 1990s, the Tuscarora healer Ted Williams spoke at a conference in Australia. Some VIPs—conspicuous latecomers to the event—were on hand, seemingly just to make the scene. After a couple of days, the social climate was getting to Ted. "I was afraid I might have to meet a bigwig," he said.

He was also starting to worry that he would spend all his time in a city building and be back on the plane before he had gifts for his kids. He snuck outside the venue and visited with some Native Australians selling their wares. One of them displayed an expensive, beautiful boomerang to which Ted came back again and again, debating whether or not to buy it. A little while after he bought it, he saw Red Earth Woman, a fellow conference speaker, look at it so admiringly that he knew he had to give it to her. This was the Iroquois custom. The spirits told him to, anyway.

A few days later, Ted made a break and traveled to the countryside, where he got to know a family of Native Australians. They fell to comparing ancient songs and rituals, and one night after dinner, they showed each other a couple of dances by a big fire in the open bush. Ted's hosts were fascinated by his Tuscarora moves, and they kept him at it a long time. When he left, they gave him a gift: a box with ten lovely boomerangs, each as wondrous as the one he'd given away. Surely, Spirit had a hand in this.

Tricks . . .

Joe Anderson—the tobacco tycoon—may not think of himself as a medicine person, but enough of them run in his family. He may have a natural aptitude for the work.

When Joe was a boy, he used to talk about wanting power and success. He dreamed of no less than the financial empire he has achieved. No one encouraged him, and there was no reason to think it was more than a kid mouthing off.

When Joe and his friends were long-haired troublemakers in their early teens, Joe's uncle Mad Bear invited a handful of them to his house where he was hosting medicine people from all over the Americas. Mad Bear introduced one scrawny, crippled, poncho-clad Mesoamerican as the most powerful of the bunch. Mad Bear insisted on each of the Tuscarora boys meeting each of these medicine men personally, shaking hands in the Western fashion. Maybe this was a form of reading.

Toward the end of the meeting, the small shaman announced to them all that *one of the boys would become great. He walked over and fingered Joe's long hair. Everyone—including Joe—was astonished. Some even laughed.*

. . . and Trouble

There was turmoil on several of the reservations in the 1970s. A number of stories from the period feature medicine people or their tricks coming between the Tuscarora and the state troopers. Joe Anderson recalls a night from his boyhood during a period when twenty troopers camped in a trailer park on the Tuscarora Reservation.

The elders had been around that afternoon talking to all the families. "Tonight is one of those nights when all the children have to stay home and be quiet. Ceremonies will be held, asking for help."

At one point in the evening, the troopers pulled out in a virtual frenzy, cruisers tearing out, one after another. It was as if war had been declared somewhere not far off, and they had all been called back to base. Or as if something had spooked them.

When things calmed down, the two sides started talking again as individuals, and word got out about how things had looked to the troopers. They had experienced such vivid phenomena—sourceless voices, ghostly pounding on the hoods of their vehicles—that they had fled en masse.

A Bit of Ritual Magic

There have been a couple of bouts of tension between the New York state troopers and the Tuscarora. By Joe Anderson's own admission, in the mid-1970s he was a punk kid, getting into the booze too young and too hard. Walking home one night well into his cups, he decided to improvise a bit of ritual magic. Snatching up a stick, he jumped out into a dirt road in front of an approaching patrol car and pointed it at the driver like Harry Potter's wand. He could well have been killed, but the vehicle sputtered to a halt as if the engine had died and the wheels had locked. The state trooper got out and pointed at him with an empty hand.

"Cut it out!" he yelled. "I know what you're doing! It's not called for! We're not your enemies. This is just what we have to do. And it's not fair, do you hear? So cut it out!"

Joe took off and watched from the house. Before long another state trooper showed up, got behind the stalled car, and pushed it out of sight.

Maybe Joe has a bit more clout than he knows.

One Girl's Mojo

Ted Williams remembers another time when troopers in riot gear were lined up outside a construction site, keeping a mass of Tuscarora folk away from a building to which they objected. A little girl came out of the throng, ran up to the troopers, and tossed a rock at them. A handful of them took off after her. She ran behind the lines of the Tuscarora into a small replica stockade: a bunch of tall poles stuck in the ground in a circle with only one entrance. The inside of it was open space, but invisible from outside.

The troopers ran into this palisade and almost immediately came running back out. They ended up back in line with their buddies, talking animatedly. The girl came nonchalantly out a moment later and wandered back to the village.

"I found out later what they saw," Ted told us. "It was a bunch of braves, warriors, with their guns drawn, surrounding that girl. And that's why they took off running."

Ted Williams chuckled when he recalled it. "That girl was alone in there. And everybody knows it."

WEAPONS OF FRIENDSHIP

Over the years, Mad Bear Anderson had gotten himself a reputation as somebody nobody should mess with. It was as if a sense of fate or karma worked on those who tried to attack him.

There was the night a fellow Native American tried to shoot him, firing drive-by volleys at the famous fortified cabin. Those in the know have the feeling that no bullets would have hit Mad Bear, even if the structure was not so materially sturdy. It was as if Mad Bear's own orenda was too much to overcome. The gunman ended up in a ditch, badly hurt.

Mad Bear's style of personal defense seems so advanced and Zen-like that it's off the chart. Whereas the most refined Asian techniques defend against forceful violence with some echo of the same violence, Mad Bear seemed simply to defuse the aggression. "He doesn't put anything back on anyone. He just doesn't receive it," someone told Mike Bastine about his techniques.

There was the council at which an enraged Native American came at Mad Bear with a knife, drawing and charging too fast for any to intercede. Mad Bear opened his arms wide as if welcoming a long-lost friend. The would-be assassin walked into Mad Bear's embrace like a mother surprised in her kitchen by a returning college kid. The knife edge slapped absently along Mad Bear's back, and the attacker returned to his seat, blinking and dumbfounded.

"Don't try that on your own," said Mad Bear to his friends out of the side of his mouth. "Took me years to work that one out."

HOUSE CLEARINGS

The Druids of Europe made a code language out of plants and animals. Every tree in the forest had a medical or ceremonial function, as well as a symbolic meaning. It was like that with the Native Americans of the Northeast Woodlands.

People were always calling Mad Bear to quell restless influences in their homes. He often used cedar for this, heating cast-iron frying pans, burning the shavings, and touring room to room with the fragrant smoke.

Mad Bear never started a smudging ceremony if children or pets were in the house. They were especially vulnerable to spiritual influences. But once a ceremony started, he could get so focused on the moment that he might overlook other details.

Whenever you cleanse a house, you're supposed to leave a door or window open just a crack, preferably higher up. This gives the unwanted presences a way to get out. An open window or two doesn't hurt, either. You want them to leave, don't you? Once when Mad Bear was smudging a house in South Buffalo, he forgot to do this. His progress through the house—and the rising heat and smoke—drove the energy upstairs. As he completed his purifying tour of the second floor, everyone heard a crack above them. They followed the smoke to the attic and found a window blown out from the inside with the smoke wafting out through it. Whatever Mad Bear was driving out left with a frenzy that surprised even him.

Mad Bear's time and energy were always stretched. When a problem seemed basic, he deputized another healer, usually someone he'd trained.

The Smoke Is Always Different

In the early 1980s, a family of Canadian Mohawks living in Buffalo asked Mad Bear for help with some trouble in their home. Their house was right across the street from the campus of D'Youville College of Nursing on the city's west side. This section of the city near the Niagara River was the scene of fighting in the War of 1812 and an earlier Native American settlement.

Many sites in the region, including various college buildings, are haunted. White families could have lived in this same house, known the same troubles, failed to sense the cause, and either moved or stayed and suffered without knowing why. Native Americans tend to be very sensitive to psychic influences.

Mad Bear sent Mike Bastine to run the ceremony. "Just be sure you have them call you and tell you what they see when you leave," he cautioned. "It's one of the most important parts of the process."

Mike went to the house in question and did a thorough smudging. It seemed a basic operation, and he left with the smoke still in the air of the house. The people called him a few hours later. "You'll never guess what happened. After you left, the smoke hovered around for a while and took the shape of a funnel cloud, like a tornado or something. When we climbed the stairs, we could see it on the second floor. Then it went straight up through the ceiling and vanished."

"Can't say I can explain that for you," said Mike. "Maybe the best question to ask is about your gut feeling. Were you scared or antsy or nervous?"

"Not at all," said the woman. "It was beautiful."

"Then I think your problem is solved," said Mike.

Mad Bear was impressed when he heard the story. "That smoke is always different. This time it must have surrounded the spirits like a tornado and took them right up and out of the house. Boy, that's the first time I ever heard of it doing that, though."

The Test of a Healer

In the late 1970s and early 1980s, there were a lot of healers in the Niagara region, who, as Mike Bastine puts it, "were real good readers." Mad Bear always claimed that his own tutor Peter Mitten was greater than he was. But too many others were in business.

"A lot of people tell you they can read," says Mike Bastine. "But a lot of them aren't very good. You can usually tell right away if you got one of those. But so many people can't."

As Mad Bear neared the end of his days, he started to wonder who might be left to carry on his tradition. On Six Nations Reservation in Brantford, Ontario, lived a medicine woman with a mighty reputation. Her name may have been Daisy Thomas. She seemed sure to last beyond him, and Mad Bear wanted to know how good she really was before recommending her to his patients. The trouble is that he couldn't do the test himself. Like medieval wizard Michael Scot and the Witch of Fauldshope, they didn't get along.

Also like the legendary Scot, Mad Bear sent a deputy to see if his rival was as good as advertised. He gave Mike Bastine a made-up ailment and told him how to talk about it. He cautioned Mike never to mention his own name or let on that the two were friends. "That just wouldn't be good," he said. "Not good at all."

Mike went up to Brantford, told Daisy his problem, and listened. Then he relayed to Mad Bear what she'd recommended: the herbs, the gathering, the processing, the recipe.

"Well, she done ya right," said Mad Bear. "The old girl's still doing a good job. Good to think there's a few people around here that'll know what they're doing when I'm gone."

The Viking in the Sky

To some Native American civilizations like the Hopi and Maya, history was a process of repeating cycles. Prevalent in the oral tradition of the late twentieth century and thriving into the twenty-first is the notion of "earth changes," as though some global cataclysm may be at hand, affecting the environment, the world economy, and social conditions. It may be purifying, it may be disastrous, it may be an upheaval, and it may be a coming together of consciousness. The only thing anyone agrees on is that it should be transformative.

One night in the early 1980s, Joe Anderson gazed up into the night sky and saw a formation he had never noticed before. He got the firm image of an outline in the stars, a craggy, bearded human profile and a horned helmet he described as a Viking. He found himself so impressed that he looked up his mystical uncle Mad Bear and told him about the experience.

At first nothing rang a bell, but Joe Anderson pressed on, even drawing something on a whiteboard that could have been such an outline. "Bear, what does that mean?"

Mad Bear looked at the drawing for a minute and asked about the part of the sky in which Joe had seen the star cluster. In a few seconds, something registered. "Wow, it's farther along now than I thought," he said. "When that figure's done, it's the next purification for the world."

Swiftie at Yaddo

In some circles it's thought that most medicine people have psychic powers that they never use for show. A display of prophecy and spirit-talking like those of today's TV mediums is presumed child's play to many of them.

Abenaki author Joe Bruchac's late 1990s circle of friends included Swift Eagle, a seventy-year-old southwestern Native American everybody just called Swiftie. To some, he seemed a lighthearted soul. Others sensed that Swiftie was an elder who may have been trained in Pueblo and Apache spirituality. Most Native North Americans tip their hats to the Southwest as the source of the continent's oldest traditions.

One afternoon, Joe, Swift Eagle, and other friends were visiting Linda Hogan and Lewis Elder, Native authors in residence at Yaddo, the writers' retreat just east of the village of Saratoga Springs, New York. It was Swiftie's first visit to the former Trask estate. He marveled at the mansion, the grounds, the setup, and the people. As others talked, the bemused Swiftie went on his own little tour.

After an hour had passed, someone wondered about him, and the group set out in search of him. They found Swiftie by one of the lakes in rapt conversation with a woman, pointing to spots in the trees, the creeks, the lakes, and the mansion itself. The guest, a newcomer to Yaddo, had mistaken him for one of the old-timers and asked him about the spirits of the place. As naturally as discussing the weather of the past week, Swiftie started walking her around, telling her the history of certain spots according to the spirit personalities he encountered. As his friends came up, he was just finishing a tale about the pair of invisible women he detected.

Joe Bruchac recalled author David Pitkin's accounts of Yaddo and suspected that Swiftie had discovered two of its most commonly reported haunters, both twentieth-century women. Joe has learned to expect the miraculous among Native elders, but this was still remarkable. Everyone looked at Swiftie with a new regard.

Ted's Dream Healing

Twice a year in April and October, Native elders lead a conference at a camp in Jackson, Ohio. Ted Williams and Mike Bastine were the speakers in April 2005. My then domestic partner and I had spent a couple weeks in the Carolinas. We timed our return trip to western New York to catch Mike and Ted in action. We drove all one Friday from North Carolina and arrived in early evening. While she took our scrappy, forty-pound polar bear of a dog for a long walk on the grounds, I sought out the two stars and found them tucking into a potluck buffet.

Mike and Ted sat opposite each other at the end of a cafeteria table. Nearby diners craned their necks to catch their conversation. A seat next to Ted had been respectfully left vacant. He motioned to it when I greeted him, and I took it.

I was surprised at how much private talk I was able to have with them both in this public setting. Ted told me some wonderful stories, such as the one about Bluedog, and he told me tales about the False Faces and the Fairy Tree. But this visit was just a greeting. My friend and I had to get to nearby Chillicothe and find an inn that would take us and our quirky cub.

That night I had a terrible dream. My mother had fallen out of her hospital bed, and I had to drive over and help the nurses pick her up. As I was starting to lift her the nurses suddenly disappeared. Her rag-doll body and the rails of the bed made the task impossible. I lifted limb and torso, but her core weight shifted like sand in a sack. A shoulder went over, a hip came back down. I was so busy trying to do it all so gently that I failed to notice, at first, that she had taken on the hide and tawny hair of a big cat, a lion or puma. She was still limp and vulnerable in her new shape, though, and trapped within her declining mind. She chuckled impishly at everything as though it were all funny. Shocked, repelled, terrified, I kept to my task with exquisite care. It was endless.

I woke with a start and sat straight up in the bed.

Like everyone, I've had the occasional nightmare. Most often I conjure a weapon and strike back at whatever the menace is, or I shape-shift and become the bigger predator. My dream mind is good at that. Once I took on a werewolf by becoming one. Another time I launched bolts from my eyes at a T-Rex like Cyclops the X-man.

I've never had a dream whose affect on me was as creepy as that one. It touched every nerve in my body. I had no idea why I had had it then. I couldn't track its occurrence to anything that had happened that day.

My mother's decline had affected me. I was at her side as she passed over. But many people go through much worse, and she had been gone for two years.

Where do these dreams come from? I think some of them are backdated flowerings of old incidents, eruptions of things that have been brewing in the mind for years. Maybe these turmoils seethe in us every night, and only once in a while project themselves into dreams that we remember. The effect of this one was awful. I said nothing about it to my companion.

We went to the morning session of the conference. When Ted was done talking, he ducked out somewhere and no one could find him. My companion and I stood with Michael Bastine and a small group of people. Thankfully, the others talked; I was only half there, still dwelling on the terrible dream. My skin crawled as though tiny electrical wires charged my clothing.

Just as we were asking Michael to give our good-byes to Ted, I felt a light, cool touch on the nape of my neck, just lifting a bit of my hair. Instantly, my preoccupation with the dream vanished. I turned. It was Ted, who had come up behind me and, with a brush up of a hand, lifted a lock so gently that it could have been done by a *puff of air. It was an odd gesture, one no American white would think of. There had to be something cultural or even ceremonial about it. Light as a breeze, it would have taken practice to copy.*

An hour later on the rural roads of central Ohio, I spilled everything out to my partner: the dream, the turmoil I could barely remember, the curiosity of it all, and that strange touch. It was as if all the grief and trauma of the past ten years were at rest.

My partner was a massage therapist, a Reiki healer, and a deeply intuitive woman. "He healed you," she said. She could have said: He knew the dream. *It's too much to think he could have seen all that. But he was of the medicine people.*

Later the same year—September 28, 2005—Michael Bastine called to tell me that Ted Williams had passed away in Asheville, North Carolina. It was a shock, since Ted had seemed in such good health. Michael was leaving early in the morning to be with Ted's southern family and friends. Memorials closer to home on the Tuscarora Reservation hadn't even been scheduled. We talked just a few minutes about Ted and all the elders leaving the world. The closeness—and the loss—was far greater for Michael than for me.

We closed, though, with him *consoling* me. *"Ted's working his medicine all over, now," he said.*

On the Rez

In August 2004, I went to the Tuscarora Reservation fair to meet Mike and Pam Bastine. I never found them. It would have been easy to miss someone. The grounds around the fair were ample, and a string of trees, if not a clump of woods, seemed to frame every area of the event—school, parking lot, fairgrounds, baseball diamond.

I walked among the displays and activities. I listened to music, looked at art, and threw tomahawks. I didn't mind being with my thoughts. As I strolled along a line of trees at the edge of the fairgrounds, two small parties crossed paths.

The first was a tiny wagon train, headed by a bandaged, older white guy in a motorized, off-road wheelchair. He was smoking a cigarette through a mouthpiece, hooked by fluid-filled tubes to a big contraption in back. I presumed the device was a filter for the cigarettes, and that the man was dying from cancer caused by the smoking he couldn't quit. Another little cart trailed him, linked to his wheelchair with chains and cables. It had to be oxygen. Two female companions, probably wife and daughter, pushed and steered the procession.

Three Native American men cut across the path of this unwieldy group. Hidden by the trees as they'd approached, they made their entrance laughing at the punch line of a joke and hurled themselves into visibility like an assault team. One of them tripped on a tree root, tumbled on all fours like a bear, and laughed the louder.

An old Native American man I hadn't noticed before was standing beside me. "Ah," he said contentedly to the air, "the white man shouldn't do tobacco, and the red man shouldn't do alcohol."

I walked and looked around a bit more and gave up on finding my friends. As I headed for my car, two young Native Americans came toward me out of the parking lot from the east. They looked about fourteen. One was probably five-three and 120 pounds, but the other was bigger and of a very distinctive body type. So much of the boy's mass pushed up under his straight shoulders and thick upper arms that he was surely destined to become one of the bear bodies I had seen among the Tuscarora men. The lad had on a black T-shirt with a bit of orange on the collar. Tipping up a bottle of a colored drink, he was grinning at something his friend had said.

Five minutes later and two miles away, I drove past two young Native Americans on the north side of the broad, sunny road, coming back toward the fair I had left. The smaller of them I didn't notice as I drove by, but to his left was the big boy I had just seen at the fair. The same black, orange-collared T-shirt, even the same gesture: smiling, raising a drink. It was him, or an identically dressed twin.

Only a helicopter could have gotten that kid where he was so quickly. I stared as long as I could, even craning to look back when I passed him. I couldn't have been mistaken. I was reminded again of the aura of the surreal that surrounds every one of my visits to a reservation.

When Michael asked Mad Bear how much of his success was due to the ingredients of his remedies and how much to psychic and psychological factors, he said that just about all of it was in the mind. He chose to use things that helped him focus his own healing powers or that of his patients. Maybe it's all in the mind.

Maybe there's no difference, anyway, between the witch and the medicine person. Maybe it's all how they do their stuff. But make no mistake about it: There are power people now and "doing work" as you read. Many of them are mature, humble-looking Native Americans. Almost none are out to impress. They aren't all saints, and they have their troubles. Some of them struggle with their health, with their families, with alcohol, or with money. But never underestimate them, their powers, or the culture that has brought these medicine people among us. How the world needs them.

5

The False Faces

The mask in a primitive festival is revered as a veritable apparition of the mythical being that it represents—even though everyone knows that a man made the mask and that a man is wearing it.

JOSEPH CAMPBELL, *THE MASKS OF GOD*

THE MEDICINE MASK SOCIETY

As long as they've been known to history, the Iroquois have been distinctive for their healing societies. Other indigenous cultures have had their doctoring clans, but there has never been anything in the world precisely like the Iroquois medicine mask society, usually called the False Faces.

Known for their goon-faced, fright-wigged wooden masks, the False Faces need to be distinguished from the local "good witch" you can hire to help you with your problems. While many individual medicine people might be members of the False Face Society, this cult of maskers differs in fundamental ways from the medicine folk of the last chapter. Obviously, there's the matter of the masks, which will be unforgettable to anyone who's ever seen one. The village healer doesn't use one of these. That shaggy mane of corn-silk or horsehair may be the most conspicuous feature of one of the classic medicine masks.

Members of the False Face Society have always been group healers, too. The national guard of the medicine people, they are mobilized as much as summoned. They come in a flock. They only do house calls. And *they* call *you,* and at special times of the year.

The old-timers held their traditional ceremonies in the spring and fall, when the collective pileup of societal ailments needed to be addressed. They made special appearances in times of special need. Their techniques were different, too, from those of the medicine people. The village medicine people, though more than simple herbalists, minister to splinters and skin rashes; their remedies can be physical and practical.

The False Faces, on the other hand, have always been fundamentally spiritual healers. They deal with the spirits of disease. And they are still at it. The healing members of the False Face Society are always male. The leader of every local group, though, is a woman. This priestess is the Keeper of the False Faces. She rules the rituals, guards the masks and paraphernalia, summons the healers, and sends them out on their missions. She is the only one who knows the identity of all the local members.

Arthur C. Parker described the accoutrements of the classic False Face Society as its members roamed the village on a healing mission. First and foremost, of course, were the masks, which every member wore. And since percussion accompanied all Iroquois rituals, the False Face healers carried rattles, often made of snapping turtle shell and hickory bark. All wore head throws—shrouds over the backs of their necks—which helped conceal their identities. The leader carried a pole on which dangled miniatures of their trademark items: tiny husk faces, mini masks, and turtle rattles. Since the customary payment for each healing was an offering of sacred tobacco, a little tobacco basket was part of their equipment.

Their ceremonies were crafted to deliver awe. Their calls could be heard a long way off, and they seemed to come out of nowhere, converging on a community at night. They stalked through the village with their gourd and shell rattles, searching for sufferers' homes. What moments those must have been, waiting for them!

Like giant predators stalking disease by scent, these healers snuffled outside the doors of homes and longhouses, deciding which one to visit. The masks amplified the sounds they made, which must have had quite an effect. Sometimes they crashed into a house and besieged beds like marauding demons. Sometimes they crawled on the floor like ominous saurians toward sufferers and jumped up tall beside them. They finished their healings with a flourish of hair, a clack of implements, and a puff of soot. Then, taking tiny bowls of corn soup as refreshment, they made their way out to the next sufferer—until the last was served and the band of healers withdrew into the night.

They needed no escorts through the spirit-haunted wood. No demon, witch, or beast would dare touch one of them as they were: behind masks and in trance.

And so often, they cured.

There's no reason to doubt the power of the False Faces. Traditional healing sometimes works where Western medicine has not, and the force of the mind can go a long way in the repair of the body. When all other treatment had failed, the False Faces offered the last psychic boost.

Some contemporary scholars aren't too sure that the False Face Society is more than a few centuries old. Arthur Parker felt sure that the outfit went a long way back, at least among his Seneca people. This society feels old to *us,* if that counts for anything. And we have reasons for thinking that.

The tradition of these maskers was fully developed by the time the Europeans discovered it. It's hard to believe that it had no backstory. And curious tiny bone and stone plaques that suspiciously resemble the historic medicine masks have been found in Iroquoian graves that go back a thousand years. These trinkets, possibly slipped into a grave in secret as the earth closed, have been interpreted as badges of honor for the long work of a healer whose name no one could know in life.

THE HEADMAN OF THE FACES

There are a number of origin stories for the False Faces, but they fall into two major categories. One stems from the creation myth. Michael Bastine tells this story wonderfully.

A Creation Myth Story

Shortly before humankind was put on the earth, the Good-Minded Spirit dropped in for a look at the region that would become the Northeast. It was a sublime, turbulent landscape full of fantastic, monstrous beings. The Great Spirit could see that these would be trouble when his Iroquois came to being as he planned. He surveyed the chaos, wondering which of the critters to keep and which to clear out.

A giant creature sometimes called the Headman of the Faces came up to him and asked what he was doing. Pleasantries commenced, and the Great Spirit kept his cards close to the vest. The giant—surely a forerunner of the Stone Giants, whose story is to come—could sense that his guest was a heavy hitter, probably from the emanations of his orenda. How heavy he didn't guess. He suggested a test of power.

"See that mountain in the distance?" said the giant to the stranger.

"Uh . . . yeah," said the Maker of All Things.

"Now cover your eyes and look away, and don't turn round till I tell you." Heaven's Holder played peek-a-boo, doubtless with a wry immortal smile.

There was a rustling of the winds and a shaking of the earth. It lasted quite a while. When the world had again fallen still, the giant being called triumphantly for the Great Spirit to turn and look. The distant mountain had moved a few notches. It was as far to the right of the sun at the bottom of the stormy sky as it had just been to the left. The giant looked very happy with himself.

"Wow, that's pretty good," said the Good-Minded One. "I can see you've really been working on your magic. Now it's my turn. You just cover up and close your eyes the way I did."

At the instant the giant's mighty paws closed over, the Creator welcomed him to turn and look. The giant had sensed no quaking earth or cyclones and thought it had to be a trick. He turned too fast. The mountain was right on top of him, with a rocky jutting cliff on the level of his forehead. As he jerked around, it smacked his rugged puss and sprawled his features all over it. Suddenly the giant realized who he was talking to.

The Good Spirit shared the information that he had been thinking about clearing the world of its rambunctious first inhabitants. He asked the giant what he made of that.

"We can't change our natures," the giant said. "But we have a lot of good to give. We could become great healers. We could learn the uses of plants and the ceremonies of restoring health. We'll get those ready for the day the people get here and figure out how to teach them." The Good-Minded One decided that the world could stand to keep a bit of its diversity. The giants did indeed become healers, and the familiar crook-nosed masks have been made ever since in tribute to the first one, the Headman of the Faces, and his craggy collision.

Another version of the False Face story takes place near enough to our own time to involve a human encounter, probably within the last thousand years.

The Stone Giants—inveterate enemies of humankind—had been removed from the world, all but one. This last of them was a mighty being who had grown mightier through his years of isolation. He had made his home in a cave in the Allegheny Mountains.

A young Seneca hunter lost in a storm stumbled into this lair. After all the centuries on his own, the giant was ready for company. He let the young hunter stay with him and taught him a variety of arts, including healing through dreams and visions. As he left the cave at the end of it all, an apparition guided the human hunter to a basswood tree on which the original False Face mask was waiting for him.

It's been said that these two myths were meant to stand for the two major classes of masks. The oldest story involving the Good-Minded

Spirit could be the origin-tale of the Great Doctor masks, generally the most revered of the bunch. The Stone-Giant tale might be the source of the Common Faces.

DOCTORS AND DOORKEEPERS

Writing around the turn of the twentieth century, Parker described four classes of masks:

- Doorkeeper or Doctor masks
- Dancing masks
- Beggar (and possibly thief) masks, not part of the true society
- Secret masks, never used in public ceremonies

The classic recent study is the one of William Fenton, *The False Faces of the Iroquois* (1987). Fenton sticks to the idea that there were two main orders of masks, of which the Doctor/Doorkeepers are generally considered a higher caste than the Common Faces. This system might not be so rigid for the people who use them. This ranking of the two classes of masks could have something to do with their origin-tales.

The Great Doctor masks were drawn from the creation song and the game between the Creator and the crook-faced giant. These grand, time-tested healing masks, sometimes also called Doorkeeper masks, were long haired and colored red or black. Their mouths were either twisted or spoonlike for blowing soot. The oldest masks had corn-silk hair, though horse's manes were used after European contact.

Iroquois masks of this holy class are more than portraits of random demons. Each one gives a definite message through its shape, color, and features. Some are mythological beings, gods of disease or wind. Old masks, veterans of many rites, passed along through centuries, have plenty of authority. Intuitives of any nationality feel a sense of awe when they behold any of these major masks, true works of sacred art.

Even among the Doctor masks, there's thought to be a pecking order. In some quarters, the red masks are considered more powerful than the black. There are even divided masks, painted half red and half black, possibly for the curing of people divided in spirit. Every year we seem to need a few more of those.

BEGGARS AND THIEVES

A ramshackle, slightly less imposing lot sometimes considered a lesser category, the common faces were rooted in stories set much more recently in time. One we discussed before involves the Stone Giants well after the Great Spirit had cleared the world of most of its demons. Others lack even mentions of the creation-days and are linked to supernatural forest beings like the Great Flying Heads.

Ethnologist William Beauchamp considered the Great Flying Heads a very likely source for the ghastly, disembodied visages these miracle masks personify. These heads could be the most dreadful bogies in the Iroquois metaphysical zoo, but they did good turns now and then for individual humans. They were also size-shifters. They could make themselves as small as a human head so as to float through a longhouse portal. In that circumstance, they would look a lot like medicine masks.

The caste system for the Iroquois masks need not be presumed to be set in stone. We hear that the oldest and grandest of the common face masks, seasoned with generations of ceremonies, are as esteemed as the Great Doctors or Doorkeepers.

Still, the common faces come in many untraditional forms. Seemingly answering to the changes in American society, some recently made masks have taken the form of pigs. Doubtless a new category of mask had to be made for consultants and career politicians.

OPENING THE EYES

But it isn't just the healers who are the subjects of reverence. A sense of awe and respect attaches to the tools of their trade, the masks themselves, that may be hard to understand for people outside Iroquois society. This is a subject of its own.

Orenda, the universal force of existence, gives the False Face masks a power unique among man-made objects. To many Iroquois, the greatest of these masks are alive. They occasionally wake. If you or someone you know has one of these, you better keep reading.

For the old-timers, no classification was more significant than that between a mask that has been used in ceremonies and one that has not. The masks that have been sold to tourists over the years are most often mere works of craftsmanship, wrought like the items in shop class. They have never been consecrated by ritual use, so there ought to be little sacrilege in selling them. While some contemporary traditionalists are starting to maintain that a medicine mask of any sort is holy and sacred, they are surely far less sensitive about manufactured False Faces.

Masks used in ceremonies are totally different. They are charged. Their "eyes have been opened." Those that have been used in generations of ceremonies have been invested with ever more of the force of orenda. They are, in their own sense, alive.

Traditionalists believe that these masks have to be handled with the respect and attention given to living things, even "fed" and continually revivified like biological beings. They pine for the community of ceremonies. They hunger for corn soup, itch for sunflower oil, and pant for the smoke of sacred tobacco. They can be pretty hot to hold.

To use any mask irreverently might curse the bearer, or whoever he or she looked at while wearing it. Most Six Nations' folk drape these False Faces when they are not in use, which minimizes the risk of riling one of them up. Masks shouldn't be left face upward, either, since this is a sign of death. The power of the mask might take the pose too seriously and start to inflict the real thing on people and pets in the home around it.

MASKS AND MUSEUMS

Every Iroquois nation keeps a store of medicine masks, to which many of the ones held in white museums are returning. The Onondaga are generally considered the specialists on the handling and repatriation of the medicine masks.

The worst imaginable environment for these masks is the one in which most twentieth-century whites encountered them: a display in a museum. To let one of these powerful objects with its own inconceivable form of life gain dust, crack, and dry in a glass pen may be as senseless and cruel as to put a lion in a cage. Do these objects live and hold consciousness in a direct sense? Do they simply project the appearance of awareness, having acquired some of the energy of the nation of their makers? These are questions that will never be answered with certainty.

Ted Williams reminded us that many of the masks in these upstate New York museums were questionably acquired, which could not have sweetened their temperaments. Some of the Native Americans who ended up selling the masks had no business making decisions with objects of national significance. And other masks were obtained by non–Native Americans in divorces and inheritances and sold from there.

The masks, though, at least the live ones, keep their power. Masks "caged" in museums get restless and agitated, cracking the glass in their displays and creating other problems. They act up, moving about during the night, trading places with other masks, making their distinctive, disconcerting whistle calls or causing poltergeist activity around them. Many a museum curator, they say, has been driven to an early retirement by these active masks. And they are known to play some part in their own destinies.

The Library Fire

In the early twentieth century, the New York State Library was housed on the fourth floor of the state capitol building in Albany. It was the fifth largest library in the United States and one of the twenty biggest in the world. It doubled as the state archives, holding a priceless collection of books, manuscripts, documents, and records going back to the days when New York was called New Netherland. It also held a trove of Native American artifacts, including some much-mistreated Iroquois medicine masks.

At that point in time, most of those masks had to be live ones. They quite likely dated back a century or more and had been used many times in ceremonies. Some may even have been taken as the spoils of conquest. They had been mounted behind glass display cases and untouched for decades. They itched under the dust that gathered on them and were offended by the gawking visitors.

The library had grown too big, and plans were made to move it by January 1911 to a larger facility. But there were delays in the construction of its new home, the Education Building, and the relocation was put off a few months.

In the early hours of March 29, 1911, a fire started. By four in the morning, a full wing of the library was a howling inferno. Crowds gathered in the streets around it, yipping and dancing like children, catching the flecks of once-precious manuscripts that soared out of the building like the snowflake of hell. It's lucky the whole structure wasn't lost.

Genealogists and researchers have never forgotten this event, certainly the greatest disaster that has ever befallen New York state's library system. It's one reason that many a passionate query into the past hits a brick wall at 1911. Lost with these records was most of a vast collection of Native American objects and artifacts. The most sacred, though, including the displays of medicine masks, were entirely untouched by the catastrophe.

The most popular explanation for the museum fire was faulty wiring. The second was the idea that a smoldering cigar butt had been tossed into a wastebasket. But the Iroquois never doubted that the conflagration's real source was the shameful treatment of the medicine masks in the collection. You don't do that to a Doorkeeper, to a Great Doctor. It was as if the masks had lashed out at everything around them and left themselves standing as a message—if the white world could read it. Not a hair on one of them was even singed. Can you imagine entering the smoking wreck of the library and seeing a set of them staring at you? This building today is one of Albany's most famous haunted sites.

We hear through the grapevine that two Buffalo museums still have masks not on display. The same source also tells us that they have arrangements with the local Seneca concerning the fair treatment of these masks. Members of the False Face Society are invited to each museum off-hours for behind-the-scenes ceremonies. Doubtless the museum folks see this arrangement as a gesture of respect to their reservation friends. The service rendered could go both ways, and the medicine people doubtless chuckle when they think of it. Both museums are haunted, by the way, and accustomed to frequent flare-ups when new Native American displays come in or old ones are moved.

The Will of the Masks

Ted Williams tells us about an incident from the 1990s. Word got out that a handful of masks in the possession of one upstate museum were to be returned to the Oneida. A representative of the Onondaga Longhouse went to the museum to see if the rumor was true. He also asked to visit with the masks in question and work a ceremony for them.

He was brought to a room in which six masks hung on a wall. He commenced a tobacco burning ceremony, and almost instantaneously the door at the back of the room flew open. No human was in sight who could have given it that kind of a shove, and the curator leaped forward to close it. The Onondaga healer, though, had gotten a look at what was behind this: Over a hundred masks not destined to be returned were being stored—"imprisoned," Ted calls it—in this room. They wanted to be part of the ceremony, too. He called to the curator not to bother with the door. "I'll tell you why later."

When the ceremony was over, the healer told the curator a few things about False Faces. One thing the Onondaga man did not mention was that he had received a vision at the end of the ceremony. As he was leaving, he ducked his head just inside the room that held the hundred masks and said to them in Onondaga, "You'll be coming home, too, within two years." It was so.

TWO HEALERS AND THE MASKS

Among the wonders in Mad Bear's cabin was his personal False Face. Usually it hung on a wall, its gnarled lips, nose, cheeks, and chin in plain view. White author Doug Boyd had learned great respect for Iroquois belief, but he admitted in his book on Mad Bear that it was hard to accept that this or any other mask was, in any sense, a living thing. Yet over the years of his acquaintance with Mad Bear, Boyd could swear that its "hair"—the yellow, wispy fibers hanging from it—dipped closer to the floor at every visit. Even its grin seemed to broaden.

Many a time there were several False Faces in Mad Bear's house, most of them on loan. Mad Bear was a culture keeper. Even people uneasy with him trusted him more than their own families to care for objects of cultural significance. It made for some turbulent nights. These masks interacted with each other like magnets. Sometimes they got restive, tossing small objects around and buzzing as if they were conversing.

To Mad Bear, the understanding that these things were energized and even filled with human sentiments was fundamental. He cautioned his human guests to behave well around them. "Don't treat them with any less respect than you'd give to another person I introduced you to," he said. "Don't laugh at them or mock them. Don't even point at them. If you get something stirred up out of one of them, I don't have the power to turn it around."

One morning, Mike Bastine came for a visit and found Mad Bear bleary-eyed. "Bear, you look awful. You been up all night?"

"Mike, you should have heard it," said the healer. "The masks were really acting up. I had to get up and do a ceremony to calm them down. Took forever. Boy, I wonder what was going on in the world last night. Guess we'll find out pretty soon." The house still smelled like tobacco and sage.

A few years before his death, Mad Bear got sick and went off for traditional healing. He loaned two masks to Michael for safekeeping. This was a gesture of respect in both directions. "I told them where they were going," he said to Mike. "They'll know you. When I come back—if I come back—I'll ask for them again, and we'll go on a few more years."

Late in his life, Ted Williams admitted to me that he was a member of the False Face Society. He told me quite a bit about it. This was something that would probably never have happened in earlier centuries, but many Native American elders have started opening up to the cultures around them. It's as if they sense a greater need in the world, as if the world has lost something it should have kept, and the time may be here for them to start bringing balance back.

Ted had made his first mask thirty years before, just after his initiation. He didn't know the ways then as well as he would later. Though horsehair and natural fibers are customary for masks, he figured to give the one he'd made more power by using his own long locks. He wasn't accustomed then to the way they "think."

Thus he blamed himself when, shortly after, his young daughter was killed in a freak accident as she carried the mask to a show-and-tell at her school. As if drawn to her by magnetism, a car had veered into a crosswalk and virtually pursued her. The stunned driver said the car had taken on a will of its own.

"Those things are just too powerful," said Michael Bastine in retrospect. "You can't take a chance on their energy going off in some direction you can't anticipate."

The founder of East Aurora's alternative Mandala School, John Newton, taught Native American children at the Onondaga Reservation in the 1980s. He liked the Onondagas' attitude to education. He admired the society he came to know. One of his ten-year-olds said something indiscreet. "I'm a member of the False Face Society."

"You are?" said John. "How do you go about that?"

"I had a dream when I was seven and I told my parents about it. They said it meant I was going to be a healer. They got me into the False Face Society. Now I lead some of the ceremonies. We did one last night."

"Ceremonies?"

"Oh, yeah. We went to see a guy who was sick. Fixed him up just right."

"How can you lead a ceremony?"

"We always have to have someone who leads the ceremonies."

"But you're ten years old."

"I am," said the boy. "But when I put on the mask, I'm a *healer*."

OTHER MASKED HEALERS

The fabulous medicine masks—the False Faces—were not the only masked healers among the Iroquois. There were two other orders of masked medicine societies, the Husk Face Society and the Company of Mystic Animals (a group of several small societies).

The Husk Face Society—sometimes nicknamed the Bushy Heads—is less organized and mythologized than that of the False Faces, and their masks look less like works of art. The Husk Face healers are water doctors. Their ceremonies end with a flourish of spritzing and spraying.

The Company (or Society) of Mystic Animals is a loose group of smaller societies whose masks are inspired by animals. Their job is to teach, maintain, and perform the rites needed to keep the goodwill of the animals in the world, which looks like a spin-off of one of the main functions of the ancient shamans. They do this by reaching to the core group of medicine animals, which doubtless includes their clan animals. The spirits of the medicine animals, had taught the founders of each dance the ceremonies needed to keep them happy and to maintain the balance of the worlds—human, animal, and natural.

Like every member of the False Faces, the conductors of these ceremonies seem to have strange powers. White guests have reported seeing the leaders of Mystic Animals rites lift red-hot stones barehanded from the lodge fire and toss them around like medicine balls. Routinely they "see" through a wooden mask that has no eyeholes and describe objects and events around the lodge. One powerful leader was reported to make a doll dance as if it were alive.

Though they may not be as legendary as the False Faces, these Mystic Animals folk are not to be mocked. If someone is persistently irreverent during a ceremony, the leader approaches him or her with a doll—even in his blind wooden mask—and cuts the string that holds its skirt. In the dimness of the lodge, it may take time for the scoffer to notice that everyone else is laughing. His pants or her dress have fallen to the floor, doubtless from the second the doll's drape was cut.

Other Native North American societies have deep and powerful traditions of sacred clowns, some of them costumed and masked. Some contemporary scholars take it as given that these Iroquois maskers belong among them.

Certainly the False Faces share some of the same features and functions. Certainly their displays are ritualized and antic. But they are more than power clowns. The awe and reverence shown the masks themselves should answer to this. Furthermore, the purpose of the medicine maskers is healing, not social commentary.

UNMASKED HEALERS

Not all the Iroquois healing societies use masks. The Little Water/ Animal Society and the Pigmy/Dark Dance Society were the most important of the unmasked healers. They were named after their traditional healing songs.

The power of the Little Water Society doubtless draws from the animal clans so significant to the Iroquois. Mythologist Joseph Campbell was fascinated by their origin story, that of the good hunter killed by humans and revived through the magic and goodwill of the forest animals. There were nine Iroquois animal clans, but many more animals were involved in the ceremonies of the Little Water healers. Members of this society keep small animal parts for use as ritual objects.

Members of the Pigmy (also Little People) Society are often called the Dark Dancers because of their habit of doing their songs and dances in dark or dimly lit places. Their rites and origins are connected to the Little People, to whom we devote a whole chapter.

THE CALL OF THE MASKS

There's a sense of destiny to the healer, even today. A new healer is called to join the False Face Society by a dream of his own that guides him to it or something a seer recognizes in him. The work is lifelong, unless another vision tells him it's time to leave the order.

Sometimes the mask he uses is inherited from another healer and given away to him with a ritual. As if it were an intelligent being, the mask is told of its journey with a new owner. The mask is adopted as much as it is received. Even that may not be the right word.

But new masks are made, and a new healer might also carve his own. This, also, is a ritual process. He begins by entering the woods and walking until he finds the right living tree. It might be better to say that the tree picks him, and it may take days.

The time of day that tree and carver finally meet will determine the mask's color. If it's morning, the mask will be red; if it's afternoon or evening, it's black. This follows the belief that the first grand False Face made a daily journey with the Sun. He would be red in the morning as he approached from the east and black in the afternoon as he looked back into the shadows from the west.

Basswood is customary for False Face masks, though pine, poplar, and maple are also used. One tree never used is the elm. Clearly there is tree magic among the Iroquois, and it seems even less familiar to the rest of the world than that of the Celtic druids.

So that the power of the tree might enter into the mask, the carver will start on a live tree. The mask has to be finished to a certain point before he can remove the block that holds it. He does the features, then strikes notches above and below, chiseling out the face in a block and working it in a more sheltered place. The mask never breaks and the tree never dies, perhaps because he's offered prayers and sacred tobacco. At almost any stage of its crafting the mask is more or less living, with sentiments and power. Once started, it can't be left unfinished.

Nature Strikes Back

A white art dealer we know tells us an odd tale from the 1980s. An old Seneca from the Tonawanda Reservation broke this taboo and left a well-formed face on a live tree. We don't know the reason. Maybe someone talked him into making the mask for money, possibly when he was drunk, and when he came to, he refused to work on it any more. Friends tried to talk to him, but he was resolved.

Then he had a stroke. His features distorted until it was clear that he was coming to resemble the face on the tree. Our white confidant claimed to have seen pictures (before and after) confirming the marvel. Finally, the mask maker gave in, and removed and ritually destroyed the nascent artifact. His appearance went back to normal before long, but he never got his walking stride back.

THE GOOD CROP

It's vitally important for these medicine masks to be renewed periodically through ceremonies and offerings of corn and tobacco. These are the rituals that would have been observed when the mask decked a living wearer, and maybe they help it to feel alive in its periods of stasis. The tobacco is often left in little pouches with the mask and needs to be changed at least once a year.

The Sacred Corn

The Midwinter Festival is the one at which the False Face masks are typically "fed" the sacred corn. The date of the rite is determined by the moons, a cycle probably intended to pay tribute to the matriarchy and female nature the way the old Celtic festivals did. It usually works out to be a late-January event, often held these days at Onondaga.

Our late Tuscarora friend Norton Rickard made a specialty of raising the old-style corn. So that his friends on the Cattaraugus Reservation might have some of their own to bring to the Onondaga gathering, Norton delivered nine bushels to the shop of a friend on the lakeside rez. The shop owner was in the middle of a talk with customers when he arrived. "Just take 'em in the back room," she said to Norton. "People will come pick 'em up."

As he dropped off the corn in the dim storeroom, he noticed twelve of the most beautiful False Faces he'd ever seen hanging on the wall in a line. Their features absolutely glowed, and their long shocks of hair trembled as if the room had its own faint breeze. He couldn't help studying them quickly. Each was a marvel. This was a master-carver! He could have stared at them all day. The shop owner was still busy as he was on his way out, but when he could get a word in he meant to ask her where she got such beautiful creations. And how she lit them! It was an artistic display.

He went to visit a friend and came back to the shop a few hours later. Social hour was still in force, but the owner told him that only eight of the bushels had been taken. The last should go back with him. When he went to get it he was surprised to see that the masks were gone. He knew the ceremonies involved in moving even a single mask. Doing it for twelve of them should have occupied several people for hours.

"You guys must have been busy after I left," he said. Nobody got the quip, and he had to explain the masks he had seen in the back room. That still didn't clarify the situation, and one or two of the listeners looked at him like he was crazy. There had been no display of masks back there—at least no material ones.

He called his mother, a clan mother, and asked her what was up. She just laughed. "You saw something, all right. The festival is late this year, and those masks are hungry for their corn. They showed themselves to you because you were bringing it. That must be a good crop."

POWER PEOPLE

The False Face healers must have possessed all the apparently psychokinetic powers observed in the adepts of other world societies. Shamans, mystics, yogis, and Zen masters may have had nothing on them. As recently as 1940, Iroquois False Face healers were seen handling hot ashes and coals, even rubbing them without effect on living human bodies.

In folklore, the False Faces are wizards when in trance and behind the mask. We don't know many tales in which they came in to save the day from evil witches and sorcerers, engaging in outright duels, but it would be logical to think some of them have been told. The Faces are presumed to have the power, and it's widely thought that, on their occasional stomp about the village, no occult evil workers will dare stick around. William Beauchamp believed that the Great Winter Feast was their usual time to march forth and purge the villages of their bad influences.

The Faces of Green Lake

West of Jamesville and southeast of Syracuse is the comma-shaped Green Lake, the traditional site of the Onondaga False Faces' greatest mysteries. In historic times, an Onondaga hunter looked over the edge of a cliff and saw below him a dancing, chanting procession of Faces coming up from Green Lake. Each member of the group was laden with so many silver fish that it seemed a miracle, but he carried them like they were weightless. They were so merry with their catch that they were crowing their joy call. ("Hoh! Hoh-o-o-oh!" writes Beauchamp of it.) The hunter decided to hold his place and get a better look at these mystery men. Even behind his mound of shiny fish, the leader of the faces sensed him from a long way off and rerouted the march, in perfect stride, up the sheer face of a cliff and right into the rocky wall. The hunter heard their calls, seeming to come from within the mountain, for a long time after. They were reputed to have a meeting hall underground somewhere near there, so maybe that was the explanation.

The False Faces may show signs of themselves in their traditional places about the state, and most of us wouldn't know what to make of them.

We hear reports now and then about apparitions of ghostly, disembodied heads in even new buildings near or on top of sites associated with the False Face healers. One of them is in a Mount Morris, New York, hotel on the site of a grove once rumored to have been a gathering spot for the False Faces. They would be ghastly ghosts, even if you knew what they were.

TED WILLIAMS'S TALES OF THE FALSE FACES

Ted Williams's book *Big Medicine from Six Nations* is, among other things, a motherlode of supernatural folklore. It is not, however a handbook, and certainly no text. In fact, Ted often told his stories to us a bit differently than they appeared in his books.

Ted was a member of the False Face Society, and he begins his section on the matter with the acknowledgment that the subject is taboo. He follows it quickly by giving us a good reason: Some of the masks are powerful, and thus dangerous.

The Skull's Warning

In his boyhood on the Tuscarora Reservation, Ted had a young neighbor nicknamed Michael Angelo. This young fellow had a middle-sized dog that was afraid of nothing. Jeese-uh, as they called him, would attack anything he thought was menacing his young master, even a pack of larger dogs. But one night as the two of them came home down a winding, wooded trail, this intrepid dog got whiny and terrified, slinking between his owner's knees. Young Michael put his hands down to comfort his dog and felt its hair standing up. By himself, he went on cautiously ahead and saw the likely source of the dog's terror: a pale, glowing skull-like face, resting on a stump by the trail, facing in his direction. His dog had felt the critter's radiance before he had even seen it. Michael Angelo decided not to get near it and took another route home.

The apparition of this ghostly head was taken as a warning from the False Faces for young Michael Angelo not to go the direction he was going. Before a full day was out, one of his young friends unexpectedly died. It was interpreted that this fate could have been his had he not taken the sign.

To be the holder of a live medicine mask is an ominous responsibility. Not all the masks we see are live ones, though; some are virtual toys, made for no other purpose than to be sold. But they are not always easy to recognize. No less than Ted's father, the famous healer Eleazar Williams, was once mistaken about a humble-looking mask.

Feed It or Else . . .

In Ted's boyhood, none of the shops on the reservation sold a single item of Native American craftsmanship. The aunt of one of his neighbors decided to remedy the situation, setting up a trading post designed to prey on tourists. All went well with the northwestern totem poles and Great Plains–style eagle-feather headdresses. Things took a turn when the shop took in a medicine mask from a desperate member of one of the Six Nations. No one knew, but he had stolen it right out of the Onondaga Longhouse.

Black and not artfully made, the mask looked like an el cheapo False Face that couldn't possibly be alive. But if there is one thing we know about these artifacts, it is that they don't always look like what they are.

One after another, all the young people in the owner's family died. Soon she lost her husband and then her own life. Then her mother was on her deathbed, where, in her last hours, she had a vision: "It's the mask! It's the mask that's eating us up!"

By then no one would touch the thing. They called in Ted's father, Eleazar Williams, and its humble appearance fooled even him. Presuming it a dime-store tourist item, he dug a hole not far from his family's home and buried it.

Outside the house was a drive-in garage near a mock orange bush under which one of the family chickens used to rest in a wooden basket. Every morning before Ted's father left for work, he came out to talk to the bird, and it clucked contentedly back as if answering him. On the morning after the mask was buried, the chicken was nowhere near its wonted basket. The False Face mask was in its place.

Ted's father presumed that the neighbor's kids had seen him bury it and pulled this prank to fool him. He made a fire and burned the mask.

The next morning the mask was back in the same basket, its black mock hair not even singed.

A picture was forming for Eleazar Williams: Against logic and appearance, this was a live one after all. He carried the mask tenderly into the house and commenced the rituals of the tobacco. "Everything will be all right," he told it in Tuscarora, and started the process of finding its true owners. He had no idea where to turn; the woman who had last owned it was dead.

In the next couple of days, the Williams household observed a handful of incidents that could have been psychic and connected to the mask. As if its work with its former owners wasn't done, a surviving nephew suffered a mysterious neck complaint. The matter came to an end on a Saturday morning when a knock fell on the Willliams family's door. A pair of men from the Onondaga Reservation had come for their mask. "This has been missing for some time," one of them said. "They have a way of coming home by themselves, but this one didn't, so we decided to do medicine and find it."

As if they felt the trouble it was causing, the two men seemed to be in a hurry. They took the mask and went straight back to Onondaga.

"You have to feed it," as the Tuscarora say, "or it will eat you up."

The Mask Keeps an Eye Out

During his forties—probably around the time of World War I—Eleazar Williams had lived at Six Nations in Ontario, Canada, and trained with Joo Gwadee, a great Cayuga medicine man. On a wall of this healer's bedroom was a large, clearly live False Face mask. It was there to keep track of things, to be a watchdog.

One night during his stay with Joo Gwadee, Eleazar Williams woke up to the sound of a sharp rattling and a tender whinny, like a puppy calling for a cuddle. He turned on the kerosene lamp and saw the mask on the wall rocking and trembling, even making the curious "False Face talk," which till then he had never heard. Moisture like beads of sweat gathered above its lips. In terror, he ran to wake his tutor.

The bed was empty and an unearthly glow shot through the window by it and lit the far wall as if hell were celebrating outside. When Eleazar looked out, he saw a neighbor's house on fire, and two forms approaching in its surging light: his powerful tutor Joo Gwadee and the old neighbor he had managed to rouse and save. The mask had woken its owner in time. It had "kept track of things."

What Goes Around . . .

For a long time, many bars and inns in the Northeast had a rule: "No alcohol served to Indians." London, Ontario, held a watering hole well known as a place where Native Americans could drink, and a certain Canadian Oneida had the habit of stopping there now and again when he was in town. This Oneida man was a wandering farm worker with very little to call his own, but he did have two very small protection masks. These were mini–False Faces, virtual plaques, and he often had them on him. We wonder which powerful old relative, knowing he would need guidance, had sent him into life with these?

After a hot day of work, this Oneida gent dropped into the aforementioned hotel during happy hour for a beer or two with fellow members of the human race. A new barmaid refused him service. "But I drink here all the time," he said.

"Not while I'm here," the girl said. "Get out before I call the police."

Missing the fellowship as much as the beer, the Oneida departed. On the way to his quarters, he talked to the masks and told them about his troubles. It was a habit he'd had for most of his life. It always made him feel better.

The next morning, he told his coworkers all about the experience with the new barmaid. "I bet she gives me a drink tonight," he concluded, thinking about his report to the masks. After work, he and two friends went to the same bar. They got a shock.

The building was a smoking pile of bricks and planks, surrounded by a crowd. "What happened?" said the owner of the mini masks.

"Big fire last night," someone told him. "Everybody got away safely. Everybody but the new barmaid."

Back at his quarters, the Oneida man tossed and turned. At last, in the deepest part of the night, he took out the small masks and talked to them like treasured friends, like godchildren who didn't know their own power. He told them not to be so rough if he ever spoke to them that way again.

The Senders

A few days before Halloween 2008, a woman called my business line for help with a psychic situation centered on her son's home in one of the towns at the edge of Erie County. Babysitting her grandchildren at the time, she was calling from the very site. She caught me while I was driving.

It was difficult to follow her. Not only was she stressed, but a funny static on the line interfered with the conversation. I attributed it to some effect caused by my cell phone on speaker-mode, but something should have cleared at some point during the fifteen-minute drive.

At first it seemed to me that she was doing a lot of projecting. She constructed messages, omens, and assaults out of the kitchen sink of effects common to haunted houses. But she was sincerely troubled, and I asked some more pointed questions.

The house she was calling from was a new building on a plot of reservation land. Her son's girlfriend had inherited the land from her Seneca grandfather. His former house still stood next door. The woman I talked to admitted readily that they were holding some sacred and ritual objects taken from the girl's grandfather's home after his death, including a couple of False Faces.

"The rez has elders and healers. Why don't you talk to one of them?"

She answered without a pause. "That's who's causing the trouble."

In spite of the situation, I laughed. "What do you expect me to do about it? A white guy with a laptop? How did you get them mad at you?"

"We're not Native American, and they want the items back."

"You have to go to the elders and make your peace," I said. "Right or wrong, that's the way to handle this."

She didn't take my advice. She turned to different sources of off-reservation help. She called people all over the western New York paranormal community, many of them friends of mine who knew nothing about the extent of her outreach. Among them was Spiritualist minister Tim Shaw. He did three phone interviews with the occupants of the house, at first thinking the matter pretty basic: garden-variety effects in an active house. Each time, though, Reverend Shaw noticed the strange static I had. It seemed that something was acting up on any phone call made from that house.

The young father reported potentially psychic activity that included sounds, moving objects, and shadows. He described feelings that ranged from sudden, quick panics in the household's residents to an atmospheric heaviness detected by visitors and guests. He was afraid things would escalate and that his children might be targeted.

The situation was causing earthly conflicts, too. The reservation side of the young woman's family was not convinced that she deserved the land. No one was persuaded by her explanations of how some of her grandfather's belongings ended up with her. This sort of thing is not unique to reservation families.

In his last conversation with the family, Reverend Shaw heard banging in the background loud enough to make him ask about it. The young father told him that the couple's kids were talking to whatever was in the house, and that it was responding, as it often did, with clamor.

Reverend Shaw knows plenty about Iroquois tradition. He visited the family and asked detailed questions. He focused on the False Faces. No one remembered when they had last been honored with ceremonies.

Alarmingly, between his visits, one of the valuable masks had disappeared. Even to the uninitiated, this doesn't sound like the work of an ordinary thief. Why take only one? A reservation healer told the couple that their problems would continue until the missing mask was found or the others returned.

While deciding what to do, Reverend Shaw started to suffer himself, at first with flu-like symptoms then a depression that he attributed to the coming winter. He and his wife experienced psychic activity in their house: whispers, footsteps, and dragging sounds. Guests saw shadow people. It was as if the reservation matter had followed him home.

The reverend had studied a lot of cases. This had never happened before. He called for help.

Buffalo Bishop James Lagona is an expert on cross-cultural spirituality. Bishop Lagona felt that there was a human "sender" somewhere, possibly one of the medicine people, shooting energy at the house, which had in turn attached itself to Reverend Shaw. Michael Bastine agreed about the concept of the sender, undoubtedly a power person, but sensed that the False Faces were adding energy to the mix. They were acting on the people in the home. Michael brought in an Onondaga member of the False Face Society at about the time the family was willing to call a truce. Reverend Shaw closed the book on the matter. Presumably the masks are where they belong, with the culture-keepers of one of the Iroquois nations.

Things were soon at peace in the reverend's home, and he felt more like himself. He later learned through some back channels that a power person, "a specialist," from the Allegany Reservation may have been recruited to send energy into this situation to ensure an outcome that would be favorable to the Cattaraugus Seneca. This force was going to be incrementally toxic to anyone who got in its way. He also reached the conclusion I did: If you are a non–Native American occultist called to help with a Native American case, feel as free as you like to be flattered. More than that, though, be on guard, especially when one of these masks may be involved.

The Song of the Faces

In the past, every Iroquois settlement of even moderate size would have had visits from a local group of False Faces. While moving to, from, and during a healing service, the False Faces would have made a number of distinctive sounds. Magnified and distorted through their masks, their snorts at the thresholds of sufferers' homes sounded like the demon bear. Other trademarks—such as their distant, high-pitched, two-toned calls—were surreal like those of marsh birds. These cries could be signals to members of the Society, calling them to gather. Others might have alerted the village that the False Faces were on their way. They could have been warnings to the workers in black magic and to the bearers of pestilence.

These healers had holy areas and vision sites to which they convened from far parts for their mysterious training. There are caves, springs, hollows, and valleys around the state where the calls of the False Faces have resounded for a thousand years. The names of other gathering places have been lost, but it's believed that some influence of the Faces still shows itself in the areas that were special to them, sometimes with a living message.

In 1995, Ted Williams was visiting his boyhood home on the Tuscarora Reservation. Nearby was a grove he remembered well. Every time he walked through this place as a boy, something had made him hear and envision the False Faces. The effect was strong when he came back as a grown man. As if there were an eternal procession taking place in some other realm, the Faces and their rites flickered into his awareness—sometimes close, sometimes dimly.

Knowing as he did the imprint these mighty healers can leave on anything they touch, he thought this grove might have been one of their ancient sacred meeting spots. As a False Face healer himself and a deep sensitive, he ought to have known. He never told this to anyone.

A party held at Ted's former home included Native Americans who lived off the reservation and worked "white" jobs. The guests represented all attitudes toward the spiritual and traditional heritage of their people. A group of them had gone for a walk in the grove that had impressed Ted, and had heard such eerie calls that they ran back completely spooked. Ted was on the porch as they came in. He drew the story out of them when they caught their breath.

Some imitated the cries they'd heard, and Ted recognized it as one of the traditional calls of the False Face healers. But not all had heard the same sounds. He asked each of them in more detail about their perceptions of the calls in the wood.

Some identified one or two forceful voices, natural-sounding calls that may have been made by human jokers having a game with them. Others heard a variety of voices in various parts of the wood. To the rest, the scene was textured with similar sounds made at different volumes and pitches and coming from all around them.

Not knowing how to make sense of the mystery, Ted next asked them about their levels of belief in Native American spiritual practice. He asked them to rank their faith on a scale and made careful note of who said what.

He found that those with little belief were the ones who had heard only a pair of callers whose voices sounded natural. Those who believed at the middle level heard many tones, volumes, and sounds. To the last, the group with the greatest belief, the whole wood seemed alive with synesthetic mystery and hidden, ancestral calls. For them, the grove was as rich with invisible, supernatural chanters as an August evening is filled with the earthly chirps and clicks of squirrels or peepers.

In seconds, the answer came to him. "This is good," he told all his guests. "The Faces have just given you a lesson. That's the way it will be with the teachings of your ancestors. That's the way it will be with the good of the world. The more belief you have in it, the more of it you'll see and receive. Don't forget that the rest of your lives."

6

Supernatural War

When you are actually in America, America hurts, because it has a powerful, disintegrative influence upon the white psyche. It is full of grinning, unappeased aboriginal demons, too, ghosts. . . . One day the demons of America must be placated, the ghosts must be appeased, the Spirit of Place atoned for . . . There are terrible spirits, ghosts, in the air of America.

D. H. LAWRENCE, FROM *STUDIES IN
AMERICAN CLASSICAL LITERATURE*

DIRECTED CURSES

As we've seen, the old-timers among the upstate Iroquois believed in the effect of curses. The curses and countercurses we have seen discussed in earlier chapters have generally been due to the actions of living power people, and directed against other living individuals with direct, specific, and usually short-term goals. There seem to be other types.

161

In fact, it seems clear from the reports we hear that the collective orenda of a nation or a site could be involved in contemporary psychic complaints. It could be aimed at anyone on one side or another of a dispute. It could affect anyone living or anyone who just happened to be in the wrong place at the wrong time. Its energy could come home to roost with those who mishandled the sites, bones, or artifacts of even the ancient dead.

This is a chapter that is not about supernatural duels, but supernatural war. It is about collective attacks, ones that can come with the force of whole nations, the dead, or even, seemingly, the land itself; they may not be exclusively things of the past. Why would the psychic force of an Iroquois clan or nation get agitated enough to lash out? The impulse might seem counterintuitive to many mainstream Americans: it often has to do with politics.

Many Americans see things in black and white when it comes to politics. Those who share their viewpoints appear hip and sinless, while those who don't look bumbling and ill spirited. To folk who see no gray areas and know the subjects of the last two chapters, it ought to be easy to predict what the Iroquois medicine people will do in any dispute: They should only mobilize around traditional and spiritual causes on behalf of all Native Americans; they would never dirty their hands with something as gritty as gas, gambling, or tobacco.

In fact, for the Iroquois, it's silly to think that politics could be separated from any other aspect of human life, including the traditional and the spiritual. Whenever there's a dispute on the reservation big enough to involve group interests, the power people get into the act, often on both sides. Ted Williams told us this from personal experience. It isn't always easy to decide which cause is the better.

There are other kinds of supernatural attacks whose roots aren't contemporary at all. Some Iroquois healers talk about a condition they call "bothered by the dead." Though the effects might look the same as a garden-variety curse, this one doesn't involve the stroke of a living witch, and it comes with a heavy spiritual depression. As Macbeth would say, your "genius is rebuked," in this case by the generations of the dead.

If you're a Native American, the cause of this complaint might be as inadvertent as failing to observe enough of the major ceremonies of your nation, hence offending the ancestors. Native Americans, at least, ought to know better.

But even non–Native Americans who mind their own business can take a hit from some ancient, indigenous power that seems beyond the natural. The offense might be as active and direct as offending a site of importance to those who had once revered it. It could be as innocent as living or working over such a site every day. This could happen easily all over New York state, and not many people would be aware that this was the case. The dead buried before the arrival of the Europeans are long gone from us, and most of the spots they treasured are invisible. Think of all the battlefields, burial grounds, and sacred sites in Iroquois country that have been unknowingly developed and built over.

How could a piece of land rebel against anyone? Again, it might be by the collective power of the offended dead. If the dead lack awareness or self-protection, the source could be a psychic mechanism set in place by shamans in ages past, like a curse on a pharaoh's tomb. When a community left a sacred site or burial ground, its power people often performed a closing ceremony to protect it.

Ted Williams talked about an unusual and more specialized condition he called "skeletally entranced." It was dangerous to mess with old human bones. He talked about young people raiding burial grounds and leaving with a couple of nuggets. If they fell asleep with these stolen bits in their pockets—"the dice of drowned men's bones" as in Hart Crane's poem—with no help near, they might not wake in this world.

It may be hard for some readers to understand this belief that artifacts, human remains, the dead, and even sites can project a force that could be active today. But many people living in upstate New York—

and not just Native Americans—have their reasons for leaving this an open question.

The Two Ball Curse

The Iroquois have always loved sports. They had a handful of games, apparently offshoots of hunting, that wouldn't seem familiar to most Americans. One that would was the game of lacrosse, which the Iroquois probably invented. The basics of the old game—ball, sticks, teams, running—would be quite recognizable to anyone today. The rules were somewhere between those of the modern game and the Siege of Stalingrad.

The Iroquois have adopted many of the sports of white society, though at some disadvantage due to the small numbers and typical poverty of their communities. One of their traditional favorites is baseball.

The Oneida William Honyoust Rockwell (1870–1960) recalled an incident from around 1900 in which the baseball-crazed Oneidas had arranged a game against a well-practiced team of white guys from Cazenovia. The Oneidas' numbers were so small, though, that between their two communities they could put together only nine able adult bodies. The Oneida figured they might need a little help. An old-timer told them what to do.

"Go into the graveyard and pick an old grave. Make a hole in the earth and reach around with your hands until you come up with an old toe bone. Take it with you to the field you're going to play on and bury it under the pitcher's box. Take some of the black dirt with you, too, and let every man on your team rub his hands with it before the game. And, finally, just before the game, the whole team has to take a swig from the same bottle of whiskey, then cork it up and put it away. When you pitch to the white men, it will look to them like you are throwing them two balls to hit."

The team decided to try the formula, but objected to only one thing: the one bottle to be used and the single swig of it apiece. All was done as prescribed, though: bone, bottle, and burying dirt were in their places by game time. The Oneida lost 22–0.

The incident had Rockwell scratching his head. When he met the great Native American Jim Thorpe (1888–1953) years later, he couldn't help getting it off his chest. *"How could we lose with so much national medicine behind us?"* he asked. *Thorpe—multisport athlete and Olympic champion—could only venture the guess that the white men were able to hit* both *balls.*

Power Line

Just after he moved into Williamsville in the 1970s, Mike Bastine was approached by a neighbor as he got into his car. Perceiving that he was a Native American, the man asked, "What nation are you?"

"I'm Algonquin," said Mike.

The man sighed with relief. "Thank God. I don't need any more to do with them Tuscaroras."

Mike laughed and asked what he meant. "There's one of them up there on the Tuscarora Reservation that's been giving me and my whole crew the creeps. Name's Mad Bear. I won't go up there any more."

"Well, that's who I'm going up to see," said Mike. The man's terror was so comical that Mike calmed him down and asked his story.

Mike's neighbor worked for the power company, which had run lines across reservation land. When some Native Americans felt that something in the original agreement wasn't being met, Mad Bear showed up to do his medicine on behalf of the nation and the land.

The project met snags, including baffling malfunctions with equipment. Fully functioning bulldozers fell utterly useless. A few had to be junked. When the lines were finally up, power wouldn't flow between two of the towers, though no perceptible flaws in the system could be detected. And the crews were getting spooked. They saw apparitions around them in the trees, dashing between the open spaces. Many chose to quit the company rather than work at the troubled site.

Mike had to laugh. "That was Mad Bear. He never was one to let something go by like that. He'd pull people aside privately and talk to them, but if that didn't do any good, he went right to the next step in a hurry. He must have done some kind of ceremony up there. I think he had help from Peter Mitten on that one."

He speaks of it like he saw it. "When they touched that bulldozer with an eagle feather and in a prayerful way, it wouldn't run again. [The whites] had to scrap it."

CALLING THE ANCESTORS

The ancient inhabitants of Europe often built and sited their religious monuments and power sites to make them fall along straight lines, often across several miles of landscape. These imaginary connectors—straight lines linking sacred sites—were called "leys." They may not have been used much as pathways.

Sometimes the leys themselves made patterns with each other. One equilateral triangle, six miles on a side, formed by leys was discovered by British astronomer Sir Norman Lockyer (1836–1920). One of the monuments on "The Great Triangle of England" is the famous Stonehenge.

The prehistoric Native North Americans had their leys, too. One of the most remarkable is a sixty-mile long trackway between two similar circle-and-octagon earthworks in Newark and Chillicothe, Ohio. Nicknamed after the moundbuilding cultures who produced it, "The Hopwell Highway" was almost surely a ceremonial path. We've been able to document very few leys in Iroquois country, but there must have been many. They were most likely used for ceremonies and vision quests, as well as marking sacred sites. They were made with vision and care, and the users altered the landscape with little but footprints.

The Iroquois were always suspicious of New York's massive "point A to point B" projects: canals, railroads, highways. They never did anything intrusive without carefully considering the local ground. "Don't you realize what you might be stirring up?" the elders would say to the state authorities. "It could be burial ground, battleground, sacred ground. You don't do this stuff with a map and a ruler."

Most of the oldest roads in New York followed Native American transportation trails. Spiritually speaking, those roads would have been all right for travel; their use disrupted nothing of sacred significance. The main streets of most of our towns were once these footpaths. They were simply widened into cart tracks in the eighteenth and nineteenth centuries and then paved for the use of cars in the twentieth. But countless new ones have been made, with no regard for local tradition. They include vastly intrusive interstate projects.

A couple of highways that go to and around Syracuse are only decades old. A lot of grading's been going on in this heart of the Iroquois territory, and not all has gone according to plan.

Cutting In on the Rez

When Michael Bastine was a boy, some highway work was done near Syracuse. He remembers hearing that it was work on I-90, but it might have been the mid-1960s expansion of Route 57 into 481, which crosses I-90 and arcs the city on the east from the south to the northwest. The eastern 481 certainly comes close to the sacred Green Lake.

"Whatever path they were taking was going to cause some kind of interference or damage," says Michael. "And it wasn't just because they were cutting in on the rez. The Onondagas knew something was under there, and it wasn't going to be good for anybody to mess it up."

The Onondaga tried talking to the state authorities. Road construction kept up in the meantime, with two crews a day. The potential pathway was already graded and covered with crushed stone when Cayuga medicine man Peter Mitten and his student Mad Bear answered the call. "And I mean, on the medicine level," says Michael. They told the Onondaga that they were going to call upon the ancestors. This was one of the heaviest ceremonies they could do.

"This was done with a lot of forethought," says Michael. "They went to the Onondaga elders and asked permission to call up the dead on their territory. They looked at the stages of the moon and whatever else. They did all the proper ceremonies beforehand, announcing their intent. They went around the day before and told everybody to stay inside after sundown and not come out until daybreak. They told people to keep a special eye on children and their animals, who could be much more sensitive to the medicine." Then they asked the dead to walk.

People in their homes felt the effects. Some heard sounds, a horde of footsteps walking on the loose stone. Others opened their shutters after dark and saw a faint migration of pale shadows and trees rocking though no wind was blowing. It was awe-inspiring—and terrible. "When Mad Bear told you this story, you got goose bumps," says Michael. It lasted into the early dawn.

The first crews to show up early that morning caught an eyeful, we hear, and immediately left work. In the words of a witness who talked to Michael, "The workers messed their pants. Stones were rolling as if people were kicking them."

"I knew Mad Bear could use the energy of other people," says Michael. "I'd seen him do it a lot of times. What came clearer to me later in life was that Mad Bear had done it with the dead." He shakes his head. "That's never done lightly. You don't go, oh, I think I'll call the ancestors tonight." The course of the Thruway had to change, with a bow in it that doesn't show on the big state maps. It may have shifted its arc only a quarter mile.

"The old cultures hang on to that stuff," says Michael. "This is what keeps us connected to the spirit world. The ancestors are here to help us if we need them. As long as we keep looking out for them."

THE LIVER TREE CURSE

Twentieth-century shaman Mad Bear Anderson was a spiritual crusader. He felt, as do Michael and I, that one of the best ways to improve the conditions of the Native Americans was to raise the consciousness of the world. As a way of accomplishing this, Mad Bear believed in uniting Native American nations in shared goals and in involving people of all origins in Native American causes. His inclusiveness helped him make his point, but it didn't work for all parties. Some Native American purists may have thought it just divided and watered down the message. Some who opposed his message surely worked against him. Many of his confidants openly believed that Mad Bear was involved in an occult cold war that now and then heated up. He was the occasional target of group attacks.

Mad Bear had lived in a couple of different houses on the Tuscarora Reservation, and at all of them he did a lot of medicine work. People who knew him wryly called each of his homes Fort Knox because of the reinforcement of the walls and the points of entry. It was widely presumed that any place Mad Bear lived needed to be fortified: When he went on his astral journeys in the form of a bear, his material body lay inert and vulnerable. Those who wanted to hurt him would never get a better chance.

It was also presumed that his homes were protected in another way, too—with medicine. His enemies were not only going to strike in material ways. In fact, the material attacks were probably only signs that the metaphysical ones had failed.

Mad Bear took special precautions, especially against what couldn't be seen. He had a couple of False Faces looking out for him, but from all we hear, he left nothing to chance. All the unusual artifacts that came with them were potential avenues for spells and curses directed against him, thus he took special ceremonial care of his place, particularly the doorway. He put medicine at the symbolic entrances, too, the windows, keyholes, and hearth, by which supernatural influences might also make their entry. He redid the work a few times a year. Still, it didn't stop people from going after him.

An Odd Mad Bear Story

In the late 1970s, when Mike was just getting to know Mad Bear, he heard an odd story from one of their mutual friends. The friend and Mad Bear had just stepped out of the latter's cabin on an early November twilight when they looked up into a tree at something odd and terrifying.

A grisly thing roosted like a balloon in the high, frail branches, so raw and biological that it could have been an internal organ. It looked "like a liver," said the man who saw it. It was twitching and making strange sounds: gurgling, coughing, hissing, like it was trying to breathe or even speak without a mouth.

"Uh-oh," said Mad Bear. "I know right away what I got to do." He ran into his cabin and commenced a mighty rite. He didn't let his friend even watch or listen. The process for Mad Bear was a long one; it took about half an hour.

When he came back out, he walked right up to that tree, still decked with its biomorphic bauble, and started talking to it in Tuscarora. The friend reported that words in a ghastly, hissing voice came back to Mad Bear from somewhere in the same language. When he was done with his inquisition, Mad Bear dismissed the thing with a backhanded, open-palmed gesture like a karate slash: "Get out of here, and go back to who sent you."

The man reported that the strange organ rose higher in the branches of the tree as if it were losing gravity by the second. A breeze caught it, and it drifted out of the branches and soared off like a weary helium balloon. He could see the thing dangling its tubes and veins till it drifted over a hill.

Before long there was a reaction. Some Canadian Mohawk suffered such a plague of accidents and illnesses that they were sure Mad Bear had witched them back. They started calling him, writing him, and pestering him to take his medicine off them. "I can't do anything about this," Mad Bear told them. "It's what you sent after me. I just turned it around."

Next they tried to bribe him, even promising to deliver an envelope full of money to his mailbox every week. "Why are you wasting my time?" Mad Bear said. "When you start things, you better be able to stop them."

At about this time Mad Bear started getting a reputation as a man of power, and this incident may even have been the start of it. Those Mohawks weren't quiet. They told everyone who they thought was after them. To this day, some people still think of Mad Bear as a witch.

Michael suspects that the curse had started with some Canadian Mohawks, possibly acquaintances of the healer Daisy Thomas. They'd gotten it in for Mad Bear because of some political dispute, wangled some medicine out of Daisy, and launched an attack, most likely without her knowledge. "They had to be beginners," says Michael. All of them learned a lesson. One may have lost his life. For quite a time, envelopes full of bills kept appearing in Mad Bear's mailbox, even though he said he didn't want them.

THE DUST DEVIL OF BOUGHTON HILL

The Celtic people of Europe associated the wind swirls and dust devils we see now and then with the passage of the Good People, the Fair Folk, and other names applied to the fairies. To them, their own Little People were powerful but not inherently negative.

Among many Native Americans, particularly of the Southwest, these curious natural wind forms were dreaded, thought to signal the passage of a witch or wizard. At other times, it was thought that a human spirit was within them, and not that of someone who had recently died. It was the mighty spirit of an old one.

Ganondagan (ga-NON-da-gan) is a New York state historic site and park near Rochester, with a preserved Seneca village. While many whites find it a spiritual place, even a pilgrimage site, others sense unrest in the area. After visits to Ganondagan, some non–Native Americans have reported troubling dreams. The young daughter of a Rochester college professor had a nightmare about an old Native American climbing the outside of her house to get at her second-floor bedroom. Some figure like him has surfaced as a ghost reported on the roads near Boughton Hill, among a bevy of less distinct apparitions not all so surely Native.

Those negatively affected by Ganondagan sense an indignation that seems vaster than that of a single human spirit. It could be the psychic echo of a battle. Ganondagan was the site of a cruel first-strike invasion from a French expedition and a collection of Native enemies in 1687. Surely that must be it. Most battlefields attract psychic folklore, and New York state is saturated with them, including ancient Native American ones. Not many of the folks who live and work over these older clash points know what went on there before them.

The late historian Sheldon Fisher (1907–2002), from Fishers, New York, was a treasure trove of regional lore. In the ninety years of his familiarity with Ganondagan, almost all the households near it reported psychic encounters of some sort. This story about a family on Boughton Hill is one Sheldon told us.

The Invisible Being

One September afternoon, members of a family were raking leaves outside their house. The youngest child went inside then ran back out, leaving the front door open. As the mother glanced up her jaw dropped, and the rake fell from her hands.

A breeze in the yard had picked up bits of leaves and dust and spun them into a man-size whirlwind. It held its shape and form so well and long that anyone could fancy a presence within it. Soon all of them were watching it. This little tornado meandered about the yard as of to throw everyone off, but the mother noticed that it kept moving as if purposefully toward the house. As it neared the porch, the mother started running to the front door, but it beat her and vanished as it crossed the threshold. It was as if an invisible being had taken up a dusty veil like a cloak and shed it as it entered the house.

The mother ran in and looked around. The house was still, but something felt different. In the weeks to come, the feeling would become a certainty.

Family members were on edge. Old problems came back. Plants died, pets acted strangely, no one slept well, and psychic phenomena broke out. Strangely, they never connected matters to the odd episode in the yard.

One family friend was an old Seneca who dropped in a couple of times a year. A mutt was his constant companion. He and his sidekick came by one October afternoon. As he waited in the kitchen for the tea water to boil, he noticed his dog tracking something across the room with its eyes, as if an invisible guest had taken up residence.

He did his best not to look concerned. "Get everyone out of the house for a few hours," he said. "Now. I need to get some things and come back."

When the family returned hours later, the house felt different, as if it had been restored to peace. Things settled down. They could only conclude that their Seneca friend had worked a ritual to banish the force, whatever it was. It was probably a housecleaning using sage or cedar.

The Cursed Circle

A doctor and his wife built their dream home on a circular cul-de-sac off the road between Lakewood and Jamestown. The house in West Ellicott was ninety-five feet long, with a full basement, rec rooms, playrooms—the works. The doctor remembers good times, especially at first. Woods and wildlife were there, and old farmhouses nearby. They had a dozen pleasant neighbors. They could walk to the southern shore of Chautauqua Lake. They skated on the pond and sledded on a hilly clearing like a ski slope. But from the start, their children were unhappy. Was this an early sign?

Soon, there were others. When they drilled their well, the plumber called the water the best he had ever tasted. Within weeks, it had turned too salty even to be used for cooking. Soon they had to run a water line in from the main road.

The doctor's wife had dreams of water; then they woke and found it in their basement. Flooding became so routine that the doctor put in a pump, which was soon clotted by gravel and rendered useless. A fine chandelier in the foyer spontaneously fell to the floor. Home at the time, the doctor's wife heard the crash.

The aged doctor was quite lucid when we interviewed him in 1997. He recalled a file of tragedies that befell others who lived on the circle. Boating accidents killed one neighbor's child and badly injured another. One neighbor lost his business, and another suffered a miscarriage. A young man had a fatal heart attack while running around the circle. A boy was killed in the woods nearby. A mother fell on the stairs in her basement and suffered migraines; soon thereafter, her big, seemingly stable family was in tatters. A heart attack killed a circle resident exercising at the YMCA. Another, who suffered a stroke, learned from his misfortune and moved. The doctor, too, finally sold his house after only four years. Two months after taking over the home, the new owner killed himself.

Families on the circle were looking for answers. The only one that made sense surfaced by accident. One of the county's first settlers had once owned the land, and a descendant still in the area remarked that it was a Native American burial ground. "Had we known," said the doctor, "we never would have built there." Was there anything else there, too?

These circular formations are suspicious. People like the circle. It's the mandala form. We tend to build circles everywhere. But when the form appears in upstate street-making, it raises the possibility that something old and Native American was there first. Many an American city plan has followed the pattern of an ancient circular monument.

The settlers shaped Circleville, Ohio, around a big henge, as did the citizens of Auburn, New York, with Fort Hill Cemetery. Joseph Ellicott's descriptions of the flat-topped, circular rise at the site of Buffalo's future center, Niagara Square, remind us of a tumulus like Silbury Hill in England.

Many of the ancient monuments that draw so much psychic karma were reported around Lake Chautauqua, whose Seneca name means "bag tied in the *middle." Maybe people just didn't handle it right, like the circle in West Ellicott. Maybe some of these sites are too strong to live on.*

As if the curse had sated itself on human tragedy, the last decades, we hear, have been happy on this ring of fine houses. It's not unusual for things to "act up" and then stop, for reasons of their own. Maybe the medicine people got word of the matter and took care of it.

Feasts of the dead have been held all over the world. The contemporary American version of one is Halloween. On this night in their society, the old Celts invited the spirits of their dead. Some Native Americans invited the corpses.

Many Native American ideas are totally unlike those of Europeans. Attitudes to the human body are not the least of them. In *The Jesuits in North America* (1896), Francis Parkman (1823–1893) describes a Huron (Wyandot) rite that would shock many of us.

As in many Native North American societies, the Huron kept the village dead in ossuaries or grand burial sites. Every couple of years, the bones were hauled up, dressed and ornamented by their former families, set at a feast, and literally "fed" bits of food. Then they were returned to the earth with gifts that beggared the village till the next such event. And so they were treated until there was nothing left of them to dig up. This ritual was a profound expression of the acceptance of all the phases of material existence, and of reverence and even tenderness to the family members whose spirits had left the world. It was also a connector of generations, a way to include the departed in life as they were in memory. The event seemed macabre and even fiendish to the first Europeans to witness it.

The Huron/Wyandot are an Iroquoian people sharing much in common with the Longhouse nations. We hear that the Neutral Nation of western New York, also Iroquoian, maintained this custom. The Six Nations may once have held similar rituals, and it may have been the influence of the Peacemaker and Hiawatha that caused them to go a different way. Could these extreme ceremonies linger, occasionally, as medicine?

The Girl without Eyes

One evening in the spring of 2006, I gave a lecture on Native American supernaturalism in a country library. One of the women attending left about halfway through. She was in the rainy parking lot when I came to my car. A forty-something woman, she had waited until the talk was over so that no one else might overhear our conversation. We talked across a car hood ten feet apart. As if afraid one of us had a contagious disease, she got no closer. She looked haunted. She started to talk, stopped, started, stopped. Then she started.

"Have you ever heard of something like the Feeding of the Dead?" I had, but I didn't say much. I wanted to draw the story out. It was hard.

The woman looked and dressed upper-middle-class white. She said she had a bit of Native American blood. She had worked as a pharmacist on one of the New York reservations not far from the building of a former Indian school, a very haunted piece of ground. She had never felt comfortable in her building. She kept hearing strange, unexplained noises and soon saw apparitions. At first they were dark, shadowy, and small, like gremlins or little demons. Then they appeared in her home.

One night at closing time, she heard something unusual in the pharmacy she had thought was empty. It sounded like an agonized cough, as though someone straining to breathe had come in looking for help. She called out, then ran into the aisles. On a shelf out of sight of her counter sat a Native American girl. About thirteen, she was very dark-skinned, with a shock of unruly coal-black hair. She wore a high-collared, many-buttoned dress that could have been a Victorian-era school uniform. In place of eyes, though, she had only a viscous, slightly reflective darkness. It was as if her sockets were filled with oil. The apparition was so solid looking that the pharmacist thought the girl was real. It made no sound as the woman watched. After a firm second or two, the image blinked out of existence.

Almost every aspect of the pharmacist's life took a downward turn after that. Even her sleep was haunted by nightmares. She would have been happy to believe her complaints were medical or psychological, but no doctors or counselors gave her the slightest help. This pharmacist was liked and respected by the reservation folk, and a sympathetic patient noticed her distress. Only then did she get the right form of medicine.

A couple of middle-aged male elders took an interest in her case. It took them months to get her right. They tried a number of remedies and cures she would not describe. What set the demons back for good was a ceremony she called the Feeding of the Dead. She wouldn't talk about it, other than to say that it was "horrible."

"I was told not to talk about this," she said, looking ghostly herself in the mist. "They said that even talking about it might bring it back. I just wish I could understand." I finished loading my books and lecture materials and gave her my card. I haven't heard from her since.

The Buffalo Curse

By 1972, "the old Rockpile" on Buffalo's east side had seen its last kickoff. War Memorial Stadium, stronghold of two-time AFL champs the Buffalo Bills, was to be abandoned in favor of a new stadium in a southern suburb. Work started on a broad country block three miles west of the village of Orchard Park. Not all was at peace.

It started in houses at the edge of the tract. Families became anxious, tense, and depressed. Pets got in on the act, shying away from spots in rooms and spaces in yards, even running away. Then there were outbreaks of poltergeist phenomena. Ghosts were sighted, inside and outside of homes. Families felt targeted, if not directly cursed. People blamed the budding stadium. They may have had reason.

Workers clearing the former farmland rediscovered the tiny 1820 graveyard of the Joseph Sheldon family. Abandoned in 1924, it was restored in the early 1970s. You can still see it—a fenced-in area in the north parking lot of the new stadium. Other graves were not so well treated.

One branch of Smokes Creek coils through the stadium plot. Along it had been much Native American habitation. Their burials were here, too. Some say the ground moaned when shovels pierced it. Word got out that this was the root of the psychic unrest.

Seneca Joyce Jamison concurred. "Things act up when our ancestors are disturbed."

"That's about what ought to start happening,'" said Michael when he heard the circumstances. "Little stuff going wrong around the house. People getting spooked, turning to drugs and stuff, families breaking up. A lot of people don't realize that

sometimes these things aren't coincidental. Sometimes they do have causes."

For whatever reason, peace returned. Graves may have been moved and offended spirits eased. To this day, we meet people who lived nearby during the construction phase, and more stories surface. ("Why did you wait so long to call me?" said a Buffalo priest upon entering a certain house.) Seneca storyteller DuWayne Bowen considered the stadium tunnels still very haunted.

It's rumored in some quarters that Seneca elders from the Cattaraugus Reservation worked traditional rites of blessing. It's been hard to verify. The Seneca we talked to remembered nothing about it. Neither did late Orchard Park historian John N. Printy (1919–2001). The Buffalo Bills' historian Beverly McQuillan found no written records, nor did reporter Mike Vogel in decades of Buffalo News files.

There's also talk that the curse just shifted and hangs now over all Buffalo sports, tantalizing teams and their supporters, keeping the word of promise to their ears, breaking it to their hopes, and snatching ultimate triumph when just within reach. It could go well beyond sports.

This region of sublime scenery, rich natural resources, and a treasury of classic architecture has seemed blighted for generations. Provided with a Masonic, symbolic street plan, Buffalo started out with visions of becoming a grand capital. Torched by the British in the War of 1812, its luck steadily improved after the completion of the Erie Canal in 1825. Buffalo's high-water mark could have been the 1901 Pan-American Exposition at which—shortly after a visit to the Devil's Hole, a Seneca bad-medicine spot—President William McKinley was shot. The Great Depression was a short hop later, and the late-twentieth-century loss of manufacturing jobs was the coup de grace. Buffalo is due a break, and soon. But what launched the blight?

Some go back to the psychic fallout of the presidential assassination. Others turn to the steady progress of New York state into a tax-and-spend, government-centered economy. Some blame developer and power broker Robert Moses (1888–1981), who destroyed the Niagara by routing expressways like defensive barriers between the citizenry and their fixed assets, their waterfront, and their splendid Olmsted Parks. Others blame a downstate power base that sees New York harbor as a local resource but Niagara Falls power as a state one.

One explanation is persistent. At some time during the settler period, the story goes, the Seneca were challenged to a foot race by the whites of Buffalo. The Seneca were marvelous runners, but through subterfuge, the whites managed to win. The Seneca medicine people drew together as one, they say, and whistled up a mighty curse. According to the story, Buffalo would never win anything significant until this wrong was righted. Some say that the curse has expanded to include the fortunes of the whole region. Like its football team the Buffalo Bills and their four-in-a-row Super Bowl losses, Buffalo will be taunted like Tantalus: After long periods of humiliation, success will come near enough to smell and taste and ever be snatched away.

Maybe it's not too late for a cure from the medicine people. We recommend Erie County folk give that a try. Then vote out of office every politician who does not work to lower taxes.

THE CURSE OF THE BONES

You can pick your own start date for this: either the ice ages, 2000 BCE, or 1997.

Western New York is the traditional home of the Seneca, largest nation of the Confederacy and the swinger of the biggest Native political bat. But many other Native nations once held the area, including Blackfoot, Eries, Neutrals, and the Iroquois' rivals, the Algonquin. Even the truly ancient mound builders could have been here. All these people rest in western New York soil.

Since the 1990 passage of the NAGPRA (Native American Graves Protection and Repatriation Act), all land development in the United States has to stop when Native burials are discovered. Human remains and artifacts have to be identified and respectfully reinterred. No project is too big to be delayed, rerouted, or even blocked. Native

American representatives have the final say dealing with the matter.

In the best cases, living descendants of the dead can be found to make decisions, and the process barely delays construction. When cultural affiliates can't be found, substitutes have to step in, sometimes from nations whose ancestors were related to the ancient ones merely because they had shared the same continent. It can be a game of give and take in which every move is calculated. Sometimes it ends up offending everyone. Even the burials of ancient non–Native Americans, like Washington state's theory-shattering Kennewick Man,* can be included in the repatriation process. In every case, though, the whites pick the Native Americans they listen to.

The Onondaga shelf, the east–west spine of Iroquois territory, can be porous or obsidian hard. The north–south Genesee cutting through it branches many a channel. All that running water and an ancient sea have left caves, tunnels, and minerals underground.

In 1885, some enterprising fellows sunk a shaft nine hundred feet down to a bed of rock salt. In just a century, the Retsof Salt Mine became the biggest in North America. Its ten square underground miles made it the size of Manhattan.

Then-operator Akzo-Nobel Salt gave up on it in 1994 when part of the mine collapsed and flooded. The state lost mining and trucking jobs, and Livingston County was short its second biggest taxpayer. In January 1997, American Rock Salt arrived to tap in from a different direction. It meant making a new three-mile spur connecting mine and railroad. The nation's first new salt mine in forty years was a high profile, feel-good affair. Work commenced around the clock at Hampton Corners.

There were some environmental protests at first, largely ceremonial, but things changed when Native American burials were found. By 1997, the NAGPRA had so big a bite that even a bark was plenty to stop a salt mine.

---

*So named for his discovery near Kennewick, Washington, "Kennewick Man" may be a ten-thousand-year-old native Japanese.

Some burials were clearly those of Senecas during the time of the Europeans' arrival. This is still Seneca country, and the state works with them all the time. But the ground also held folks from Blackfoot and other Algonquin-speaking nations who haven't lived in the region since the time of the Crusades. They could have been sent to their graves in the first place by the Seneca. Finding representatives for them wasn't going to be easy.

The new work area turned out to be a prehistoric power point: the site of at least one sacred earthwork, a village or two, the junction of ancient trails, and a multicultural burial ground dating back at least four thousand years. Trains, tracks, digging, and paving would destroy it all. This was an unwelcome new twist.

We know mound-building societies like the Hopewell and Adena only from burials, artifacts, and the massive earthworks that mystified the Senecas when they came to this valley. The Viper Mound, a Genesee riverside earthwork and possibly a Hopewellian style snake effigy, had already been paved over during the mid-1970s work on I-390. It is hard to identify the living ancestors of the Hopewell. Who rules on their remains? NAGPRA, we have a problem. The suits, of course, just wanted work to go on. Enter, according to the story, a certain prominent Seneca.

This gentleman has devoted his life to teaching the world about his ancestors. The government turns to him in many matters. Some of his decisions have been controversial. He looked the site over, did some of this and that, and gave the OK for work to resume.

The way some tell it, artifacts, remains, and even the GOK (God Only Knows) piles from the salt mines fell largely into his lap. With his OK, the bones, every last nub of them were, in theory, relocated to nearby portions of the property or elsewhere in the valley. The mine opened with only reasonable delays. Talk of backroom deals, political intrigue, and payola ran amok. White activists, alas, may have been shouting the loudest.

What happened to the bones and artifacts? Since a Native American handled them, it wasn't of white concern. It was other Native Americans who asked the questions. There was grumbling about moving Algonquin remains to Seneca territory, even simply dumping them. Protests came in from many quarters after the reports of bulldozers piling up grave goods and even human bones.

Surely, some justice awaited this desecration. There was talk of curses and mine disasters. Suicide, death, substance abuse, madness, and ruin plagued local politicians who had been involved. Even passersby suffered. One local who took an artifact lost a leg in an accident. Another touched a piece of skull and found her mother dead at home. Mystery lights and altered animal forms were reported on nearby stretches of road. Auto accidents were common. It would be interesting to know what the late motorists saw before spinning out of control. The pattern sounded like an upstate King Tut's curse.

One of our Native American friends is a woman of Blackfoot ancestry. An activist, she is also mystical, versed in traditional lore. She gets pretty riled when we come to the subject of someone who may have disposed of her ancestors' remains. "He makes the deal, he takes the money, he does *what* with the pots and bones?" she said. "Do they go into his museum? Does he sell 'em? They aren't his ancestors. They're mine!"

After all we've heard about curses befalling whites who picked up bones or greased the skids for the political process, we'd expect far worse to befall a Native American who knew better. "How does he avoid the karma?" I asked.

"Oh, he has protection," she said. "Every year he has a certain deal he has to make to keep himself out of the way."

I was aware that I was getting only one side of the story. I called Ted Williams and caught him on one of his western New York forays. He met me at his beloved disc-golf course on another sunny afternoon. When I started in, he didn't seem to have heard of the case. How could he not have? The matter of the mines had been making shock waves in local Native circles. Ted's good friend Michael Bastine had been involved in some of the protests. I thought it might be another of his tests, drawing the student out to see what he thought he knew. But Ted had been down south most of the preceding year, so maybe the ignorance was sincere. I gave him a few of the outlines. "I hear there were curses," I said, wrapping up. "I hear people got attacked because of their involvement."

In what? he said with a bit of indignation. I gave him a few more details about the burials, the disposal, and the protests. I still felt like I was being tested.

Ted gave one of his checked laughs. "Seems like some of those protesters were from nations that don't even have *chiefs*." He said his last word with such exasperated stress that it rhymed with "sheaves." "The mining people probably went to some reservations and couldn't find anybody to talk to." He had a point. The embassy of Austria is easier to find than that of the Olmec.

"You know, what everybody would like is that the chiefs decide, the representatives. But you can go out to some reservations, and there's no government to be found. Or else there's two of them, the spiritual authority and the political authority. Some reservations have representative government. Sometimes greed gets involved."

He looked at me hard. "How would you get rid of those remains? Fella you're talking about up in Rochester might have been the only person they could find willing to take it on. If he's got a thick hide, he ought to just let the stuff rain off him. That's what I'd do."

He squinted off in the direction of the sun. "Doesn't surprise me there might be some energy at those mines."

I didn't feel like I was at the bottom yet of this cycle of curse and countercurse. I went to Michael Bastine. At first he thought I was curious about the Seneca individual who had reburied the human remains. "He's an OK guy," he said. "I've been in the same sweat lodge with him a couple times. We don't have any problems."

"But people we know do have problems. What's your take?"

"He's gotten himself the reputation as the type of *Indian* whites can do business with," said Michael with a bit of a grin. "He's made a few bad decisions."

"Bad decisions?"

"There might have been a time or two that he got called in by his bosses, and they might have said to him, 'You're being a bit too *Indian* here to get this job done.' I know what I'd have done if somebody had said that to me. I'd have said, 'Well, that's who you hired.' But he didn't say that, and he got himself caught between bad options."

"Like some of those arrangements with the ancient remains?"

"Some of that. And so much more I can't even talk about."

"After all I've heard people say about curses," I said, "I was wondering how this guy can escape them."

"Well, there's *deals* you can make," said Mike with a knowing look.

After all the damage had been done, a prominent Onondaga elder visited the region. He gathered members of the Native community. "This is a battlefield as well as a burying ground," he said of the area of the mines. "Ask permission if you have to pass through."

He showed people the troubled areas and told them to keep children away after dark. "Kids are vulnerable. They'll see things the parents won't." He worked a ceremony to ease the site and minimize harm to the living innocent. Then he headed up to Rochester.

The old healer found our Seneca friend toiling in his office over a block of stone studded with bones and artifacts. Without a word, the elder took up one troublesome femur like a piece from a jigsaw puzzle. It popped into his hand like the rock had decided to spit it out. Then he put it back. The Seneca went to pull it out again and found it as stuck in the stone as King Arthur's proverbial first sword.

"It's all about the intent," the old healer said. "If your intent is for the good of the world, a lot of these problems will go away for you. If you're selfish, the old ones will know it. And they'll never get out of your way."

SIGNS OF SUPERNATURAL WAR

The undercurrents of an occult culture clash could be seismic in some sensitive circles and yet run far beneath the radar of almost every white. How would you know if something is brewing behind the scenes? How would you know if war has been declared? If the clash is a stalemate or just one eruption in a long series, you may never know for sure. But you might learn to spot the signs of an unrest that may be the omens of a conflict.

It could be when a diminutive old Native American man is spotted pitching powder on the city hall building in Albany. Was it witch or medicine powder? What did he want the city to do or stop doing?

It could be when an otherwise responsible nineteen-year-old from one of the Niagara region reservations steals a car and tears out inexplicably into the night, howling east toward Batavia on a road that follows a trail that was already ancient when the whites arrived. As if some devil came after him, he may have hit eighty-five in the village zones and stopped only when he was killed in a crash. Who sent what after him? Why?

It could be when a middle-aged Seneca man is found killed with no explanation on the Cattaraugus Seneca Reservation. Was it a simple crime?

It could be when the heads of dozens of dogs are found on the St. Regis Reservation. Someone, it seems, in Mohawk country was sending someone else a message, with at least the signs of a powerful spell.

It could be when a man is found in his car in the parking lot of an Onondaga country hospital, drowned in his own blood, his face and upper quarters so badly slashed by fang and claw that authorities are at first unsure what animal could possibly have done it. Maybe to keep things at their simplest point, a pit bull attack is publicly blamed.

It is up to you if you believe or fail to believe in the power of any of the subjects of this book. One thing you cannot deny, though, is that the tradition of an ancient and indigenous supernaturalism is still active in New York state. It would be best to respect it.

7

Power Spaces

It demonstrates . . . that there was once indeed something
strange and irresistible, which can be seen today in legend,
symbol, and ruined monuments.

FRANCIS HITCHING, EARTH MAGIC

Landscape Magic

In 1955, South African travel writer Laurens Van der Post (1906–1996) tore off
into Botswana in search of the mysterious, ancient Bushmen, who these days are
often called the San. As his expedition neared the fabled region of the Tsodilo Hills,
their African guide warned the whites not to do any sport hunting. Word didn't get
to a small advance party, who shot an antelope and a wart hog who had doubtless
loved their lives. Such an uncanny plague of calamities commenced that even the
skeptics among the whites suspected that their troubles might be supernatural.

Their African guide Samutchoso drew off by himself and sat in the sun. He gave
the appearance of holding a solemn ritual, then a dialogue with invisible presences.
He returned with the counsel that "the spirits" were angry with the whites for

approaching the holy region with blood on their hands. The whites were starting to believe in African landscape magic, and the misery didn't let up until they all performed a ceremony of contrition—signing a letter of apology, sealing it in a bottle, and burying it under an impressive ancient rock painting. Still, the spirits had a message for group leader Van der Post: Soon he would hear bad news. So it was; at the first village he came to, a telegraph was waiting to inform him that his father had passed away.

We could cite a twentieth-century story like that on every one of the continents. The sites of traditional ancient power places like these were once everywhere about us in upstate New York. Some were sacred, and any of them could operate negatively if offended. How many of us are camped above them, meeting inspiration and spirituality every day and not knowing why? How many of our haunted houses and cursed zones could be atop them? This is a chapter about some of the ones known in Iroquois country.

Folklorists have known for a long time that supernatural folklore tends to cluster about certain sites or regions. A dramatic example of that would be Stonehenge, attributed in medieval legend to witches, giants, wizards, dragons, fairies, and possibly even the devil. Paranormal scholars—the good ones—notice the effect today. As strange as it may sound, reports from the modern mythology—including mystery monsters, UFO sightings, and unusual earthly energies—tend to pile up in small zones.

Once you identify one of these power places, you can just about presume there will be a story or two about a ghost. Another constant comes in the fact that the most prominent American paranormal places usually have some connection to the people who were here before us. Most of the power places in New York were spiritually significant in one way or another to the precontact Native Americans.

British scholar Paul Devereux has made a study of Native American shamanic landscapes. "It is often difficult to separate spirit haunts," he writes, "from more generalized American Indian concepts of sacred places." As we said at the start of this book: Where do you draw the line between the sacred and the spooky?

The classical—Greek and Roman—world believed in two kinds of sacred places. The most obvious were man-made, what Sig Lonegren calls "sacred enclosures": churches, temples, altars, and monuments people had designated as holy through architecture and devotion. Some were as simple looking as a pile of dirt. Some were as elaborate as the Parthenon or as monumental as the Great Pyramid.

Like all the territory at the underbelly of the Great Lakes, New York state was once dotted with earth-and-stone monuments much like the ones of Europe. Most of them were simple burial mounds, but others were geometric shapes like circles, ovals, and octagons. Some were even human and animal effigies. Virtually all were built by people who preceded the Iroquois. Not many were left by the start of the twentieth century, but some of their former locations are known. These sites tend to pick up folklore, even when no trace of the monument remains.

Another kind of sacred place is natural. One knew the gods had made these places to be special by the way they looked or felt. Fountains, falls, faults, caves, hills, and mountains predominate. Others are simple groves and inconspicuous springs. Something in the energy or ambience of a site projected to people that this was a great spot to get closer to the spirits. Iroquois country is rich, too, in these.

In his 1992 study of Native American sacred places, Andrew Gulliford detailed some styles in the pattern, which include:

- Sites associated with traditions and origin stories
- Trails and pilgrimage routes
- Traditional gathering areas
- Offering areas (altars and shrines)
- Vision-quest and individual-use sites
- Group ceremonial sites (including sweat lodges and singing spots)

- Ancestral habitation sites
- Battle, burial, and massacre sites
- Sites of pictographs and petroglyphs
- Observation and calendar sites

Gulliford makes his observations in the broad American West. Only sites meeting the last two categories—pictographs and calendar sites—are hard to find in Iroquois country.

Human activity can sacramentalize a place. Think of battlefields, forts, religious monuments, and burying grounds. Human activity can also outrage it. We'll take a look at sites in Iroquois territory that have attracted supernatural folklore and tradition. These places are all spooky. And visionary.

WITCHES' WALK
(Seneca Country)

The whole region of Allegany State Park is one of intrigue. Stone ruins, strange artifacts, and curious writing on rocks have gotten more than one writer speculating about undocumented aliens of the ancient kind: Celts, Vikings, or even Egyptians, traveling, trading, and maybe even colonizing in this region of abundant water transportation routes. Today, this is a mother lode of paranormal folklore: UFOs, Bigfoot, mystery monsters, and ghosts. No part of it is richer in tradition than a rural stretch by the Allegheny River by Salamanca.

The Seneca had legends about the region between hill and river. The first of them to venture here found countless skeletons, all bearing the marks of violence. Thousands of young warriors had lost their lives in an event storyteller Duce Bowen suspected was a civil war between communities. The energy of brother killing brother made it more than an ordinary clash. Angry, confused, cut-off souls are thought still at work, giving their energy to the land over their bones.

Witches' Walk may get its name from a single old trail winding through it, the proverbial route of the only folk who dared walk here at night. Only then was it so easy to spot them, huffing along on a frosty eve, red glows like inner fires coming out their mouths and nostrils, fanned fuller with every exhalation. Anyone who happened to be near at such a time—a hunter frozen in a stalking crouch, a lover awaiting a tryst—held pose, even breath, hoping stillness and cover would hide them. Bear, wolf, and panther turned aside and went their ways—unless, they, too, breathed the internal fire and gave greeting.

Supernatural folklore was vivid here throughout the nineteenth century, and the twentieth got a taste of its power, according to Duce Bowen. The train used to go through along the route of the current expressway by river and hills. One night a conductor saw something odd on the tracks ahead and got off to check. He never got back on.

Witches' Walk today is a bushy, low area of Allegany State Park. The state has since routed an expressway through it, the picturesque I-86. The best way to get to Witches' Walk is to ask directions at the Seneca Nation museum. If you belong there, they'll tell you. And don't go off the road at night.

HILL OF THE CROWS
(Cayuga Country)

Owasco Lake was the center of gravity of the Cayuga. Auburn, New York, just north of it, was their major community. Two of Auburn's distinctions overlap. One is the illustrious Fort Hill Cemetery based around the burial ground and earthwork of a pre-Iroquoian culture. Upstate pioneers and national heroes, including Harriet Tubman, are buried here. The other distinction is unwelcome, the infestation of migrating crows that besets this historic burying ground twice a year.

It's no surprise that Auburn would have been an ancient civic center. Many upstate cities were Iroquois capitals. Even in the prehistoric Northeast, the natural features that made for community growth pertained to commerce and travel.

It's no shock, either, that Auburn's Fort Hill would have been burial ground to prehistoric Hopewellians, contact-era Cayuga, and contemporary whites. We see this pattern in New York more than most would expect. Sites sacred to one culture tend to be adopted by each supplanting one. We see nothing like these crows.

For as long as we have records this biennial bio-bomb has perched at the cemetery every autumn and ravaged the city before setting off to its winter rest. All the months that the snows sweep or settle the upstate, countless coal-black scavengers breed and season on Mexico's Yucatan. They return from Maya country and blacken our skies every spring.

Earthworks are clustered at the top of the high ground above the Owasco Creek. Early settler James McCauley studied the remains of the Cayuga palisade Fort Osco in 1820 and judged by the trees growing through it that it predated Columbus. Fort Allegan, right around it, was a Hopewellian fort at least 1,500 years old. Similar in style to the megalithic constructions in Europe, this ring fort held eight open spaces that might have been entrances.

Maybe as a sign of its mystical heart, the city of Auburn was passionately involved in some of America's nineteenth-century movements: Spiritualism, women's rights, and abolition. Today's Fort Hill is a grand cemetery in which psychics, suffragettes, and abolitionists rest. Dedicated in 1852, it's spilled well beyond its original bounds. But at the core of it is the famous earthwork. Much like a British henge, it's a piled dirt monument that makes a ring and a ditch. It's almost invisible today due to the development around it and its settling under all those winters.

But it's easy to find. It's the Fort Allegan section, rooted by the fifty-six-foot, local stone monument to Cayuga chief John Logan, a fighter against white expansion into Ohio and Pennsylvania. At the end of Lord Dunmore's War (1774), Logan gave a short, noble, remarkable speech whose text made its way to Washington and impressed Thomas Jefferson as much as Caractacus's address to the Roman senate.

Psychic folklore is often a sign of power places like these. When you

Logan's Monument in the Fort Allegan section of
Fort Hill Cemetery, Auburn, New York

see the flowers—apparitions—you wonder what sort of bed lies under-neath. The whole cemetery seems, of course, to be haunted, just not by clear Native American ghosts. The apparition reports we get about Fort Hill are those of many New York graveyards, archetypal images like the seemingly omnipresent little girl ghost and the woman in white. Mystery lights and a pale horse or two are legion in upstate New York, and they have no known explanations in the folk tradition of this cemetery.

A region's ghosts are seldom frozen onto either the natural landscape or the one of folk memory. Psychic folklore is so plastic a thing that the reports you get of a site or region can vary radically depending on the day or decade you interview. In a morning of driving the streets around Fort Hill, I came up with rumors of "Indian chiefs" buried inside its trees, of the sound of the hooves of invisible horses, of someone's grandparents reporting the images of old settlers. I notice that none of the reports were personal, but were instead recollections of what old-timers had said. The site may no longer be active. I keep coming back to those crows.

Vögel der Seele, Rilke called his angels, "birds of the soul." Birds are symbols to most world societies, often as emissaries of the spirit. Intermediaries between the realms of earth and sky, they rise, vanish, and rest again. Some have been messengers and prophets, and others totems of warrior cults.

The battlefield birds, though, crows and ravens, are usually more than that. Associated with war and destiny, they know where death is soon to come and bodies to be had. In their visits with the eternal, they learn the fates of heroes and the ends of empires. Why do the real ones keep coming to Fort Hill?

The old name of the outlet of Owasco Lake was Deagogaya, "the Place Where Men Are Killed." Was this a memory of some tragic event that took place at Fort Hill, even a battle that preceded the Iroquois? What have the crows learned to remember?

GREEN LAKE
(Onondaga Country)

Nine miles east of downtown Syracuse is a state park holding comma-shaped Green Lake. In the heart of Onondaga territory, it lies just a short walk north of the Great Migration trail that lies under today's Route 5. The lake may have been made by a titanic waterfall spilling off a retreating glacier, hence its preternatural two-hundred-foot depth. One of its first white names was Lake Sodom, possibly linking the tale of Lot's calcifying wife with the heavy sulfides in the water. Green Lake is meriomictic, meaning that the top layers and the bottom—like human society—don't readily mix.

The lake is aptly named. Its color is depths beyond green, an effect caused by low plant life and lack of suspended matter in the water. That explanation doesn't take away the wonder.

The Power of Green Lake

Green Lake is a gem, an emerald, a crystal. This is a power lake whose dominant legends concern a gigantic serpent, a snake being that partners with a human-size shape-shifter or else takes a human form itself. In this guise, it beguiled a young mother into trading her infant for the serpent's own beglamoured bairn. A few moments later, she felt something clawing at her; the changeling infant on her back had become a hatchling crocodile. She heard her own babe crying in the swamp.

She pondered suicide by jumping off a high point into Green Lake, but a voice within told her to live. She presumed it was the Great Spirit. She went to her husband.

The couple consulted the medicine man. Their little son was at peace, he told them, with the Good-Minded Spirit who had decided to break the power of the snake of Green Lake for good. He needed their help, though. Could they draw it into the open by making offerings of sacred tobacco from a high point above the lake? This they did. The water dragon reared and roared, and the Good-Minded Spirit made his appearance. It went under, never to resurface.

The Onondaga name for this lake was surely a reference to this legend: something like Kiayahkoo, meaning "happy with tobacco."

SQUAKIE HILL
(Seneca Country)

Squakie Hill is a ridge in Letchworth State Park just north of the village of Mount Morris. It's a place of mystery—sacred, for one thing.

It hosted the White Dog ceremonies that some whites were allowed to witness. When the Seneca dispersed for their reservations in 1827, Squakie Hill was the site of their farewell dance to their ancestral valley, the Genesee.

The hill had a reputation for trauma and witchery, too. It was dimly remembered to have been a concentration camp for captives. *Squakie* could be an Anglicization of the name of a nation the Seneca blamed for bringing witchcraft among them. The name could be derived from Kahquas, the name for the Neutral Nation, rumored to have lived there once. It could also come from that of the Sac, or Sioux (the Fox nation), some of whose members may have settled here as prisoners. All this could account for the hill's occult legacy. (Magic is typically the resort of society's underdogs: slaves, servants, and the dispossessed.)

Even the "ancient mysteries" connection comes in at Squakie Hill. Seneca old-timers were sure that a mystery population, possibly even pre-Columbian whites, lived here before them, speaking a different language. The Great Slide of the Genesee River took place nearby in 1817, and a bank-side burial mound spilled non-Native bones and goods into the drink. Odd stonework found at the top of the hill in 1915 was sensed to be Hopewellian and even much like the oddities at Bluff Point. One of our confidants reports handling an ancient European-style sword taken from Squakie Hill.

The UFOs seem to hone in on Squakie Hill. A local confidante tells us of the mid-1970s UFO sighting by a scout troop camped on Squakie Hill and even provided the names of the investigating New York state troopers. This sighting was far from the first. In fact, while the UFO business might seem a high-tech matter to its believers, its connections to other paranormal phenomena are solid. As if they navigate New York by its watery alleys, the UFOs like the long north–south lakes and river channels: the Niagara, the Genesee, the Seneca, and the Hudson.

At least the appearances of Iroquois supernatural bogies have been reported at Squakie Hill. Doctor Seaver's *Life of Mary Jemison* mentions it as a traditional home to the Great Flying Heads. The Seneca always figured the hill was haunted because the witch John Jemison—Mary Jemison's serpent-blood-sipping son—was bushwacked there in 1817. Jemison had killed two of his brothers on Squakie Hill, and his two murderers took their own lives there as well. With that pedigree, it ought to be haunted.

Squakie Hill today is partly wooded parkland with a couple of roads. Its rolling terrain and the occasional grove make for short sight lines. It can be gloomy. Wiccans go there, we hear, to celebrate their rites, maybe tapping John Jemison's indignant power. Many a Letchworth camper has reported apparitions that could be the altered animal forms of Iroquois legend. Are they shape-shifters, ghosts, or the ghost forms of a witch? It would be no wonder either way on Squakie Hill.

FORT HILL AND BLUFF POINT
(Seneca Country)

Shortly after the American Revolution, the whites moved en masse into central New York. The landscape itself attested that the Iroquois were not the only people who had lived here. Some of the most problematic earth-and-stone constructions ever discovered in the Empire State were in Yates County around Keuka Lake.

Keuka Lake is shaped like a big natural Y with the forks to the north. In the middle of the forks is a V-shaped high ground called Bluff Point. Some of the most spectacular vistas in New York state are to be had from atop this promontory. Man-made spectacles even more unique could have stood until the middle 1900s.

On behalf of the Smithsonian Institute, a couple of detailed (for the day) studies were made of the monumental Bluff Point stonework. In 1880, the father-son team of Dr. Samuel Hart Wright (1825–1905) and Professor Berlin Hart Wright (1851–1940) surveyed and mapped the fourteen-acre site at the summit of the promontory. The son revisited them in 1938.

The Bluff Point ruins were a set of low stone ramps and marking stones that might have suggested archaeoastronomy to the two men, had the discipline then been understood. The stones and their placement were so bizarre as to be indescribable. We can only suspect that a lot was stripped away before the first studies were made. The rest was taken for road fill and even building foundations in the later twentieth century.

Ten miles to the north and clearly visible to the Wrights from one of Bluff Point's pillars was an elliptical earthen structure often called Fort Hill. The Old Fort in Sherman's Hollow was 545 feet long north to south and 485 feet across, enclosing ten acres. Its dirt embankments were 4 feet high and 10 across a century ago, and they had probably settled quite a bit.

Fort Hill may have been aptly named. There were twelve breaks in the walls where gates, presumably wooden ones, could once have been, and it had a spring, which would have been vital for withstanding a siege. Near it is a tall hill with steep sides, nicknamed the pinnacle. Smoke signals or fires from this spot would have been visible at Bluff Point, implying line-of-sight communication with a sister settlement, part of the reason we profile them together.

There are many Fort Hill place-names in the eastern states. A military use was surely made of some of these virtual henges or ring-ditch earth circles, but they may not be only what they seem. Many may have been places of ritual and commemoration. A deep, wide trench ran around the *inside* of Bluff Point's bookend earthwork. In essence, Fort Hill's moat is within, which implies a ceremonial use, possibly a water barrier to pen in the spirits summoned until their eventual release.

Historic Native American groups in this part of New York were not thought to build elaborate stone-and-earth structures. The influence of the mound-building Adena or Hopewell cultures of the Mississippi and Ohio valleys may be seen in the Yates County sites. It was known that their influence extended into western New York.

Other curiosities were found at both sites. A hundred yards southeast of the Fort Hill enclosure was an ancient graveyard in which skeletons had been buried seated, facing south back toward Bluff Point. There is talk among Yates County historians about a bronze sword taken from a nearby mound. Only two Native American cultures were known to be working in bronze before the Europeans came, and neither was in North America. The ground around Bluff Point was reputed to have disgorged other out-of-the-way artifacts, some implying a Mesoamerican influence and others—bits of iron—ancient Europeans.

Many are tantalized by the prospect that a mystery community may have settled this region, a possibility that Seneca historians do not discount. "We've kept the tradition that we had visitors from other parts of the world," DuWayne Bowen told me in 2003. "The idea is nothing remarkable to us."

One thing that may be remarkable is the way white supernaturalism gathers around these ancient sites. Fort Hill in Sherman's Hollow is a short walk from the home of the mystical community of Jemima Wilkinson (1752–1819), the Publick Universal Friend, in a town even called Friend. And all the evidence we have implies that as long as both these sites were intact, they were folklore batteries. Howling ghosts, mystery lights, and buried treasure were rumored of both sites.

"These were old, abandoned places that have always been mysteries. Everybody's trying to figure out who did them and why," said Michael Bastine. "I think if I sat down with some tobacco and asked for some more information, I'm pretty sure it would come with time."

THE VALLEY OF MADNESS
(Seneca Country)

They say the word *kanakadea* means "where heaven and hell meet earth." Whatever that might point to, the Kanakadea Creek valley holds two New York colleges, SUNY Alfred and Alfred Tech. The region has another nickname, more direct and more sinister: the Valley of Madness. It points to the sense of an age-old suspicion to this valley that may predate the Iroquois. The lore doesn't let up there.

An ancient Seneca burial ground is reportedly covered by the Alfred campus. They talk about it being a more recent battlefield, possibly from General Sullivan's Revolutionary campaign. People hike and hunt in the woods and report strange "things" in the trees at dawn and dusk, strange sounds at dawn and twilight, strange images at the eye corners. After dark, some say you can see spectral figures carrying their dead to the sound of deep drumming. Something must be behind it all.

Allegany County historian Craig Braack observes that the folkloric bedrock here is shifty. For one thing, there's no earthly peculiarity about the region of Alfred University. It's a creek valley, but not with a dead end. While you can't rule out scouting and skirmishing, there was no battle here in 1779 nor at any point in Sullivan's campaign. Native American burials are possible anywhere in New York state, but Braack doesn't know of any in the town. There were, however, ancient earthworks in the region. Visible from Braack's Belmont office is a house situated on top of a mound. Bones were found when its foundations were laid.

We've heard it suggested that the Valley of Madness, like much other Alfred folklore, is the invention of college pranksters, possibly no older than the 1970s. The cycle indeed has a murky feel, and we often see that the mere hint of such is enough for skeptics to declare victory and stop questioning. A rumor cycle so strong and prevalent about one of the stops on the Forbidden Trail—to come—at least deserved a mention.

THE HILL AND THE STONE
(Oneida Country)

Primes Hill is about six miles south of today's town of Oneida, at the heart of the Oneida Nation territory. It had held an Oneida village, including a two-acre, twelve-foot-high, double-walled fort that could have sheltered twelve hundred people.

The Oneida needed their forts. They had sided with the colonials in the Revolution, helped turn the war, and been relatively abandoned by the young United States. They had also earned the outrage of the

British-allied Mohawk, who burned and sacked a pair of Oneida forts. Oneida lash-backs took out three Mohawk forts and drove the survivors into British-controlled Canada. Many Oneidas relocated to a reservation near Green Bay, Wisconsin, still a center of Oneida culture. By the early 1800s, the New York Oneida gave the appearance of a shiftless, beaten people with little purpose or cultural core.

In 1813, Thomas Rockwell bought one of the first farms on Primes Hill. His new tract held the former Oneida Council ground and Council Rock, which, so far as any whites of the day could discern, was *the* Oneida stone. This object is interesting.

The Oneida are the People of the Standing Stone. Though a mighty tradition has developed about their national symbol, it may not have been just figurative. There appears to have been one central "true" stone and a host of lesser ones, one to each Oneida village. It's as if this original stone, should one exist in reality, was a big emanator of orenda from which all the others drew their power.

Early New York ethnologist Henry Rowe Schoolcraft (1793–1864) visited Primes Hill in 1845 and was most impressed by the view, at the top of the highest point in the Oneida Creek valley. A beacon lit here would be seen a long way. Schoolcraft found it the focal point of some elaborate white folklore, chiefly of the "ancient mysteries" school. The evidence of battlefields and reports of very large human skeletons—common rumors about upstate New York—got them speculating about metal-using giants and a prehistoric culture clash. Human giants are associated in legend with ancient power sites all over Europe. Primes Hill, site of the fabled stone, was surely one of them.

So far as he knew, Schoolcraft was looking at the stone that clear day in 1845. He was impressed mightily by the view and his romanticized notions of the site, but he was let down by the stone itself. In Schoolcraft's sketch, this object, set heavily in the earth, is far more of a quadruped than a bipedal standing stone.

It's no wonder Schoolcraft might have been let down; these mythic relics on all the continents can seem humble to whites, raised on grander and more recent monuments. But there is mystery about the Oneida stone. Other sources describe the original as a slender, crystalline seven-footer sounding suspiciously like a European-style menhir.

The Primes Hill site was surely still holy. William M. Beauchamp's confidants remembered scenes from their childhoods, of small groups of Oneida, foreigners in their own lands, drifting about looking for seasonal work like today's migrant laborers. Twice a year they returned to Primes Hill and camped within easy walking distance of the Council Grove. They never bedded down too near the stone, people recalled, and they only approached it at night. A woman remembered spying on them as a child and observing some "strange rite" by the stone.

In a gesture intended to convey inclusiveness and respect, something taken publicly to represent the Oneida stone was moved to Utica's Forest Hill Cemetery in 1849. In the century-old photograph, it doesn't look anything like either Schoolcraft's sketch or the natural obelisk others described. The whole situation leads many to wonder if the Oneidas said everything they knew to the whites. In 1974, this object, too, came back to Oneida land and rests today quite close to their casino—Turning Stone—which may even be named for it. But obviously its former Primes Hill site was still sacred to the Oneida of the middle nineteenth century, and we wonder if the stone itself was the whole point of the thing—or if another one is out there.

KINZUA
(Seneca Country)

Because of repeated flooding of towns and cities downstream—like Pittsburgh—the Kinzua Dam was authorized in 1963. It backed up the Allegheny River, turned a valley into a lake, and flooded loads of Seneca history.

Somewhere under the Allegheny Reservoir is Cornplanter's grave, a simple tree under which the old warrior was buried in 1836 at the age of one hundred. Probably only the Seneca knew which one it was, if it was still standing, but what a tragedy it was for them to lose access to it. Cornplanter's village and Handsome Lake's vision site were here as well, now under water.

It's hard for non-Iroquois to appreciate the anguish this caused the Seneca. All through the cycle of protests, lawsuits, and construction, the whole region was a zone of psychic folklore. Phantom horses, fabled bogies, and even the archetypal Great Snake of the Allegheny were spotted, as if the unrest among the Seneca had sprung their supernatural circus. Even High Hat, the cannibal giant in the Abe Lincoln stovepipe, was reported, and sometimes by white construction workers. The place is still spooky, a zone of paranormal folklore of most imaginable types: mystery lights, UFOs, mystery critters, ghosts.

Two of the most-talked-about aspects involve the water. Salamanca historians tell us that not too long ago, U.S. Army Corps of Engineers divers didn't finish the underwater part of a dam inspection. Shadowy shapes buzzed them by the dam wall, many of them bigger than human size. The divers surfaced and refused to go back under. Surely these shadow figures were natural critters like lake sturgeon or muskellunge. They can grow . . . almost that big.

THE GREAT FALLS
(Seneca Country)

Waterfalls are sacred all over the world. There is only one this big—Niagara Falls—and its creation was an act of fury.

The geologists tell us it was a single cataclysm, an ice block of the melting glaciers that let loose the water of a vast prehistoric lake, shearing the Niagara Escarpment into the tortuous form we have today. The old Iroquois thought it was made by the death rolls of a titanic serpent, caught in the open by a Thunder Being and fried with a single bolt. Everywhere, though, the Great Falls of Niagara are counted as something special. The first whites who saw them just stood and gaped. No wonder: The area is packed with vision sites.

Goat Island just below the great falls is joined to the American side by a small bridge. To the Iroquois this was Turtle Island, named for their image of the world as a great body resting on the back of a primal turtle. It was sacred to them as an omphalos, a world still point or navel. Their shamans prayed and sacrificed here over the graves of great warriors. At its western edge are small islands, the Three Sisters, one of them three hundred yards from Horseshoe Falls.

Anyone who doubts the falls' reputation should remember the famed harmonic convergence, almost single-handedly launched by art historian Jose Argüelles, author of a series of books mixing Mayan mysticism and New Age thinking. On August 16, 1987, the planets fell into the shape of a double triangle or Star of David, and a metaphysical Woodstock was proclaimed. Seven global power sites were chosen for the first dawn of the New Age. Among the elect: Machu Picchu in Peru, the Great Pyramid in Egypt, Stonehenge in England, Mount Olympus in Greece, Mount Fuji in Japan, the banks of the Ganges in India—and Niagara Falls in New York state.

Buffalo mystic Franklin LaVoie observes that waterfalls are symbols of the dissolving process in alchemy, thus purifying in emotional senses. Niagara Falls are for lovers and newlyweds: The falls' energies dissolve rigid patterns in lives. They can be a new start in relationships.

Like all great forces—fire, electricity, wind—this one can be edgy. The bloodiest night in Canadian history—the 1814 Battle of Lundy's Lane—took place within earshot of the surging waters. Freak accidents happen here with depressing regularity, and more people than we hear about take the plunge. Not every one of them is killed. When the survivors can talk, the first question they have to answer is usually, "Why did you come here to kill yourself?"

A good part of the time, the answer is, "I didn't." They remember coming to see the great falls, looking in, admiring, wondering, adoring, and . . .

Contemporary psychics say that anyone who listens long enough can hear ancient spirits in the natural hiss-roar. They must hear something. Ted Williams's father, Eleazar, used to tell him about places on the Niagara *that can just take you*. "You look into them, they haul you in, next thing you know you are gone." Anyone who has ever stood close to a speeding train and felt the pull of the wheels may understand. And this is vastly grander.

SNAKE HILL
(Mohawk Country)

Spook, snake, or devil: These are scarlet-letter place-names in the Northeast. Whenever you come across one of these in reference to a site, it bears examination.

Most of the early white settlers who developed these place-names were nurtured on the dualism—the good god, bad god—of Christianity. Anything that didn't compute as saintly defaulted into the satanic. Calling something Spook Hollow, Devil's Punchbowl, or Snake Hill might be a sign that it held an immeasurable power to an earlier society, a power that even the early settlers could feel.

Snake Hill is one of the most conspicuous natural monuments in the state. You can't miss it as you drive or boat around Saratoga Lake. On a promontory that juts out from the eastern shore, it is a curious piece of geology, and it is coupled with others.

Locals will tell you that in most places, Saratoga Lake is no more than a dozen feet deep. Boaters can usually see the bottom on bright, still days. But just offshore from Snake Hill are declivities said to go 250 feet down. The fish breed and grow down there, they say—a fine place to wet a line. Something dropped into that abyss would be there a mighty long time.

Some conjecture that Snake Hill was named for a resident who liked his privacy. To keep it, he generated a legend of rattlers bigger, badder, and more profuse on Snake Hill than anywhere else in the region. Other stories feature a white man who raised and trained the snakes and showed them off to the public. (One day he got bit, and that was the end of that.) Still another rumor concerns an Algonquin who collected an abnormal bounty turning in just the rattles, taken as evidence of death. It turns out that he wasn't harvesting the varmints, just trimming the rattles and waiting for them to grow back.

At the northeastern edge of Iroquois territory, Saratoga County was hunted and fished by Mohawk and Algonquin groups. By all accounts, Snake Hill was a legend site to them, too, and many familiar motifs are attached to it. The Mohawks have a tale about a brave old chief tortured to death here by the Algonquin. The Algonquin get even with a "lover's leap" tale about a brave of their own delivered from the Mohawk stake by an infatuated chieftain's daughter. The cornered pair are said to have plunged from a high point on Snake Hill.

Behind the scenes, people talk about an ancient earthwork on Snake Hill, private property now. It was likely a mound, and one neither archaeologists nor residents want us to know about. If it's a burial, it's both monument and graveyard. It's also a mystery. The mound-building tendency (if *influence* isn't the word) wasn't thought to get this far east and north of the Ohio Valley.

From the right vantage, Snake Hill looms against the starry sky. The lights of houses glisten like the eyes of unknown animals in a bush. Strange luminous spheres are reported moving about Snake Hill at night. A classic, unnatural, sky-high moving light—a UFO—has been spotted buzzing Snake Hill, and there are even witnesses who report a touchdown. We see once again the connection between ancient human power sites and the UFO cycle. This is clearly a power hill.

THE ANGEL'S MOUNTAIN
(Seneca Country)

We've all heard the story about the American farm boy who went on to found a major new religion. Born in Vermont in a region of strange stonework, Joseph Smith (1805–1844) moved with his family to Palmyra in upstate New York. In his teens, he poked around Cumorah Hill, may have dug into an ancient monument, and turned up tools, trinkets, and a pair of crystals he used to read a set of mysterious golden tablets no one has been able to find since. New York's Burned-over District had one more founding tenant.

Joseph Smith would spin a strange tale of a hidden cave, dialogues with an angel, and the golden plates that make a virtual new Bible. This Book of Mormon tells of lost tribes from Israel, ancient American civilizations, climactic battles, and biblical allegories. In only a few years, Prophet Smith (like Jesus Christ) died an early death at the hands of a mob, and his inspired supporters formed a new religion. His devout followers suffered persecution, built their New Jerusalem in the western wilderness, and founded one of the world's most successful young religions. This tale of fantastic achievement is rooted in a serious mystery. What did Smith find, and why was it on Hill Cumorah?

"This is a special place," said Salvator Michael Trento, the Oxford-trained author who's studied North America's sacred places. Trento found "a major aberration" of Hill Cumorah's "total magnetic field" and electro-magnetic curiosities like those reported at the world's other major sacred monuments. Supernatural folklore tends to follow such sites, as with Smith's Palmyra hill: UFO sightings, apparitions, and even witchcraft-inspired murders.

His followers think Smith talked to angels and spoke for God. Our Seneca contacts agree that he found *something* on Cumorah Hill, and that it may be no easy place. They say their ancestors knew something powerful was hidden in that hill, and that it was medicine no one wanted to mess with. It was like the bottle holding the genie: Open it right and at the right time, and it works with gratitude; open it wrong or too late, and you had best not have opened it at all. Surely this counts as one of North America's hot spots. The Seneca, we hear, still mistrust that hill.

TAUGHANNOCK FALLS
(Cayuga Country)

Cayuga Lake drops south of Seneca Falls, home of the women's rights movement. At the bottom of it is Ithaca, an eclectic city and home of Cornell University. Between Ithaca and Trumansburg on the southwestern shore is one of the state's most unusual features.

As much as today's tourists revere sublime views, the old Iroquois loved them more. They walked vast distances to commune at these special scenes. Taughannock Falls was known to be one of them.

Taughannock Falls, a sacred spot for the Iroquois

Taughannock is far from New York's biggest waterfall, but its 215-foot drop makes it the highest. It's the focus of a number of tales.

Some believe that *Taughannock* may mean "great falls in the woods." In some tales, it's the name of an Algonquin hero who made forays into Cayuga country. In others, it's the name of a Delaware invader killed and tossed over the falls. Still another version of the legend stars Taughannock as a righteous local defender against Iroquois oppression whose daughter married a defeated Cayuga chief at the falls.

There is also a Cayuga "lover's leap" tale set here, fundamentally identical to a Mohawk legend of Snake Hill, an Onondaga story about Skaneateles Lake, and a Seneca romance about Canandaigua Lake. There could quite well be story-variants that we haven't heard of. In recent Internet folklore are unsigned reports of mystery lights and a female demon somewhere in the park. Take those as you will.

Taughannock Falls has a curious doorlike space, about eight by ten feet, in the cliff wall to the right of the water. Of course, it's created by a falloff of a layer of rock, but it jumps out, even on the Internet photos. It looks like the entrance to a secret space inside the rock-ribbed mountain.

The Six Nations folk presumed some magical force was at work in truly curious natural features. Either the spot attracted the supernaturals, or it was made by them. Queer clefts in rock faces were wizards' hideaways. Doorlike spaces in cliff walls were the gates of the Little People. This spot at the top of Taughannock Falls could have been either, and we would know which if we could solve the spell and get the smooth barrier to open for us.

LOST NATION
(Seneca Country)

There's some kind of mystery going on here, but we're not sure what.

For much of its existence, the Confederacy was at war. As the

Longhouse nations expanded their territory, they met obstacles in single tribes. These groups were absorbed or cleared out.

The Europeans changed everything, including the scale and objectives of war. In the 1600s, the Confederacy fought sustained wars on many fronts with large Native American groups, chiefly fellow Iroquoians like the Huron and Algonquin speakers like the Adirondack and Abenaki. Mini world wars, these conflicts sprawled all over the Northeast, the Great Lakes, and the Atlantic states.

Many New York nations disappeared in the pass and fell, as Hamlet would say, of mighty opposites. None did so with greater mystery than an Allegany County group remembered as the Lost Nation. What else do we call them? They vanished from history in a heartbeat. All that remains of them is the name set to their former territory, a 1,500-acre tract in the town of Centerville.

Scraps of rumor lead us to deduce that these folk were admired as craftsmen and settlers. Nothing tells us why they left in such a hustle. The Canandaigua Treaty of 1794 lists the tribes and territories in western New York; none could be the Lost Nation.

The name *Tutelo* has surfaced in some sources. The Tutelo were a Siouan people from the American Southeast who did some wandering. Some were in western New York in the mid-1700s and may have been absorbed by the Cayuga. But who lived in Lost Nation? And why are there no signs of what happened to them? Did the UFOs beam them up?

Lost Nation today is still undeveloped and used for hunting and other outdoor sports. Its enigmatic ruins—stone foundations and fireplaces—inspire the imagination but have recent origins: the CCC's (Civilian Conservation Corps) Depression-era work camps.

Still, something about Lost Nation nurtures folklore. Almost every figment of the paranormal surfaces today in the region: mystery lights, ghosts, witchcraft rumors, and mystery critters, including an excellent Bigfoot flap. Every few years it's something.

THE DALE
(Seneca Country)

The Cassadaga Lakes are three tame water bodies eight miles south of the Chautauqua County college town of Fredonia. They make a rough C-shape nestling today's Lily Dale, concentrated just south of Upper Lake.

Lily Dale is the capital of Spiritualism, a young American religion based on the idea that the spirits of our dead are still around us and can be reached for communication. While the Dale today is a freethinking community that hosts a summer program of talks and events on many metaphysical topics, what we see is only the flower on the vine. A series of eclectic movements ran behind today's Lily Dale. The constant is the site.

The whites settling here in 1809 found a number of ancient earthworks. Scholars reported odd skeletons and an ancient road, possibly even a European-style *cursus,* one of those short, still mysterious, roads to nowhere. These old monuments drove the belief that Lily Dale had been a cross-culturally sacred, conflict-free zone for ancient Native American societies and even a necropolis, a city of the dead.

In the Lily Dale archives is an ancient works map, which Brad Olsen used for his own write-up in *Sacred Places of North America.* The southern Lower Lake was the focus of the ancient energy, featuring fire pits, causeways, palisades, and earthworks on the north, south, and east sides. We only wish we had the words of the ancient societies. We can only judge by the monuments they left us and the reactions we have to them.

There's still an earthwork somewhere at Lily Dale, inconspicuous, much settled, and in a tree-shaded yard. There seems little doubt that the spirit of place, the genius loci, is still active. Paranormal folklore abounds from the nineteenth century, including mystery lights and a couple of wonderful reports of a UFO and a Bigfoot. The psychics and mystics at Lily Dale are prone to seeing vortexes and power points there today, as well as spirits.

Surely by design, Lily Dale encourages meditation. It has many nurturing nooks on its grounds. The most powerful may be Inspiration

Stump, the atmospheric, reconstructed tree in an amphitheater amidst old-growth forest. Michael Bastine recalls the rumors among the Iroquois that this was a Little People place.

Canadian psychic Gwendolyn Pratt recalled a midnight walk to Inspiration Stump just after a rain. In glistening steam and moon-spattered foliage, the bole in the grove was covered with white butter-flies. All they took of the moonlight they gave back. What drew them all here, only here? Not another was in sight, anywhere. It took the breath away. Were they natural? In many cultures of the world, includ-ing some Native American ones, it's thought that souls often return as butterflies.

LAKE ELDRIDGE
(Seneca Country)

Four hundred years ago, the junction of the Chemung and Susquehanna rivers was hunting territory for Native American nations from as far away as the Atlantic coast. This was not unusual. The Northeast Woodlands were being overhunted, and communities had to send far afield for game. Sometime before the Europeans arrived, the warlike Andastes took hold of the region and gave it up only to the mighty grip of the Seneca. Odds are good that this was Seneca territory when the whites arrived, eventually setting up the city of Elmira.

Somewhere in today's city limits was the Iroquoian village called Shinedowa. Mount Zoar to the southwest dominates the horizon. Just south of it and along the Chemung River was a grove of evergreens that held the burial mounds of these Iroquoians and who knows who before them. The Seneca had legends about what's called today Eldridge Lake.

A dangerous swamp once surrounded it, and it had many myste-rious residents. The Bird of Doom was a giant green creature whose eerie calls drove men back from the trails. Men knew they were fated to be wounded or killed when their paths were crossed by a certain huge black wolf, doubtless a shape-shifter or some wizard's emissary.

A chief's son met a strange, seemingly supernatural woman here and was haunted and fey afterward. The Celts would say that this was his fairy lover. He lost all his taste for life among mortals and was found dead in this swamp. He may be buried under a mound that could still be here—somewhere.

Eldridge Park today is an urban oasis just north of the core of Elmira. Its small lake is so deceptively deep that the Native Americans believed it was bottomless and that it might be connected by underground channels to Seneca Lake, and thence to Lake Ontario, the St. Lawrence River, and the Atlantic. Maybe that explains its most dramatic legend, the one about its monstrous serpent at perpetual war with the local villages that the Thunder Being resolved to save. A chief's son and his bride-to-be bravely tempted the critter into the open, walking dangerously close to Eldridge Lake. When it reared to strike them in full sight of the lightning hurler, the trap was sprung. A single bolt ended the monster's reign.

HIGH ROCK SPRING
(Mohawk Country)

For thousands of years, on all the continents, springs have represented healing and inspiration. They are also associated with visions. Many Christian miracle sites, including those of Marian apparitions, are natural fountains. It was no different in Iroquois country.

The British Empire's Indian agent in North America was Irish-born Sir William Johnson (1715–1774). Revered by the Mohawks, he had a thing for Mohawk women and left a long line of multiracial descendants. He led the Mohawk men against a French and Algonquin force at the 1755 Battle of Lake George. He took both the honors of victory and a musket ball in the thigh that acted up ever after. It was so bad by the summer of 1767 that the Mohawk took Sir William in a litter to their most private and holy site: High Rock Spring in today's Saratoga. He got there one morning in August.

In the Mohawk style, he offered ground tobacco to the earth and winds, to the ancestors, and to the four quarters. He used more to fill and light the calumet, the peace pipe that may have been a gift from Ottawa chief Pontiac. Then he walked shakily to the sacred fountain. For four days he drank from it and lay in its waters.

Letters arrived calling him home, and he stood with a pleasant shock. Not only was he no longer at death's door, he could walk well enough to make much of his journey on foot. High Rock Spring's notoriety may date to this visit. Other new springs were found in today's Saratoga village, and all over this part of Saratoga County. The towns of Saratoga Springs and nearby Ballston Spa thrived as resorts based on the healing industry.

Today, High Rock Spring nestles in its pavilion below the prominent fault that runs right down Saratoga Springs' most important street. Its chief supernatural distinction today may be the wake of hauntings that spreads all around it. Noteworthy but not unexpected is its nearness to the famous haunt the Old Bryan Inn and the reputed territory of the late Angeline Tubbs (1760?–1865), the Witch of Saratoga. (She resurfaces, too, as a worthy ghost.) "You always have sightings at springs," says Abenaki author Joe Bruchac. "We've got so many stories."

THE GREAT HILL
(Seneca Country)

The south end of Canandaigua Lake is a region of paranormal mystery. Here a Seneca-Onondaga army was rumored to have defeated the Massawomeck, a fierce nation whose name means "great snake." A big mica-flecked rock cut with unexplained symbols may commemorate the event. Algonquin settlement was here, as well as strange and ancient stonework, something that always fills people with awe. Giant lake-serpent sightings have been so prevalent since the whites moved in that lakeside innkeepers took their validity as a matter of course into the late nineteenth century. This lake is also a zone of sanctity. Somewhere here, a nation was formed.

THE SENECA NATIONAL CREATION TALE

The Seneca national creation tale begins with a pre-Iroquoian boy who made a pet of a queer worm found in a creek feeding Canandaigua Lake. At the start it was cute, and it had two heads in some of the tale's sixty-something versions. It ate ravenously and grew so big that soon it was a monster that people were afraid not to feed. When the forests had run out of animals, the devil snake turned on its patrons. By the last night, it had encircled the community in their fort like a living henge and eaten every human but the boy who raised it—and a girl. The human pair huddled behind the palisades after sunset. Their reward was to be the serpent's last Canandaigua brunch. The Holder of the Heavens had other ideas.

In a dream, he told the boy to fletch an arrow with the girl's hair, then face the beast, draw bow, and take aim. A single stroke of this fatal charm took the monster down. Its death rolls cleared the hillside below of its trees. As it subsided into Canandaigua Lake, it disgorged the skulls of its victims. The two young survivors started the Seneca Nation.

The Seneca name for themselves, Nundawaono, means "People of the Great Hill." There's debate, though, about the exact site of the sacred mountain, and no wonder; the Seneca have repented many of their disclosures to the Europeans, not least of which might be their sacred stories.

It might be what's commonly called Bare Hill, on the east side of Canandaigua Lake and five miles from the head. That's what the Seneca told the early whites. It could also be South Hill, this one, too, thin of tree. It could even be Parrish Hill, where Arthur C. Parker made his home at the end of his life. Whichever mountain it is, if you head to Canandaigua Lake and look south, you will be sure to see it.

Much that we know about Parker's ancestors comes from his work. In the 1930s, Parker and his wife spent summers in a farmhouse on Parrish Hill near Naples, high over the valley legendary as the birthplace of the Senecas. This home became their residence when they retired. Parker was sure this was the hill down which the legendary serpent rolled.

Possibly because of his success in the white world, Parker never felt accepted on the reservation. Still, when the death owl hooted by his door, he was Seneca enough to know what it meant. He went to the reservation and made his peace in the traditional fashion, then returned to his home on New Year's Day and left this life at his people's most sacred place. A lucky man, he was, to know it. Oh, reader: *Where is yours?*

RING OF HONOR

Sketchy legends of monsters, witch lights, and supernatural battles help us recognize New York's ancient power places; they don't touch the richness of the traditions the old societies maintained about them. Now and then we get a hint.

Sig Lonegren is a Vermont native who lives today in Glastonbury, England. Our paths crossed a lot in the 1980s when I taught English at the Gow School in South Wales, New York, and Sig was one of its most distinguished graduates and board members. A big, lighthearted, graying-blond man, even in a suit Sig would have the look of someone who was once a hippie. Sig is also an authority on diverse topics and has written world-renowned books on dowsing, labyrinths, and ancient mysteries.

Sig is a pretty good man to ask for insights about any paranormal subject, and as a longtime student and friend of Seneca wolf-mother Twylah Hurd Nitsch he knows plenty about Iroquois country. In November 2009, I asked him what he knew about ancient monuments in New York. "I was taken to one on the Cattaraugus Reservation," he said. "I don't think the archaeologists know this one."

"What's it like?"

"Very impressive. A big earth circle, maybe on the oval side. It had a couple of openings in it that could have been entrances."

"Where is it?" I asked in the tone of asking the time. We made eye contact, and I forget who smiled first. He knew I had to ask; I didn't think he would answer. Then he went serious.

"If I remembered how to find it, I couldn't tell you," he said. "But that was a long time ago. I honestly don't remember. I do remember what I was told about it, though. The Seneca I was with said, 'This is where we honored our handicapped.' They honored people of different abilities because they presumed that they had extra gifts."

I know he looked at me again, but I was gazing off into space. *Ceremonies and monuments to the disabled!* There are people in my society who resent them getting a few parking spaces.

"The Creator never takes something from any of us," says Michael Bastine, "without giving something back. The Native peoples of the world have always believed that. We don't look down on our handicapped. To us they are powerful, but in ways that aren't easy to see. They were put here not only to enjoy their own lives, but as spiritual teachers to the rest of us. If we can only learn how to listen to them."

8

The Supernatural Zoo

Pan, the goat-footed god, is not so funny when you encounter him.

F. W. HOLIDAY, *THE GOBLIN UNIVERSE*

THE CELTS AND THE IROQUOIS

The Iroquois imagination filled the upstate woods with psychic characters and a supernatural bestiary. Some were figures of religion. Some were more important than others. In coming to grips with Iroquois tradition, it might be useful to think of the Celts of Europe. There are parallels.

Both words, *Celtic* and *Iroquois,* represent a language group rather than an empire, a nation, or even a distinct ethnicity. The climates and physical environments of the two groups were roughly similar, and their people lived in small, often widely separated villages, not cities. Neither always played well with their linguistic cousins, and when unity came, it was often too late. Though centuries apart, both met with a crash higher-tech, urbanized cultures—for the Celts, it was the Romans—that wanted something of them. Both were storytellers, both were thought by the world to be the bearers of psychic gifts. Both supernaturalized their landscape. Both held traditions of Little People.

All speakers of Celtic languages from Austria to Ireland shared a handful of head gods, usually with similar names. All Celts had a solar deity, a father god, a horse goddess, and probably a fate queen (the dread Morrigan to the Irish).

Individual Celtic nations had their own gods, too, patrons of them and them alone. Very often these tribal gods were visualized as zoomorphs—able to take animal forms—likely related to the totems of the tribe, hence tribal identity.

But within the territory of each Celtic nation were scads of highly localized lesser divinities whom no one outside the immediate region could have known of. It's been thought that they were associated with local landscape features.

The cultural, the national, and the local. . . . The supernatural system of the old Iroquois of New York was almost surely something like that.

All Confederacy nations shared a cultural mythology of religious/creation-related figures. They had their Creator, often taken to be identical to their "Good-Minded Spirit." Their thundering god and their mighty serpents were in perpetual opposition. They had their great New York water snakes, their World Turtle, and their Three Sisters (vegetation spirits of corn, beans, and squash). The pan-Iroquois culture-hero the Peacemaker is nearly deified. All this seems to have been high and sacred, not spooky.

There were shared figures of storytelling. All Iroquois nations had their Stone Giants, vampires, Flying Heads, and Little People. They were clearly supernatural but not fully divine, though some—like the Little People—turn up in ceremonies that are quite sacred.

Each of the nations had its own supernaturals. Only the Seneca have their creation hill. Just the Oneida revere their self-operating power stone.

Then there were the bogies that may have been associated with specific natural features and unknown outside the range of a single village. Longnose, the Legs, and High Hat could be such highly localized figures. If any of them made it into print 150 years ago, it was a coincidence.

As regards this subject, the supernatural actors of the Iroquois, this book doesn't have room for what could have been obtained. Ten this size couldn't hold what has been lost. This chapter is only a profile of some bogies from Iroquois tradition. Some of the garish characters may have spun off the high divinities, figures from Iroquois religion. They are clearly separate from that now. Some are pure figures of folklore that haven't been heard from otherwise in centuries. Some of them are as real and immediate as a contemporary paranormal report.

THE FEARSOME FOURSOME

Stone Giants, Flying Heads, Vampire Corpses, and Little People: Folklorists have found this supernatural quartet the dominant characters in the Iroquois forest tales.

Other beasties have come and gone. The Mohawk made offerings to *this* near Lake Champlain. The Seneca steered clear of *that* along the Allegheny. But all Iroquois nations—even North Carolina newcomers the Tuscarora—talked about these four, and variants are found in Iroquoian groups as far-ranging as the Cherokee and Wyandot. Most folklorists think these cycles are quite old, predating European contact.

Note that all are variants of the human form, and many, such as the Iroquois giants and vampires, have counterparts all over the world. Their Little People look even more like the elves and fairies of Europe. Only the curious Flying Heads lack off-continent parallels.

We don't know a living Native American who claims to have seen or encountered Stone Giants, Flying Heads, or Vampire Corpses. They seem figures of folklore, and we'll discuss them in this chapter. The Little People may be different. They have their own chapter.

THE STONE GIANTS

The Iroquois nations have legends about a tribe of ancient enemies whose name is usually translated as the Stone Giants. They were monstrous cannibals in skintight coats of weapon-proof scales.

Once the Stone Giants were a northeastern tribe content to live and let live, but they endured famine in their wanderings in the cold of the north. They turned to raw meat for sustenance and came into New York with a taste for fresh Iroquois. It was the source of a serious culture clash, and the then Five Nations were getting the worst of it when the tide turned. There are two versions of the matter.

One starred the famous Skunni Wundi, or "he crosses the creek." Skunni Wundi was a trickster hero who'd grown from an impressionable boy into a resourceful young man. He'd made a legend for himself in his own village, but his fame was not yet international when he made his vow to rid his nation of the trolls. He had been doing some scouting in their territory and had left his belongings on the bank of a creek. He came back to them to find a woman of the Stone Giants inspecting them. She picked up his tomahawk as if it was a marvel, even licking the edge with her tongue. Then she set out to see what it could do. The weapon shocked her by splitting a boulder at just a touch.

One of the fundamentals of world myth is the premise that talents or qualities can sometimes be transferred by touch. Unaware that her own act—and her saliva—had given the weapon some of the special powers that protected every member of her tribe, the Stone Giantess presumed that the weapon's owner could whip them all. At that point, the Iroquois hero showed himself, in no hurry to correct her. He added that he'd give her folk some of the boulder's medicine if they troubled his people again. The giants packed up and left Iroquois territory for good.

In another version of the Stone Giants' demise, the Creator disguised himself as a studly young Stone Giant and persuaded his new colleagues to gather into a single army in a valley at Onondaga. The avalanche he started from above overwhelmed them. When the elaborate hoax called the Cardiff giant—a ten-foot man carved out of a block of stone—was found and exhibited in 1869, the Onondaga were not surprised that it was unearthed in this valley so near the site of their legend.

Like the Little People, the Stone Giants display a number of powers. The Stone Giants had several types of magic, including the ability to bestow luck in hunting. Healers as well as fighters, the Stone Giants are sometimes associated with the lesser caste of False Face masks. Transferring magical power to a human artifact is another common motif. Most storytellers agreed that the being inside the flinty coat might be a normal looking, if large, human. Though statuesque, Stone Giant women could also be seductive, doffing their armor coats piece by piece in a mineral striptease by a young hunter's fire.

The giants have peculiar weaknesses, though. Individual Stone Giants who went to live with human families were often chased by members of their own nation and needed human help to win a titanic duel. Though normal clubs, spears, and arrows couldn't hurt the Stone Giants, certain types of wood were said to pierce or shatter their flinty armor. Red willow osier (a type of bush) and basswood (the lime or linden tree) were among these.

Another weakness involved the stiffness of their armor. The Stone Giants couldn't tilt their heads back to look up. A good way to befuddle them was to climb a tree. The trickster hero Skunni Wundi pulled a move on a couple of them near the Oatka Creek near Leroy. Some Stone Giants had snuck up on him and his sister as they played by Buttermilk Falls. Skunni Wundi hid himself under the falls, snuck up behind them, and gave a sudden yell. As they turned their heads, their necks snapped.

The last of these Stone Giants lived for many years in the region of today's Allegany State Park. A Seneca hunter took shelter from a blizzard in a cave and found the giant, who took pity on him. He taught the young man about the history of his nation, then let him depart as a friend. This was the source of one origin tale for the False Faces.

The Stone Giants seem likeliest of the four major Iroquois creatures to have had some origin in reality. So many Native nations of the Northeast have legends about ancient giants that some people interpret them as ancestral memories. The evidence of forts and battlefields attests to prehistoric wars. Some even interpret the Stone Giants to have been European visitors, possibly Vikings, who may have worn metal armor. Tuscarora historian David Cusick never doubted these giants and placed them in dim antiquity, estimating that they came from the north about twenty-five hundred years before Columbus.

A sense of the unknown past of their territory surely had to affect the Iroquois. Some vanished culture left stone-and-earth monuments all over upstate New York, ones that have fed the imagination of all subsequent holders of the land. (The builders had to be giants!) Pre-Iroquoian flint points are sometimes found in Iroquoian burials, often imbedded in masks representing Stone Giants, as if the Iroquois connected the antiquity of the points with the mythic beings.

Giant human skeletons have been reported at dozens of sites in Iroquois territory. Some were buried with artifacts that looked strange to the white settlers. Some skeletons were said to have been the remains of people who would have been nine feet tall. Add to that the regional mythology of Bigfoot, and it could make you wonder how real the Stone Giants were.

THE GREAT FLYING HEADS

The Iroquois have a penchant for direct description. The name says it all about these Great Flying Heads: bodiless, enormous, humanoid heads who either shot through the air where they wanted like Superman or flew by means of tiny, hyperactive wings. The height of a man, they were fitted with dreadful saucer eyes, huge jaws, tusklike teeth, and bear-size arms with wicked claws. Wild, flaring manes trailed behind them.

A ravenous meat eater, the Flying Head was one of the most dreaded beasties of the Northeast. Often drawn to fires in the woods and fresh-cooked kills, it shoveled anything it wanted down its gullet.

The original Flying Heads were envisioned as spiritual beings, zipping about the world before the time of mankind. Associated with the power of wind, they may even have been miniversions of a god whose Seneca name is Dagwanoenyent, meaning "whirlwind" or "cyclone." When an overnight storm mowed channels through a forest, laying trees about like twigs, it was thought that a couple of Heads had been at work.

In most tales, the Flying Head was a dim bulb. One we see in a common tale peered through the window of a cabin and saw a young girl roasting chestnuts in the coals and plucking them out with tongs. The Head figured that the coals themselves were a delicacy and barged in, determined to have its share, perhaps an appetizer before the main course of the girl. It wolfed down a cropful of red-hot coals and soared off in agony. No one in that village ever saw the beastie again, so maybe it burned to death.

The Flying Head had shape-shifting magic. It could make itself the size of an ordinary human skull if it needed to, in which case its mane would have made it look much like a medicine mask. There are stories of it flying in its small form into human homes and interviewing the inhabitants it had not yet decided to kill and eat.

The Flying Head may have been a brute, but there was more to it. In some tales, the Heads are grudgingly benevolent. Later tales pictured them as material beings who, when they weren't eating people, might intercede for them against other monsters. Usually this means standing up for human beings against Stone Giants or witches in a wizard's duel, a common northeastern motif.

In other tales, the Heads can work as healers, serving as a source of inspiration for the common faces of Iroquois medicine masks. They come to hunters in the woods or as visions in dreams, often long enough to direct the making of masks and even serve as models.

We haven't heard contemporary reports of these Flying Heads anywhere in Iroquois country. Even in the settler days, according to

Mary Jemison, the Iroquois talked about them as if they were things of the past. There were regions, though, groves or hills, known once to have been special to them. I've heard of one in Seneca country near Letchworth State Park.

THE VAMPIRE CORPSE

The Iroquois had a lot of stories about evil, semidead, humanlike beings sometimes called vampires or cannibal corpses. Not all of the Six Nations' variety are bloodsuckers like the Romanian vampire or the Scottish *glaistig*. Still, they were so similar to the human predator of European folklore that we have to call them vampires. Variants abound.

The culprit can be a dead human, a simple corpse that something overtakes. It may be the body of a witch or sorcerer so full of its own otkon that the force lasts on after physical death. Sometimes the demon is an airy specter or ghost, physical enough at the business end for a bit of chewing. The Iroquois vampire can be a virtual skeleton, sometimes even what seems to be a separate species that only looks human. It could even be a servant of the otherworld like the monsters that wait along the perilous course of the human soul in Egyptian mythology.

It's hard to tell if these are different tales—regional variants—or if the subject of them has different forms. Ah well, the European vampire is a shape-shifter, too, at least within a range of animal forms: bats, wolves, rats, moths. Maybe the stories are about the same critter. But forget the suave Victorian counts or runway models of the twenty-first-century vampire industry. The Iroquois bogie is a reanimated corpse that wouldn't score at a zombie festival.

The Vampire Man

There were rumors about the old man. He lived by himself far from the village. In his last sickness, people came to make his days easier. Just before his death he said, "Put me in a bark coffin and set me in the backroom of this house. Leave everything as it is, and travelers can shelter here." He added in a tone that should have registered, "But no woman or child should ever sleep here. It will be just too dangerous."

Sometime later, a poor traveling couple and their baby girl came upon this deserted house. They saw the body in the birch-bark coffin, but made little of it. This was a normal custom for many Native Americans.

The husband lay down in the backroom to rest. His wife prepared the evening meal, her daughter slung at her side. She heard the sounds of breaking bones, chewing, and slurping. She knew instantly that her husband had been killed, undoubtedly by some supernatural presence related to the corpse. Hope lay in deception.

"Your daughter and I are going to the stream to get water for the broth," she cried out as merrily as she could. "We're coming right back." She took the pail, left the house casually, and started running along the well-worn footpaths. She was a long way toward the nearest village when a furious howl came from the direction of the cabin.

She ran even faster through the dim woods. Her pursuer was coming. The next bestial vocable she heard was closer than the first; the vampire man was gaining. She threw off a scarf. In a little while, she heard it ripped to tatters. She threw off other pieces of clothing, and each time the same thing happened.

She saw the walls of a stockaded town and called out the traditional distress cry, hoping someone might hear it. Some women finishing their last chores took it up, not knowing what emergency was at hand. But the sounds were near. The young mother could hear panting.

She collapsed outside the village, fearing it was too late. But a party of young men burst from the gates. They hovered over her, glaring into the night, and they were armed. Even a vampire knew he was beat. A half-human voice howled from the thicket.

The next day the young mother told her tale, and a war band set out for the cabin. The body of the husband lay just as he had slept, but with a big hole in his side. Next to him in its coffin was the body of the hermit, fresh blood on its face. It was the most contented corpse they had ever seen.

The warriors pounded the vampire into pulp and piled logs about the house. Soon after they set the fire they could hear yipping and howling within. A big jackrabbit slipped out, dodged weapons, and dashed between the legs of warriors.

This may or may not have been the vampire spirit, but if it was, he had learned his lesson from the Iroquois. They never heard of him again.

SUPER SERPENTS

The snake is a universal image: its emotionless gaze, its stony torpor, its earth-cool blood, its inexorable slithering, its coiling, enveloping kill. As a symbol, it has powerfully impressed the conscious and unconscious mind since people started to create their lore, art, and mythology. The snake permeates dreams, all over the world.

Snakes that appear in conflict with the powers associated with sun, air, and sky—birds, lightning gods—may be different from the giant ones that appear solo. This bird-versus-snake imagery is heavy all over the Americas, including among the Iroquois.

In art, mythology, and literature, almost any big slithery evokes a dragon. Legs, wings, and fire or not, the twain are often taken as one.

The Asian snake/dragon is usually a symbol of the earth force and intertwined with the power of fate. It is not meant to be confronted, any more than other indomitable natural forces like gravity or the wind. It's best worked with. Despite the occasional variant tale, the Native American snake is more like the Asian one.

Although the pre-Christian Europeans' view of the snake may have been more in keeping with the Asian and Native American version, the European snake/dragon we see most often in art and literature is something the hero, the representative of consciousness, needs to master, carve, or skewer. Monstrous and inimical to human society, the European dragon is often interpreted as a symbol of something terrifying within the human mind, possibly the bestial unconscious—or older societies, an earlier way of life, and even the Devil.

Bearing in mind that their folklore shows some influence from European Christians, the great snakes that populate New York legend have a bit of both continents in them. Suffice it to say that the lore of the Iroquoians seems to participate fully in this pan–Native American and global mythological cycle.

In the Iroquois site tradition of New York, there are great lake snakes, little lake snakes, shape-shifting mythological snake beings, and landscape energy snakes. In general, the bigger the snake, the better it is for human society. Let's talk about a few of them.

The Welsh word for *man* is related to the Latin *vir* and sounds like "were." A werewolf is a man-wolf. One class of Iroquoian snake beings are were-snakes, shape-shifting serpent fairies, an alternate race like the *selkies* (were-seals) of Scottish lore. They may be related in some form to something the Seneca called the Blue Lizard, a man-sized servant of the greater snakes.

Some of the time these were-snakes are in league with a gigantic lake monster. They lure people near it for a meal. In other scenarios, they are altered forms of the big critter. Many Iroquois supernaturals are size-shifters.

Sometimes they come to us as lovers. They look pretty slick in their human forms. Seductive, on-the-edge beings, what about them entrances us so? They're a lot like the Lamia of European folklore and Keats' famous poem. They're like the Lorelei Jung talked about, figures of dangerous sexuality. They are sublime—psychologically threatening. They look too cool for us. Then they show an interest. One hangout session with one of them and you are lost—*fey*—spiritually taken by the fairies, as the Celts would say.

If a man meets a female were-snake, he wanders the marshes at the borders of the human world that no longer interests him. Then he's mysteriously found dead.

For a woman, it may be more complex. She goes off as a bride with the fast-talking, elegant stranger. Before long, she discovers his beastly, size-shifting nature, but what's she to do? He's as potentially hostile as he is amorous. But a Thunder Being just waiting for this moment comes to her and gives her the guidance to flee her demon-husband. As he pursues in his true form, the massive, hypnotic snake comes into the open and is killed by a bolt of lightning.

With the big-lake snakes, we start in the realm of folklore and step into that of the paranormal.

The Great Horned Snake of Lake Ontario is a figure of Iroquoian legend. Sometimes his horns are the shape and spread of the antlers of a massive buck deer. Sometimes they're like those of the buffalo, though many times larger. This being is not by nature evil. He helps outcast human beings in many a tale. Still, he's at war with the Thunder Being and his allies. For some reason these two have it out for each other, and whenever old horny flashes his hide under open sky, he risks taking a bolt. Many geological features around the state are reputed to be the work of the climactic clash. Ironically, a big slithery has been reported many a time in Lake Ontario. Soldiers stationed at Fort Niagara have called it in.

There is a two-hundred-year-old string of reports about a less religious mythological creature in Lake Erie. Back Bay (or South Bay) Bessie is a variably sized critter blamed in at least one boat capsizing and attack in 1992. (We have not interviewed witnesses of that event and have to tell you that this is an Internet rumor.)

Then there is the famous Lake Champlain monster. While it's rumored to have been mentioned first in the 1609 journal of French explorer Samuel de Champlain, that water-critter sighting most likely took place in the ocean waters of the St. Lawrence estuary. Still, the Mohawk and some Algonquin-speaking nations thought there was some big animal in the long lake, nicknamed Champ after the French explorer. The legend continues to grow.

Several of the Finger Lakes and some of the smaller lakes and rivers have both Native American serpent legends and recent paranormal reports.

The 1850s flap over the serpent of little Silver Lake in Wyoming County was as much a hoax as the man-made Cardiff or Taughannock giant. The perpetrator claimed to have gotten the idea from a Seneca site legend. Even tiny Findlay Lake in Chautauqua County has its serpent tales.

Lakes Seneca and Canandaigua have both Iroquoian serpent legends and fairly current white reports, some of them well documented. We know the Seneca great serpent legend associated with the south end of Canandaigua Lake. In August 1891, many white Canandaiguans reported seeing a gigantic snake that could have been its twin, negotiating the lake's beautiful waters. Lakeside innkeepers claimed that sightings were routine.

Likewise a feature of legend, the Seneca Lake monster was spotted in 1899 by a boatload of Geneva citizens. This one came so close that a geologist on board believed he could identify the species—a *Clidastes,* a finned croc nightmare. It was of modest size, though: twenty or thirty feet long.

A bigger *something* was seen on Seneca Lake in the summer of 1995. A responsible, educated woman on a Geneva hotel porch reported seeing a monumental form leap out of the water, lunge like a column, and lapse like a tree back. The distance from her she estimated at six hundred feet. She was so shocked that other aspects of the experience are foggy. Another curiosity, which could be related, is the Seneca Lake drums—massive, seemingly geological percussions occasionally heard coming from the lake.

Lesser-known "underwater drums" are also reported in Cayuga Lake, which has its own serpent legends and reports. Old Greeny, the whites call the eel-like thirty-footer. According to the *Ithaca Journal* of January 5, 1897, they've been seeing him since at least 1828, and the most recent sighting we've heard of was 1974. Cayuga is the longest and widest Finger Lake and maybe the best candidate for such a critter. Since both these lake bottoms dip below sea level, the possibility of underground channels between them, the Great Lakes, and, hence, the oceans comes into speculation.

Also in Cayuga country, Owasco Lake was the subject of big snake reports in 1889 and 1897. A lakeside farmer reported a fast-swimming critter. Two men in a boat saw a fifty-foot reptile with a huge girth.

The 1828 pamphlet of David Cusick, Tuscarora historian, memorializes a gigantic serpent legend based around Onondaga Lake near Syracuse. Cusick had spent midstate time with the Oneida, among whom it was said that this stenchful, venomous critter attacked and killed two hundred people.

There are also the serpents of outrage, of offense to the Native people and the face of the New York landscape. In this sense, they seem projections of the collective unconscious, if not the earth itself.

During the late-1960s turmoil over the Kinzua Dam, Salamanca residents reported all the bogies of the Iroquois zoo in the natural landscape, including the Great Snake of the Allegheny. It had apparently climbed the banks of the river and done some foraging in the hills above the construction site. Most witnesses were offended local Seneca, but not all. Such an image was also reported at and about the 1930 damming of the Sacandaga Creek, creating the Sacandaga Reservoir in Saratoga County. Though this was far less of an offense to Native American sovereignty, it produced plenty of local paranormal folklore.

The Kinzua snake may not have left us. In 2001, a local college physics professor and two friends reported seeing a gigantic snake in the reservoir water below them. It may not have been a match for Godzilla, but it was at the least the biggest natural python in the world and completely out of place and clime. From hundreds of feet away, it was visible, forging its mighty course through the waves.

Asked for a material explanation for these critters in lakes that widely freeze over—like the Erie and the Champlain—and that could hardly support a single big predator, much less a breeding population, we are at a loss. We can only point out the significance of the big snake in both mythology and Jungian psychology. We will also say that these big critters are reported in other deep, cold, mind-defying places about the world, like Loch Ness. There is probably something going on that we haven't figured out yet, and whatever it is, it is not as simple as a "true or false."

THE THUNDERERS

In so many world mythologies, there is a clash between fire and sky forces, symbolized by explosive flame and lightning, and earth and water forces, personified by enormous snakes, reptiles, and lizards. We see this with the Iroquois.

One of the great Iroquois gods was called, in Seneca, Heno. Parker tells us that it means "he great voice," a pretty apt name for this power of the sky. So esteemed was this Thunder Being that it's not clear that he and the Creator are totally separate entities.

In a striking parallel to the Indic thunder god Indra, the Iroquois Heno keeps an entourage of thunder boys. At least some of them are probably noble orphans, lost children ruined by disaster or fate, saved from death and raised by another Thunderer. Sometimes the orphan of a chief favored by the Thunderers will be so honored. Others are love children of wayward Thunderers.

One of these Thunderers is pretty hard to resist when he comes in the form of a splendid young chief. He tells his mortal bride not to let their boy play with other kids. Just a slap from him would kill a natural human; he's that full of juice. Soon he goes back to the heavens and joins the apprentice Thunderers. Their jobs are to patrol the world on the lookout for evil magical beings.

They are also the Thunder Beings' spies, one each inside a thunder cloud, on the lookout for the otkon forces of the earth. But they're a frisky bunch. It's hard to see how anyone sleeps in their part of the Iroquois heaven.

Now and then one of these formerly mortal Thunderers comes back to the world with extra abilities. They're really good at straightening out a lawless village or a pack of witches terrorizing a community. Sometimes they pitch in with the Little People and launch a bolt or two at the giant underground buffalo when they are on the loose.

A former mortal raised and trained as a Thunderer is of special use to the high one. The head Thunderer himself and his mightiest minions can be scented a long way off by their enemies on the earth. Riding a cloud, packing a magical bow and a quiver of bolts, a mortal-born Thunderer is just human enough to fool them.

So strong was the faith that mortal children might be raised to the ranks of Thunderers that some Iroquois had no fear of lightning storms. "We have a relative there who makes the thunder," an Oneida woman told Hope Emily Allen in the early twentieth century.

THE MONSTER BEAR

Most feared of beasts in the magical Iroquois zoo is this big, devilish-looking critter. He isn't even built like a natural bear. Sometimes the alternative form of a wizard, he loves running contests, luring men and swift boys to bet their lives on a race. These marathons last from sunrise to sunset, and second place for the mortal means *dinner.*

Like Achilles, this demon bear has a weak spot on the pad of a foot. A spike or arrow here can kill him. In a tale or two the Little People take him down when they pity his human quarry, as does the right tricky hero with red willow weapons. Others whip him with wits or magic and maybe talk him out of a couple of his teeth—the bounty of generations. His bones are medicine. Just the powder in a potion makes a human unbeatable as a runner. Such a heavy totem is the monster bear that he's the focus of a whole dance society, one of the few mythic animals so used.

We don't know any Iroquoians who claim to have met the demon bear in our woods. There are enough Bigfoot reports to make you wonder if people are taking one for the other. There are those who think all myths are distortions of real events. Some suggest that Australia's dawn beasts live on in the dreamtime images of its own native peoples. Could the demon bear be a memory? Was there a natural parallel in the northeastern woods?

In his dreams, Edgar Cayce (1877–1945) raved that the Atlanteans shunned North America because its mammal predators were so nasty. Archaeology half supports the twentieth century's "sleeping prophet": The ice age's meat eaters were dreadful. There was the American lion, *Panthera leo atrox,* much bigger than lions of our day. There was *Canis dirus,* a loping assassin we call the dire wolf. The saber-toothed tiger was an ambush-slasher, and outsized hyenas and wolverines were stalking terrors. The top killer, though, seems to have been *Arctodus,* the giant short-faced bear, a rangy goon that ate not a thing but flesh and marrow.

Nicknamed the bulldog bear for its strange, pushed-in face packing so mighty a bite, Arctodus could run forty miles an hour. Its five-foot limbs and eight-inch claws could rake or club any foe. When it stood on two legs, its stubby chin would have rested on a basketball rim. The first Americans had to face it. Was this the demon bear?

Zoologists note the curiosity that big cats are spooked by the bark of dogs. It's not the dogs they dread; it's the sound, evidently like that of a once-real animal so fearsome that its chuffing cough resonates in the ancestral memory and sets generations of tigers a-quake. Some think it could only have been the short-faced bear. Little wonder if the Iroquois remember.

HIGH HAT

Many Native Americans testify without hesitation that there is some large, humanoid critter on the prowl in our wooded regions. Most of us have heard of the giant apelike being, variously named Bigfoot, Skunk Ape, or Sasquatch, that's been reported all over the United States. While its SAT scores may not get it into Duke, to the Iroquois it's no simple brute. To them, it is a very old, august being with the wisdom of the woods within it. Its power makes it capable of being dangerous.

Iroquois country has a surprising number of sightings, and a few beings in Iroquois folklore might be the same thing. The last of the Stone Giants fled to the Allegheny hills, and there may be some connection to High Hat, a bogie of the same region memorialized in the tales of Seneca storyteller DuWayne Bowen.

High Hat is a giant, bestial humanoid fond of the taste of human children. We seldom hear of him far from his swampy haunts. His oddest feature is a stovepipe hat that reminds people of Uncle Sam, Abe Lincoln, or the archetypal image of a white undertaker (tall, craggy, and lank). Not only Native Americans see him.

White construction workers spotted him at dawn and twilight during construction of the Kinzua Dam, usually at the edge of bodies of water. Abe Lincoln, they nicknamed him because of the hat. We wonder how old he is.

This man-animal morph makes us think of other shapeshifting beings, including witches, shamans, and even the Christian Devil. Around the year 2000, reports started surfacing from the Tuscarora Reservation about some big, speedy beastie they called Tall Man. It played high-speed hide-and-seek with reservation kids on ATVs, which calls for some pretty slick running. It also takes a lot to spook the Tuscarora.

"There's definitely something out there that can kill us," says Michael Bastine. "If you decide to take a shot at one of those, you better be sure it's a good one."

THE LEGS

One of the oddest bogies in the New York forest was this critter called the Legs. There may be no more descriptive term in the Iroquois psychic lexicon.

These legs are described as a body-sized pair of human gams with just a bit of torso visible. They may have an eye or two on them toward the hip or one apiece on each upper thigh. Sometimes there is just a single big eye, presumably at the navel. This cyclopean single orb sometimes bulges in and out as it studies its much-amazed humans. Other witnesses notice no eyes at all, just . . . legs.

It—or they—show up only after dark, typically running by you in the woods. Normally that's the end of it, but sometimes they drive you crazy running circles around you until you try to get away from them, collapse exhausted, and—more on that later.

In the early 1900s, Parker interviewed people who claimed to have seen the bogie in action. No one has ever been hurt by the Legs, but things don't usually work out too well for people who see them. It's often a forecaster of disaster.

While the Legs could probably clean up at the Special Supernatural Olympics, it's questionable exactly what their purpose may be. To many who have spotted them aimlessly running, the only point would seem to be getting a workout.

In reservation circles, Michael Bastine has heard a bit about these critters, and some of it is for adults only. It seems that a female version of these legs stalks philandering men on their way home, scares the devil out of them, catches up to them, and lays a big wet one on them in a way that must be imagined. This kiss holds its own distinctive, lingering redolence. *Ahem*. The wife will have no doubt about where he has been—for the last time.

Maybe this was part of the original picture of the Legs, and turn-of-the-century commenters were too prudish to say it. Maybe the spooky stems have a variety of pursuits. Forgive us for uncertainty on this point. As Arthur Parker observed sagely of the bogie, "No one has ever made a complete examination of one."

THE MISCHIEF MAKER

Like the shaman, the image of the Native American trickster has been immensely captivating to contemporary whites. Figures more or less like the trickster are found in literature and folklore all over the world, but the character seems nowhere as important as it is in Africa and North America.

The Iroquois have their own trickster-figure. His Seneca name is

Shodisko, and he's a lower-level deity. Sometimes called "the Brother of Death," this Iroquois Loki loves playing practical jokes on people, not always caring if they do harm. He has a vast array of tricks and can turn himself into many different forms.

While Coyote, the animal-like trickster, stars in cycles of tales among southwestern Native Americans, this figure seems of far less importance to the Iroquois. Even near neighbors the Algonquin make a lot more out of their own tricksters.

LONGNOSE

Many of the bogies of the Iroquois woods come with some lesson to teach. This seems to be a major point of some of the tales, maybe none more so than with Longnose.

Longnose is a humanoid critter whose tapir-style snout and other head-borne appendages—nozzles, tubes, and tentacles—remind us of fantastic, ornamental Aztec drawings. In some tales, this Longnose is a simple monster, a stalking nocturnal predator. One of the most terrifying sounds in the northeastern woods would be his snuffling calls behind you on the trail or around you in the trees. Thankfully, there might be only one of him, so he can do only so much damage. He's not often described as being above human size, but he's at home in the dark woods, and he's got some way of getting you if you're out alone.

In other tales, though, Longnose's terrible reputation is only for show, a game of adult storytellers. Longnose needs this reputation, since his main job seems to be to scare rebel teens and wayward drunks back to their homes at night. They get out and think about mischief, and then—the sounds drive them home.

DuWayne Bowen told a number of stories about Longnose. He felt them pretty strongly since he was nurtured on them in his own Allegany Reservation childhood.

THE GIANT MOSQUITO

Once upstate New York had formidable marshes. They sent up such hordes of mosquitoes that malaria was a serious plague, even for the incoming whites. Not until the nineteenth century were most of the marshes drained and managed.

In one of his occasional helpful moves, the trickster set up a smudge to get rid of the mosquitoes. All it did was tick them off. The whole swamp full of them pulled together into the form of one gigantic mosquito. The trickster made tracks. The beastie stayed behind, terrorizing the village nearby. It could drain a man with a single sting.

There are a couple of stories about the critter's demise, including enchanted arrows launched by inspired boys or girls. In one variant, the Creator sends one of his mighty eagles, which so shreds the brute that it reverts again to the hordes of tiny bugs that had made it. This story has many settings, including ones near Batavia, Syracuse, and Conesus Lake.

THE WITCH HAWK

While the cloud eagle of the Great Spirit is one of the most admired of supernaturals, the legends are full of big wingers neither noble nor good tempered. Some hover over swamps and lead hunters to doom. Some whip packs of warriors into a battle frenzy. Others circle fields and snatch babies from the backs of mothers. Some take the forms of gorgeous people and win love only to crush it.

This Witch Hawk is one of these shape-shifting figures. His namesake form is that of a huge raptor. Don't trust him, though. A pitiless fate alterer, he plays with lives.

Once he appeared as a young chief to a sultry Iroquois woman. Something otherwordly in him both charmed and repelled her, and she wedded a man of her nation. For years the Witch Hawk bided.

When the woman gave birth, he snatched her child and left her to die. Nurtured in the wild by the animals, the girl grew to be as lovely as the mother. Then the Witch Hawk came to her, too, in his mortal form. He took her back to her village where he knew she would launch a new cycle of love and disaster, thus doubling his revenge on her mother.

Fey and otherworldly as she was by then, cursed with this life between the worlds, she hurt so many others.

THE SERVERS

In Harriett Maxwell Converse's rendition of the Iroquois creation myth, two mighty, primal spirit beings dueled for the rights to rule the world. It's the Evil-Minded Spirit who wanted the fight, and the Good-Minded One wasn't silly enough to fall for the choice of weapons. The Good One pitched the Evil One into a cave deep in the earth, where he has to stay through all eternity. Only in spirit form can the Evil One return. He can do a surprising amount of damage that way, alas. And he has servants.

These emissaries of the Evil One are called the Servers, and they remain on Earth, in all its quarters. When they rise up to do the Evil One's bidding, it can be at any time and in any place. When they report for duty, they show themselves as mixed human and beast.

One wonders if American horror writer H. P. Lovecraft (1890–1937) might not have heard about these Servers. His tales featured echelons of morphing beings, all working for a common goal. It's another reason to be suspicious of altered animals.

THE EVIL-SOUL GATHERER

We can tell from their stories that the old Iroquois believed in several components to the psyche, the immaterial part of a human. The good and bad parts were detachable and given different destinations. Somebody needs to separate them.

Like many Iroquois supernaturals, Dehohniot—Seneca for "evil-soul gatherer"—is a zoomorph. He has human and animal forms. He's here to gather the evil parts of souls. One of death's emissaries, most of the time he courses the Milky Way, the pathway of spirits. You can't see him on the wing when he comes to Earth; from below, he's the color of the sky. When he settles outside a longhouse door, he has a wolf face, a panther's body, and a vulture's wings and talons.

The sick and the dying hear him clawing. He whines like a cat when the spirit is on its way. He snarls like a wolf when it makes him wait too long. But the Evil-Soul Gatherer can seize only the spirits of evil-hearted people, and most human souls have protectors. Even if the evil of a soul is overpowering, just a bit of good might be enough to save it—if it puts up a hell of a struggle as Dehohniot carries it across the skies. Once out of his clutches, other invisibles guard the path of the soul, guiding it to its future home.

THE UNDERGROUND BUFFALO

The center of the earth was thought to be a vast cave full of winding chambers, surging rivers, bottomless troughs, deadly gases, and steaming springs. By the time of the Iroquois, the Great Spirit had penned there many of the creations of the Evil-Minded Spirit. Banished, too, were evildoing mortal creatures: greedy beasts, venomous serpents, poisonous insects, and noxious weeds. The most dangerous of all the critters here were the great white underground buffalo. They are forces of primal chaos.

Little would be left of the upper world if these titans got loose from under it. The main duty of the mighty and elusive third tribe of Little People, the Hunters, was to guard the doors of this underworld.

Once in a while, a couple of these mammoth buffalo-beasts stormed out, and a mad pursuit commenced. Some underearth elves tried to hunt or herd them. Others raised the alarm to the clouds, a sunset so red and unique that all Hunter fays in the world were put on guard. Whenever you see one of those faerie skies, you know somewhere the chase is on.

Late one afternoon in June 2010, I looked to the south outside my East Aurora house and saw one of those odd, mixed skies. Clouds coursed the watery horizon like icebergs in the North Atlantic. All above hurled into the gray of coming night, but out of the turquoise bed and miles-distant whiteness forged one truculent cumulus, striding like a promontory that dared the waves to beat. A stray beam from a sun in some quarter of the sky hit him and lit him such a martial pink that he stood alone in the billows and aerial waves. I wondered if the underground buffalo were at their game in the Alleghenies.

WHITE DEER OF THE GENESEE

In his code, Prophet Handsome Lake mentions a pair of deer representing a new species. The buck is spotted white and the doe so striped all over her back. These deer are the sacred creations of the Creator. Not only is it commanded that these animals are not to be killed, but no "pale invader," no white, will ever see them. Cornplanter says these deer were killed by one of the prophet's jealous rivals. Maybe so, but a few of the faithful have reported seeing them at night in the woods.

There may be a place you can see these deer today, on an old army base along Canandaigua Lake. The white deer are interpreted as a pair of albinos that miraculously survived and reproduced. Maybe so. Fenced in as they are, they are far safer from predators of all types. Or else maybe the times are changing. When the whites start to value the teachings of the Native Americans, the world may be entering a new phase.

9

Talking Animals

This whole day have I followed in the rocks,
And you have changed and flowed from shape to shape . . .
W. B. YEATS, "FERGUS AND THE DRUID" (1893)

SPECIAL ANIMALS

There are stories about talking animals in many world cultures. The ones we encounter in European tradition are diverse as you might gather, but they are almost exclusively folkloric and literary. No one runs into them anymore, at least that I've heard of. And when they appear in a tale or story, the narrative almost always bears an explanation for them: They are enchanted people, much of the time, or even supernatural beings who can take many a form. Sometimes they're just special or magical animals.

We come to other talking animals in twentieth-century reservation stories and recent paranormal reports. These have a distinctly unnatural cast; they are curiously animal-like humans or the reverse. They play things a lot closer to the vest. They don't stop and explain themselves.

Few upstate Iroquois doubt that talking animals like these can still be encountered from time to time. Now and then we may catch them at it. Some of them are familiar horses and cattle, maybe even beloved dogs and cats. Always their speech is in the native lingo, never any European tongue. You doubt us?

If you walk by a pasture at night and see farm animals that don't appear to have noticed you, be still. You might see something that astounds you.

Keep an eye on your cats sometime when they don't know they are being watched. Do they look like they are having a conversation?

Keep a window open as you let your dog out at night; see if another is waiting, and look and listen as quietly as you can. Do they draw close and nuzzle like they are conversing?

Maybe a witch or wizard is disguised among your trusted animals. Maybe your pets had hidden talents all along. But if you live in the Northeast and like those long nightly hikes, even around your own village, be courteous to whatever approaches you.

"You don't want to walk by and see two horses talking to each other," said Seneca storyteller Duce Bowen. "You don't want to have an animal ask you why you're out and invite itself home with you." Decline courteously, we suggest. Better yet, stay in on those nights that don't feel just right.

WITCH AND SHAPE-SHIFTER

As with Celtic wizards, one of the distinctive powers of the master witch was shape-shifting: the ability to become another being, usually an animal, and continue to think as a human. Most of the wacked-out animal forms we encounter in Iroquois story and report were thought to be dangerous. When they weren't apparitions projected by the witches or the back-off signs of a negative site, they were thought the alternate forms of great witches, most of whom had a favored critter into which to shift.

"Spirit of Victory" by Tom Mullany (1989) in Joseph Davis
State Park, Lewiston, New York

Still, tradition doesn't give us a reason to presume that witch and shape-shifter are one. For one thing, there are shape-shifters who aren't witches. For another, there are witches who don't shape-shift. The occasional worker of a love charm or a hex may be technically a witch, but no metamorphosis is involved.

Some good power people can be shifters, too. The shamans, forerunners of the great medicine people, were thought to take animal form. The most exceptional contemporary medicine people are thought to do it, too, but the transformation could be psychic. (The material body lies at rest; the astral form's at work.)

But you can spot a shifter. One of the oldest pan-Amerindian strictures concerning these people-animal forms is that they can never fully hide what they are. A shape-shifted animal will always show some feature of what it used to be. Even the ancient rock art of the American Southwest depicts animal forms with human feet. You just need to look closely enough.

The morphed human will have an animal tooth, ear, or tail. The full animal will walk funny, even on two legs like a human. Fully morphed animals may turn to each other and talk in human poses. Pay attention. This may be your one edge on them.

But these altered animals don't stop and explain themselves. All you can know for sure about them is that the matter is wondrous strange. And people still say they see them, all over upstate New York.

The Witch Dog
(Late Nineteenth Century)

A woman suffering with a wasting disease told her family that every night something peered in her window. Some thought it was just the delirium of her ailment, but often when the ground was soft her husband found big dog tracks outside. Once after a snowfall, he followed them to the dirt road where they got lost in other tracks.

The morning after that, an old woman was among the friends who called. She lived in a little house near the creek and asked about the wife so suspiciously that the husband wondered how she knew so much. When she left, his wife was worse.

That night his wife screamed in her sleep: "She is looking at me!" The husband jumped up, saw nothing, and thought it was another vision. Outside, though, he saw widely spaced dog tracks under the window, as if the animal that made them had run away. A neighbor saw a dark, fast-moving form leap a fence and run into the trees toward the creek.

In the morning, the husband followed the tracks of a big dog to the creek. On the other side were human footprints, leading to the house of the old woman. That afternoon, the old woman came again, and the husband accused her of witchcraft. She acted shocked, but her performance fell flat. No member of any Iroquois nation would be that surprised by the idea of witchcraft. "Stop witching my wife," the husband finished. "I'll fix you if you don't."

That night, the husband camped in the woodshed. Sometime after midnight he heard an ominous huffing and dog feet coming from the trees. He looked through a crack in the shed and saw a huge hound looking in on his sleeping wife, its paws on the windowsill. Its snout glowed in the glare that pulsed from its jowls with every breath; its spittle lit like molten metal. It had picked a bad night to come witching. The husband had his rifle.

It was sleighing time, and the moon was out. Lots of people saw the witchdog hurdle the fence as the husband fired. They heard a yelp and the sound of a tumble on the other side. They saw something taller and two legged run to the nearest cabin and jump through the window. In the morning, they saw blood spatters in the snow.

Three days later, the old woman was found dead in her bed from a bullet wound. Everybody was sure she had been a witch. Her intended target recovered.

The Twilight Walker of Marble Hill
(Late Nineteenth Century)

Between Syracuse and Utica is the town of Oneida where utopian socialist John Humphrey Noyes (1811–1886) set up the first of his alternative perfectionist communities in 1848. Ever after called the Oneida Community, it thrived for three decades and was the flagship of a handful of others in North America. Noyes was far from the only white to find inspiration on Iroquois ground. The small bit of Indian land he picked had an otherworldly rap sheet before he got there.

A short walk east of Noyes's massive mansion is a high ridge called Marble Hill. It's just south of the eastern edge of the village called Oneida Castle, named for the fort once here. In the late 1800s, the area of Marble Hill was awash with reports of a strange twilight walker. Tall and slender, he carried a satchel and wore a stovepipe hat. That chapeau makes him sound suspiciously like a bogie the Allegany Seneca personify as High Hat.

Anyone walking about at night might see him, though they might not hear him. He walked noiselessly. Few got close to him, probably for the good. Those who did saw the two big animal ears partly covered by the hat. Some noticed one normal foot, in a walking shoe or boot. The other was the hoof of an animal. If Iroquois tradition surely held an indigenous devil, this might be one sign of him.

An Oneida farmer on Marble Hill had a bit more of this character than he wanted. His cows were developing an unwelcome habit of wandering off at the end of every day. One dusk, their owner was looking for them when he met a tall longhair who could only have been another form of this stranger. The minute the pair met, the twilight walker commenced launching such verbal abuse that the two fell into a terrible fistfight. They clinched, and the sturdy farmer got the edge, twisting one hand solidly into the stranger's mane and, like a hockey fight, using the leverage to belabor him with the other. Suddenly, as if bespelled, he fell asleep.

He woke by daylight, his joints stiff and his clothes wet with the dew. He noticed, though, that his hand was firmly tangled in a patch of the coarse marsh grass the Oneida call the devil's hair.

CHANGELINGS

Some reservation folk talk these days about changelings. They seem to be using this old European word to mean shape-shifters, shamans or witches who take on animal forms, but with an odd twist. These changelings seem never to be a single whole critter. They are either animals that are complete morphs of others or people with critter features: fox tails, bear ears, horse hooves. We keep open the possibility that they could be shape-shifters, spotted in the process of shifting into shape or careless about shifting back.

We'd like to know how long this word *changeling* has been in use among the Iroquois. We can't tell if it's an English word being used for an old Iroquois folkloric critter or if the term has infiltrated reservation folklore through contact with whites and been misapplied. We suspect the latter.

The changeling of Celtic folklore isn't a being who changes forms. The word means something *exchanged,* usually a fairy baby left in place of a stolen human one. Loud, sickly, ugly, ravenous, and developmentally challenged, this changeling is a world of hurt for its adopted parents. There are usually two ways to be rid of it and get the mortal child back:

either to make the changeling think you're crazier than it is by doing something silly—like making tea out of brewed eggshells—or scaring it by threatening to abuse it. ("I'll boil the water for the baby's bath," the mother calls cheerfully to the father. "You get the steel wool and bleach to rub him.") It bolts out the window like it could fly, and the mortal child is heard cooing in its crib.

In one description, these Iroquois changelings, from the front, look like people, normally dressed for the rez. But the back half is animal-like, with tail or fur. The surreality of this description makes us wonder if the whole thing is an illusion.

The Iroquois aren't the only ones who see these altered critters. I met a white trucker who once cut through the Tonawanda Reservation every morning on his way to work. One misty dawn, he rounded a bend and caught a look at something strange: a human figure in a long coat and hat, with a big, bushy animal tail billowing out behind. It froze just long enough for him to see it, then darted back into the woods. He never took that shortcut again.

In another description, a changeling is an altered animal but with frightening powers. In the early 1990s, one of these popped out on winding Sandhill Road and chased a man on a chopper, one of the biggest men on the Tonawanda Reservation. People referred to him as "that big mean biker dude." It was his turn to be intimidated.

He could see it in his rearview mirrors, a forty-pound animal with fox ears and a tail. It chased him upright, though, like an enraged fireplug. He ran stop signs and sped around bends. It gained on him at fifty. He didn't see the last of it till he was off the reservation. Maybe it was a changeling, out to get him, losing its power on white man's land. Maybe the medicine people sent it to him as a message: *cool it.*

There are parallels all over North America. Around the upper Great Lakes are legends about *bearwalkers.* Obviously witches in their theriomorph forms, they pace as shaggy humanoids that huff and puff smoke and sparks. Author Tony Hillerman (1925–2008) recounts the southwestern mythology of the *skinwalkers,* who can move pretty fast.

Late one night a white trucker saw one of these pull alongside him on a highway. A lean, grinning Native American man under a coyote-head hood kept up with him on foot and motioned him to pull over. He didn't outrun the figure till he reached a terrifying speed down a hill.

SHAPE-SHIFTERS

For the old Iroquois, shape-shifting witches usually took the forms of forest critters like wolves, bears, and owls. These days, it's often livestock or pets: dogs, horses, cats, and pigs. In these forms, they stalk and curse their human enemies. They also get hit, whipped, or shot. Somewhere a human usually turns up with a matching wound.

Duce Bowen talked of shape-shifters like they were real. "Have you, or anyone you know, ever seen one of these things in the process?" I asked him once.

"No shape-shifter will ever let you see them," he said firmly. He seemed to feel that as recently as his own childhood there were people known to use this power. It's probably a fading art. As of 2004, he knew no one he suspected, at least none he would talk about. Maybe we only hear about these folks near the end of a life, after many occult feats.

But the old-timers can recognize them in their final shape. Any time you see an animal behaving unnaturally like a person—walking on its hind legs or talking—it's a sign of supernaturalism and usually trouble. Even an animal that looks normal but displays a humanlike sense of purpose—perching outside a home and staring fixedly day after day—is probably either a wizard in disguise or something sent by one. Even a natural animal out of place might be such a critter. Horses grazing in a neighborhood that lacks them. Sheep wandering without an owner.

In the 1930s white writer Carl Carmer (1893–1976) got a couple of Tonawanda Senecas talking about shape-shifting. They gave him an earful.

"There are a good many witch stories about humans changing themselves into animals," Jesse Cornplanter admitted. "I could tell you the names of two or three who actually do it if reports around here can be believed."

Cephas Hill, a college-educated plant foreman, recalled that once, in his boyhood, strange pigs were heard rooting in the shed of Willy Abrams, a Seneca man who had just died. An old woman told young Hill that he'd better watch out for them, that they might be witches. She said this as if they might have had something to do with the death and had come back gloating on the funeral day. Young Hill gave them both barrels of his shotgun, and they ran off squealing. Later some younger children who had been with him at the time told Hill that they'd seen a man by an abandoned cabin in the woods picking buckshot out of his backside. "Witch!" they yelled, and off he ran.

Cornplanter remembered an old man who went to the Lockport Fair on a hay wagon with some Tonawanda folk. He wasn't ready to leave with the rest, so they left him. Later a pig came trotting along behind the wagon. As it passed, the driver gave it a crack of the whip. The pig stopped and looked at him with an eye so evil that it gave him the creeps. When they passed the old man's cabin an hour later, his lamp was lit, and on the porch he sat. He never said how he beat them all back.

"I knew an Indian fellow who took a girl to a dance who was not his regular girl," said Hill. On the way home, he and the girl were following a path along the top of a ridge when a galloping horse came up behind them. It nearly ran them over. As it went by, the lad shot it in the shoulder. It whinnied and ran into the woods. Soon after, his regular girl's mother died. When they laid her out for burial, they found a bullet wound in her shoulder. No one knew how it got there.

The notes of Irving historian Everett Burmaster tell us of one early twentieth-century witch who lived on the Cattaraugus Reservation. She could transform herself and spent much of her time in a pond as the consort of a huge black snake. This reminds us of the Olympian

Zeus who amused himself by getting it on with his conquests—usually mortal stunners—in the forms of different animals, sometimes even transforming them as well so as to deceive his jealous wife Hera. The Greeks didn't tell us which animal does it better, but in Seneca country the snakes must have had the mojo. As if a testament to the witch's eternal flame, when she finally died and was buried, a witch light or ga'hai was seen over this pond. I think I know where that pond is, or at least used to be. It's not far from Irving, New York, and on a point always reputed to be haunted. It was her house in which Burmaster found his witch bag.

ALTERED ANIMALS

On October 12, 1870, the *Livingston Republican* ran an article about a strange beast seen by several different people. It was large, bipedal, and, from the description, a bit like a crazed kangaroo. The residents of Livingston County would have recognized such a beast, though, and this one's temper was hardly that of a vegetarian. It attacked a number of dogs, rearing on its back legs and striking out with its forepaws. A few weeks later, another article claimed that the beast "literally tore the feet and ears" off the hound of a doctor in the Livingston County town of Moscow (now the village of Leicester). On the last day of 1870, the *Nunda News* reported what had to be the same strange animal, spotted again outside Moscow. The accounts make no mention of critical details: its skull size and shape, its tail or lack thereof. They describe its motion as virtual hopping and its paw prints like those of a dog.

In 2003, there was a flap in Niagara County. Near the Tuscarora Reservation is a campground around which people reported seeing bizarre animals, including deer walking on their hind legs. The white folkloric imagination latched on to the idea of radioactive waste dumps and mutating wildlife. There has been some deplorable contamination at many points along the Niagara and radiation has been the deus ex machina—sudden artificial plot device—for movie monsters like Godzilla. But the critters have parallels.

They see things like this on Ga'hai Hill near Salamanca, where images of deer—sometimes gutted—have been reported, rearing up like people and walking on their spindly rear legs. Are these the altered animal forms of the Iroquois variety?

One of our favorite Native American bogies is a sinister, silent little devil from the lore of the American Southwest. Hillerman skillfully retells the stories of these critters, assassins from the spirit world who take over the bodies of animals and can appear in any natural form. The favored ones seem to be small, like owls, rabbits, and foxes. Killing the animal will only kill the host, and the bogie will show up in an equivalent version soon enough. Though they terrorize through their inexorable stalking, they usually kill through simple bad fate: accidents, sickness, and the like. They may walk on their hind legs like humans, and it's no good sign if you see that. The only sure way to tell them is by the eyes, flat and unreflective like those of dead fish. It's presumed they are animated by the *chindi,* malevolent spirits of dead humans.

There was the story of a rich Navajo family that had asked a heavy favor from an old shaman and crassly refused payment. He set this sort of altered-animal demon on them. At first, only the old and sick died. Then accidents and ailments struck the middle-aged. The young ones met with the shaman. He agreed to think things over but died before he had a chance to undo his work. Most of the family was gone by the time the story was recorded.

These southwestern chindi can be dispatched for personal reasons, but they seem to be impersonal beings, however sinister they might be to their targets. They go where they're sent; they address matters of balance, and they have in some sense the force of nature behind them. This outline is similar to some Iroquois beliefs. I've asked my confidants if the Iroquois have a supernatural assassin like that animal filled with the chindi. Occasionally there's been a telling look, but no one has wanted to talk.

Once I brought the subject up to Duce Bowen, and he didn't say much. He did look at me like I'd come across something I wasn't supposed to know. Even Michael Bastine got a little terse. "Yeah, they got . . . something like that."

The last story of my second book *A Ghosthunter's Journal* is "A Question of Levels," a tale about the curses that accompany reservation politics and the altered animals that sometimes embody them. It reminded a fellow I know of something he'd experienced.

When this gent was a kid, he used to play at a hill in the village of East Aurora called Old Baldy. Not far from a known ancient Native American settlement and the site of reputed earthworks, this was a hill whose prehistory is incalculable. He and a few other kids encountered some kind of animal that seemed put together out of many others. It probably weighed forty or so pounds, but it was a platypus of the Northeast Woodlands, an interspecies Frankenstein composed of impractical and unrelated parts. Even its behavior was unnatural. It scared the kids. One of the mothers arrived by surprise and shepherded them all away. They talk about a mother's instinct; this one was in no mood to analyze the situation years later.

When the same witness was in his twenties, he was hunting with some buddies about two miles from the former site. Again they encountered an altered animal, one whose actions were incomprehensible. It danced, it pranced, it frolicked. Its gestures made no sense along any patterns of animal behavior, and something about the encounter spooked the hunters. Afraid even to shoot at it, they withdrew in a hurry, leaving the animal to its distempered celebration.

The Big Dog Changeling

These days, the Iroquois do most of their infighting over "gas and gambling," in the words of a Seneca friend. On one of the reservations north of Buffalo, a woman got uppity in council. While hanging laundry later that week, she noticed a big dog in her yard. Its profile was strange, and when it turned to look at her, it had partly human features. Its face was that of a Native American man, with long droopy ears.

She ran in the house, locked the doors, and pulled the shades. She thought it might be a changeling, a shape-shifter who had chosen to come in this form. One thing was sure: It was a dangerous situation. These things had been known to haunt people until they died.

She stayed inside all night. She waited till afternoon before looking out. The monstrosity was gone. She almost doubted herself, but the neighbors reported hearing a godless howling all that night, like that of a soul so tortured that it turned angry. The sound had no parallel in anyone's memory, though the elders didn't seem to be saying all they thought. Maybe this was one of their changelings, sent on another mission.

The Horse on the Roof

On the night before they moved out of their trailer on the Tuscarora Reservation, a family of women—two sisters and their daughters—heard some terrible banging on the roof. It sounded like a heavy being crashing and rolling from one end of the metal surface to the other. The mother leaped up, grabbed her .22, and came out shooting. Nothing was found, but the next day some neighbor boys who had heard about the ruckus came over and inspected the roof. On it were the prints of horses' hooves. No one let the little girls look up there.

The Strange Old Man
(Early Twentieth Century)

When they were boys on the Allegany Reservation, Duce Bowen's uncles were always getting into trouble. Their neighbor was a solitary old man many suspected of being a power person. The boys set out to goad him into a display.

They played pranks on him all summer. They were peeping toms, hoping to catch him in some magical practice. They threw rocks at his house at night, hoping to make him steam out after them in an altered form.

One night, they looked in the old man's windows and saw him asleep in a chair, the paper folded across his lap and his lower body in shadow. One of the boys swore his legs were hairy, the feet hoofed like those of a goat. They left him alone for a few weeks.

One night shortly after they'd started back at it, they heard a big racket behind their house. They ran out expecting anything, but found only a little black-and-white dog poking around the back porch. They shooed it off and thought little more of it.

A few nights later, they heard their neighbor's screen door open and figured it might be something too good to miss. They snuck through the trees and saw the old fellow come out, stretching as if he'd got up from a nap, and head toward the outhouse. It seemed a golden opportunity to throw rocks at the roof or lock him in with a stick across the latch. They watched him pass by the structure as if he were going in. They crept to it.

They were just by the door when the black-and-white dog they'd seen the night before tore around the little building. It was tiny, but its fury was terrifying. It had the eyes of a devil! Before they could think, they were scampering home in a fright, the little demon snapping at their ankles. They were out of breath when they got inside.

"Come to the window," their mother said. They saw the form of their aged neighbor strolling back up the path toward his house, smoking his pipe. In a minute, his lights came on.

The boys learned a lesson. They started to look at people with new respect, even outcasts who seemed powerless. They were also good friends to their old neighbor in the coming years, showing as much energy to help him as they had formerly spent teasing him. Duce Bowen always wondered if this scare was what straightened them out.

DuWayne Bowen heard this tale from the grandmother of the girl who would become his wife.

A Walk Home
(Mid-Twentieth Century)

A Seneca soldier came home after World War II. He'd seen some of the hottest action of the Pacific. Friends had fallen all around him, and he hadn't been scratched. His first night in Salamanca started a party that wasn't done till every one of his relatives had him over for dinner. The first week was for brothers, sisters, and grandparents. By the second week, he was visiting cousins. He was a hero to the kids and couldn't leave without playing with them. After that, he told the elders all about the war and the Pacific. It was almost midnight when he started for home.

His cousins urged him to stay the night. His route home would take him through Witches' Walk, they said. But he laughed. Salamanca held nothing to scare anyone who'd been through the war. He put on his army coat and started walking.

In a few yards, he was wondering if there could be anything to worry about. The neighborhood was dark, as if the Seneca knew a witching night. But it was warm and still, and the moon was bright. The young veteran kept walking.

At one point on a dirt road near the Allegheny River, he heard voices from a pasture, speaking in Seneca. He heard the word for apple. He kept still and heard a phrase that sounded like Ak hide nay *("Be quiet!"), and then in Seneca, "There's someone on the road." He froze.*

"Let's go to the other end of the field," another voice said.

"OK," said the first. "The apples are better there, anyway." Out of the darkness behind the trees came two horses. They walked peacefully across the pasture.

The soldier ran home. His parents had forgotten to leave the porch light on. He was in such a hurry to get in that he banged his head on the door.

One of our favorite characters from the tales of DuWayne Bowen is this "man the animals talked to." Bowen always said that the fellow had been real and that he had known him.

The Man the Animals Talked To
(Early Twentieth Century)

In the 1930s an old Seneca man moved to Salamanca from one of the other reservations. He made his way doing odd jobs for a few bucks and the occasional meal. People got to know him through the work he did. He spent most of his time with his animals, several cats, and a pack of dogs. He was a curious character.

He walked wherever he went, a couple of dogs always with him. The understanding between them was uncanny. In his presence, these pets seemed more composed than typical animals. There wasn't the frisking, the sniffing, the reflexive behavior common to cats and dogs. There was a sense of mission about them.

People passing his house often saw him in his rocker on the porch, animals always near. Sometimes he spoke to them, always in Seneca. It scared people more to hear that he paused to listen. Others swore they saw the other animals lean in when a single one had its say. People wondered if these were witch animals, but there was no report of trouble from them, and when the old man wasn't around they acted like well-mannered pets, not wizards in disguise. Word got out that he could talk to animals and that he was the man to call whenever an animal was sick.

Many could recall him leaning near the head of an ailing horse or cow as if conversing with a patient. He usually made up a potion, and most often the animal got well. He never accepted a fee for work like this.

People never visited him after sundown. The lights in his house were never on at night as if he could see in the dark like an animal.

The Dark Gray Stallion

One summer in the 1930s trouble came to the houses on the hill.

At all hours of the night people heard horses' hooves on the roads and on the wooded paths behind the houses. Soon they started seeing a strange horse. One old woman reported coming out on her porch at night to find a well-groomed, dark gray stallion, standing still and looking at her with a more-than-natural focus. She screamed, and it trotted into the woods.

Her husband came out a night or two later for a pail of water and saw the same horse staring at him. The night after, he looked out and saw it stalking the house. He shined a flashlight through the window at it and it took off.

The community was worried. The old-timers considered this a witch that had come among them in the form of a horse. They were about to call a council of the elders when the man with the dogs paid a visit to the old couple. Some of the neighbors joined in. Everyone told him what they had seen and heard. When they were through, he told them they might see the horse again and that it would be bolder. He didn't say much when they asked him how he knew.

Two nights later, a loud thump on the side of the house woke the old couple who had first seen the horse. The woman looked out the kitchen window to see the critter looking in, a foot or two away. She let out a yell and it vanished. The next morning, the man with the dogs came back, heard them out, and decided to stay with them that night.

Around sunset he and four of his big dogs came back. He carried a bag, a walking stick, and a hunting knife. He and his dogs sat on the dim back porch and waited.

Around midnight, the dogs perked up their ears. Sure enough, it was the sound of hooves coming down the slope on the path that approached the house. The dogs ran out silently in four directions, and soon the man and woman of the house heard a commotion. They came to the door and looked out on the scene.

Barking, snarling, and snapping from all directions, the dogs had surrounded the horse. It stomped, snorted, and whinnied fiendishly. It reared and lashed out with its hooves, but it could not break away from the dogs. Their owner came out and spoke a single sharp phrase in Seneca, which made the horse stand still and look at him. The man walked into the woods, followed by the horse and its escort of dogs.

The old couple waited on the porch, the man holding his shotgun. In an hour, the four dogs ran back to the house, quaking and looking back into the woods as if they had seen something terrifying. The couple worried that the witch horse would be coming back to finish whatever work it had with them. Then the dogs perked up their ears again as if they had heard something and ran back into the woods. The exhausted old pair went to sleep, hoping for the best.

At the end of the next day, the man who talked to animals was on his porch as always, smoking his pipe and rocking in his chair, animal friends beside him. He never said anything about his night in the woods. No one saw or heard the witch horse again.

A neighbor, though, recalled something strange on the morning after the incident. He had been driving to work and passed by an old church just as the sun was rising. He spotted the man who talked to animals coming out of the woods, four dogs alongside him. A canvas bag on his shoulder held something heavy enough to make him totter as he walked. No one could guess what was in the bag or what the medicine man's dogs had seen that scared even them.

The Allegany Seneca still remember the night the dogs cried together. Even Duce Bowen couldn't give us a date, but it was a cold one in the autumn, most likely in the late 1930s. It was a night when all the dogs of the valley and all the communities around it set up a keening, as if motivated by some collective grief that they could voice in no other way. There had been signs of it the day before.

The Night the Dogs Cried Together

The man who talked to animals had been working for a family, and when he was done, he was asked to look at a dog. The inseparable companion of the boys, the big hound had lost interest in anything, as if he were sick to his belly. The animal man spent a few moments near him on the back porch.

"Something strange could happen tonight," he said to the family. "I can't tell you much about it yet." On his way home, he stopped at other houses. Sure enough, all the dogs had been listless for a couple of days, and some had started to whine with no apparent cause.

The man who talked to animals had a lot to think about on his walk home. He fixed meals for himself and his animals and sat a long time with them on the porch. Then he took his usual chair, two cats on his lap, the dogs in their spots. He fell asleep that way.

Two hours after midnight, he jerked awake to the sound of a dog howling somewhere outside the house. He went to the door for a look. All the dogs in the neighborhood, inside or outside, were carrying on just like it. Their varied tones, pitches, distances, and volumes made an awful, surreal sound that absolutely haunted the valley. His own dogs came close to him and commenced their own whining, but they calmed when he spoke to them. He told them in his Seneca tongue that they did not have to cry out to the world, because he knew their hearts already. Soon they were still.

He put on his coat and went out. The pale moon, the silver clouds, the deepest turquoise sky, all looked down on the valley of crying dogs. Their songs told him a story. Tears were on his cheeks when he turned back into his own house.

The next morning a group of people sought him out and asked him about the strange night. Tears came to him again when he started to answer. He told them to prepare their hearts, because a big war was coming, bigger than any that had ever been.

"Somewhere across the seas, events are in motion, and it's finally too late for

them to be turned around. Many of our sons will leave us, and many will not be coming back. The dogs know this, and they cried by the doors and windows because they love their families, especially the sons who ran with them as boys, who will be with their families only a little while longer."

The Dogs Who Saw Too Well

One summer night in 1954, two young men were coon hunting near the Wyoming County town of Gainesville. Both were already veteran woodsmen, and with them were two blueticks—medium-sized hunting dogs.

The woods were misty after a day of rain, and they felt unsettled. Every snap and click in the glistening trees sounded like something stalking the two youths. Still, they were armed, and perhaps too young to get as scared as they ought to.

At one point, the dogs tore off howling into the underbrush. The two hunters followed the racket to a medium-sized tree that stood alone in a circular clearing. The dogs thought they had something, almost certainly a raccoon. They were coon dogs, and they were usually right. The ample flashlights revealed nothing but branches and leaves.

In hunting, this experience is called "a false tree." Old raccoons are good at scooting up one tree and crossing branches into another. The ruse works with dense trees and young dogs.

The tree was the first problem here. Not even a squirrel could have hidden in that one, and nothing the weight of a raccoon could get out on its thin branches. It stood a long way from any other trees, too. The two friends looked until they were sure the dogs were wrong and hauled them off, by their leashes, still baying for their imagined quarry. They had never seen veteran dogs so sure of themselves at such an obvious false tree.

A change came over both those dogs almost immediately after that incident. They grew afraid of the woods at night and never hunted again. Our storyteller wondered if the dogs had indeed chased something up that tree that was still there when they left, simply invisible to humans—or whites—and if it had left a parting lesson for the dogs who could see so well.

ANIMAL CLANS

The precontact Iroquois had to kill animals to live. Without the life of the animals, they would have had none of their own. This led to a mix of admiration and pragmatism. Life was revered, even as it was taken. It was not to be taken needlessly. It was also believed that each animal in the woods had something vital to teach every human.

All Iroquois nations have animal clans, and everyone born among them or adopted into them belonged to a clan. All Iroquois nations have three clans in common: wolf, bear, and turtle. Other clans varied by nation, with the Onondaga having the most (nine), and the Mohawk and Oneida having just the basic three. The animals are based on their domains: the earth (bear, wolf, and deer), the water (beaver, eel, and turtle), or the air (snipe, hawk, and heron). Clan affiliation is always matrilineal, determined by the mother; if you don't know your ancestry, or no one knows it, you are automatically one of the turtles, sort of the default-clan for the Iroquois. As if the spiritual bond between human and animal could even be physical, it was considered a sort of incest to marry within a clan, even of another nation. Eel Clan Cayuga were uncomfortable with the idea of marrying an Eel Clan Onondaga.

Undoubtedly, this clan affiliation was another bond of unity among the Iroquois nations. Seneca Turtle Clan members would fall in quickly among Oneida Turtles. It also encouraged good behavior. Showing cowardice or scurrility was letting down one's clan, as well as one's family, village, and nation.

There was, of course, a lighter and highly imaginative side to this. Members of these clans were thought to represent or take on some of the traits of the totem animal. This led to a host of associations and supplied the lifelong fodder for quips and routines. "Come in if you're fat," a member of the Wolf Clan might call at a door upon which someone had knocked.

This clan thing is still a factor. Most Iroquois even living off the reservation know their clan, and they act accordingly. Mohawk members of the Bear Clan do not kill bears. The fine Buffalo State College scholar Bill Englebrecht (author of *Iroquoia*) heard of a Turtle Clan member who stopped his car on the shoulder of a highway to carry a turtle safely across.

While the Iroquois we've interviewed don't directly believe in reincarnation, so strong was the theme of identification with the clan animal that it might be presumed to go on into another life.

Ron Schenne of West Falls remembers visiting the Canadian Six Nations Reservation as a kid in the 1940s. His dad had become friends with Chief Jamison, and whenever they visited him, they brought him American coffee and hot dogs, which he much preferred to what he could get locally. The chief's son Arnold was about Schenne's age, and the pair used to hunt together. The shooting could get a little wild. "You know, when you're a kid with a gun, you shoot at anything," said Schenne.

At his Erie County home raptors were considered a nuisance, and Schenne was paid to shoot them. It was a reflex to pop one in a tree. While he and Arnold were out hunting, they spotted an owl in a nearby tree. Before he could fire, the son of the chief reached over and flipped the barrel up into the air. The shot soared into the sky.

"That could be my grandfather up there," said Arnold. His father's father was of the Owl Clan.

THE TENDER OF THE FLAME

The old Iroquois hunted to live. They loved life, though, and had a code by which they took it. Their tales tell us that living according to this code both took and gave great virtue and displayed such respect that even animals destined to lose life were grateful to humans.

If there was a single thing that set mythologist Joseph Campbell (1904–1987) on his course, it was an Iroquois story often called "The Grateful Animals." Campbell was spellbound by the theme of the hunter chief killed by humans and rallied to life by animals. Though he had killed many of their brethren, each animal of the wood mourned him like a sibling, each giving something of its nature to bring his body back to life. Maybe they still have their ways of showing appreciation.

A Story in Himself

Every spring, the men of a western New York family fish and camp in Quebec above the Kahnawake Reservation. By 1998, their guide had become a trusted friend. He's a story in himself.

A completely self-sufficient woodsman, he lives only with his pet companion, apparently a full-blood wolf. He makes the money he has by leading tours and selling tools and jewelry made from natural products. He barters for all else. When he takes people on tours, they abide by his almost religious code: Take only what you'll eat or wear; leave nothing but footprints. It isn't for everybody. Many a tour he cuts short because some high-rolling slickers can't learn respect. Once he pointed a raft of them toward land and told them to take their money and get lost.

Every day of this trip, a father and son went out with their guide on the lake in kayaks, catching their dinners and brooding into water and sky. Often they were so far apart as they fished that they couldn't see each other. Always they left a huge, slow-burning fire by their campsite so they could find it. This beacon was vital. Evening comes early that far north, and even April is winterlike. A night without shelter was a life-or-death situation.

As they met in their kayaks at the end of one day, they realized that they could hardly see the fire they had left as a beacon. A faint snow in the air was almost a mist, and the fire seemed likely to go out before they reached their cabin. They paddled desperately toward their last glimpse of it, to no avail.

They met a mile from shore and agreed on a plan to find what was left of the fire. The father would paddle well to the left of their last sight of it; the guide was to head right. Then both would cruise along the shoreline back toward the middle. The youngest would head straight toward it. Coals could still be glowing, and whoever came near might rekindle a beacon. Still, they didn't have much hope. Land, water, and sky were a marginless twilight.

The son saw nothing when he was a hundred yards from shore. He cruised back and forth along the waterline and was about to double back again when he saw the flare of a fire.

Shocked and gladdened, he drove his kayak toward it. He was not mistaken. The fire was roaring in surges and then falling dim as though an invisible bellows was at work. When he got closer, he spotted what could have been a human figure beside it, arms and body heaving, fanning it with a cloak or blanket so cumbersome that it could have been bear or buffalo hide. The figure's size, build, and long hair made him think of a woman. He called out with a laugh.

As he neared shore, though, their savior drew back. As she left the glow, he thought he saw the forms of waiting animals, escorting her into the trees and darkness.

The youth whipped the blaze into an inferno, and his father and their guide soon found it. He told his story. The father was amazed; their guide was mighty quiet and didn't say much about what he was thinking. He went to bed early.

Late that night, the young New Yorker saw the guide and his wolfy friend go out, as if for a rite or meditation destined to be private. It was hours before the pair returned, and nothing was said about it in the morning.

The Men by the Fire

Early one Sunday evening in August 2004, a young East Aurora man drove by the lakeshore not far from the Cattaraugus Reservation. A few hundred feet off the road, he saw the glow of a fire and human forms around it. He followed a couple of sets of tire tracks in sandy soil through the grass, hoping to see what was going on.

A dozen Seneca men between seventeen and forty sat around the fire, drinking a variety of their own spirits. They greeted Ken when he pulled up, and he decided to visit. He brought some of his own Scotch whiskey from the car, and the ice seemed fully broken when an observation of his sent a laugh around the circle. "Ken-man, you're cool," the oldest of them said. From then on he was Ken-man.

Ken thought he was fitting in, but soon noticed that most of the laughter and conversation came from the older fellows. He couldn't help but study one young longhair who'd said nothing since he arrived. A lean fellow with the graceful build of a boy, he couldn't have weighed a hundred forty pounds. He fell in upon himself, shaded his features in his mane, and muttered.

Soon he glared at Ken whenever he spoke as if he had no right to have an opinion, join a laugh that circled the fire, or share the lakeside air. Once he spat after Ken said something, and others spoke to him in Seneca. He said something short back and looked at Ken.

"We having some kind of problem?" Ken said. The young man rushed at him, and the two clashed chests in the glow. Ken's weight threw the lad back. The oldest of the men, the one who had first used the name Ken-man, said something sharp to the young fellow.

"What's wrong with you?" said Ken. Others tried to hold the whooping, snarling lad, gaining frenzy with each second like a Scandinavian berserker. The young Seneca fought through the arms, closed in again, and clutched with fingers like claws. There was something more than crazed about him. It was hard for three men to hold him. In the struggle, his torso showed. ("Talk about a six-pack, he had a twelve-pack," Ken said later.)

A brawler himself, Ken had been the aggressor against bigger men. Something in that moment was terrifying. "What's wrong with you?" he said. "I'm not fighting you."

"Run, Ken-man," said the oldest, struggling. "Get out of here! He's proving himself on you."

"Run!" yelled others. Ken strode quickly to his car. A shadow fell near him as his hand was on the door. He spun, lashed out, and landed a perfect right to a jaw.

It was the young Seneca. Sense left the astonished eyes while still open.

Not every man gets all his weight into a punch. Ken is one of the ones who can do it. That tag should have dropped anyone for hours. Still, the blow felt odd. The young Seneca's jaw had felt like something fixed to a leather saddle. The body had none of the give of other bodies he had struck and fell to the sandy soil tense like an animal's.

Ken started the car and was turning onto the path when something pounced on the convertible roof, seeming to grab it at four points like a lioness tackling a buffalo. It had to be the young Seneca, trying to tear through the top.

Ken backed up, stopped, and turned, tossing the body over the side. He tore down the trail that he thought was the way he had come in. It was not. It actually *went along the beach, curved a mile around marshy woods and thinned till it was invisible. The car hit something sandy and slowed. Ken got out and stood in the headlights, studying the situation. A shadow came out of the trees fifty yards off and flowed toward him.*

It was the young Seneca. He'd run a mile or more in three minutes through black woods and come into the headlights, shirt in tatters. He bounded toward the car.

Ken started rocking and flooring his vehicle. Just as the young Seneca reached for a door, one of the wheels caught traction and spun the car onto hard dirt. Ken took off, leaving the young Seneca running again, watching his form recede in the glow of the taillights. It took a surprising time to be clear of him. He came to a paved road that led to Route 5 and made it away with no more incidents. He woke the next morning with a swollen hand and a knuckle that would turn out to be broken.

When he reflects about that night by the fire, he remembers things the commotion distracted him from noticing. Some of the other men, too, fell silent and lolled back. A time or two he thought he saw a pair of canines gleaming in the light and something clawlike in the position of a hand. What would have happened if he had stayed? Some nights he wonders if the dark form could still be running and if it will someday find him.

Granny Wolf

Mike Bastine remembers a woman, an old storyteller from Allegany, who knew someone who could shift her shape. It was her grandmother.

When she was a girl, she used to like sleeping over with her grandmother, but many a time she woke late at night with the feeling she was alone in the house. When she checked it was always true. Where had her grandmother gone?

When she was older, she tried to stay awake to see her grandmother come back. She never succeeded, though once near dawn she heard someone come in and go straight to her grandmother's room. That afternoon as she played with the other children, she found wolf tracks all around her grandmother's house.

One night when she heard the sounds of her grandmother leaving on the other side of the house, she looked out her window. She believed she saw the form of a wolf lope off through the moon shadows into the trees.

One morning a short time later, her grandmother didn't get up. The girl found her in bed with a wound in her leg. There was blood leading from the window to the covers.

"Don't worry, dear, I'll be all right," said the old dame. "I just need to rest awhile."

The girl asked about her leg. "Darn it. I was walking in the woods and there was this sharp stick out. Got me right here. I'll be all right."

The little girl took a breath. "Uh, Grandma. . . . One time when you left at night I'm pretty sure I saw a wolf run into the woods. I've been meaning to ask you about that for a long time."

At first the grandmother dismissed the matter, but the girl wouldn't let it go.

"I always knew you were a smart little girl," she said. "Well, I have to tell you something just for you. You're right, honey. There have always been some of us who've gone around like that at night. I'm one of the only ones I know any more who still does it.

"But that's how I keep an eye on the neighborhood and make sure everything's all right. You can't go all over the yards and woods like that like a person. I make sure people are treating each other right, and if I have to get involved, well, I do it my own way. Sometimes I wonder why."

She groaned. "That old Mr. Jamison would just drink all his money away and there'd be nothing left for the family. Somebody has to scare him into keeping home at night. Mary Snow is out at all hours with her boyfriend and just about anything could happen to those little kids of hers if somebody didn't keep an eye out. And if Davey Green ever hits his wife again, he has to know something's coming for him.

"Now this story is just for you," she finished. "If this got out and around in the community," she shook her head, "it wouldn't be good. It wouldn't be good at all."

She rolled over and groaned. "That's all for now, honey. I have to get some rest. You run home and tell your mom to come over later. Boy, it's lucky that darn farmer's such a bad shot, or he'd have got me for good."

The Dog and the Wolves

A Seneca man and his dog lived in a cabin far from a village. They got along well and fairly with each other, certainly no worse than people and dogs ought to. One evening, the dog ran into a pack of wolves outside the house.

"We've been watching this place for weeks," said the leader. "If you know what's best for you, you'll ditch this guy now. We're coming back tomorrow night to knock him off when he brings in the water. Then we'll eat up all his game. The same thing will happen to you if you get in the way."

"If I were you, I wouldn't try any of that," said the dog. "You know, that guy blows smoke and fire out of his lungs every night. You want to mess with a witch like that?"

"You are some kind of a liar," laughed the head wolf. "Still, it's worth a look, if he can do a thing like that. But don't forget what I said. If we catch you here tomorrow, you'll get the medicine he gets."

"Don't forget what I said," said the dog. "Make sure you're watching tonight around sunset. That's when he shows off his power."

All went as the dog expected. That night the wolves returned, looked in on the cabin, and saw the man enjoying his pipe, apparently breathing fire. They presumed him a great wizard and took off running. His dog sleeping comfortably at his feet, the man never knew of this.

We should always be good to our dogs. We will never know how many times they have saved us.

THE ANIMALS TALKING

While you're waiting to hear from the supernatural talking animals, Mike Bastine will tell you it's important to listen to the natural ones. You shouldn't need to be a medicine person to hear them.

"It kind of started with the geese," he commenced in a recent talk. "When I grew up, in the spring and the fall you'd hear them migrating. You'd look up in the sky and they were the tiniest little dots. So high up in the air. Now they're flying just over the tree line. And they're everywhere. Those Canada geese, they're a nuisance. You can walk right up to them.

"It surprises most people to find out that coyotes live around us almost everywhere. They are the shyest, most secretive animals. You only see them when they get hit by a car or when they're mangy and they're almost dead. Even then you might not know it. They look so much like dogs. Coyotes are getting aggressive out West. I've heard of it happening around here.

"And there's the red-tailed hawk. When I was a kid, if I heard the whistle of one of those, I'd run out and try to find it. You couldn't get within half a mile of one. Today, they just perch there on a telephone pole and look at you. You can get right under one.

"There's the blue heron. It used to be that as soon as you saw one, he'd fly away to a point so far off that he couldn't see you. Pam and Bailey and I were by this farm pond, and five feet behind them there was a blue heron standing in the water. *I don't believe this,* I said to Pam. I had to get our camera out and take a picture.

"One time we were on our way to Springville. There was this pasture behind a little fence with thirty turkey vultures on it. We pulled over and turned the car off. Pam said, 'What were those?'

"I said, '*Turkey vultures.*'

"She said, '*What are they doing?*'

"'Waiting.'

"'What for?'

"'Dinner.'"

He turned to his audience. "What do seagulls eat? Coyotes? Vultures? What do they eat? They're scavengers. Their assignment in life is to clean nature up. Nature isn't preparing—making their presence so well known—for no reason. If things don't start to change, I'm kind of thinking there's going to be a major die-off. That's what they're saying to us. That's what they're here for. They're going to clean up all the stuff.

"If I repeated to you what Mad Bear said to me toward the end of his life, some of you wouldn't be feeling so comfortable. He wrote a poem, *A Warning to White-eyes.*

"There are too many levels, too many indicators. . . . What they're all saying is that we humans better pay attention. We better start watching. The stuff we're doing to the world, it's not going to be sustainable for very much longer."

The Altered Beasts

It could be that all the mythology of the psychic zoo is based on fleeting paranormal encounters, seasoned richly by storytelling. But I think these critters exist. I am pretty sure I saw one.

It was a gaudy dusk in September 1995. I was driving from the bike trails at Allegany State Park down into Salamanca. I was where the road curves downhill and to the right, just before the hill falls away, throws open the river valley, and lays Salamanca across it. On the right twilights at this point, the lights spread out and shine the whole city up. On that one, the sky arched before me with a low red-gold gleam like a segmental pediment, etched and burnished over the entrance to a temple. As if the shield of Achilles lay behind the horizon and tossed its rim behind the sun's corona, I might have visualized creation and prophecy had I stayed long enough to catch the moment. By the road I saw a strange animal.

On my left between the road and tree line was a critter about the size of an adult groundhog. I gave it a hard look in the clear twilight. It had the features of many other animals, and its eyes were drilled at some spot on my side of the road.

It stood comfortably on its hind legs like a bear, and its ears, eyes, and snout were bearlike. It was too small, though, for even a cub. Its dangling, shriveled front paws were those of a dog or rabbit. Its chest and skull were flat like a badger's. My best guess was that it was a morphed woodchuck, with pert bearlike ears. Its stare was the giveaway, trained with human focus across the road and right through the mountain. I'd never seen a look like that, and I drove through its laser gaze as if I didn't exist to it. I even looked into the trees on my right to see what it could be watching.

I considered turning back for another look but saw in my mirrors that it was already gone. I filed it as a simple curiosity. Any natural animal could disappear quickly. It was only when I considered where I was—a haunted region in Seneca country—and thought of the legends that it occurred to me that I might have seen one of the alter-beasts.

I'm not a naturalist, but I know the animals of the Northeast and have an excellent visual memory. This image is in my mind. I don't know what it was. I've never seen an animal like it.

The Choirs of the Shape-Shifters

An East Aurora woman spent childhood time on the Tonawanda Reservation in the 1980s. Her mother worked up there in some capacity that called for her to be "adopted" into one of the Seneca clans, which put her into a position of special trust. When the woman I interviewed was a young girl, she and her family spent a lot of social time up there, too, not all to her liking.

"Why do I have to come up here and spend the whole day at a festival?" she always used to ask. "I want to stay home with my friends. I don't even like corn soup." But she saw and learned a lot.

One evening a clan mother drew a number of her guests together outside her house, including the young woman's family. "It's time for you all to go," she said.

The East Aurora woman, then a girl, remembers asking why. "The shape-shifters are out tonight," she was told.

Their hostess cautioned them to walk only in the light between the buildings and their cars, and not for any reason to walk into the woods or off any road. From there they were to drive safely and not to stop or get out for any reason until they were off the reservation.

This was so different from anything she was taught in school. The girl was ready to laugh. "How do you know they're out?"

"We can hear them. Listen." Everyone fell silent and strained their ears into the wooded land around them. To this day, the woman swears she remembers the sound of the shape-shifters howling, the eeriest thing she has ever heard.

I'm always fascinated to talk to nonpsychic people about paranormal experiences they've had. I take them down to the last details. "What did it sound like?" I asked her.

"It was like . . . a choir. Choirs. In the night."

"Choirs?" I said, I'm sure with a wrinkle of the brow.

"Yeah. Choirs of people, all howling together like wolves. Like fifteen human voices. Mostly human voices."

THE SONGS OF THE DOGS

Some readers might find it silly to think that human speech could reach any animal. They did not see Michael Bastine set our newly rescued West Highland terrier onto his lap and talk to her, an hour after my companion and I had adopted her. Michael had dropped in on us by surprise. He tends to show up when he's most needed or can do the most good.

After years as a breeder, this dog had been discarded after dropping her last litter. Her belly was still distended. She was also undernourished and had no trust for human beings. "You're going to have a nice home here," Michael finished up. She had kept up eye contact with him as if every syllable registered. It may have been the first tenderness she had received in her life.

The dog was the only animal domesticated by the old Iroquois. They lived with dogs and had mixed attitudes to them. The dog was an animal that would work with humans to hunt other animals, a little bit of a traitor in that sense. It was also dependent on people. Bears, deer, and other forest animals needed nothing from people. To some Iroquois, it seemed shameful to see the village dogs snarl and worry among themselves over bones and body parts, the remains of noble animals who gave their lives after struggle so that people might live. There was no dog clan.

But no other animal was this kind of messenger between the worlds of men and of animals, between village and forest. It would be natural to think of dogs as intermediaries of worlds in other senses, between the earthly and the spiritual. It may also be natural to think of them as human companions, after the life of the world.

The Iroquois sensed, as do we, that the bond between a human and a dog can be something marvelous. It's thought that for most of the Iroquois, dogs were regarded as psychopomps, guides for human spirits to the afterworld. Other Iroquoians like the Huron may have believed that, when dogs died, their souls' course was alongside that of the human souls, the Milky Way.

The Onondaga, oldest of the Iroquois, have a tradition about their dogs. If it's true, we may see our own again after they have passed.

For the Onondaga, at least in one traditional tale, the human soul after death undergoes a period of wandering in a stormy night world. After passing through a hazardous forest, he or she comes to a vast abyss, the last barrier to the grounds of the Happy Hunting, the land of the ever blessed. For the soul fortunate enough to get this far, the only passage is across a massive log, which two gigantic doglike beings hold steady at each end in their teeth and claws. The bridge is easy footing if they keep their hold, but their focus is wobbly. It's then that the voices start to chime and call. They are the souls of the dogs the humans knew in their lives.

If these souls say things like, "He loved us, he fed us, he sheltered us," the mighty beings grip the log hard, holding it steady for the passage to the Land of Souls.

But if the voices say, "He starved us, he beat us, he drove us away," the mighty beings lose their attention. The log teeters, and the human soul tumbles into confusion.

If you cannot find it in you for the sake of the world to be kind to all life, be kind for your own sake to your animals. You never know when they will be speaking for you.

10

The Little People

He used one argument which was sound, and I have never forgotten it. It is the fact that it is not abnormal men like artists but normal men like peasants, who have born witness a thousand times to such things; "it is the farmers who see the fairies."

G. K. CHESTERTON, CONCERNING AN
INTERVIEW WITH W. B. YEATS

THE WEE FOLK

Traditions of diminutive, magically powerful human beings are found in many parts of the world. The wee folk that come first to the mind of the average American are certainly the fairies of Celtic tradition, but many Native American societies had ancient, elaborate, and apparently indigenous traditions about their own Little People—as did the Iroquois.

In the colonial period, the Iroquois Little People were thought to be powerful and real. Culture keepers—elders, storytellers, historians, and medicine people—revered them as forces of the natural world. They were envisioned as humanlike devas somewhere between the status of human beings and that of the spirits or the gods.

Today's Six Nations folk regard the world with twenty-first-century minds, but not all of them believe that the Little People are completely folkloric. For a contemporary Iroquois, the experience of seeing them or their work is rare and awesome. It's like what witnessing a UFO or a mystery monster would be for a typical white. The reason so few whites know the power of this tradition today is because so few Iroquois will talk about it in their presence.

In the 1950s, Edmund Wilson remarked upon the reluctance of the Iroquois to talk about their ancient mysticism. That goes double for the Little People, still among the most sacred and private traditions of the Six Nations. Do not ever press any Iroquoian about this subject. Some take it far more seriously than you could believe.

Late Allegany storyteller Duce Bowen was a friend of mine, and he wouldn't say a word about the Little People with me. Even Michael Bastine won't say everything he knows, especially about the Little People.

"I don't own this knowledge," he said years ago—before I got it—when I pushed him too hard on a certain point. "Even though I happen to have it, it's not my property to give away." Maybe this was the reason the Celtic Druids didn't set their wisdom to writing: It was meant to be kept for those to whom it was sacred and shared with only those who were ready. Or maybe the Little People could be listening. We aren't publishing anything that wasn't published before, or anything even remotely off-limits that wasn't told to us by whites.

I started my publishing career writing about the supernatural history of western New York. As a ghost-story collector, I have interviewed thousands of people about their sightings. One of the most interesting patterns that comes up across New York state is how often the whites see the Little People, reporting them first as ghosts.

White Little People reports come in a few styles:

- *Site-specific encounters.* New York's ancient site tradition has been lost. There are probably sites and regions all over the state once associated with the Native American fairies. Most of the Little People places anyone remembers are on reservations. Whites who visit these areas sometimes report seeing them.
- *The imaginary friend.* Many American children report conversations and encounters with beings no one else can see. The syndrome of this "imaginary friend" is well known to psychology. (Sometimes the classification is expansive enough to include personified toys, but this seems to be pushing it.) Some of these encounters are mere sightings, but sustaining relationships do develop. Typically the phantom pals these children see are their own size or smaller. Some of them in upstate New York sound just like the Little People of Iroquois folklore.
- *Ghosts.* When I interview an eyewitness about an apparition, I ask a lot of questions, including specifics of the visual qualities. When I come to the size, a very few witnesses do a double take to remember that the apparition was unnaturally small. Sounds like they had been seeing Little People. Little wonder in Iroquois territory.

Everywhere they exist in world tradition, the Little People have three general traits:

1. *They have a connection to nature.* They are of the woods, lakes, and hills. They move easily among the animals and speak to them in their languages. They guard and honor special places in the world. They help the seasonal cycles and other processes of nature.
2. *They are associated with the human dead.* It's not as if they *are* the ancestors in any world tradition, or that the spirits of our

dead go to join them. It's more as if the fairies and the dead share the same indefinite realm where they occasionally cross paths. The otherworld, apparently, is big and indistinct enough for both of them.

3. *They have a special interest in human children.* They come to children, they protect children, and sometimes they take children away.

THREE NATIONS

The invisible Little People, called the Jo-ga-oh by the Seneca, are nicknamed the Jungies today on many reservations. They were thought to live in three tribes, whose names in Seneca were the Ohdowas, the Gahonga, and the Gandayah. Each tribe has its own role in the world, so distinct that the attempt has even been made to place them into European categories such as gnomes, elves, and fairies (which are not absolute and settled terms even in the world that gave them birth). Each Iroquois language has different names for the tribes, but other essentials seem to hold. We know them best from the Seneca tales preserved by Harriet Maxwell Converse (1836–1903) and Arthur C. Parker.

The Hunters

We don't see them much anymore, "The People of the Underground Shadows," "The Hunters," or "The Little Folk of the Darkness." These *Ohdowas* (in Seneca) are mighty, kindly sprites who carry out the will of the Good-Minded Spirit. Their territories are the sunless realms under the earth. They are the doorkeepers of hell.

Were the underworld a concentration camp, these Hunters would be its guards, watching the passages to the upper world and keeping down the monsters penned there by the Good-Minded Spirit. They are especially on guard against the Great White Buffalo. Not much would be left of the upper world if these chaos beasts were running loose.

When the stampede is on, the shadow hunters thin the herd. When one of the creatures breaks into the daylight, the sunlight elves send up a red cloud as an alarm, and the Hunters take up the chase above ground. To the old Iroquois, such an inspiring, discordant sky was a sign of the Little People on the job.

The underworld has once-earthly prisoners, too, ones who transgressed against the natural order: stinging, slithering, and venomous critters; cats who kill more than they can eat; witches or wizards in animal forms—all rounded up by the Hunters. It's their role to know that their proper places are here, but many still hope to break out. There they would poison springs, blight trees, and cause plagues.

While the Ohdowas are skilled at almost anything, it's hard for them to hunt most natural animals who have gotten used to their scent. This is why the members of the Iroquois Pygmy Society save their nail clippings, sew them into bags for hunting medicine, and leave them outside or toss them over cliffs for the Little People. The hunter fairies make a broth out of these human parts and bathe in it to disguise their scent. In gratitude for favors like these, the Ohdowas often warn human communities of trouble. Sometimes they join their elfin kin above ground at nightly festivals in the deep woods. We know this by the rings left behind in the grass.

The Stone Throwers

The Gahonga, the Seneca "stone throwers," live in caves beside lakes and streams. They care for the natural balance, freeing fish from traps and leading them to deep caves if people take too many. They're as mighty as they are small. They can uproot trees and pitch big rocks, and they often challenge human warriors to tests of strength. Sometimes they visit people in dreams or visions and take them back to their dwellings. Associated with water, they are particularly common in the Mohawk territory by the Hudson, the Mohawk, and the Champlain.

Iroquois elders and medicine people appeal to these spirits in times of drought. They head far from the villages and look in mountain streams until they find signs of the Gahonga: little cup-shaped hollows in the soft earth at the edge of the stream. They scoop these out whole, dry them in the sun, and take them back to the lodge. These are the "dew-cup charms" that kick-start other fairies to work in the ground or garden.

The Stone Throwers are thought to be the ones who come most often to people. They like pranks, but not ones played on themselves. If you offend them, you better find an elder and placate them immediately with the proper ritual.

The Plant Growers

By far the favorites of the Iroquois are the Little People of the Fruits and Grains sometimes called "the Plant Growers." Their Seneca name is Gandayah. They hide with the seeds and shoots in their long winter beds. In spring they whisper to the stems to wake and show all growing things the way to the sun. They watch the fields, ripen the fruit, and lead the crops to their autumn harvest. They quell blights and disease. These little folk of the sunshine are the universal friends of the Native Americans.

The strawberry is their special plant. Its first ripening is the sign of their work and a call for thanksgiving to the community. The priestesses of the Honondiont, or the Company of Faith Keepers, hold meetings of praise at night, make strawberry wine, and save a special vintage for the singers and dancers. The old ceremonies were probably held around the time of the solstice and Midsummer's Eve, a high fairy night in Europe, too.

Some old tales tell us that when the fruits first came to earth, an evil spirit being stole the strawberry and hid it underground for centuries. A stray sunbeam found it at last and released it to the fields of the day. The Gandayah are on guard against another captivity.

The Gandayah visit the longhouse in animal guises. As robins, they bring good news. As owls, they give warning. Since the tiniest bug or worm could be the bearer of "talk" from the Gandayah, the Longhouse folk never uselessly harm little creatures. One of the old Iroquois proverbs says it best: "The trail is wide enough for all."

When the Iroquois Little People come to mind, many presume that the influence of the whites could have been involved. After all, few Iroquois stories saw print until the golden age of Iroquois folklore (1880–1925) when some fine white story keepers and researchers were at it and the Iroquois were still talking to them. By then, the white influence had had three centuries to permeate Iroquois storytelling.

The Little People are older and indigenous. We think this for several reasons.

One is that a European influence is not needed for the existence of fairy-lore. It's developed all over the world. Another is that apparent tributes to the Little People—tiny tools and weapons—have been found in Iroquoian graves that far predate the coming of Columbus. Finally, Iroquoian speakers in far parts have their own Little People traditions. The Cherokee, for instance, have their own Little People legends, and they broke off from the ancestors of the New York Iroquois thousands of years ago. The Huron/Wyandot waged wars against the Iroquois, and they have similar lore about the northeastern woods.

It was the Little People of the Fruits and Grains who set the rule that the Iroquois should save their fantastic tales for winter nights in the longhouse when nature was at stasis. Storytelling could do harm at other times of year. Suppose a poor beast were to be spellbound by the wondrous tales and stay listening too late to stock its winter home? Birds might forget to migrate, and burrowers skip their digging until the ground is frozen. Even the vine over the lodge door might forget to change with the cycles of the year. True storytellers obliged, lest a bird or bee hear them and take word of it back to the Gandayah.

But this rule may not be so strict for the greatest human storytellers, maybe because the need to hear is so dire in the human world. Duce Bowen gave a session one night in July 2002, and it was real stories he was telling. Surely the Little People will let you slide, whatever time of year you read these.

IMPARTING A RITUAL

So often in Iroquois supernatural tales, the human characters ask the beings they encounter, "What sort of dance can I bring back?" It would seem that one of the most significant features of any individual mystical experience was the ritual it might impart to the nation. Many tales serve as origin myths for cultural rites, one of the most solemn of which is the Dark Dance.

The Dark Dance
(Traditional)

Long before the coming of the Europeans, a Seneca boy looked down from a cliff in Zoar Valley and saw a strange scene. Two tiny boys at the base of a tall tree were firing needle-sized arrows at a big black squirrel. Their shafts didn't even reach the creature's perch. The human lad launched his own bolt from above, dropped their quarry, and climbed down to find the fairy boys examining the big mortal arrow. They were delighted when the Seneca boy presented the critter to them. The "buffalo squirrel" was their nation's favorite prey. They invited him back to their village.

The human boy joined the family of his tiny hosts and shared their meal. No matter how many times he drained his thimble-sized bowl, it never ran out of corn soup. Their berry juice was intoxicating, and their sacred pipe hallucinogenic. Soon he barely noticed the difference in their sizes. The father of the boys told him about the three nations of the Djogao, or the Jungies. Then the drumming and the dance started, and through the smoke, the forms of many Little People joined them. They told him to learn the dance well enough to teach it, since it could bless his nation. He stayed what seemed like a few days and saw the rite enough times to remember it.

When he got back to his village, he found he'd been gone so long that everyone had given up hope of him. The boy was a leader, though, who soon had his village ready for the rite. True to his promise, the tiny father came to sit beside him during the first Dark Dance, though only the boy could see him. The Dark Dance is still held by the medicine society named for it. In honor of the invisible Little People, it is highly private and done in almost total darkness. No one but the celebrants knows what it is like.

Some Who Met the Stone Throwers
(Traditional/Contemporary)

A Seneca lad of seven was out playing with his toy bows and arrows. He longed for the day that he could use the real ones.

He was beside a stream, taking aim at birds and bugs, when he noticed something coming toward him in the water. It was so fast and small that he thought it might be an otter swimming with its head out of water. When it neared he was shocked to see that it was a tiny canoe with two men in it, each with a miniature bow and a quiver of finger-long arrows. They paddled right up to him.

"Like to trade your bow and arrows for mine?" said one of the little men.

"That's not much of a deal," said the mortal boy. "Look how small they are."

"Not all big things are better than little ones," the other paddler said. "You'll learn that someday about life." He took aim and fired straight above him. The arrow took off like it could hit the sun and vanished into a cloud. The tiny pair paddled off.

The boy told his grandmother about the event. "Don't be so quick to judge things by the way they look," she said. "Those bows are enchanted. With that bow and quiver you could have had any game in the world."

The Ways of the Stone Throwers

Orphans are the heroes of many Iroquois tales. Centuries before Columbus, a scrawny orphan boy was cared for—as it were—by an uncle. He was so neglected and slovenly that the other kids called him Wrapped in Crap. No wonder he played by himself.

One day he was at the riverside when one of the Stone Throwers paddled by and offered him a ride. The canoe looked too small to seat him or float him, but the paddler was persuasive. At last the boy set foot in it, and the world seemed to shift. With a single mighty stroke, the little rock thrower swept the canoe off the river, up in the air, and into a cave on the side of a cliff. The boy went with it.

Inside was a whole community of Stone Thrower folk, who started their dance and song of welcome. The boy stayed for what seemed like days. He learned their songs, their dances, their mysticism, their rites, and their stories about other tribes of Little People.

Time came for him to go. He was given a bit of each bird and animal—a wing, bone, or claw—and told how to use it in ceremony. If things were done right, corn, beans, and squash would grow at his bidding. Berries and fruit would ripen, harvests would be full, and flowers would bloom as he walked the land. Even as they chanted to him, he floated down to the valley from which he had come. The vision of the Little People faded, and he was back where he'd started. Things had changed.

He'd been gone for years. He was a man so big and good-looking that folk in his village didn't know him until he called them by name. He taught them the ways of the Stone Throwers, and they've passed through the generations. Hunters and fishermen know their customs. Girls hear the stories from their grandmothers and sing the songs to their dolls. The words echo still in the chants of the medicine people.

Three Little People in a Stone Canoe

Living Native Americans in Mohawk country refer to this Stone Thrower group as "real ugly when you look at them." Though not ill tempered, they have skinny, fishy faces.

While canoeing on the Sacandaga Reservoir, some of Abenaki author Joe Bruchac's Native American friends were shocked to find themselves overtaking three Little People. They usually move faster in their stone canoes than any human boat and even slip under the water when they choose. This trio was clearly up for a little fun with the humans.

"Look at those guys behind us," said one of the Little People in the Mohawk language. "Somebody's got to say something to them. It's only polite."

"We don't want to scare them," said the one in back. *"I'll do it. I'm the best looking."* He turned to the humans and grinned as if posing for his picture. His face was narrow and streamlined like that of a fish. The stone canoe submerged smoothly, taking the little man and his grin with it.

"He was real ugly," said Bruchac with a grin.

NINETEENTH-CENTURY LITTLE PEOPLE

Little People were seen often in the old days, reported Onondaga Wesleyan minister Thomas La Fort in the early 1900s. Often they were at work helping the Iroquois, he said, but they had virtually disappeared since the coming of Christianity. White author William M. Beauchamp asked his old friend what he made of that and did not record for us the answer.

M. R. Harrington (1882–1971) found few nineteenth-century Oneidas who doubted the existence of the Little People. When they wanted little favors from the fairy folk—say, a good round stone for a hammer or a corn crusher—they placed offerings of sacred tobacco under flat stones by creeks. The next day they went back to the spot of the gift and often found whatever they had asked for a few feet away.

Arthur Parker interviewed Seneca adults who reported sightings of the Little People as very rare. Hearing some of the sounds they made, such as the "water tomtom," was far more common. When an initiate of the Pygmy Society hears these distinctive drumming sounds, he knows the Little People are calling a council. He heads back to the village and gets his crew together for rites of their own.

Parker found many Iroquois children who reported seeing these Little People as they played in the woods. They were about a foot high, and moved so fast that it was hard to be sure what they wore. Some dressed normally for Native Americans of the day.

Author David Boyle informs us that the Little People most often reported in Canada were about three feet high and pale yellow in color. They were fully clothed even in the hot weather. This made them quite different from the summer-clad fays of the Iroquois.

White New Yorkers who report seeing Little People do not find the dress remarkable. They either fail to notice clothing or describe it as "a little old-timey." It's as if the Little People's dress is a couple of generations back in time of the society of the observer. This pattern was fairly common in the British Isles during the nineteenth and twentieth centuries. The Little People are always out of style. They have better things to worry about.

Dealers of Fortune
(Traditional)

La Fort remembered stories about the Little People from his boyhood. He told Beauchamp an old tale about a poor Onondaga man hunting deer, hungry and miserable at his post in the woods. He had to keep at it. Times were hard, and his wife and children were in need. He prayed to the powers of the sky and forest to help his family. He had been still for hours when he noticed a tiny old woman standing right in front of him. How had she come upon him so suddenly? How had she found him?

She said she could make him happy. She offered him his choice of rewards: gold, silver, or successful hunting. He took the hunting. If she was surprised, she didn't show it. "Enjoy your venison," was all she said. He took a deer shortly after she left and was a fine hunter for the rest of his life.

Why the Girl Looked Back

In 1899, La Fort told Beauchamp a story his grandmother had told him. One morning when her grandmother was a girl she was out walking with one of her own grandmothers. A strange-looking tiny woman appeared out of nowhere and spoke. "You've been a good woman your whole life. Now you're unhappy because you can't walk like you used to. You can be young again if you do what I tell you. Have your grandchild keep walking straight ahead, and don't let her look back till I give the word."

The grandmother sent the little girl ahead. The fairy woman took a bone comb out of her coat and said, "Comb your hair with this as far out as your hands can reach." The old woman did so and found her hair getting longer and darker. Even her skin changed color and tone the more she combed. A year turned back with every stroke. She stood straight for the first time in decades. She must have laughed.

Maybe that's why the girl looked back. The fairy comb powdered into dust in her grandmother's hand, and in a breath or two, her joints were stiff again. "My dear child, you have destroyed me!" she cried, raising her arms to her head, suddenly gray again. She dropped dead on the spot.

The Largesse of the Little People

A Seneca family recounted a strange happenstance to Edmund Wilson about one of its late uncles, probably from the early 1900s. As a boy of ten, he'd disappeared into the Allegany woods for about four weeks. When he came back to his family, he had no recollection of where he had been or how the month had been spent. He was pretty well cared for, for a kid who'd been in the woods that long. His clothes were clean. His hair was even combed. Everyone presumed he'd been taken by the Little People in order to save him, as they were thought to do, from some illness or danger. To the end of his life, the matter remained a mystery.

Little People to the Rescue

Seneca author and storyteller Leo Cooper (1909–1976), known as Hayendohnees, tells of an instance from his twentieth-century boyhood in his book Seneca Indian Stories. *One of his neighbors took a shortcut home after a night of drinking. On the railroad tracks, he ran into a couple of gents with whom he was not on good terms and came out the worse for it. Knocked cold, he was left lying on the tracks where he was likely to be frozen stiff or hit by a train. A flock of Little People tugged him awake and saw him home. The frost was still on his coat when he woke the next morning. Doubtless he had rendered some service either to the natural environment or to the Little People themselves.*

In 2006, a white friend of ours got friendly with the staff at the Seneca Nations Museum in Salamanca. They fell to talking about folklore of all types, and the museum guide confided in him that the Jungies had actually been seen on sunny mornings near a picnic bench under the trees of the little park outside the building. They must not be easily distracted. This park is right across from the entrance to I-86 and "strip-mall city." It's also only yards from a casino. What fortunes have they made and lost?

Supernatural folklore is common in Europe in association with the megalithic monuments. There is always some tale about a witch, dragon, or wizard to explain an earth circle or a standing stone.

The Little People vs. the Iroquois

Michael Bastine has heard people suggest that some of the mounds and earth rings in Iroquois country were constructed by the Little People for purposes that are not clear to us. He recalls hearing about an incident in which one of the Little People, possibly a young and trusting one, was captured and mistreated by some band of the Iroquois. He died in their custody.

The response of the Little People was extraordinary. They trapped the young son of the nation's chief and penned him inside a geoglyph monument, most likely some sort of ring ditch. They altered it in such an ingenious way that his people could watch the boy thirst and starve but do nothing to get him out. They had to make a deal with the Little People, and it took a long time to patch relations up. Rumors are that this event took place with the Senecas, and that the Little People in western New York may not have gotten over it quite yet.

The Hunters and the Salt Lick
(Traditional)

A small party of Iroquois hunters was on its way home. They got into a clash in hostile territory, and one of them was wounded too badly to walk. His friends huddled around him with prayers and embraces and left him by a salt lick near a cave.

The injured man thought he was dreaming when he saw some little men come out of the underbrush. They bustled around for a few minutes, communicated with nods and gestures, and took up positions by the mouth of the cave. There they drew their tiny, powerful-looking bows and waited in ambush. The warrior just watched. So the stories about Hunters were true! His last hours on earth would be rewarded with a spectacle if he could only hold on to see it.

He must have fainted. He woke to feel the ground rumbling. Something was shaking the trees near the mouth of the cave. Two enormous, blocky animals burst forth, mowing down the trees with an awful cracking. He could only presume they were the famous Great White Buffalo. Stomping and snorting, they stood, looking with their red-rimmed eyes as if treasuring a moment of anticipation before a charge into a helpless world.

But the massive animals shook their hides and moaned as if attacked by poisonous insects. The man saw the tiny arrows of the Hunters dart in and out of shade toward their targets. In seconds one fell, then the other. The little men came up to the human warrior.

"Thanks for not giving us away," one said. "Let's take a look at you." They sat with him, opened their packs, and shared a meal. He took only a few nibbles of the fairy food but felt full and very quickly better. The chill passed from his bones, and his joints felt as if he'd just come out of a peaceful sleep. His wound was by then only a scab that healed as he watched.

The little men packed up and said their farewells. The warrior made his way back to his village and, after the rejoicing, told his story. A large party of his comrades went with him back to the salt lick where his adventure had taken place. Around it were strewn the giant bones of the animals the little Hunters had killed, already starting to settle into the earth.

The Fairy Healers
(Traditional)

One spring day, the members of an Onondaga community were making maple sugar in the woods. The village was empty except for one young man home sick. He stretched out on a couch, hoping to sleep away his aches.

In late morning, he woke to the sensation of something stroking his temples and forehead. He didn't see anything when he opened his eyes and thought he was dreaming, but the feeling continued. He decided to stay still as if he were sleeping *and try to sort the matter out. Soon he was sure of it: these were tiny human hands and fingers, massaging him gently.*

The hands worked their way along his neck and head and patted his shoulders. Then they went down his chest, and at last as he rolled his eyes without moving, he could see a small, well-proportioned human arm coming through the wall of the wigwam. His curiosity got the best of him. He grabbed the arm and gave it a tug. It pulled out of his grasp like the tail of a running buffalo. Something hit him on the head, and everything went dark.

He came to in a few hours and noticed that his head and shoulders felt fine, but his torso and legs still ached. Wherever the little hands had touched him, he was a lot better. He told the story to his mother when she came home. She listened sadly. "My boy, I should have told you about this before. You had no way of knowing, but you have offended one of our family's best friends. I'll see if I can make things right."

She took the finest deer hide she had and cut it into pieces for twelve pairs of moccasins. She set them all out in the center of the wigwam with beads, thread, and colored moose hair. "Go to sleep, and lie quietly this time, no matter what happens," she said.

Around the middle of the night, the boy woke to sounds coming from the direction of the skins. He felt the fingers on him, but this time he let them do their pat-down without moving and fell asleep before they were through. He woke healthy in the morning to find that all the objects were gone. In their place appeared a marvelous pair of moccasins, crafted and ornamented far beyond the skills of the Onondaga. They fit the youth perfectly.

TWO NATIONS

Arthur Parker summarized the three types of Little People as those who deal with hunting, those who work with natural cycles, and those who come most to people. Those categories may have been superseded.

In the 1950s, Edmund Wilson conjectured that only two nations of Little People were appearing in the lore and report of his mostly

Tuscarora confidants. Wilson broke them down into Healers and Tricksters.

Without directly confirming these categories, Michael Bastine generally backs the two-tribe impression among today's reservation folk. One branch of Little People—presumably Wilson's Healers—has only goodwill. These smallest of the fairy folk, only a few inches high, are preservers of the natural environment and all life in it. They are by far the strongest of the Little People and can protect humans from the others if they choose. Full-sized living people almost never see them any more.

The larger kind—a foot or two in height—are likely to be Wilson's Tricksters. They are the type people most often report—small enough to be miraculous but too big to be stepped on without notice. You'll see this kind on the road once in a while and at the edge of the woods. These may be the ones whose artifacts and even body parts are kept in a few very private collections. They are not always goodwilled. These are the ones who come to people in dreams, making their hearts race. They are the ones who come to children.

It's hard to be sure where the Little People we hear about fit into the classic categories of literature: Hunters, Stone Throwers, and Plant Growers. We don't seem to be hearing from Hunters anymore. If what's left are Healers and Tricksters, well and good. But today's Tricksters are playing rough.

Little Tricksters
(Contemporary)

Mike Bastine and Mad Bear were on one of their cross-country forays in the late 1970s. They stopped somewhere in the Ozarks for dinner, took the leftovers, and set off driving again. At a ridiculously late hour of the evening, they neared a remote motel. Mad Bear told Mike to pull in. "We've got to get some sleep." Mike had trouble understanding that, since Mad Bear had been snoring all night beside him as he drove, but he let it pass.

Mad Bear jumped into the shower. As Mike unloaded the car, he kept hearing

an odd sound effect—blurry, abrupt, and melodic. It was half zip, half laugh—
zzzzzhee-hee!—like a needle scratched across an LP of the voices of indigenous
children. As he settled into the room he could hear them through the windows. He
yelled into the bathroom for Mad Bear.

"It's just the Little People," yelled Mad Bear back. "They're as common around
here as they are back home. Boy, they're really out there tonight."

"Are we in trouble, Bear?" said Mike.

"Mike, take that leftover chicken and biscuits and leave them in that little
circle of trees out there. You remember. You saw it when we parked."

"Uh. . . . Bear, do I really want to go out there?"

"It'll be all right," said Mad Bear, sticking his head out the bathroom door.
"They really like it when you do that. Just take the tray out there and make the
leftovers look nice. Put them in a circle real neat on the napkin and come on back
in. And don't look out there right away."

Mike did as he was told. Soon the sounds turned steady but softer, like
appreciative murmuring. Then they stopped. Mike parted the curtains and looked
out. Sure enough, the vittles were gone. That's no proof of anything supernatural,
of course. A raccoon could have gobbled them as neatly and almost as quickly—if
it had been waiting. But it wouldn't have sounded like that.

Impressions of the Little People

The Tonawanda Reservation has a couple of traditional sledding hills. The most
popular is by the Baptist church, but there's another spot off Sandhill Road. A
group of children went there one January afternoon in 2003.

Most of the kids went up and down an open slope, but the youngest hopped on
his disc, took off down a wooded trail, and disappeared. Soon the others heard him
calling wildly and ran down to look for him.

As they got closer, they heard him yelling something about Little People. Sure
enough, when they found him by his saucer in a clump of trees, they saw them, too:
hundreds of tiny human footprints the size of rabbit feet, making blue shadows in
the sunny snow. This grove by a creek must have been a playground for them the
night before!

The Fading Light

Abenaki author and teacher Joe Bruchac lives in Greenfield, New York, in the home of his grandparents. He has a marvelous library and bookshop in the house and has turned the land around it into a nature preserve. He taught his children to love the natural environment and not to fear the night or the woods. They spent many hours running, playing, and hiking about the area. They even had a family game, sort of a tag/hide-and-seek/treasure hunt, running through the woods at night.

One night, one of Joe's boys came home gushing about mystery lights and Little People. "Dad, I followed one of those lights," he said, breathless. "It came down in a clump of trees. I watched it till it faded out. There were Little People, all around it." He was five at the time. A few years later, he had no recollection of the event.

An Odd Little Fellow

Indian Hill on the Tuscarora Reservation is a sprawling, wooded area famous for Little People sightings and psychic events of other kinds. Joe Anderson hunted there as a boy and remembers places that were outright spooky. "There were times when my dogs wouldn't go in a certain direction, and I figured it was time to get out of there."

An artist friend of his was painting one morning on Indian Hill when he looked up from the easel and saw one of the Little People through the undergrowth from about thirty feet away. He held his breath. The little man was like a tiny Native American, but there was something as primal about him as an animal or the tree beside him. The artist couldn't see him closely enough to notice clothing or other particulars.

The optical conditions were queer. The exact spot in which the Jungie appeared was just a foot or so from the base of a big maple, in the slanting fall of a sunbeam. The artist moved his head as stealthily as he could, hoping for a better look, but the Jungie was invisible from other positions, even ones not blinded by foliage. Only when the man looked at him just so where the sunlight became visible in the shimmering dust motes could he see anything of him at all.

The merry little fellow stood and basked in the light, preening in its warmth, like a groundhog on its hind legs, as if he could taste every second of existence. He was visible for fifteen minutes before he started to fade. He may not have moved, but the beam changed its fall around him, and he was soon gone.

No wonder so few of us see them.

THE FAIRY FISHERS

Eleazar Williams was one of the great Tuscarora medicine men. It was widely said that he had good friends among the Djogao. This magical friendship has parallels in other traditions.

In Celtic legend, an acquaintance with the fairies can bestow great powers upon a lucky human. Scotsman Thomas the Rhymer or True Thomas (1220–1297) was thought gifted with prophecy and poetry due his seven-year dalliance with the fairy queen. Blind Irish harpist Anthony Raftery (1780–1835) was suspected of having midnight tutorials with the Fair Folk. Legendary King Daniel O'Donohue even joined them at the end of his life.

In Celtic tradition, the fairies disliked being seen, even by those to whom they wished well. They often communicated and even played pranks by tossing tiny flint shards nicknamed elf shot or fairy shot. One historic witness reported a gentle rain of pebbles on the roof and windows of an old house that troubled people's sleep all night. In the morning, piles of tiny Neolithic arrowheads and chippings were found beneath the windows, suggesting that some mysterious pranksters had gathered these obscure objects and used them as projectiles. Where did the Little People—if such they were—find piles of these impossibly ancient artifacts? Maybe the fairies *do* know the dead. Something of the sort in both senses may be going on in Iroquois tradition.

The Sound of Pebbles Tossing

One dim night, Eleazar Williams and his young son Ted were spearfishing along the Niagara River not far from Lewiston. An eddy formed a pool a few feet from a feeder stream, creating a fine place to look for lake sturgeon. These fish could be big, and if one were taken that had a bit of roe in it, it could fetch a good price. It had to come in pretty close to the spearfisher, and he would have to know just when to launch.

"How are you going to see a fish?" said young Ted. It would have been hard enough to see anything under this water in full daylight.

"Just wait and you'll learn something," said Eleazar. "I've got some helpers."

"If you catch a sturgeon on this kind of night, I'll carry it home myself."

"Watch what you wish for," said the father, standing poised with raised spear. He stood that way a long time.

Ted started to notice some faint noises in the brush around them at the edge of the creek mouth. Soon, little ticks came to his hearing as though drops of rain were falling, but there was no rain, and the sound came from objects softly striking the metal point of the spear. The tone of these impacts was more like the friendly tap of little flecks of stone. It sounded exactly as though someone with an uncanny aim was tossing pebbles at the tip of the spear. The healer held his pose. Almost like the code of a ticking Geiger counter, the rhythm of the percussion changed. Eleazar made a sudden rush and a lunge into the water. The pitchfork spear came back out with a squirming, flapping critter that gleamed in the dim moonlight. It was a sturgeon! It weighed over a hundred pounds.

Ted's father helped him carry the monster, but this event remained a curiosity in Ted's memory to the end of his days. What or who had been throwing those tiny stones?

The 1927 dam on Caneadea Creek created Rushford Lake, a summer boating and resort community off Route 243 in Allegany County. It also flooded two tiny villages, East Rushford and Kelloggville.

Every winter, they drain the lake, aiming for an ideal depth. Once in a while they go too far, and if you're there at just the right time, what's left of the buildings comes into view. It has to look pretty eerie, and clearly someone agrees. *Ghost Lake* was filmed here in 2004. This is also hilly country. It feels strange, as you drive through it, to look for a lake.

The Boys and Girls Got Me Out . . .
(1976)

A friend of ours and her family often visited Rushford Lake in the summer, staying with a cottage owner. When she was seven, they paid a winter visit. The point of the out-of-season trip was to get a look at the odd lake emptied. She's sure of the date: December 21, 1976. Thick snow was everywhere.

Our storyteller, her brother, the son of the cottage owner, and his cousin were inseparable summer companions. They dedicated the bright December afternoon to sledding on a hill they had only heard about, somewhere above the highest cottage. As they set out, the only girl tore off ahead of them, calling back a promise to beat them all to the top of the destined hill.

She crossed a creek on a makeshift bridge, a thin wood panel. She cut through a stretch of woods, a cornfield, and a clearing. Then she stood before it. She waited at the bottom for a quick, admiring rest. Then up she ran.

She remembers getting to the top and simply staring. This hill was like a plateau, its summit high enough to be scary. She could see into the valley below. She could see to all the four quarters. The sun, the clouds, the other hills. It was intoxicating. All she had to do for a whole new look at the world was run to another side of the hilltop and gaze! The slopes fell below. Which would they be sledding first? When the boys arrived, she wanted to show them the best. From one side to the other she ran.

She got a jolt. The snow fell through under her. She felt icy water coursing over her ankles and sloshing between her toes. She must have stepped into a puddle hidden by the snow. She hurried to get over it.

Then she heard something she'd never heard before, a loud cracking sound muffled by snow. She foundered, knee deep. She kept going.

Next she was in up to her waist. The best course seemed to be to go forward. She'd learned to swim the summer before and wasn't afraid to test her new skill. She went under, snow spilling down around her.

She came up, but the billows came in on her as she tried to swim. It was as much a barrier as the ice at her chest. The ground under her was rising, though. Soon her upper body rested against a bank, but she stalled trying to climb out. Rubber boots slid on sloping, underwater rocks. The snow on the bank choked and chilled her as she tried to grip it. And that full-body snowsuit, logged with stinging water, doubled her weight. She struggled until she was exhausted. Ice daggers went into her legs.

She called out, but, ringed with snowbanks, her cries went nowhere. The boys could have been ten feet away and not seen or heard her. Were they still coming? The sky above her was desperately bright.

Her trunk under water, her head on her arm, she collapsed and sobbed. Soon her legs didn't hurt. But she couldn't lift her head! Her cheek had frozen to her sleeve. Where were the boys? They'd played other jokes before. She was so tired she could sleep forever. Then something happened.

She heard a sound she described as "rushing horses," increasing in volume as if coming toward her. Then she heard light, stray human voices like children on a playground fading in strangely. None of this made sense at the top of a snowy hill. She turned her head as much as she could and rolled her eyes.

She saw small children running toward her, moving over and across the hilltop in huge, half-flying strides. A boy jumped over her in a bound as big as he was small, landed in the water behind her, and started trying to push her up. He smiled as if her danger were play.

Another child took her by the hood, and other boys and girls tugged at her arms. Not even wearing winter clothes, they were as cheery as the first bold boy. They seemed at the start no stronger than they looked, but something pulled so hard and well that the mortal girl went airborne, soaring over the top of the bank and landing several feet from the water's edge, as safely and softly as if the others had leaped or flown along with her. She was suddenly, completely alone again in the sunlight, astonished enough to forget the cold.

Her companions soon arrived. They loaded her soaked and shivering on a sled and took her back to the cottage. After a long process of thawing her out, their host commenced an interview session that went over the simple facts again and again. At the end he shook his head.

There were three ponds on the broad top of that hill. They'd been drained a bit so the spring thaw wouldn't cause them to flood the field below, but they were death traps. Climbing out should have been impossible for a snowsuited seven-year-old. "The boys and girls got me out," was all the girl could say.

When she was sent to bed, her Irish-born father took over. He turned to the boys and asked carefully about these other children.

"There was no one else up there," his son said. "She was already out of the water."

THE SECOND NATION

Storyteller Leo Cooper grew up on the Allegany Reservation near Salamanca and Allegany State Park. In his boyhood, his little sister used to talk about playmates no one else could see. On a day that seemed like a dream to Cooper, he was close to seeing them himself. His sister stood before him and announced that she was going off with her friends to play in the woods. She was halfway down the walk, arms out exactly as if hand in hand with small, invisible presences. Their mother looked from the house, rushed out, and took her youngest child inside.

The Little People Zone

A house that had been a funeral home once stood on Paine Street in East Aurora. A family that lived next door to it in the 1980s ran into some problems. They centered around a first-floor bedroom facing the old funeral home and a window with a low sill.

This was the bedroom of a four-year-old. If the blinds to the window were closed overnight, the girl always slept peacefully and well. If the blinds were left open or raised and the little girl woke and could look outside, she started to scream bloody murder.

The first time it happened, the parents rushed into the room, expecting to interrupt a break-in or kidnapping. They found their daughter out of her bed, her tiny body backed against the wall. She was pointing out the window and shrieking hysterically, "The Little People! The Little People!"

When she calmed, her mother tried to get the details. She thought Little People came onto the lawn at night and paraded outside her window, grinning at her, mocking her, enticing her. They wanted her to come outside so they could pull her under the ground where they live. They laughed because, sooner or later, they would get her. Her descriptions of them and the events were unusually coherent. She showed her mother where they tried to grab her forearms.

Some nights the girl was afraid to sleep in her room. She spent many an hour in bed with her parents.

The family soon moved and had no further issues at their new home. The house that was the focus of it all was demolished in the 1990s to make way for the new wing of the Boys' and Girls' Club.

But stories of children's encounters with Little People have surfaced about another house on Paine Street, and a few hundred yards to the south, on King. These reports come to us with less development, and we have not been able to interview witnesses. But what a Little People zone the core of East Aurora must have been! Could there be any connection to the rumor that the village had once been a prehistoric battlefield? There are plenty of ghost stories in this area as well.

The Strange Jungie

One of our Cayuga confidants remembers an aunt who, when a girl around 1960, had a Jungie as a friend. He came to visit her now and then at the Tonawanda Reservation and talked about things that had happened in her life. Usually they met outside, but sometimes he came to her family's trailer on Shanks Road. He was her strange, beloved companion. Sometimes he warned her about things she needed to look out for. He could be jealous, though, of other friends. Once when some of her schoolmates were visiting, he bit a little white girl on the leg.

The Tuscarora Girl and the Little Man

One young Tuscarora girl used to think she saw a little man now and then in her grandmother's house when she went over to spend nights. The grandmother always told her it was nonsense, but the little girl thought she knew more than she was saying. After a particularly traumatic night, the girl confronted her in front of the rest of the family. "I saw him in your bedroom, Grandma, right on your dresser. And he was bad!"

The girl was a fine natural artist and did a drawing of the little fellow she'd seen. It was not a hopeful one. He had a thatch of tangled, coal-black hair, pointed ears, and jagged teeth.

The girl was tragically killed in a shotgun accident in 2003. People who live in the murder house still report a dark, blurry shape a foot or so high that streaks across the floor now and then. One of the local elders called the case "bad energy."

A Discerning Native

A friend of ours was one of a handful of white teachers on the Cattaraugus Reservation. He got along well with everyone and was a particular favorite of the children.

One day, the teachers took their classes on a field trip around the reservation. Community elders were stationed to explain the history of certain spots and buildings. One of them started to talk about a certain grove that was special to the Little People. He caught himself, looked around, and locked eyes with our friend. "Are you Native?" he asked.

Our friend is dark eyed and olive skinned and could probably pass for part Native. But he conceded that he was not. "I'm sorry," said the elder. "We're not allowed to talk about some aspects of our tradition with people who are not members of our society." He scanned his eyes over the children. "We'll get to that another time." The discussion moved to another topic.

The Lucky One

In 1995 a white friend of ours was living in Riverside near Buffalo. He worked at an auto parts shop on the Tuscarora Reservation. His colleagues were all Seneca and Tuscarora.

His young son started to complain about visits from little human beings in his room at night. He described their sly little faces grinning at him, their little hands clutching. They wanted to take him away.

For the first few weeks, the parents thought it was just night terrors, but the matter escalated, and the boy's descriptions sharpened. In every Little People dream he went deeper with them along a trail into a woods at night. He didn't want to go, but they cast a spell on him, and he couldn't resist. They were heading for the mouth of a cave. If he ever got into it, he believed, he was never coming back out.

The visions and dreams scared him so much that he was afraid to fall sleep. He could wake terrified after even a few seconds. The only rest he or his parents got was during the day. The situation exhausted the whole family. After an especially troubling night, our friend overslept and came late to work on the reservation.

"Man, you look terrible," said his Tuscarora boss. "What happened?"

"I might as well be honest with you," he said. "We're really worried about my little boy. He's having all these dreams and visions about Little People—"

At that word, his boss cut him off. "Let's take a walk." In a grove out of the hearing of their colleagues, he retold legends and stories about the Little People. "It's OK about you being late today," he concluded. "Go home and get some rest. I'll get some help for you. But don't ever say anything about Little People around those guys again."

In a few days, a call came to his home. A woman with the accent of the reservation was on the line. She seemed uncomfortable, as if she'd made the call only to repay a debt. She asked my friend what was wrong, listened to his answer, and waited before she spoke.

"We Seneca people have legends about things like these," she said, "these Little People. I'm not sure anybody really knows what they are. Sometimes they show themselves to children like this, though, and then we think they're up to no good." She hesitated before she spoke again.

"There's nothing you and your wife can do but wait. Some children stop seeing these things as they grow, and these children are OK. Some children don't stop seeing them, and . . ." She paused and took a breath. "I hope your boy is one of the lucky ones."

As if an afterthought, she spoke again. "Oh, and one more thing. Be sure to watch your boy. Never leave him alone outside. Never let him out of your sight, especially near woods or bushes or trees—at least until he stops seeing these things."

Within a few months, the boy stopped mentioning these visits from Little People, and the case seemed closed. What happens to the children who aren't so lucky?

The Seneca language reminds us of Latin in some regards. It's a subtle, complex, old tongue that only a handful of people speak any more. One does not learn Seneca in a long weekend. Like Latin has become to

Christians, Seneca is a language of traditional spirituality, used mostly in reservation rites, dances, and prayers by people who cannot always converse in it. Due to its use in the incantations and spells of reservation power people, Seneca, like Latin, could be considered the voice of magic, of supernatural beings.

The Children Who Came Back
(Seneca, Contemporary)

In the late spring of 2005, a young white man, his Seneca wife, and their two children were at a family gathering on the Tonawanda Reservation. After dinner, the couple's boy and girl, then six and four, played with some reservation kids. The husband lounged outside, keeping half an eye on the brood. When the mass of them headed off for the railroad trestle, he saw no reason to object. The tracks were unused, and they were in clear sight, one hundred yards away. He relaxed, enjoying the slow merge of day into night.

He found himself studying some odd lights by the overgrown tracks at which he'd last seen the children. They were delicate, fist-size, and incandescent, sashaying a foot or so off the ground in open spaces, moving as seamlessly through the patches of brush as if they could both fly and climb lightly. He realized that he had been seeing them for some time without noticing. Did the children have flashlights?

But this was a different form of light. Their texture was odd. They were light spheres, too diffuse to be man-made, but too big and steady to be fireflies. They stayed mighty low to the ground, too. They lasted as long as he looked and drifted off into denser wood. He could think of no natural explanation for them.

Just before full dark, his two children came back. The four-year-old didn't have much to say for herself, seeming bemused, even a little sly, as if holding a secret she needn't share, but the boy was beside himself. "Dad! Dad! There are Little People that live by those tracks! Little People!" For his age, he was quite descriptive. Wonderful friends, they were full of tricks and fun. They told him about the sounds the animals made and what they were saying by them. They made life in the woods seem like a never-ending amusement ride. He was also amazed. He was old enough to have a picture of reality and to fall into wonder at the violations of it. No one at school had told him that the world held anything like Little People.

The boy's Seneca grandmother came out in the middle of this conversation and caught the drift instantly. She scolded both children harshly and told them not to be playing with Little People. Her attitude was as if "they ought to know," as if she might have told them this before. Then she turned to the parents. "Take them home, and don't say any more about this," she said. "Call me if anything strange happens." The white father found it all puzzling. It was just children telling tall tales.

A dozen miles away, the dad spent one of the worst nights of his life. Every five minutes he jump-started. It wasn't exactly material sounds that woke him, just the sense that something was in the driveway. Time after time he got up to peer out the broad second-floor window. He never saw anything. Another room overlooked the spot: the one in which the children slept.

In the morning, the six-year-old described a remarkable night of his own. "Dad! Dad! You know who came to see us last night? It was the Little People from Gramma's! They were outside all night in the driveway! They were trying to get us to come out and play! I really wanted to, but I was good. I remembered what Grammy told us. I didn't think you wanted us to go out there, either, Dad."

The father called his wife's mother and gave her all this. She told him to leave the house quickly with his wife and children and not to return before the end of the day. When they came back, something about the apartment felt different, and a faint, natural fragrance lingered in the air. The couple could only figure that a reservation healer must have come to the house and worked a ritual, possibly going through every room with a smudge of sage or cedar.

That was the last the father said or thought about Little People for quite some time. When they were on the reservation even in daylight, the family's children stayed away from the questionable trestle and before long had forgotten the incident. One night, though, a year or so later, the father found himself in the same chair outside his mother-in-law's house, again gazing toward the tracks at twilight. He saw the light spheres again where he had seen them seasons before and recalled the strange incident. He was tempted to stalk off after them and challenge their mystery. As if she could hear him thinking, the grandmother came out of the house, *took a seat by her white son-in-law, and told him why the reservation folks were on edge about Little People.*

A few years earlier, a reservation lad the same age as his boy had disappeared. He was lost for three days, apparently outdoors. That seemed the only possibility for where he had been; they had turned the reservation upside-down looking for him.

Everyone was glad just to have him back when he walked up to someone's house and knocked on the door. There were curiosities, though. For someone who had been outside for this period of time, he was pretty well cared for. He was clean, and he wasn't hungry. Other than not remembering where he'd been, there was another oddity: He was speaking fluent Seneca. It was months before English came all the way back as his natural language.

LANES OF THE LITTLE PEOPLE

The Little People were probably only spotted by humans when they chose to be. They're even more withdrawn nowadays, offended by the plight of the Native Americans, the wrecking of the natural environment, and the racket of contemporary culture that breaks into their woods. All that said, there are a handful of spaces reputed to be homes and playgrounds of the Little People. You had better know how to spot them. People who mess with these spaces often pay a price. The pattern is familiar in Europe.

One of the best-known contemporary Celtic fairy anecdotes concerns automaker John DeLorean (1925–2005), who against a warning had a certain tree felled as he was clearing a plain for his Dublin factory. He ended up broke, divorced, and in jail. This is a familiar theme in Iceland, where the locals are very protective of certain stones sacred to the Hidden People. An American Army base in England during World War II encountered a pattern of disasters when they moved a standing stone to widen a road for their tanks. (The locals eventually put it back in the same spot, and the Americans moved the road.) Don't mess with these Little People places.

It's interesting to note that upstate New York's folkloric patterns follow those of most of the rest of the world. These Little People places often fall inside zones of folklore of all other paranormal types: UFOs, mystery critters, ghosts, occultism. Is the whole thing set off by some energy at the sites, or is it all just the tricks of the Little People? They're known for that sort of thing everywhere else.

The Cattaraugus Creek flows northwest through Gowanda and the Cattaraugus Reservation and empties into Lake Erie at Irving. Thirty-five miles south of Buffalo, it branches to form the sublime Zoar Valley.

The origin story of the Seneca Dark Dance is set in Zoar Valley, long associated with the Little People and apparently all else paranormal. People say the valley hums at night, as if it breathes orenda or some other vast force. They talk about how hard it is to build roads that last through it. They talk about hunters and hikers who go missing in the valley, curiously and seriously lost. It took a full day and a massive search to find a group in 2003; they said they'd gone far into the park following other hikers, who just . . . disappeared. Others rescued report that familiar trails and landmarks looked completely different; they'd been "pixie led" as the Brits would call it. It would be no wonder if the Little People had a hand in it.

The Genesee Valley had many sites and monuments that were special to ancient societies. The only ones we can write about are those the Seneca described for the first whites, if those whites went on to list them in the histories. Wherever these sites are, they are magnets for psychic folklore.

The Genesee River flows through Rochester, New York. Three of its waterfalls are within the city limits. General mystery spots to the Senecas, these falls were special to the Little People. We don't expect to learn much about them beyond that.

A bit further upriver and south of Rochester is another waterfall in Letchworth State Park, also associated with the Little People. When the beams of sun hit just right, the merry spume makes earthy rainbows, tossing light and color. The Little People were fond of natural psychedelia everywhere. It's no wonder that this was one of their places.

John Billington was the manager of Beaver Island State Park on Grand Island in the Niagara—longtime Seneca country. Billington was not a talkative fellow, at least around his white colleagues. Those who told us about him were not sure of his nation, but it's a good bet that he was Iroquois. He used to point out a certain patch of ground in the park that his workers were never to disturb. He was so emphatic about this that more than one of them got interested in the reason. All he would ever say of it was that it was "because of the Little People." The man we interviewed remembered it as a curious area, a little mound in the grass in a natural clearing, before a unique-looking tree.

Though upstate New York is historic Iroquois territory, there were settlements here of the Algonquin, the big northern alliance that was the Confederacy's age-old rival. The Algonquin word for the magic force is *manitou*.

Manitou Road in Parma, west of Rochester, seems haunted by some frisky demon that could surely be one of the manifestations of the Little People. Something scratches at the glass on moving cars, pecks on farmhouse windows, and rushes at observers.

Late Rochester historian and author Shirley Cox Husted (1931–2004) recalled waking to the sound of scratching on the bedroom window of her brother's Manitou Road farmhouse. Something ugly rushed at her and disappeared at the moment it would have struck the glass. She screamed, and the household came running. She'd imagined it, her brother and sister-in-law said, as they said years later when a child was spooked by the same freaky image. Yet when Husted's sister-in-law passed away, her brother, living alone in the house, never raised the shades after dark. Maybe he didn't want to look out the windows. Maybe those who named the street knew something.

The Tonawanda Reservation has a couple of haunted lanes. One that comes up in Little People folklore is Sandhill Road, a roughly north–south stretch that changes its name a couple of times. North of Bloomingdale Road, Sandhill is called Meadville. South of there, it takes turns as Hopkins. Many of the folkloric roads in New York have this configuration: cutoffs, with funky name changes.

One of the area's first sawmills was here on Sandhill proper, and the famous Seneca Ely Parker—grandfather of Arthur C. Parker—was born in a Sandhill Road cabin overlooking the Big Falls of the Tonawanda Creek, doubtless a Little People place. It may be worth pointing out that Sandhill Road on the rez is a corpse path, connecting a cemetery and the Tonawanda Baptist.

The Onondaga didn't expect to see the Little People often but were grateful to them for the work they did. They had their own special site associated with the Little People, a ravine west of Onondaga Valley not far from their traditional capitol near Syracuse.

Gistweahna, "Little Men Valley," is one Onondaga name for the place. We have no certainty where it was. There are rumors that it may have been east of Syracuse by Indian Hill in Pompey. William Beuchamp suggests that it may have been the area of a series of ravines west of Onondaga Valley. By the road passing through it two hundred years, almost surely today's Route 20, is a slick, steep bank of boulder clay—an ice age clay deposit decked in places with big stones. The Little People were said to have worn this smooth in the sled-pinball event of their metaphysical X-games. They liked the bounce the big stones gave them.

Between Utica and Albany is Palatine Bridge. Between Palatine Bridge and the nearby village of Mohawk is an area that members of the community of Stone Throwers were thought to frequent. "These little men could appear and disappear whenever they wished," it was said.

Onondaga minister La Fort saw one here around 1869 as he was on his way to Albany. The little fellow sat on the top of a hill above the road, doubtless today's Route 5, and just watched the reverend as he passed.

Homage to the Little People

On the western shore of Lake Champlain is a certain beach that the Mohawk considered special to Stone Throwers. (The Flint People called them Yahkonenusyoks.)

It was reported in the Jesuit Relations of 1668 that, as three French fathers traveled on a trail along the lake, a solemn mood came over their Native escorts. A little north of Ticonderoga, they found a beach littered with shards of the flinty material the Native Americans of the Northeast preferred for tools and weapons. A remarkable quantity of this raw stone was ready for use as projectile points, knives, and gunflints.

Without a word or ceremony, the Mohawks started gathering pieces of this flint. Their moods were not those of toolmakers, but of people working a holy duty, even receiving gifts from the other world. Used to rituals of their own, the Jesuits just watched.

When the journey resumed, their escorts explained that, whenever they were near this spot, they stopped and paid respects to the village of invisible Little People under the water. They had made these flints ready for use, and they'd do so as long as the humans gave them tobacco in their ceremonies. If the nation used a lot of tobacco, they got back a lot of these flints.

These little water men, they told the Jesuits, travel on the lake in canoes. When the leader arrives, dives into the water, and leads the troop to his palace, it makes a shocking noise.

The Mohawks named Lake Champlain after a white man they called Corlaer. He ridiculed Mohawk customs about the Little People and ended up drowning in the lake.

In a way it may be silly to list Little People sites at all, at least specific ones. Who knows how many landscape features could have been credited to them by the Iroquois who lived here so long? A little run-off down a slate cliff giving the appearance of a staircase. A tiny pool in the forest clearing, never empty even in times of drought. A crack in a cliff that looks like a tiny door. A special tree.

A young Cayuga friend of ours recalls a spot in a creek near Delevan in a campground his family used to visit. A big flat stone had a missing piece, a rectangle as neatly incised and removed as if twentieth-century tools had been used. Leading down through it was a slender, spiraling chute like an umbilicus to a watery underworld. No one knew where it went. The children and other bathers used to play with it, and it was rumored to be special to the Little People, a place where they could be seen frolicking in the moonlight on tender nights. They vanished if they knew they were being watched. The children got into the habit of being quiet as they came to this part of the creek at night.

THE DJOGAO SKULL

One prominent American curiosity is the well-photographed mini-mummy from Casper, Wyoming. In October 1932, a dynamite blast opened a small natural cave in granite, and when the smoke cleared, a humanlike figure, seated with arms folded, came into view. The leathery imp was fourteen inches tall and, according to X-rays, had adult development. What this—and his entombment in natural rock—says about the Little People is anyone's guess. The little fellow has not been seen in public since the 1970s and no one is certain where he is.

There are tales, even current ones, about rare shamans keeping mementos of these elusive and magical folk as concrete as the Casper mummy. Though Michael Bastine has learned never to completely discount any Native American belief, he never thought he would see one of these.

Once when he was helping Mad Bear move from his trailer to his new house, Mike noticed a small, purple, plastic box on a closet shelf.

"Open it up and take a look," said the shaman. Wrapped inside it was a tiny human skull, perfect down to the complete set of teeth. The cranium was the size of a ping-pong ball. Mike knew bone when he saw it and was in no doubt that this object was made of it. "It scared the hell out of me," he says. Mad Bear never showed him the skull again.

Mike badgered him constantly for an explanation of the wonder. All Mad Bear would ever say about it was that a cache containing the skull and other tiny bones and artifacts had been found in the 1820s during the digging of the Erie Canal near Syracuse. It drove a couple of dozen men—possibly all Irish—to run like mad from the spot and flee the business of upstate excavating for good. The collection made its way into the hands of the Onondaga and the skull ended up with Mad Bear a couple of generations later.

FAIRY TREES

Everywhere in the world, human folkloric tradition has associated certain natural features and regions with supernatural beings. In Iroquois country, the Little People are the most prominent sacred supernaturals, and the rocks, groves, springs, and waterfalls once linked to them are impossible to list. Had the people who maintained tradition about them not been displaced, it's certain that many more of them would be remembered. The larger sites and zones are usually the ones that stand out still, but sometimes a scrap of information about even the smallest of them can be found. Sometimes it's even a single object, like a tree.

The Fairy Tree

Late Tuscarora healer Ted Williams told me a story about a fairy tree on the Tuscarora Reservation.

One day when his father Eleazar was a boy, there was no one to watch him but his own father. He, however, was on his way to dangerous work felling trees. Afraid that his venturesome boy would get hurt at the lumbering, he dropped him off one morning at the special tree. "Just wait by the tree till I'm out of sight," he said. "You'll have playmates all day."

The future healer was completely alone for the first time in his life. As the horse and carriage pulled out of sight, tiny human beings came out, first one, then others, from around the tree, as if they had a door behind it. The band of them played with Eleazar the whole day. It was magical and delightful. The wildlife, the trees, even the passage of the sun and its changing moods were more fascinating than they had ever been before. The little folk taught him to understand the talk of the birds. It was the brightest day in his memory. What a wonder was this world around us! He made many friends. One special one was at his side every moment.

Sunset found them back by the original tree. As the clops of horses' hooves and the clacks of the carriage harness came into hearing, Eleazar's playmates bid him bright farewells, and one by one disappeared behind the tree. By the time the carriage was in sight, even his special friend, waving to the last, was gone. Ted's father never saw them again, but he always said that the story was true.

When he first heard the story in the 1940s, young Ted wasn't so sure. "Were the Easter bunny and the tooth fairy there, too?" But Ted never forgot the fabled tree, and it was standing forty years later when three illumined Iroquois walked by it.

The Double-Stemmed Oak Tree

In March 2006, Michael Bastine took a documentary TV film crew to the Tuscarora Reservation to meet some of his friends, including the elders Jay Claus and Norton Rickard. I was along. We visited the graves of Mad Bear Anderson and Ted Williams. Mike had a moment by himself at Ted's grave. I think it was his first visit to it since the November service. When he was ready to talk again, he came up to us, and our little procession got walking.

Jay is a pony-tailed, wide-chested, fiftyish man of middle height. "You know, Ted Williams's father was a medicine man," he said to the whites.

"A great one," said the sixtiesh Norton with a nod. Norton had a short haircut, but he was built a lot like Jay.

They led us on a dirt road through some woods and came to a curious double-

stemmed oak on a slope, the fairy tree of Eleazar's boyhood. Michael Bastine recalled a more recent story about it.

In 1975 three illuminated Iroquois—Ted, Mad Bear, and the Seneca Beeman Logan (1919–1979)—were walking by the very tree. The two Tuscarora, Ted and Mad Bear, let us say, did not need metaphysical bodyguards when they walked at night, and Beeman Logan was a celebrated mystic. Logan was, however, a Seneca, and not of this reservation. He shouldn't have known much about its lesser curiosities. At one point after they had passed the tree, Ted and Mad Bear noticed that they were now a duo. A hundred yards back, their companion was studying the tree and the ground around it as intently as if looking for a lost ring.

Mad Bear and Ted came back to him and asked what was up. "I think the Little People live here," Logan said. "I could swear they've been around here."

Winter stayed late in 2005, and Easter came so early that part of western New York was still covered in white on the holy Sunday. In midafternoon, I went for a long ski tour in the hilly country south of Buffalo. Usually I like to keep a pace on fast tracks at a park or touring center, but a couple of times a winter, I go for tours like this.

Five minutes after I started, I was on an old logging road. To my right was a creek, on my left a short, steep slope. Something low to my left caught my eye: a perfect wheel of wet snow, a foot across, like the stone hoops high on the walls of the Mayan ball courts, and perpendicular like they were to the course of human activity. This one was at the base of a steep, white bank, twenty feet high. Its symmetry was remarkable, its sides five inches thick, the same as the hole through which passed its axle of air. I could have flicked it with my pole from the center of the road. I came back to study it.

It was the oddest natural thing I had ever seen in the woods. It seemed spun by wind or magic. A four-foot groove ran from it up the white slope. If nature had made it, it was most likely that something had fallen from the tree above it and rolled itself into this snow wheel. Still, it looked improbable. Human artists could only have made it with a mold. It should have collapsed under its own weight. And the snow that held it was so old, it was moist and gray at the edges. The night before had been turbulent. How had it lasted?

Curious works of nature or ones cleverly wrought, particularly into the shapes of circles, were thought works of the Little People by old cultures on both sides of the Atlantic. I could envision the fairy children at play, scooping into the white and rolling themselves a snow wheel, casting their baby spells to hold its form, fixing it like a marker or a monument to bemuse passing humans.

The Thursday before had been a full moon, and Michael Bastine and I had been storytelling in East Aurora. Maybe the fairy children had been working even then and heard themselves called. Almost expecting to see the prints of tiny hands and feet beside the snow wheel, I looked up from the groove to the tree from which it came.

The chief of the bank, this maple was strange in itself. It stood like a champion, bigger and bolder than its line of neighbors, a king to the whippy bushes that huddled at its roots. Its bare fellows were smooth barked and full-set on top of the bank. This one's truculent roots showed like a maw of tangled teeth where the bank had worn away, either that or a gate to a world behind it. Pockets in its surface looked like little mouths or caves. Knots and gnarls in the bark above were the features of merry gnomes. What were they like at midnight! Did they grin, and move, and laugh with other trees! Did their squinty eyes glow! A thought came to me, something that Michael would probably say if he saw it: This tree was of the Little People.

I started skiing again, wondering if a bit of Mike's intuition had rubbed off on me. That snow hoop had seemed like a gate or an arch marking the entry to another realm.

The skiing was surprisingly fast for so warm a day. The top inch was soft, but March's freezes and thaws had left a hard, heavy base. In wooded areas, it could feel like full winter again. Still, connecting patches were thin, and rain was counted on for that night. This would be the last day anyone could ski this loop, surely the last long tour of the year in these parts. The thin sun alone might settle it that afternoon.

Ah well, that tour was a good one for good-bye; I'd said farewell to other winters on that course. I thought about the seasons.

It's rare for one to turn so dramatically, I thought, to be so clearly winter full of natural skiing and then snap to climatic spring overnight. A clean cut was better, I thought, one last ceremony of good skiing, than weeks of to and fro.

The winding, wooded trail opened on a bare hillside facing north. The city was there, as bright as where I was, but warmer and snow-less. The streets were full of people coming and going from churches and gatherings, the women in their flowers and pastels, maybe hoping through their imagery to encourage the April to come. They'd had enough of snow—as had the world.

It was after equinox, and the whole continent hurled itself away from winter. I had skied back into it as if for a breath of time, a point of stasis in which things might fall clear, as if to catch back some important thought or mood whose only chance to be understood was to feel within it, while it could still be imaginatively held. Maybe this gesture into the natural cycles was what my life as a writer is about, to bring back things that should not be lost and hold them until people learn from them.

By the time I came out under open sky, I realized that I had been thinking about ancestors, and my own elders, all passed to the other side. On days like that—Easter—they seem close. Their memories passed before me.

The men in my family had dropped quickly, and to no pattern. The women had lingered past their capacities to enjoy anything in the world but the love for them that came back from it. I loved my sports, my movement under the open sky like this, my books, my friends. I pitied the two women I had seen to their ends, that they had nothing like this anymore in their lives. As they aged and weakened, I found myself paying special attention to them on holy days like that one, affirming images of renewal and hope for them any way I could. Every long winter either of them survived seemed to promise that one more summer would beckon and charge their fading lives into another full-year cycle. The last of them was gone, though. My mother had crossed over two months before.

I looked up and across the open fields and reflected on family, on the family each of us chooses to create, creates without thoughtful choosing, or never creates. It seemed a loss to me that I have had no children, and that I have no plans to. Even nieces and nephews are no likelihood. I have no siblings.

Most of us are born into the embrace of families. Through children and partners many of us re-create it around us as the elders fall. That's what we think our duty is. Some with those responsibilities envy those who seem free. There's another side.

For those none will ever look to as ancestor, that community is gone when the elders leave the world. I realized that the true honoring of ancestors may well be children, gifts of continuity and love coming back to them from the world. I wondered if I had wasted the preceding twelve years in an indirect cycle of stress and grief, and if by then the true remedy was too far away. Leaning on my poles, I looked to the sky, then looked down for a good long while. I saw that my books may be the gifts I give to the elders and started to ski again.

These Little People are quirky. Like children, their gifts and short-comings are not those of adults. Their size and whimsy make them childlike; their powers and understanding are supernatural. This con-trast may be a testimony to the archetype of the child.

The child mind has immeasurable inspiration and creativity. Its limits are those only of its species, but it lacks experience. It needs help to do simple things, but its talents—its imagination, its play, its gifts of seeing past boundaries—can only be recaught by the greatest artists. This could be the model for these forever children.

As if powered by the boundlessness of every child mind, these Little People are forces of nature—of growth and fertility—to every culture that holds them in tradition. They drive the seasons' turn. They are also with the ancestors, as if either the spirits of the human dead can, after some transformation, join the Little People, or the Little People as they are know other otherworld realms.

Messengers from both the worlds, of nature and of spirit, these Little People may be closer to you than you think. See them, hear them, when they come to you.

11

The Land of the Elders

At night when the streets of your cities and villages will be silent, and you think them deserted, they will throng with the returning hosts that once filled and still love this beautiful land. The white man will never be alone. Let him be just and deal kindly with my people, for the dead are not powerless. "Dead" did I say? There is no death, only a change of worlds.

CHIEF SEATTLE, IN HIS 1854 ORATION

THE OLD SPIRITS

The paranormal is a broad field (UFOs, cryptozoology, earth energies, ancient mysteries). The division of it presumed to originate with the human mind or spirit is called psychic phenomena: ESP, poltergeists, mind over matter, and, yes, apparitions. Ghosts. This chapter is about haunted places and psychic experiences related to the New York Iroquois.

Today's Iroquois don't tell a lot of ghost stories, at least not in any writer's hearing. They talk about seeing the occasional curt supernatural image and give it the name of a once-living person if they can. They talk about their own psychic experiences. They talk about buildings and sites that host spectrums of paranormal effects, including these apparitions we call ghosts. They talk about dreams, visions, and psychic experiences, many of which seem related to the spirits of humans who have passed over. In this, they are the equal of any people known to history. Ghost stories of the popular type, though, are told about the Iroquois by others.

The great folklorist Louis C. Jones (1908–1990) was well aware that not all of New York's Native American ghost stories originated with the Native Americans. "These are neither the tales the Indians tell of themselves nor tales that have taproots in the white man's past." It makes sense that it would be this way, from several perspectives.

While we know of no treatise developing the Iroquois concept of the soul, the Iroquois seem to believe that the human organism had several levels of spirit-self. They aren't the first world society to have thought that. The classical world, for instance, thought there might have been layers to the immaterial part of the human being. The fine contemporary paranormal scholar Colin Wilson gets quite close to this with his "ladder of selves" theory.

As Arthur C. Parker concluded from the classic stories and his interviews, the Iroquois didn't consider all ghosts to be sentient, self-actuated beings. For the Iroquois, the ghost is, like the Roman *manes,* the body-spirit. The full psychic personality is long gone into the spirit world when the material body dies.

In our mix are some stories the Native Americans do tell. Our tales fall into four categories:

1. Traditional Iroquois ghost tales
2. Profiles of cross-cultural haunted sites that feature folklore of Native ghosts
3. White folktales and reports about Native American ghosts

4. Contemporary Native psychic experiences, including dreams, messages, and sightings

Native American ghosts are reported all over the United States. They are especially common in New York, where, if you checked hard enough, you could come up with some Native American–related ghost tale in almost every village or patch of city.

Our settlers reported Iroquoian ghosts. Just check the eighteenth- and nineteenth-century files. You won't fail to come up with some anecdote, however cryptic, about a haunt of relevance to New York's first nations. We've done our best to reconstruct a few such ghost stories. Not all of them may be current.

Apparitions of chiefs, shamans, and buckskinned maidens are scarce in some quarters, like Times Square. Little wonder. The period of reporting of an identifiable ghost is typically less than two hundred years, and Native American societies have been displaced from the territory of our cities at least that long.

A lot of ink has been spilled over America's Native ghosts. Their apparitions are often analyzed as manifestations of societal guilt. "Europeans take possession of Native American lands," noted Renee Bergland in *The National Uncanny* (2000). "But at the same time, Native Americans take supernatural possession of their dispossessors." As Jones pointed out, when the rest of us stopped slaughtering the Native Americans, we started to supernaturalize them. It may also be, though, that the ghosts are there; that the Native Americans, quick or dead, represent the spiritual conscience of the nation; and that, until we come to grips with something we haven't collectively faced, they will be here to remind us, like Banquo's ghost, of our debt, especially in New York state.

FIVE IROQUOIS MOTIFS

Doubtless there is a European influence in some of the most familiar Iroquoian ghost tales. There is also something original to them, not least of which is their attachment to precise upstate sites. In his 2005 book on Oneida folklore, Anthony Wayne Wonderley notes "how consistently [Iroquois supernatural stories] relate to space and local geography."

As we see everywhere else in the world, stories told by and about the Iroquois tend to fall into generic forms called motifs. In the matter of ghost lore, we find a couple of these story forms everywhere in Iroquois country, almost always affixed to local landmarks. Below are five of the major upstate Native American ghost motifs. They could have been sited in almost any county in the upstate. If we see an Onondaga tale in one of these motifs and find that a Seneca version has not been preserved, not to worry. We can presume it was there.

The Offended Lovers
(Seneca Country, Rochester)

A young Seneca couple journeyed along Lake Ontario to join their families on the Niagara River. They made camp near Long Pond in today's Greece. A handful of fellow travelers soon joined their fire.

Their guests were a party of renegades who at first shared only fire and conversation. Soon they stopped even addressing the husband and drew closer to the fair young wife. One started going through the belongings of the couple, looking for anything of value. Others started pawing the woman and told the husband to scram. They must not have known he was Seneca.

The only weapon near the young man was his knife, which he drew and instantly commenced to use. His wife fled the firelight. A scoundrel turned after her and was struck dead. The young Seneca fought like a panther, but his assailants had numbers, clubs, and tomahawks. He took many wounds. When sure his wife was clear, he dove into Long Pond, singing his death song, and went under.

All was still, all but, from an invisible grove, a woman's voice, chanting the bitter words of a curse. The renegades never reached their destination. Maybe they were finished by a party of avenging Seneca. Maybe it was something worse.

Apparitions are common by bodies of water and moonlight. The one at Long Pond could be anything. But a legend has developed that it's the Seneca husband reappearing as a sheeny spirit in the water. Whatever it is, Rochester historian Shirley Cox Husted recalled seeing it.

THE HAUNTED BATTLEFIELD
(Mohawk/Algonquin Country, Ballston Spa)

Until the advent of the car and modern highways, water has always been the preferred method of travel in the hilly, woody Northeast. When lakes and creeks didn't connect, there was a canoe-hauling march between the points called a portage, usually marked by a well-worn trail.

Kill is a Dutch word for creek, found often in Hudson-region place-names. Mourning Kill is a stream at the northeastern edge of Mohawk territory. Today it runs through the town of Ballston in Saratoga County and winds into the Kaydeross River. Between the creek called Mourning Kill and the outlet of Ballston Lake was a portage on one of the trails between the Mohawk and St. Lawrence Rivers. A thoroughfare for thousands of years, Mourning Kill was a natural meadow, a likely place for Native American groups to cross paths—even those who didn't get along.

The Trickster Raptor

One morning during strawberry time, centuries before Columbus, five hundred Mohawk men entered the Mourning Kill portage en route to the St. Lawrence River. As they did, the first handful of an Adirondack band approached from the other direction. An eagle landed on a high branch and looked down as if for a show. A fight broke out in the flower-rich meadow.

Packs of men in small parties pounced on one another. Clubs, spears, and tomahawks clashed. Archers' work was no less deadly. Both sides were shocked by the carnage in the trees, but neither gave ground. The eagle hopped and gloated on its perch. It rose and circled whenever parties lagged and cheered them when they rushed again. Both sides took it as a sign urging them to courage. The day would be remembered! New songs would be made and, for centuries, danced for their eagle!

But as the day stretched with no resolution at Mourning Kill, the men started to look at the raptor with revulsion. One by one the idea came over them that they had been killing and dying for nothing. As the last beam of sunlight tipped the high pines, five hundred bows lifted, and that many arrows launched as if by a single impulse. Blood, feathers, and bones, the bird fell to the earth. It had hardly touched ground before a bright dove rose out of its tattered form and flew up and away. The men parted and went their ways with only glances at those they had been trying all day to kill. No man of this battle at Mourning Kill ever raised a hand against folk of the other nation again.

For generations, the landscape remembered. The wild roses that sprouted in strawberry time came no color but red in memory of the loss and sacrifice. For years, the ghosts of the warriors showed themselves at their old battleground at the end of the occasional day. The sounds of their cries may have troubled the nights for centuries. The effect may linger today in reports of mysterious lights, likely witch lights, at dusk in Mourning Kill.

A story like this teaches us to understand the Native American reverence for human remains. They believe the spirit has some connection still to the body, possibly one too profound for human philosophy. In this case, though, the returning dead person is less ghost or spirit and more of what's called a revenant: They're back—in the flesh.

In the old days, the Iroquois often wrapped their dead in skins and left them above the ground in trees or on open scaffolds. This way the natural processes could do their work in the clear air and give back to nature what it had put together.

The Specter Wife
(Seneca Country, Western New York)

A young hunter had a pretty wife to whom he was much attached. She sickened and died within days, leaving him and his young daughter. Even after the accustomed ten-day mourning period of the Death Feast, the husband was beside himself. He wandered about the village aimlessly, sitting by himself, crying and muttering, their sad little girl in tow. He recovered enough to join the rest of the men for the hunting season. He left his daughter in their home, telling her that her mother's spirit would look out for her.

In a few days, he came back and was surprised to find the fire already made and his daughter looking happy. He wondered about this, but the girl was too young to talk. The next day when he came home, the fire was made as before. Furthermore, his daughter's hair was combed and her face was clean as if a mother were caring for her. The next day he came home a bit early and found the fire made, the girl groomed, and the meal started. The man wondered if the Great Spirit had taken pity on him.

He came home still earlier the next day and caught a glimpse of his wife's dress darting around the lodge as if she had just left their home. He pursued it, but saw nothing.

The next day he rejoiced to himself, hardly able to think about his hunting, sure that the Great Spirit was returning his wife to him. Sure enough, when he came home that day he found the meal almost ready to serve and his wife at her appointed tasks. He could hardly believe it. He rushed to embrace her, but she stopped him with a gesture.

"It's true that I've returned. I've been coming back to our daughter all along. I loved you both so much that I couldn't rest in the other world. I'll stay with you and care for you both, but I'm still one with the spirits. You must never try to touch me in any way."

The young man was overjoyed to have her in any capacity, and the family spent many a month together. At the end of the hunting season, though, the small family was sharing a meal when the mother cut loose with a scream. "My burial place has caught fire!" she said, horror in her eyes. "I have to go. I love you both, and I will see you on the other side!" And she vanished.

The hunter ran madly through the woods to his wife's scaffold and saw indeed that it had caught fire. Her body was almost entirely consumed. It might have been the work of lightning. That was the beginning of the time that the Iroquois started to bury their dead. It's from events like these that societies like the Chanters for the Dead originated, intended to ease the earthbound spirits.

The Old Chief's Grave
(Onondaga Country, Skaneateles Lake)

It was the fall of 1696. Frontenac's massive army had landed near Onondaga Lake and was on its way to the Onondaga Castle. The huge force had guns and cannon. Open battle was pointless. Even a traditional Iroquois ambush was a poor idea. These invaders had Native allies serving as their own keen scouts.

The Onondaga leaders called their century-old chief to the council fire. His name Thurensera was said to mean "dawn of the light." No one watching him on a litter would guess how agile he'd been in his youth.

"Not until you join with the other Longhouse nations can you fight this force," he said. "But the invaders must learn a lesson. I will stay to show them how an Onondaga can die." The whole camp took a breath. Thurensera would be tortured and killed.

The old chief told them how he wanted to be buried: with his pipe, his canoe, his tomahawk, and his bow, on a hill overlooking Skaneateles Lake. When they returned, they would find his bones, doubtless by the torture stake. He made his good-byes, declaring them the last words he would speak. Then he took a Zen-style pose, faced the direction from which the invaders were expected, and waited for an army alone. His people fired their homes, loaded their belongings, and filed by him with their last words.

All that Thurensera foretold came to pass. His burial, too, went as planned. Today, Skaneateles Lake, including any of a dozen potential gravesites, is a region of paranormal allure. What one of the mystery lights on any hill about that lake is a blink of the orenda of the old chief? That spectral form they report, rising from the shallows on moonlit nights—is it the Dawn of the Light?

The Lovers' Leap
(Seneca Country, Canandaigua Lake)

For many years the Algonquin speakers and the Iroquois had waged war throughout the Northeast. A valiant Algonquin, Hondosa, had killed in a fair fight the son of the Seneca chief into whose hands he had fallen. The handsome guest was awarded the honor of proving his national courage at the torture stake. Till then he was treated with the utmost courtesy. Among his privileges was the attention of the fairest maids, including the chief's daughter, sister of the man he had killed. Many days she waited on him and talked to him. She came to love him.

The guards slept, the escape was made, and the pair paddled across Canandaigua Lake into the reflection of the fabled mountain Ganundowa, most likely today's Bare Hill. Pursuers came, swift young warriors not weakened from weeks of captivity. The pair reached the eastern shore first.

"Run," the girl told her chief. "Run to your people. I will face them."

"We run or stay together," said the man. They climbed the hill over the lake and looked down from a steep crag. As their pursuers closed, the pair leaped to the rocks below. Ever since, their spirits can be seen in the waters of the lake as reflections, and sometimes, in the right light, as images, hand in hand, on the edge of that same cliff.

ROGERS ISLAND

There are two Rogers Islands in the Hudson River. The one in Washington County just off Fort Edward is where Major Robert Rogers trained Anglo-American forest fighters for the French and Indian Wars. About fifteen miles north of Saratoga Springs, this is "the spiritual home" of American special forces. Don't be shocked that something spiritual could be associated with war. Companies of men who risk their lives together develop intense bonds that span generations, including psychic traditions.

Eighty miles south, also in the Hudson, is Rogers Island, Columbia County. Archaeologists have found six-thousand-year-old signs of hunting and fishing here. The battle was far more recent.

The Last of the Mohicans

The Keepers of the Eastern Door, the Mohawks, were expanding their territory. They met in battle in 1628 with an alliance of Algonquin-speaking nations, including the Mohicans, whose domain was this part of the Hudson Valley. The Claverack woods resounded with yells and groans, the clack of weapons, the arrows' hiss.

The Mohawk got more more fight than they bargained for. At sunset, they withdrew in apparent despair to Vastrick's—now Rogers—Island. Their foes ringed them and waited.

The Mohawk made campfires, wrapped sticks and logs into bundles, arranged them like sleeping warriors, and lay waiting in the dark. The Mohicans crept to the scene, jumped the bundles, and sprung the trap. This was the last of the Mohicans, at least as national players.

A century ago the visitor to Rogers Island could still see the spot of the struggle: an open green ringed with pines old enough to have witnessed the clash. For years, arrowheads and trophies turned up, and Rogers Island was one of the Hudson's most haunted spots. It was said that, on the right night, the old battle resounded on both sides of the river. No one dared get close enough to see if the source was visible.

It would be no wonder if you were to visit Rogers Island and find the marvel over. Against logic, there seems to be an expiration date for ghosts. As we've observed, two hundred years is it for most of them. We've already crossed that mark for most of our New York Native American sites.

THE DARKNESS ON THE HILL
(Seneca/Cayuga Country)

Where the name *Spanish Hill* came from is a question. This bread-loaf-shaped hill is a stone's throw south of I-86, about ten miles east of Elmira by the cross of the Chemung and the north branch of the Susquehanna. Fortifications found here were said to be quite like those at the mystery site Bluff Point, fifty miles to the north. European-style artifacts suggested the visit of gold-hunting conquistadors, even the last holdout of besieged buccaneers. French explorer Champlain wrote about Carantouan, a Native American fort some suspect was Spanish Hill. It would be hard to find a place in Iroquois country with a reputation like it.

Writer Carl Carmer found Spanish Hill a mystical place that fully engaged the circuits of wonder. To white settlers in the late 1700s, it was a hill of dread, and no Native American would set foot on it. Historian Deb Twigg calls its energy "the Darkness on the Hill."

Once this formation was presumed a titanic, man-made earthwork. It's clear now that it was formed by retreating glaciers. It may have been the site of a battle, and a legendary curse.

The Iroquois Confederacy cleared New York of the Huron, Eries, and Neutrals. The Andaste community at the southern edge of Seneca/ Cayuga territory may have given them more trouble than all the rest. An Iroquois attack in the spring of 1662 found the Andastes behind a double-walled fort and a handful of European cannon. They hoisted the Iroquois ambassadors over the walls and killed them slowly in sight and sound of their fellows. The Iroquois considered Spanish Hill haunted, and then cursed, ever after. The Andastes, stricken by plague, were later overwhelmed by the Iroquois. Their refugees were shamefully massacred by white vigilantes called the Paxton Boys.

Spanish Hill today is a tough place to collect folklore. It has a fine house at the top and posted signs about it. Still, there are newspaper reports of haunted houses (1930) and suspicious construction accidents (1971). There are still rumors of mysterious fires afflicting whatever has been done up there. Earlier forms of legends included strange caves, buried treasure, and giant skeleton reports—a New York state fixture.

The Mohawk sided with the British during the American Revolution, and things didn't go their way. Most of them headed to Canada, but one diehard stayed near Schenectady.

The Phantom Paddler of the Mohawk (Mohawk Country)

The old Mohawk lived on the Hill of Strawberries and came now and then to the Dorp—the Schenectady Stockade Historic District—with fish and game for trade.

On those occasions, he revealed his other gifts: He could shoot and drink as well as any white.

One day in 1789 he came to town and did a couple of strange things. For one, he shunned the tavern. For another, he gave his load of fish to a friend and refused payment. All he said in explanation was, "Great Spirit call. Indian no need." Then he got into his canoe and headed up the Mohawk River.

Boys swimming off a sand bar saw something odd the same day: the old Mohawk in his canoe, moving against the current without paddling. Like Pharaoh in the stern he sat, head up, arms folded across his chest. Next day the canoe was found far down the river.

A week later a white who had known the gent was out fishing when he looked up and saw his old pal sitting on a high bank of one of the river islands, arms folded and gazing "toward his departed people," according to Louis C. Jones. This may have been a look toward Canada, but possibly it was toward vanished riverside villages that might have been considered the Mohawk homeland. The white guy paddled over and offered him a lift to shore. The Mohawk—clearly a ghost—faded from view as his head turned.

In the accounts of longtime Schenectady historian Percy Van Epps (1859– 1951), this old Mohawk was one of the longest-lasting ghosts of the region. Many reported seeing him in this pose, knees hugged to his chin—a common burial position—and looking to the upper reaches of the valley. We only wish his name had been preserved.

It seems logical to link him with the phantom Indian paddler who with his canoe has been reported recently on the Mohawk River between Utica and Schenectady. On the right night, you could probably see him from many spots on the I-90 and Route 5.

The Ghost-Riders of Coxsackie
(Mohawk Country)

In the settler days, a white hunter and trader named Nick Wolsey lived along the Hudson in Green County near Coxsackie. Honest and fair, Wolsey got along well with his Native American neighbors.

To one village in particular he kept returning, and few needed the medicine people to know that it was more than trade that brought him in. In fact, it was a lovely lass whose name Louis C. Jones remembers as Minamee. She was sought after by the young men of her nation, but became the wife of the white trader.

Wolsey was so well thought of in the village that no one disapproved—no one, that is, but one jealous suitor. There was one bitter outburst between the two contenders for Minamee, possibly on the wedding day, but otherwise the matter seemed forgotten.

It was a happy year for Nick Wolsey and his new bride. Every day when he returned from his hunting, trading, or trapping, the welcoming smoke of the hearth drifted over the clearing. Light shone in the cabin, and his wife and her babe waited in the open doorway.

One day he came home to find trouble. The door was open, but no one stood in it, and no blue haze or sweet smoke lingered. On the cabin floor, he saw the baby's decapitated head, and in the shadow, eyes glazed, beaten and bruised, his young wife clutching the tiny trunk. She died sometime that night, but not before telling Nick Wolsey about the drunken rampage of her former suitor and the horror he had visited upon them.

Wolsey rode to the nearby village and told the tale. The murderer was brought forth, and Wolsey allowed to name the punishment. "You wanted Minamee," he said, "so badly that you would kill. Then have her now!" The murderer was lashed face to face with the body, then mounted on a crazed horse. The grisly burdens on its back, it tore off into the woods along the ancient trails. It was never seen again.

They say that for many years after, the ghost horse and its desperate riders were dreaded apparitions in this part of the Catskills. Even today if you are in the region some night and hear hollow hoofbeats and a godless howling, you may know that Wolsey's revenge lasted longer than life.

THE WAILING SPIRITS

The old Iroquois had clearly developed a concept of the soul that was detachable from the human body.

They also believed that, on occasion, the souls of the dead can be invited back from the afterlife to enjoy the love, tribute, and even goods of this world. This is the night of the dead familiar to many world societies. The Iroquois version seems to have had no fixed solar date. The dead may also come back uninvited.

Seventeenth-century missionaries and travelers reported incidents reflecting the Iroquois dread of offended human spirits. A servant girl of the Erie Nation was impulsively killed by her Onondaga mistress in December of 1656. A couple of captives were executed in a Seneca village in 1677. In both cases, the communities sent word all round that so-and-so had been killed that day. That night, the village set up a ritual racket—howling, screaming, pounding, and banging, hoping to distract, reorient, or even scare off the presences of the indignant dead.

The Caged Spirit

Early one evening in February of 1807 a Leicester man started heading for the western shore of the Genesee River. This meant crossing the river at its shallows where it freezes easily. About halfway over the Genesee Flats, he was shocked and terrified by the sounds of human screaming, seemingly coming from the sky above him. He hustled home and told his neighbors.

A handful of suspicious Genesee farm folk came back to the spot the next night. The gusty shrieking returned, this time for multiple witnesses! Word spread, and people came from far parts just to hear it. Every night for two weeks no member of the ever-increasing crowds was disappointed by failing to be scared silly. Oh dependable prodigy! At least once there may have been two thousand onlookers. Among the multitude of rustic spectators were several prominent, educated gentlemen ("very aged and very reliable," according to the article in the Genesee Valley Herald*). They, too, vouched for the phenomenon.*

This wonder needed an answer, and someone thought of consulting the Native Americans—a remedy we'd recommend today for many American problems. The Seneca dwelling at nearby Squakie Hill held a council and came to the conclusion that this was the spirit of one of their elders who had recently died. Apparently it had lost its way on the journey to the Iroquois heaven and was caught in this sort of nether land. To help the disoriented soul, a hundred warriors were chosen, armed with rifles, and placed as directly under the noise as possible. At a signal, all of them fired their guns at once into the air. The echoes faded, and the wonder was no more. It was not reported again after the Senecas' ceremony, so maybe their explanation of it was the best. It would be far from the first time.

THE ONTARIO COUNTY COURTHOUSE
(Seneca Country)

At the north end of Canandaigua Lake was a village of Great Hill folk and other Native American communities before them. Its name in Seneca means "the chosen spot," and Canandaigua is still one of the most gorgeous towns in New York state. It's long been a place of power.

Somewhere in today's village the first whites found a big old fort—a term for both a palisaded town and an oval or circular earthwork shape. Canandaigua was one of the frontier's early capitals, nucleus of a huge tract that stretched westward and became many of today's counties. Canandaigua was the seat of Ontario County's government and a frontier center of population and trade. Its star was high until the Erie Canal turned cities like Buffalo, Rochester, and Syracuse into metropolises.

Canandaigua's original 1794 courthouse administered frontier justice from the square at 27 North Main. New York's first jury trial west of Albany was here. (It was over the theft of a cowbell.) By a big rock still here was signed the Pickering Treaty (1794), the oldest still-honored pact between the United States and the Iroquois.

The splendid Greek Revival courthouse we see today was wrought in 1857 by architect Henry S. Searle (1809–1892), most likely on the spot of the earlier one. Searle's original was squarer than what we see today. The wings that make the courthouse rectangular were put on in 1908 by another Rochester star, J. Foster Warner (1859–1937). Both tended to design buildings that would someday be haunted, and this one does not disappoint.

Some memorable guests have made in-life appearances here, which always gives a prod to psychic folklore. In the original courthouse on this square, Red Jacket defended a Seneca accused of murder in 1794.

(Stiff-Armed George was convicted but later pardoned by state governor George Clinton.) Cult leader/community founder Jemima Wilkinson was tried here in 1800 for blasphemy. Batavia's famous William Morgan (1774–1826), allegedly kidnapped and murdered by the Masons, was jailed here in 1826. In the updated courthouse, suffragette Susan B. Anthony (1820–1906) was tried and fined in 1873 for voting in the

The Ontario County Courthouse, Canandaigua, with a stone marker commemorating the 1794 Pickering Treaty

presidential election. Two executions that took place here—those of Charles Eighmey (1876) and John Kelly (1889)—involved illicit love affairs and unseemly gallows scenes. We have many candidates for ghosts. This is one of the liveliest sites in the upstate.

Every courthouse has its cast of mortal grievants. We have here a diverse and nether legion. One comes in the image of a Native American male, rumored to have been hung for some crime or other. A ghostly black man appears, too, suspected to be a runaway slave returned South, if not local abolitionist Richard Valentine (1798–1874), still blaming the system over the court case that had ruined him. Even an image identified as Red Jacket is reported here now and then, maybe lamenting one of the few cases that got away from him.

One curious thing is the way the building itself has been supernaturalized. When the verdict against Anthony was announced, they say, the scales of the statue of justice atop the building clattered to the ground. Faces are said to peer and arms reach out of the courtroom walls. Men working near the dome have been stunned by the building's reactions, shuddering and moaning like a giant organic being under attack by hammer and chisel. It's as if the Iroquois sense of the power of place spires up through its foundations.

This is not by a long shot the only upstate site to represent a human train wreck of history, a place or zone at which memorable events tend to pile up; nor is it an exclusively Native American site. But what in New York is exclusively anyone's? We're all just passing through, or over. This psychically energetic site illustrates again that the Native American element cannot be separated from any aspect of New York life. The clearest ghosts at this site may be figurative ones, the ghosts of a ceremony.

Go back to that fortnight in 1794 as the Pickering/Canandaigua Treaty was made. Between October 18 and November 12, sixteen hundred Native Americans camped about the well-wooded region. Hunting parties brought in one hundred deer a day. Native witnesses included a Longhouse all-star team: Farmer's Brother, Cornplanter, Red Jacket,

Little Beard, and Handsome Lake. Sometimes called the Calico Treaty, it declared peace, set aside reservations of land, and provided the annual delivery of a batch of cloth—calico—from the U.S. government to the Seneca. The hand-off still takes place. Drop by that stone outside the courthouse any November 11 and see for yourself.

THE KICKING CHIEF OF COOPERSTOWN
(Mohawk/Oneida Country)

Cooperstown ought to have ghosts. Founded in the late 1700s, it's one of the older villages in this part of the state. Today's village doubtless covers many unknown Native American burials, and at least one ancient earthwork still stands along the Susquehanna River. They say that on the right full moon, long Otsego Lake above it still reverberates with the sounds of centuries of Native American canoes paddling across the water.

On the west side of River Street near the estate called Greencrest and at the edge of Cooper Park is a stone wall that's gone through a lot of changes. For most of the twentieth century, it was smooth. By the 1960s, the stones bulged toward the street, as if the wall were buckling—or something inside was trying to get out. Some Cooperstonians got curious, broke through the wall, and found a skeleton, with pipes, weapons, and artifacts. Most presumed it the burial of a Mohawk chief, though he was just as likely to have been an Oneida. Otsego Lake is the boundary between their former territories, and Cooperstown roots it like the dot of an exclamation point. This burial is on the Oneida side of the town.

The townsfolk could have saved themselves the trouble if they had read Ralph Birdsall's (1871–1918) 1917 history. The skeleton was found in the late 1700s by Judge William Cooper (1754–1809), father of the Leatherstocking Tales author. The novelist's grandson, also named James Fenimore Cooper, told this tale to folklorist Harold W. Thompson (1891–1964). How the body got into a wall in the first place is left to conjecture.

It seems likely that the wall's first builders may have found the old chief exactly where he was and decided to keep him near his original spot by putting him in the wall. Many thinner walls fell around the bones, and a stronger one was made. It lasted into the Woodstock era and merely buckled.

In local tradition, the buried chief's posthumous kicking expressed his fury at the white takeover of his lands. Other supernatural theories involve a weeping skeleton whose saline tears undermined the wall and a thrashing one trying to get a bit of leg room. This guy was folded close: in a virtual squat, knees to chin, arms round his shins.

Not the least of the controversy is the whereabouts of the chief's remains today. Did they put him back, with a little repositioning, and reform the wall? Did they sell the artifacts? Did they give the bones to a local museum? Heaven help whoever holds them, if his or her heart isn't pure. At least the wall is still behaving.

THE FIVE GHOSTS OF RED JACKET
(Seneca Country)

The Six Nations were not metallurgists, painters, city builders, or engineers. Their distinctive arts were those natural to their place and lifestyle, those of mind and word: storytelling, song making, and speech giving. They were particularly famous for their orators, and the man we call Red Jacket was one of the greatest. When he was born near Keuka Lake in 1750, Iroquois lifestyle and landscape were much as they had been for a thousand years. When he died at Buffalo in 1830, he was afraid for Native American survival.

The name Red Jacket likely comes from the British officer's coat he often wore. His birth name Otetiani is often said to mean "always on guard." By the time he stood with the Six Nations counselors he was Sagoyewata. That could mean "he keeps them awake," but it's also been taken as "he can't shut up." No translation implies that he withheld his opinion.

Red Jacket's monument at Forest Lawn, Buffalo

Many whites considered Red Jacket a genius, an orator ranking with Cicero and Demosthenes. He campaigned against selling land to whites and taking alcohol from them. He caught the liquid plague himself, and most of the comical episodes in his file come from it. George Washington's silver medal on his chest did sobriety no favors, making Red Jacket one of the few Native Americans allowed in a white pub. He was at the least a great wit, who, even through the language barrier, came up with some of the best lines of the day.

All kinds of invective get thrown around in political squabbles, and Red Jacket had his share of them. One image of him that's stuck in history is coward. No one who called out Joseph Brant and Cornplanter could have been a chicken. Eyewitnesses described Red Jacket leading a devastating guerilla operation at the 1813 Battle of Chippewa. Some Iroquois maintain that Red Jacket founded a deadly Seneca assassins' cult, the Red Tips, named for the red-tailed hawk, little brother of the eagle. (The Mohawk correspondents are the Black Hand. They choke you in the night and leave only sooty marks on your throat.) Red Jacket a coward? That's silly on the face of it. He was Seneca.

In his last years, Red Jacket was filled with gratitude to the Great Spirit for his days on earth. Hoping to honor him with the ceremony of one last hunt, he plunged into the Genesee Valley, probably in Livingston County. He was expecting the old-growth forest he remembered, streaked with footpaths and dotted with villages. Before long, he came to a fence and saw cleared land and whites plowing. He went off in a different direction and came to another fence and another farmer's field. He sat down on the trail and sobbed.

After a round of farewells to friends and relatives, Red Jacket died at Buffalo Creek in 1830, "exulting that the Great Spirit had made him an Indian" and dreading a white burial. His Christian wife, however, ruled his rites. He was originally buried near many Seneca luminaries in the Old Indian Graveyard at Buffum Street in Buffalo, but his remains did a spell in a cherry wood chest on the

Cattaraugus Reservation until they were reinterred—allegedly—in 1884 at Buffalo's Forest Lawn Cemetery, resting now by a fine martial monument, tomahawk in hand.

Some Seneca believe that Red Jacket got his wish and that the bones under the monument are not his. In one week of May 2010, I met two whites claiming to know where his true grave was. (One proposed site was in West Seneca and the other Elma.) With so many questions about Red Jacket's bones, it's no wonder his ghost might be acting up. After-life protests are thought customary at troubled graves. (The wretch Caligula was said to have haunted his Roman villa until someone treated his remains fairly.)

Folklore hangs the name *Red Jacket* on ghosts in his section of Forest Lawn, by the sites of Canandaigua and Batavia courthouses at which he spoke, and at still-standing Williamsville and Lewiston inns at which he might have been overserved. The best report of a sighting comes from a folder of notes willed to the Buffalo Museum by volunteer archaeologist and Erie lakeshore antiquarian Everett Burmaster (1890–1965).

As a boy around 1900, Burmaster and a pal cut through the Cattaraugus Reservation on a foggy night. As they passed a ruined house, they heard strange rustling sounds and saw a mass of mist take the form of a man in a heavy coat and beaver hat. The apparition drifted right through a fence and became indistinct, then invisible. It turned out that this had been the home of Red Jacket's stepdaughter. The box holding his bones had once rested there, and the locals had seen him many a time. They see him still—in a young, vigorous form.

My Seneca contacts also think Native burial ground was emptied as fill beneath Buffalo's streets and roads, hence Red Jacket's spectral reappearance may be an afterthought. Maybe a bit of him is everywhere with us, then, under our feet, in the air, in the trees. The image of Native Americans as spiritual counselors of white Americans may, after all, be what this book is about, but still, it's a mite trite the way countless Victorian-era mediums hauled Red Jacket up as a spirit guide. Blessings on you, old He Keeps Them Awake, wherever you rest or return.

THE TONAWANDA PRESBYTERIAN
(Seneca Country)

Buffalo scholar and preservationist Austin Fox (1913–1996) (*Church Tales of the Niagara Frontier*) figured that 1868 was a good year for the construction of the Tonawanda Presbyterian Church. It's been remodeled and looks younger than that would make it, but the Seneca operate with the assumption that its core is decades older. Some say that Reverend Asher Wright (1803–1875) transcribed at least part of Seneca Prophet Handsome Lake's Code in a building on this site, possibly an older version of this one. (The prophet himself died in 1815.) Whatever its age, the building has an illustrious legacy, including a psychic one.

Some Seneca consider this the most actively haunted building in western New York. People who visit the church routinely see and feel things out of the normal. Even in the middle of the day, something raises their hair; something touches them on the arm; something brushes their shoulders. At night when the building is empty, something plays the piano. In 2005, our Mohawk friend Andy Printup recalled rumors that the lights of the church turn themselves on at night. "This is no high-tech church with automatic lights," he said. His brother used to go by there frequently and reported the effect himself.

This church became so proverbial as a haunt that the reservation had to recruit security to watch it for periods in the 1980s. White thrill seekers came here routinely in hopes of witnessing something spooky.

Our favorite report is one from a Christmas season, remembered for us by Seneca Jean Taradena in the late 1990s. A dozen members of a choir were getting ready to practice. The doors opened and footsteps came down the aisles behind them. Thinking it no more than fellow choristers on the way, they kept their eyes ahead of them on the minister. "Let's wait for them," he said, looking down at his music. The footsteps stopped, as if a party were waiting, and the singers turned to look. No one visible was there. "Well," said the minister, packing up with a feeble smile. "I guess we won't practice today." They got up and filed out. Through the back door.

HAUNTED ROADS

Buildings and battlefields aren't the only things that get haunted in New York state. There are streets and sections of road in every community that pick up formidable bodies of supernatural folklore. Many of them had deep roots in Native American tradition and have to be considered power sites, of a different sort than a haunted human enclosure.

New York's most prominent old footpaths are well known, and most have been turned into numbered highways by now. Many of our haunted roads were once stretches of them.

Some of our psychic highways may also be what are called (in England) corpse paths, the routes the human dead in their coffins traveled to their last rest. All across medieval Europe, these often short paths from church to graveyard were considered wonderful places for spirit spotting on the right nights of the year, generally power nights relevant to the specific society. (The night varied. In Germany, this would have been April 30, Walpurgisnacht. In Scandinavia and much of England, it might have been June 24, the traditional Midsummer's Eve or St. John's Day. In Celtic countries the night would have been the variously spelled Samhain, our Halloween.)

While in old Europe, the corpse path was usually a walkway with little other use; today our village streets often fall into the configuration. Some city streets link several churches and graveyards in a single mile. We drive over them every day. We live on them. Funeral processions take them, too.

Short stretches of some of these New York power tracks are also leys. This is a much-used term in today's spiritualist New Age. Depending on whom you talk to, leys are:

- Lines of spiritual force along the landscape
- Sacred pathways
- Alignments of sites (both naturally sacred or man-made and religious)

The only definition that can be proven to an open-minded skeptic is the last. Preindustrial people *did* set up their sacred sites in alignment with each other. (An Inca term for these connectors—ceques—means something like "a row of things.") The typical ratio is still, we believe, six sites on a line ten miles long.

Leys collect supernatural folklore, especially where they cross. While leys were rediscovered and popularized in England, an island dense with both antiquarians and cross-cultural sacred sites, they can be found worldwide. Native American societies in the Andes, the Chacoan (Four Corners) region, Mexico, and the Mississippian/Ohio Valley were known to have established these dead-straight sightlines across impressive distances. Some were dramatic and visible pathways like the Hopewell Highway in Ohio and the Four Corners' region's Chaco Meridian.

Surely leys existed in ancient New York state. We know of no authoritative study of our potential leys, and I don't see how a comprehensive one could be done, since so many of the ancient monuments are gone and their exact locations are unknown.

Few of these haunted roads are true leys; they aren't all straight, for one thing. Still, many short stretches may be leys—or corpse paths. The haunted sections themselves may be stretches of ancient trails. We mention here a few of the power trails we know that have Native American roots—as if anything in New York state doesn't.

DELAWARE AVENUE
(Buffalo, Erie County)

The turn of the twentieth century was likely Buffalo's peak. One of its grandest streets was called Millionaires' Row. For a short stretch,

Delaware Avenue was one of the truest leys we know of in New York state. It connected an apparent earthwork at the core of Joseph Ellicott's old city plan with the powerful natural fountain at Gates Circle before plunging into today's Forest Lawn Cemetery and several ancient burial mounds. All three of these sites were legitimate power points to the Native Americans of the area, defining Delaware Avenue as a ley. It also has plenty of churches and current or former graveyards.

American Freemasons and landscape planners tend to be sensitive to Native American site traditions. The work at Delaware's south end—by Ellicott—and that of Frederick Law Olmsted a few miles north certainly commemorate this configuration.

Delaware, a Native American ley, is one of Buffalo's most haunted avenues. We venture to say that if you did five-minute interviews up and down the street between Niagara Square and Delaware Park, you would collect psychic reports from half the buildings. So far the only named Native spook we hear of is Red Jacket at Forest Lawn Cemetery. The idea of a ley in a modern city might seem strange, but, as Hamlet says, as a stranger give it welcome.

BLACK NOSE SPRINGS ROAD
(The Tuscarora Reservation, Niagara County)

Urban legend has an explanation for the juju on short, cutoff Black Nose Springs Road: the massacre of a family whose bodies were thrown into a nearby pond. As if reminders of their murderers' guilt, their light, pale, wretched faces kept appearing just under the surface, even decades after the event. If so, their influence radiates. Living witnesses driving on the road at night report scary faces in their mirrors and sounds on the outside of the car as if something alongside it is either keeping pace and tapping a message or hitching an unseemly ride.

These massacres keep coming up in the folklore of hauntings, seldom with any background. If there's truth to the theme in this case, the event likely happened as some offshoot of the War of 1812. Both sides in that war had Native American allies, and this reservation along the underbelly of Lake Ontario was ravaged by attacks out of Fort Niagara made by British-allied Mohawk and Great Lakes nations. The ghostly backdrop could also have been a lash back by the U.S.-allied Tuscarora upon white Loyalist agents.

THE FORBIDDEN TRAIL
(Allegany, Cattaraugus, and Chautauqua Counties)

East–west Iroquois trails were paths of peace and commerce. They ran between the New York Iroquois nations. North–south trails were ones of war; invaders usually came from Pennsylvania or Lake Ontario. That way they could hit one Iroquois nation without having to fight through the territory of others.

The ominously named Forbidden Trail is a tweener, a gnarly diagonal flowing from the core of the state to the Allegany region. Sometimes called the Andaste Trail after some Iroquoian enemies, this was a military shortcut, a warpath that Iroquois warriors used to respond to emergencies to the southwest.

The Forbidden Trail connects old paths at Tioga Point with ones at Olean. It flanks creeks and rivers—the Genesee, the Allegheny—and coils through a lot of Southern Tier villages, generally as their main street. Towns likely to be on it include Alfred, Almond, Angelica, Canisteo, Corning, Elkland, Hornell, and Painted Post. Other than that, its exact course is a matter of debate. This figures. It was meant to be a secret: You stray, you pay.

We can hardly summarize the psychic and paranormal folklore that comes from the region of this trail. Visions were reported along it in historic times, including prophetic images on the moon. Otherwise, let your imagination run free: Bigfoot, UFOs, ancient mystery ruins, as well as haunted buildings along it in every village it bisects. It's hard to imagine what this trail would have been like at night in the old days.

13 CURVES
(West Syracuse, New York, Onondaga County)

Winding and narrow, 13 Curves is a stretch of Cedarvale Road south-west of Syracuse. It's creepy for natural reasons. It has no shoulder, and trees crowd the asphalt as though reaching for motorists. The effect is squared at night. Every accident adds to its reputation. At the middle, there's even a dead man's curve.

The traditional ghost of 13 Curves is an archetype, what I call the woman in white. Most New York state villages have a handful of them. There is even a folkloric motif, a 1940s car crash on a wedding night, behind the one reported at 13 Curves. The place has become a Halloween hotspot. Thrill seekers report ghost faces in the car mirrors. Others drive right through a faint form on the road and sense a chill permeating the car.

13 Curves might seem no more than a simple haunting were it not so suspiciously located on something called Onondaga Hill. As it is, we interpret 13 Curves as one of those wonderful cross-cultural morphs we get in New York state, a power place acting up and frying the circuits of the observers. To those who fail to see the Native American connection to this folkloric figure, it should be remembered that, whatever the melanin-content of the skin of the living, ghosts are often on the pale side.

WEST ROAD
(Oneida, Oneida County)

Like a lot of haunted roads, this stretch a mile or so west of Oneida Castle changes its name a bunch of times. It's Smith Road at the bottom, Creek Road north of that, then Highway 10, Highway 54, and Pine Ridge Road. It's also called Creek Road and County Highway 29 in other places.

Our contemporary Anthony Wonderley sifted many Oneida tidbits from the papers of Hope Emily Allen. In one of them from the early 1900s, Electa Johns recalled the haunting of her parents' derelict house on West Road: "A stone rolls through it and then a ball of fire follows." According to Johns, many West Road houses kept their hauntings even after the Oneida left. West Road may be just as famous for witchcraft as for ghost lights and psychokinetic stones.

ROUTE 5

Route 5 is the daddy of New York power roads. A three-hundred-mile track from Albany to the Niagara, it is a rib, a spine of psychic energy that runs along the Onondaga Formation. This trail, the spine of Iroquoia, is ancient. There's a good possibility that the foot-wide track the first whites encountered was made by beasts migrating east to west with the seasons. They could have been mammoths and short-faced bears. Paleo-Indians who hunted them used the track along the underbelly of the Ontario once the glaciers receded. The Jesuits called it the Iron Path since it was packed so hard and so much military hardware clanked along it. Only the Hudson Valley could even be suggested as the broker of that much New York state energy.

Today, this old track is paved over and massively traveled. In places, it is a virtual highway. In others, it is the main street of quaint villages, holding historic sites and buildings. Visit any one of them on the route and walk each side with a clipboard. Do a few interviews at any building older than fifty years. The ghosts you hear of may not all appear as Native Americans, but you will hear of ghosts. The effect doubles in stretches where 20A and 5 overlap. Sections outside Canandaigua get reports of altered animal forms. Other stretches are considered cursed and accident-prone.

While this was a migration trail, a hunting trail, and a warpath, it was also a vision trail. If it surprises the reader that something could be strongly all four, remember that the Native American mind was not nurtured on the Socratic dialogues, which arrive at many of their truths by winnowing down and excluding nontruths. The Native American mind had no trouble with one thing being strongly of one quality and also strongly of another.

THE SPIRIT WORLD

Without question, the Iroquois grieve when a loved one dies. If we had to give a character to it, we would say that their grief tends to be a melancholy and a sense of tribute, not the utter despair displayed by some whites. It could be because their faith in a life to come is so strong, seemingly like that of the old Celtic warriors, who borrowed from each other in life with the promise of repayment in the afterworld. This belief may not be a thing of the past among the Iroquois, and it could be with them from their earliest years.

Though not as famous as Davey Crockett or Daniel Boone, New York "Indian Fighter" Tom Quick (1733?–1795) was a similar figure. There was a real man, and there is a pile of folklore about him. Not all of that said about Quick is heroic. Though Quick is associated with Milford, Pennsylvania, the site of his birth, most of his adventures were in Iroquois country.

Quick's Revenge

Quick grew up around Native Americans and was a great woodsman, in that sense the proverbial "white Indian" like the Deerslayer of Cooper's fiction. His greatest gift, though, was an uncanny ability to sense danger.

In the turmoil of the colonial wars, Quick's family suffered under Native attacks. Quick might have blamed fate, mankind, or war. He might have blamed the French and then the British Empire who launched these allied attacks. He might have blamed first Algonquin speakers or Iroquoians. He might have blamed individuals. Instead, he blamed all Native Americans.

Quick's revenge was so drastic and bitter that it set off a cycle of retribution that lasted long after peace was declared. Quick never knew which Native American he encountered might be remembering a death he had dealt a brother or comrade.

One winter night in a tavern, Quick found that he had a sudden new friend. Drinking, joking, laughing at everything Quick said, a young Native American man proposed hunting together on the morrow. Quick doubted that all was as it looked. In the middle of the night, he emptied his new friend's rifle of most of its gunpowder and reloaded it with ash from the fireplace. He did likewise with the powder horn.

The next morning, the brave inspected the loading of his flintlock with a bit more care than that of a man out for some sport hunting. "Why don't you walk ahead of me awhile and break the trail?" he said when they set out. Quick obliged.

The pair were no sooner out of sight and hearing of the lodge than the white heard the pointless click of a rifle behind him. He looked around. "What did you see?"

Making an expansive gesture, the brave replied, "A fine buck on the other side of the creek." Misfirings were common in the black-powder era. Apparently making no more of it, the Iroquois reloaded carefully from his own horn.

Awhile later, the scene was repeated. "What did you see this time?" said Quick.

"An eagle soaring above us," said the brave.

Quick kept his own gun at the waist, casually trained on his companion. "Why don't you walk ahead of me this time."

They came to a grove even more sheltered than the rest, and Quick cocked the hammer. "So, my deceitful friend," he said. "Tell me what you see now."

"The spirit world," said the brave, stepping in front of the barrel and standing tall.

One afternoon in the 1980s, white teacher John Newton was walking on the Onondaga Reservation with some of his young students. A pickup truck went caterwauling by them on a bumpy dirt road. As it passed, he was startled to see a couple of young men bouncing precariously in the back, legs hanging over the tailgate. "Boy, they ought to be careful," said Newton. By their lack of reaction, his students let on that it wasn't such a big deal.

Newton couldn't understand this. He may even have raised his voice. "Well—somebody could get killed! Doesn't that matter to you?"

One of the boys shrugged and summed up the attitude of the others. "He'll just go into the spirit world a little early."

I FEEL MY FRIENDS HERE

The notion of acculturating the Native Americans goes back to George Washington's administration. It was presumed that progress was the natural goal of societies, and that the proper gift to Native Americans was what the whites would have wanted for themselves: religion, education, jobs, and life skills—in short, more white medicine. Indian schools were established across the United States.

Most of them in the East were orphanages for the care and education of children orphaned because of the collapse in their societies brought about by white incursions. Some in the West were shock military schools intended to modify ancient attitudes by reworking a single generation.

Supported by Baltimore banker Philip E. Thomas (1776–1861), Quaker missionaries Asher Wright and his wife, Laura Maria (1809–1886), built a combined school and orphanage on the Cattaraugus Reservation in 1856. Tycoon William Pryor Letchworth (1823–1910) gave a financial hand in 1875, and by 1898, the Thomas Asylum for Orphan and Destitute Indians came under the supervision of the state's Department of Social Welfare. That's when most of the buildings we see today were constructed.

Like many a college campus of the day, they were Georgian Revival redbrick structures, with appealing cornices, dentils, and cartouches, most featuring Native American images with classical styling. Today, a handful of the buildings stand, and probably, in some form, the tunnels and passages that connected them all. By 1905, it was known as the Thomas Indian School.

By 1956, the centralization of New York schools was under way, and the Thomas, as it was called, closed. The site and some structures did a five-year spell as part of the Gowanda State Hospital, an insane asylum. Decline, dilapidation, and many demolitions followed.

The experience of these Indian schools was traumatic enough— away from nature, language, villages, families, play. The discipline of the era would qualify today as abuse. These "forgotten" children returned to their villages as adults, often neither fully white nor Native—"neither wolf nor dog" as the Seneca say—and unable to deal with the world.

Over the years, we've interviewed old-timers who remembered family members traumatized by their years with the schools. Our Tuscarora friend Jay Claus had an uncle who had never been right, due, Claus was sure, to his experiences at the Thomas.

No wonder the Thomas is haunted. We know a graveyard was here, probably under the whole campus. Skeletons were discovered in 1900 during excavations for new construction. That should have told them something.

Only a couple of the original Thomas buildings still stand, and the most prominent is the former infirmary, right out there on Route 438 across from the library. Today the site is used for office space by the Seneca Nation, but no one likes to be in it at night. We know many a Seneca who lists it as a top haunt in the region.

Seneca librarian Pam Bowen tells the story of a Cattaraugus woman doing some late-night painting on the top floor. Just after her male colleague ducked out for an errand, she heard the old-time elevator kick in ominously and start clattering up. She didn't wait to see what would come out the door. She bolted down the stairwell and waited outside for her partner.

One old lad we interviewed used to drop in on the place whenever he was in the area and walk around mournfully near the resting places of his chums. Many had died during their time at the Thomas, and some were buried, according to him, in "lost" graves. The place was, to him, horrible, but the way old warriors revisit battlefields, he went back now and then to honor the fallen. "I feel my friends here," he said.

The Ghost Talker

In the 1970s, Mad Bear and friends were out viewing rock carvings when their young guide found a magnificent, ancient flint point. He offered it to Mad Bear. "You found it," said Mad Bear. "There must be a reason." The boy put it in his pocket.

"Whoa!" said Mad Bear. "You can't take it like that. Either put it back where you found it or make some kind of offering. If you can't offer something, make a pledge."

The lad held the arrowhead up to the sun for a minute and put it in his pocket. "I made a pledge," he said, grinning. "I promised the Great Spirit I'd quit drinking."

Mad Bear cut him off. "A pledge is sacred," he said. "You've got to mean it."

A few days later, Mad Bear called his friends together to tell them that the young man who had taken them to the rocks was dead, killed by the stroke of a knife. Few thought it would take Mad Bear long to find the killer. He went to the boy's family.

At dawn he called his circle together, which included the white author Doug Boyd. "The ceremony went pretty good," he said. "I got hold of him, and he recognized me." Mad Bear led the young man's spirit around the house where he had lived, showing him his room, his things, his friends, his family. "This is where you used to sleep, but no more; this is who you used to live with, but no more."

"You got to get everything closed out," he said. "That's the purpose in a ceremony like that." Confused spirits can be "trapped something terrible. Time was, everyone in the world had ceremonies for that. Now it's mostly lost—especially where there's no traditional medicine people left." He got up. "I'm tired. I done a lot of work tonight."

"How did he get stabbed?" shouted Boyd. Mad Bear sighed as if the grief was new and he'd seen it through the young man's eyes. The boy with the flint in his pocket and the pledge on his lips had walked a long trail to a store. When he came out with a six-pack, a dog that had always been friendly went after him. A fracas ensued, and the dog's owner drew his knife to stop it. Mad Bear's young friend kicked out at the dog, maybe even at the knife. That was how he'd been hit. The wound had seemed just a scratch in his hip, but it bled as he walked. He weakened, rested by an old cabin, and fell asleep. The steel point had come in over the flint one in his pocket. It must have sparked off it.

BLOODY MARY

One of the Niagara's best-known Native American ghosts haunts the Saylor Community Building on the Cattaraugus. Her fame is so widespread that even Tuscarora and Tonawanda folk will tell you about Bloody Mary. Still, her story is counterintuitive.

The fact that they give this ghost a name presents the first problem. The Iroquois seldom personify their ghosts. They know the apparition of a late person when they see one, and they'll give it a name when they know it. But the site ghosts they report, named or not, behave not like the ghosts of entertainment, but like those of parapsychology: quick, quirky images, not always fully formed, seldom dramatic or self-aware. So often no one knows who the apparition may represent.

Problem two is the name itself. Bloody Mary is a white contemporary bogie—the ghost of a woman who either killed her children or whose child was stolen. (Stand in front of a mirror and call her name three times and she just might appear as a reflection.) This urban legend may be only a quarter-century old. It's also a cocktail named for an English queen, the daughter of the notorious Henry VIII. Mary I (1516–1558) could have gotten her nickname from a couple of false pregnancies or abortions. More likely, it came from her penchant for killing Protestants.

The Saylor's Bloody Mary is a character—and a player who may have a connection to the fabled bogie the Legs. An edgy babe, dark-haired, seductive, dressed in black and red, she turns up at the occasional dance. The Saylor is dark, and the music rocks. She catches the eye of a married man who likes to run around on his wife. She's a quick laugher, and he's impressed by his own form. His friends are watching. Who knows what she looks like to them? Like a vampire or the European fairies, she has *glamour,* the power of casting visual enchantment on herself or other beings and objects. She goes to "freshen up" and agrees to meet outside. That's the last he sees of her—in this form.

The man walks home, dejected, and soon uneasy. Trees stir around him; footsteps follow. If it's his would-be conquest, she doesn't answer his weakening calls, and those strides are not those of a woman in heels. Soon a massive pair of female legs and pelvis races round him in the dark. He detects the smell of menstrual blood, a dozen times greater than normal. There's a collision. He gets home, out of breath and terrified, but the effluvium is with him. His appetite for conquest is dimmed. Even if his wife lets him live.

THE CHIEF OF THE BLUE HERON

Leon Shenandoah (1915–1996) was the Tadodaho of the Six Nations. This is a title, and a different word in all the Iroquois languages, but there's no mistake about the man who bears it. The leader of the Longhouse folk, the Tadodaho, is the Fire Keeper of the Onondaga and the only member of the Six Nations to wear the single feather of the great blue heron. This inspiring bird and its feather in the ancient head-dress have come to symbolize this chief of chiefs. The man who bore it to the end of the twentieth century had power in his hands and play in his heart.

Mike Bastine and Ted Williams used to visit Leon often at Onondaga. One thing that impressed Michael the most about him was his forgiveness. Leon's daughter was killed in circumstances that looked like murder to many. It was the direst event of his life. Still, he swore off vengeance and never gave way to bitterness, even when people around him vented against murderers. The worst Leon ever said was, "Sending them to the Land of the Elders is too easy. Let them stay here awhile longer." His verdict was always final.

The Graceful Bird

On the night of July 22, 1996, Mike and Pam Bastine were driving home from a camping trip in the Catskills. It was about ten, and they were on Route 20A near Varysburg, about twenty miles east of their Wales Center home. One of those long

Erie County hills bottomed out at an intersection by a streetlight. A pale shape was ahead of them, at the very edge of their side of the road. Michael had to swerve to miss it. Still as a coatrack in a sheet, it could have been a ghost, and one that didn't fear the brush of cars doing sixty. Michael had a funny feeling about it. He turned to Pam. "Did you see that?"

She did. "It looked like a little old man."

They turned and came back. Their headlights showed it to be a great blue heron, as calm as a mailbox and standing perilously at the edge of the road. These rare, inspiring birds dominate the scene where they appear. You feel them when you peer down those long, wide creeks. You are drawn to look at them no matter how still they are. They keep quietness about them; they hate the commotion of machines and highways. Michael had never seen a heron do as this. It would be killed if it stood where it was.

He got out and came close to the graceful bird. He stepped into its animal gaze and spoke. "You can't stay here," he said. "You have to go somewhere else."

The bird was unaffected. Michael appealed to it. "You can't stay that close to the highway. The cars don't care about you. They'll run over you, they'll kill you." The bird just stared. Only when he tried to shoo it, coming a bit closer and making sweeping gestures with his arms, did it react. It flew up and landed, assuming an identical position on the other side of the road.

Michael crossed the road. "This is no time for fun and games," he said. "I got whatever message you have to give me. I may not understand it till later, but now you have to let us help you. You don't belong here any more. You have to go to a place you do belong." The bird processed this in its own way, then flapped its wings and took off above the man-made glow of the street. The two humans followed it with their eyes into the deep turquoise of the summer twilight. Within their sight was a farm with a spotlight over a pond. The bird landed by the sheeny waterside, and Michael smiled. "Better fishing there, anyway," he thought.

When Mike and Pam reached their home, an hour-old message was on the machine. Leon Shenandoah, chief of chiefs of the Longhouse folk, had crossed over. He wore the feather of the heron in the next world.

The Powerful Dream

In 2001, Michael had another of his power dreams, and this one involved Leon Shenandoah. The visual effect reminded him of a 1960s TV show.

Some of us may recall The Wild, Wild West, *sort of a cowboy James Bond show. One of its trademark effects was the way each ten-minute segment ended. Live images of interacting characters froze—with appropriate music—into cartoonish stills, always at climactic moments and just before commercial breaks. The scenes did so in Mike's dream. But this dream was about ancient Iroquois ceremonies, and the antique freeze-frames fell at the close of iconic rites. They were clearly meant to be teachable moments.*

In his dream, Michael looked into darkness as if through an old-time theater or viewing device. He saw lit scenes of Native American people at dances and chants. During the live parts of the dream, a voice narrated, explaining what Michael was supposed to learn from what he was watching. It was a familiar voice, clearly iconic. It was Leon Shenandoah, majestic and mighty from his seasoning in the other world.

At the end of each scene, the active image froze into stillness like the commercial breaks of the old-time TV show, and Leon's voice said urgently, "You got that? You got that?" Before Michael could answer, the next teaching scene started, and the voice went formal again. His dream mind tried so hard to take it all in. He knew what an honor this dream was and how precious these ceremonies were. He marveled; he cried in his sleep.

At the last, Leon's voice came in, addressing Michael alone. "Don't ever forget those ceremonies. There's a time to come when you won't have to see them done anymore, when others can take over for you. But you have to work until then. Don't ever forget them."

The feeling hit him deeply. When Michael woke up, this dream was as powerful as any he had ever had. It was one more confirmation of the course he had taken in the world, possibly why he would consent to help this book be written.

THE LAND OF THE ELDERS

Many Native American societies believe that some dreams are messages from the spirit realm. Often when an old-time Iroquois or Algonquin had a dream that felt exceptional, he or she consulted the medicine people in search of an explanation. Some dreams were so strong and direct that they had to be obeyed. Some were so impactful that the whole community had to be enlisted in a ceremony made to re-enact them and "close them out."

A Dream Story

In 2005, Michael had a dream that he calls "really interesting." It opened with him walking in a natural environment that became a redwood forest like those of California. He looked up and realized with a sense of awe that he couldn't see the tops of the trees.

He started to explore the forest. Before long, he sensed that things other than trees were above him. He reached overhead, felt something soft and furry, and looked up to find the belly of a deer, big enough to loom like an arch. Reaching up to its snowy underside was like touching the lintel of a doorframe.

There were other animals, tame and trusting as the trees, and proportionally as big. There were turkeys whose bellies he could barely touch. They walked over him like he was a low bush. He had been among them for minutes. Why had he not noticed them before? It was as though the awareness of them faded in, as if they were only visible from well within the forest. They had been blurry forms at first. It was as if the ability to see them was something that had to be learned.

And they were talking! They were all conversing in a language some part of his mind understood. They savored the play of light through the leaves; they joked about the silly squirrels, the forest children. The squirrels joked back and scampered off to their endless play. The animals' language was basic and effortless to understand. The meanings of their calls was like a childhood memory so commonplace that he had never bothered to bring it into focus. Why did he have to come to a dream to learn that he should not just hear the animals but listen to them? This was the most comforting place he had ever been. He wanted to be sure to find it again. A thought came to his dream mind: "Get the name of this place." He kept walking, hoping to find someone to talk to.

Soon he sensed a little fire. He heard the crackle and saw a bit of smoke. He came to a clearing and found a little old Native American man tending a fire with a stick. He gave it a prod just as Michael's dream self entered. They made eye contact, and the fire keeper nodded. As if already sensing that he was in the dream and fearing that he might wake, Michael said to himself, "I have to ask him the name of this place."

He watched awhile, admiring the man's contentment with his trust, sensing that he knew the question in Michael's mind. At last, he said, "What do you call this place?"

"You know," the little man said, with a little smile.

I hate dreams like this, *Mike said to himself even as the dream went on. "I did know it, but I couldn't come up with the words," he concedes. "It was like that language of the animals." But the effort of bringing it into focus would wake him up. He had to be told. He had to hear it.*

"Look, I want to come back here someday," he told the fire keeper. "If I don't know the name of it, I can't ask directions."

The little man just smiled as if this was some formality in a game he was used to. "This is the Land of the Elders," he said, giving the fire another poke.

Of course, *Michael started to think.* That would figure. It was all so big, and the animals were talking. They had all crossed over and become elders. Elder trees, elder deer, elder turkeys. *Then it was over.*

For years, Michael couldn't tell anyone about that dream, because he choked up trying to get the words out. It was that powerful. It's only been in the last year or two that he can make it through the story.

"You have no idea what it's like on the other side," he said to me. I wish I could write that look in his eyes. "You have no idea what's coming."

Your Buddy Was Here

When Mad Bear was in the hospital, Mike got a call from one of the other guys who helped look after him. "You better go see Mad Bear. He's in pretty bad shape."

When Michael reached his side, the old shaman was about to have surgery for a bleeding ulcer. He had something urgent on his mind that he kept trying to say through the sedation. He could only get a word out: "Call!"

"Call who, Bear?" said Mike. "Who?" He had to shout in Mad Bear's ear to

get anything through. The answer was never different, a mumble and a trailing off after, "Call. . . ."

Mad Bear made it through the surgery, and the operation seemed to be a success. His heart, though, wasn't strong enough to pull him out of the sedation. It was the anesthesia that killed him. He passed on December 20, 1985.

Michael went in to pick up Mad Bear's clothing, and Mad Bear's brother made the funeral arrangements. It was a difficult couple of days, pondering the last word Michael heard from his famous tutor. It's never been clear to him what this might have been about.

Some time in the depth of the night of December 23, Michael woke out of a sound sleep. Something was in the room with him. He sat up, looked toward the door, and saw in the ambience of a streetlight a full-size, lifelike image of Mad Bear at the doorway. His arms were folded, and he leaned on the frame wearing a jaunty smile. It seemed a younger form, like the fifty-something Mad Bear he had first met. It lasted a good long time for a ghost, five or ten seconds. "I sat straight up in bed," Michael said. "It was incredible." He fell back to sleep, pondering it.

About ten the next morning, a call came in from the Cherokee John Pope (1920?–1997), a friend and colleague better known as Bob Dylan's crony, the famous Rolling Thunder. "Your buddy was here last night," was how he started.

"He was here, too," said Mike. "I could see him standing right there. I guess he was making the rounds."

RT, as they called him, got a real big kick out of that.

The Clipboard Dream

When Michael first visited Mad Bear, he heard so much of value spilling out that he started bringing a little pad with him and writing in it every few minutes. Mad Bear couldn't have failed to notice, but it was the fourth or fifth such visit before he leaned over and looked at Mike. "What do you keep writing in those pads?"

"I'm hearing a lot of great stuff," said Mike. "I like to write down what's really important."

"Is there something wrong with your brain?" said Mad Bear.

"I don't think so," said Mike.

"Then why don't you use it? What do you think is going to happen if you

lose that pad?" After that, Michael learned to rely on his mind and his memory. He has such a strong recollection of so much that his old tutor said to him that it would take a dozen books to get it all out. It's also a little disorganized. More comes out every time I talk to him. So fixed in him was this concept of focused listening that it might have affected his unconscious. Maybe it's time to let the lesson go.

One night in the spring of 1995, Mike had a series of strong dreams. Every hour, the presence of Mad Bear came to him, a ghost in a dream. Every time Mad Bear held a clipboard out to him and urged him to take it. He remembered the old lesson, even in his dream mind, and, as if this was a test, kept putting it off. All night the sequence went on.

"I keep kicking myself over that," he says today. "He was trying to tell me something. I might have just had that one chance, and I think I let him down."

He blinked with real feeling. "He won't keep coming to me like that. As there's constraints to being in the physical world, there's constraints to being in the spirit. He'll have to find somebody else to give it to. I just wish I could figure out what that meant."

"He told you to put away the writing pad before," I said to him one night as we conferred about this book. "Now he's trying to get you to take one up. Maybe that's what we're doing here. Looks to me like you heard him."

THE SPIRIT CHOIRS

We judge from their stories that the psyche had several components for the Iroquois. A ghost would be only one of them. Some form might even journey the earth in animal shape, undoubtedly the clan totem of the recently deceased. Then there's the everlasting presence, the seat of reason and personality, that, after some process or another, dwells with the higher spirits. Whatever reaches back to loved ones now and again with a message and maybe even an appearance would probably be a manifestation of this.

Could there even have been another aspect of the being, a nature soul, one that, at times, comes back to the places it knew in life? If so, it's most often on one of those shy twilights, when people relax in their yards or stroll the tree line. If so, this part of the soul tenants a twilight state in which it thinks and feels as an essence and responds to the rhythms and scenes of nature, in which it chimes with the chants of the ancestors, like Yeats' "lasting, unwearied Voices" from some realm in which nature and human poetry are one.

The Allegany Seneca may think so. On those special eves, the elders among them, so often the grandmothers, notice them and guide others to listen, maybe even to hear.

"As a child," recalled Duce Bowen, "it was a most impressive thing to sit down on those old porches. A grandmother would say, 'Be quiet, because so-and-so is singing.' And off in the dark, you'd hear a person who had been dead for ten years."

You may not get a look at them. They may not be ghosts. They may not be full spirits. They may be only feelings, expressed as sounds that at first you mistake for natural dusk noises—breeze, leaves, birds—conspiring with light, congealing like liquid to make a rhythm that at first seems nothing. Listen long enough, and then you hear. Some nights they come clearer—faint, half-melodic tones, even voices, chanting the ancient songs. You may spot the voice of someone you knew. To those reservation communities where their ancestors lived, where descendants dwell, they come back.

These voices we ought to be hearing, everywhere in New York. How many of us do?

Think about life and consciousness today. How many Americans live where their elders lived or near any place they might return? How many live anywhere quiet enough to hear deeper than the sounds of the living? The highway roar, the static hum. How far into the woods do we have to go? When we do, how many sit still enough? How many would listen, if they did? What have we traded for the ability to hear? What songs would your ancestors be singing?

"Every night when I burn tobacco," says Michael Bastine, "I listen for the elders. I give thanks that I have spent time with these elements, these living people, these ancestors who bring such fullness and under-standing to this life. There's no time for fighting about so many of the things we fight about in this world."

Even after they have left the world, we have our debts to the elders. One of them is to preserve their teachings. This is also part of our debt to those who will come after us, to hold those teachings so they will not be lost for them.

The Iroquois have not lost their elders' songs, but for too long they have not been heard outside their figurative Longhouse. Maybe the gift of them is greatest to those who can no longer hear their own ances-tors, who may not even think to listen for them. The teachings of these People of the Longhouse, of all indigenous elders, can lead everyone to see the richness of the world, if not look into the world beyond it—even those whose elders' songs are lost. This is something Michael and I will always believe.

Bibliography

Historic information about the regions of this book came from just about every old county history available in our target area of New York state. Insights and information more specific to our stories and subjects came from the following books and periodicals.

Abrams, George H. *The Seneca People*. Phoenix, Ariz.: Indian Tribal Series, 1976.

Anderson, Mildred Lee Hills. *Genesee Echoes, the Upper Gorge and Falls Area from the Days of the Pioneers*. Castile, N.Y.: F. A. Owen Publishing Co., 1956.

Beahan, Larry. *Allegany Hellbender Tales*. Snyder, N.Y.: Coyote Publishing of Western New York, 2003.

Beauchamp, William Martin. *Iroquois Folklore: Gathered from the Six Nations of New York*. Syracuse, N.Y.: Dehler Press, 1922.

———. *A History of the New York Iroquois, Now Commonly Called the Six Nations. New York State Museum Bulletin 78, Archeology 9*. University of the State of New York, State Education Department, 1905.

Bergland, Renee. *The National Uncanny*. Hanover, N.H.: The University Press of New England, 2000.

Birdsall, Ralph. *The Story of Cooperstown*. Cooperstown, N. Y.: Arthur H. Crist, 1917.

Blackman, W. Haden. *The Field Guide to North American Hauntings*. New York: Crown Publishing Group, 1998.

Blanchard, David. "Who or What's a Witch? Iroquois Persons of Power." *American Indian Quarterly*. University of Nebraska Press, 1982.

Bolton, Jonathan, and Claire Wilson. *Joseph Brant, Mohawk Chief.* New York: Chelsea House, 1992.

Bord, Janet, and Colin Bord. *The Secret Country.* New York: Warner Books, 1976.

Bowen, Duwayne Leslie. *One More Story: Contemporary Seneca Tales of the Supernatural.* Greenfield Center, N.Y.: Greenfield Review Press, 1991.

———. *A Few More Stories: Contemporary Seneca Indian Tales of the Supernatural.* Greenfield Center, N.Y.: Greenfield Review Press, 2000.

Bowman, Don. *The Witch of Mad Dog Hill.* Greenfield Center, N.Y.: Greenfield Review Press, 1999.

Boyd, Doug. *Rolling Thunder.* New York: Dell, 1974.

———. *Mad Bear, Spirit, Healing, and the Sacred in the Life of a Native American Medicine Man.* New York: Simon & Schuster, 1994.

Brandon, Jim. *Weird America.* New York: E. P. Dutton, 1978.

Briggs, Katherine Mary. *The Vanishing People: Fairy Lore and Legend.* New York: Pantheon, 1978.

Brinton, Daniel. *Myths of the New World: The Symbolism and Mythology of the Indians of the Americas.* New York: H. Holt, 1876.

Britten, Evelyn Barrett. *Chronicles of Saratoga.* Saratoga Springs, N.Y.: Bradshaw, 1947.

Bruchac, Joseph. *Turtle Meat and Other Stories.* Duluth, Minn.: Holy Cow! Press, 1992.

———. *Stone Giants and Flying Heads, Adventure Stories of the Iroquois, As Told by Joseph Bruchac.* Trumansburg, N.Y.: Crossing Press, 1979.

Burich, Keith R. "'No Place to Go': The Thomas Indian School and the 'Forgotten' Indian Children of New York." *Wicazo Sa Review* 22 (2) (Fall 2007): 93–110.

Burmaster, Everett R. Unpublished papers in the possession of the Buffalo and Erie County (N.Y.) Historical Society.

Canfield, William W. *The Legends of the Iroquois Told by "The Cornplanter."* New York: Wessels, 1902.

Cariou, Warren. "Haunted Prairie: Aboriginal 'Ghosts' and the Spectres of Settlement." *University of Toronto Quarterly: A Canadian Journal of the Humanities* 75 (2) (2006): 727–34.

Carmer, Carl. *Listen for a Lonesome Drum*. New York: William Sloane Associates, 1936.

———. "Carantouan." *American Heritage Magazine* (Summer 1952): 17–19.

Cayce, Edgar Evans. *Edgar Cayce on Atlantis*. New York: Hawthorn, 1968.

Clark, Joshua V. H. *Onondaga or Reminiscences of Earlier and Later Times Being a Series of Historical Sketches Relative to Onondaga With Notes on the Several Towns in the County and Oswego*. Syracuse, N.Y.: Stoddard and Babcock, 1849.

Colden, Cadwallader. *The History of the Five Indian Nations Depending on the Province of New York in America*. Ithaca, N.Y.: Cornell University Press, 1980.

Coleman, Loren. *Mysterious America*. Winchester, Mass.: Faber & Faber, 1983.

Conklin, Susan L., and Judy Stiles. *Supernatural Genesee*. Kearney, Nebr.: Morris Press, 2004.

Converse, Harriet Maxwell. *Myths and Legends of the New York State Iroquois*. Editor and annotator Arthur C. Parker. *New York State Museum Bulletin* 125 (1908).

Cooper, Leo. *Seneca Indian Stories*. Greenfield Center, N.Y.: Greenfield Review Press, 1995.

Cornplanter, Jesse. J. *Legends of the Longhouse, by Jesse J. Cornplanter of the Senecas, Told to Sah-Nee-Weh, the White Sister, With an Introduction by Carl Carmer, Illustrated by the Author*. New York: Lippincott, 1938.

Curtin, Jeremiah. *Seneca Indian Myths*. New York: E. P. Dutton, 1923.

Cusick, David. *Sketches of Ancient History of the Six Nations*. Lockport, N.Y.: Turner & McCollum, Printers, 1848.

Dennis, Matthew. "Seneca Possessed: Colonialism, Witchcraft, and Gender in the Time of Handsome Lake." In *Spellbound: Women and Witchcraft in America*. Wilmington, Del.: SR Books, 1998.

Densmore, Christopher. *Red Jacket, Iroquois Diplomat and Orator*. Syracuse, N.Y.: Syracuse University Press, 1999.

Devereux, Paul. *Earth Lights Revelation: UFOs and Mystery Lightform Phenomena: the Earth's Secret Energy Force*. London: Blandford, 1989.

———. *Fairy Paths and Spirit Roads*. London: Vega, 2003.

———. *Mysterious Ancient America: An Investigation into the Enigmas of America's Prehistory*. London: Vega, 2002.

———. *Secrets of Ancient and Sacred Places: The World's Mysterious Heritage.* London: Blandford, 1992.

Durkee, Cornelius. *Reminiscences of Saratoga.* Salem, Mass.: Higginson Book Co., 1928.

Engelbrecht, William. *Iroquoia: The Development of a Native World.* Syracuse, N.Y.: Syracuse University Press, 2003.

Evans-Wentz, W. Y. *The Fairy Faith in Celtic Countries.* New York: H. Froude, 1911.

Fanton, Ben. "Where the Ghosts Walk: Storyteller Duce Bowen and the Spirits of the Seneca Nation." *Buffalo News* (1993).

Fenton, William N. *The False Faces of the Iroquois.* Norman, Okla.: University of Oklahoma Press, 1987.

———. *Masked Medicine Societies of the Iroquois.* Ohsweken, Ontario, Canada: Iroqrafts Iroquois Reprints, 1984.

———, ed. *Parker on the Iroquois.* Syracuse, N.Y.: Syracuse University Press, 1968.

Fox, Austin. *Church Tales of the Niagara Frontier: Legend, History and Architecture.* Buffalo, N.Y.: Western New York Wares, 1994.

Gehring, Charles T., Dean R. Snow, and William Stama. *In Mohawk Country: Early Narratives About a Native People.* Syracuse, N.Y.: Syracuse University Press, 1996.

Goodwin, Arlene. "The Legend of Roger's Island." *Catskill Examiner,* July 19, 1884, Number 1.

Green, Miranda J. *The World of the Druids.* London: Thames and Hudson, 1997.

Guiley, Rosemary Ellen: *Atlas of the Mysterious in North America.* New York: Checkmark Books, 1995.

Gulliford, Andrew. *Sacred Objects and Sacred Places: Preserving Tribal Traditions.* Niwot, Colo.: University Press of Colorado, 2000.

Hauck, Dennis William. *Haunted Places, the National Directory: Ghostly Abodes, Sacred Sites, UFO Landings, and Other Supernatural Locations.* New York: Penguin Group, 1996.

Haring, Sidney L. "Red Lilac of the Cayugas: Traditional Indian Laws and Culture Conflict in a Witchcraft Trial in Buffalo, 1930." *Spellbound: Women and Witchcraft in America* Lanham, Md.: SR Books, 1998.

Hawley, Charles. *Early Chapters of Seneca History: Jesuit Missions in Sonnontouan,*

1656–1684; With Annual Addresses 1883–84. Collections of Cayuga County Historical Society 3 (1884).

Herbeck, Dan. "'A Nation of Warriors'; Seneca Nation President Maurice John has no shortage of battles." *Buffalo News* (2007).

Hewitt, J. N. B. *Seneca Fiction, Legends and Myths.* Washington, D.C.: Bureau of Ethnology, 1918.

Hillerman, Tony. *Skinwalker.* New York: HarperCollins, 1986.

———. *The Shapeshifter.* New York: HarperCollins, 1988.

Hibbert, Alfred G. "The Forbidden Trail." *The Crooked Lake Review* 40 (1991).

Hitching, Francis. *Earth Magic.* New York: Morrow, 1977.

———. *The World Atlas of Mysteries.* London: William Collins Sons & Co., 1978.

Husted, Shirley Cox. *Valley of the Ghosts: Folklore and Legends from the Storied Genesee Valley Region of New York State.* Rochester, N.Y.: County of Monroe, 1982.

Johnson, Elias. *Legends, Traditions and Laws, of the Iroquois, or Six Nations, and History of the Tuscarora Indians.* Lockport, N.Y.: Union Printing and Publishing Co., 1881.

Jones, Louis C. *Things That Go Bump in the Night.* New York: Hill and Wang, 1959.

Jung, G. G. "Flying Saucers: A Modern Myth of Things Seen in the Skies." From Volume 10 of *The Collected Works of C. G. Jung.* Princeton, N.J.: Princeton University Press, 1964.

Keel, John. *Strange Creatures From Time and Space.* Greenwich, Conn.: Fawcett Publications, 1970.

Kennedy, Roger G. *Hidden Cities: The Discovery and Loss of Ancient North American Civilization.* New York: Maxwell Macmillan International, 1994.

Ketchum, William. *An Authentic and Comprehensive History of Buffalo, With Some Account of Its Early Inhabitants, Both Savage and Civilized, Comprising Historic Notices of the Six Nations, or Iroquois Indians, Including a Sketch of the Life of Sir William Johnson and of Other Prominent White Men, Long Resident Among the Senecas. Arranged in Chronological Order.* Buffalo, N.Y.: Rockwell, Baker and Hill, Printers, 1864–1865.

Klees, Emerson. *Legends and Stories of the Finger Lakes Region.* Rochester N.Y.: Friends of the Finger Lakes Publishing, 1995.

————. *More Legends and Stories of the Finger Lakes Region.* Rochester N.Y.: Friends of the Finger Lakes Publishing, 1997.

Lankes, Frank J. *An Old Ebenezer Graveyard Mystery.* West Seneca, N.Y.: West Seneca Historical Society, 1965.

Larsen, Stephen H. *The Shaman's Doorway.* New York: Harper & Row, 1976.

Leland, Charles G. *Memoirs.* New York: D. Appleton, 1893.

————. *Algonquin Legends of New England.* Boston: Houghton Mifflin, 1884.

Markusen, Bruce. www.cooperstownghost.com/stonewall.html. Accessed April 24, 2010.

McCarthy, Richard L., and Harrison Newman. "Prehistoric People of Western New York" in Adventures in Western New York History 7. New York: Erie County Historical Society, 1961.

Merrill, Arch. *Down the Lore Lanes.* Rochester, N.Y.: American Book-Stratford Press, 1961.

————. *Land of the Senecas.* Interlaken, N.Y.: Heart of the Lakes Publishing, 1986.

Michell, John. *The View over Atlantis.* New York: Ballantine, 1972.

————. *The New View over Atlantis.* San Francisco: Harper & Row, 1983.

Mooney, James. "The Swimmer Manuscript: Cherokee Sacred Formulas and Medicinal Prescriptions." Edited by Frans Olbrechts. *Washington, D.C. Bureau of American Ethnology Bulletin* 99 (1932).

Morgan, Lewis Henry. *The League of the Ho-de'-no-sau-nee or Iroquois.* 2 vols. New York: Burt Franklin, 1851.

Olsen, Brad. *Sacred Places North America: 108 Destinations.* Chatsworth, Calif.: CCC Publishing, 2010.

Parker, Arthur C. *The Code of Handsome Lake: The Seneca Prophet.* Albany, N.Y.: University of the State of New York, 1913.

————. *Seneca Myths and Folk Tales.* Buffalo, N.Y.: Buffalo Historical Society, 1923.

Parkman, Francis. *The Jesuits in North America in the Seventeenth Century.* Boston: Little, Brown and Company, 1912.

Partner, Peter. *The Murdered Magicians: The Templars and Their Myths.* New York: Barnes & Noble Books, 1993.

Pierce, Frederic. "Fifth Stop: Thirteen Curves." *Strange Central New York.* From Syracuse.com. http://blog.syracuse.com/strangecny/2007/11/fifth_stop_thirteen_curves.html.

Pitkin, David J. *Ghosts of the Northeast*. Chestertown, N.Y.: Aurora Publications, 2002.

———. *Haunted Saratoga County*. Chestertown, N.Y.: Aurora Publications, 2005.

———. *New York State Ghosts*. Chestertown, N.Y.: Aurora Publications, 2006.

Powers, Mabel. *Around an Iroquois Story Fire*. Buffalo, N.Y.: Buffalo Museum of Science, 1952.

Reid, William Maxwell. *The Mohawk Valley: Its Legends and Its History*. New York and London: G. P. Putnam's Sons, 1901.

Reis, Elizabeth, ed. *Spellbound: Women and Witchcraft in America*. Lanham, Md.: SR Books, 1998.

Richardson, Judith. *Possessions*: *The History and Uses of Haunting in the Hudson Valley*. Cambridge, Mass.: Harvard University Press, 2003.

Robinson, David D. "Mysterious Ruin at Bluff Point." *The Crooked Lake Review* 68 (1993).

———. "Saint George, the Serpent, and the Seneca Indians." *The Crooked Lake Review* 71 (1994).

———. "Who Built the 'Old Fort' on Bare Hill?" *The Crooked Lake Review* 103 (1997).

Robinson, Rosemary. *Gannagaro: Stronghold of the Senecas*. Pittsford, N.Y.: Wolfe Publications, 1976.

Schoolcraft, Henry R. *Notes on the Iroquois: Or Contributions to the Statistics, Aboriginal History, Antiquities, and General Ethnology of Western New York*. New York: Bartlett and Welford, 1846.

Seaver, James Everett. *A Narrative of the Life of Mrs. Mary Jemison*. Canandaigua, N.Y.: J. D. Bemis and Co., 1824.

Shimony, Annemarie Anrod. *Conservatism Among the Iroquois at the Six Nations Reserve*. Syracuse, N.Y.: Syracuse University Press, 1994.

Smith, Carroll Earll, and Charles Carroll Smith. *Pioneer Times in the Onondaga Country*. Syracuse, N.Y.: C. W. Bardeen, 1904.

Smith, De Cost. "Witchcraft and Demonism of the Modern Iroquois." *The Journal of American Folklore* 1 (3) (1888): 184–94.

Smith, Erminnie A. "Myths of the Iroquois." Edited by William Guy Spittal. Originally published in *The United States Bureau of American Ethnology* 2nd Annual Report, 1880–1881. Washington, D.C.: United States Bureau of American Ethnology 1883 orig.

Snow, Dean. *The Iroquois*. Oxford and Cambridge, Mass.: Blackwell, 1996.

Snyderman, George S. "Witches, Witchcraft, and Allegany Seneca Medicine." *Proceedings of the American Philosophical Society* 127 (4) (1983).

Squier, E. G. *Antiquities of the State of New York: being the results of extensive original surveys and explorations, with a supplement on the antiquities of the west*. Buffalo, N.Y.: G. H. Derby, 1851.

———. *The Serpent Symbol, and the Worship of Reciprocal Principles of Nature in America*. New York: G. P. Putnam, 1851.

Stone, William L. *Reminiscences of Saratoga and Ballston*. New York: Virtue & Yorston; Salem, Mass.: Higginson Book Co., 1875.

Stonehouse, Frederick. *Haunted Lakes: Great Lakes Ghost Stories, Superstition, and Sea Serpents*. Duluth, Minn.: Lake Superior Port Cities, 1997.

Sylvester, Nathaniel Bartlett. *History of Saratoga County, New York: With Biographical Sketches of Some of Its Prominent Men and Pioneers*. Philadelphia: Everts & Ensign, 1878.

Thompson, Harold W. *Body, Boots & Britches: Folktales, Ballads, and Speech from Country New York*. New York: Dover Publications, 1939.

Trento, Salvator Michael. *Field Guide to Mysterious Places of Eastern North America*. New York: H. Holt & Co. 1997.

Tucker, Libby. "Spectral Indians, Desecrated Burial Grounds." *Voices: The Journal of New York Folklore* 31 (2005).

Turner, Orsamus. *Pioneer History of the Holland Purchase of Western New York: Embracing Some Account of the Ancient Remains. . .* Buffalo, N.Y.: Geo. H. Derby and Co., 1850.

Twigg, Deb. www.spanishhill.com. Accessed June 13, 2010.

Van der Post, Laurens. *The Lost World of the Kalahari*. New York: Morrow, 1958.

Walker, Deward E., Jr., ed. *Witchcraft and Sorcery of the American Native Peoples*. Moscow, Idaho: University of Idaho Press, 1990.

Watkins, Alfred. *The Old Straight Track*. London: Methuen & Co., 1925.

Williams, Ted C. *The Reservation*. Syracuse, N.Y.: Syracuse University Press, 1976.

———. *Big Medicine from Six Nations*. Syracuse, N.Y.: Syracuse University Press. 2005.

Wilson, Colin. *Mysteries*. New York: Putnam, 1978.

Wilson, Edmund. *Apologies to the Iroquois. With a Study of the Mohawks in High Steel by Joseph Mitchell*. New York: Farrar, Straus and Cudahy, 1959.

Winfield, Mason. *Shadows of the Western Door: Haunted Sites and Ancient Mysteries of Upstate New York.* Buffalo, N.Y.: Western New York Wares. 1997.

———. *Spirits of the Great Hill: More Haunted Sites and Ancient Mysteries of Upstate New York.* Buffalo, N.Y.: Western New York Wares, 2001.

———. *Haunted Places of Western New York.* Buffalo, N.Y.: Western New York Wares. 2004.

———. *Village Ghosts of Western New York, Part 1: Actors in the Half-Light.* Buffalo, N.Y.: Western New York Wares, 2006.

———. (with John Koerner, Rob Lockhart, and Tim Shaw.) *Haunted Rochester: The Supernatural History of the Lower Genessee.* Charleston, S.C.: The History Press, 2008.

———. *Supernatural Saratoga: Haunted Places and Famous Ghosts of the Spa City.* Charleston, S.C.: The History Press, 2010.

———. *Ghosts of 1812: Folklore, History, and Supernatural Tradition from the Niagara War.* Buffalo, N.Y.: New York Wares, 2009.

Winfield, Mason, John Koerner, Rob Lockhart, and Tim Shaw. *Haunted Rochester: The Supernatural History of the Lower Genesee.* Charleston, S.C.: The History Press, 2008.

Wonderley, Anthony Wayne. *Oneida Iroquois Folklore, Myth, and History.* Syracuse, N.Y.: Syracuse University Press, 2004.

Index

Page numbers in *italics* refer to illustrations.

BOOKS OF RELATED INTEREST

Dreamways of the Iroquois
Honoring the Secret Wishes of the Soul
by Robert Moss

Walking on the Wind
Cherokee Teachings for Harmony and Balance
by Michael Garrett

Medicine of the Cherokee
The Way of Right Relationship
by J. T. Garrett and Michael Garrett

The Cherokee Herbal
Native Plant Medicine from the Four Directions
by J. T. Garrett

The Cherokee Full Circle
A Practical Guide to Ceremonies and Traditions
by J. T. Garrett and Michael Tlanusta Garrett

Meditations with the Cherokee
Prayers, Songs, and Stories of Healing and Harmony
by J. T. Garrett

Sacred Plant Medicine
The Wisdom in Native American Herbalism
by Stephen Harrod Buhner

Narrative Medicine
The Use of History and Story in the Healing Process
by Lewis Mehl-Madrona, M.D., Ph.D.

INNER TRADITIONS • BEAR & COMPANY
P.O. Box 388
Rochester, VT 05767
1-800-246-8648
www.InnerTraditions.com

Or contact your local bookseller